Jagdish Kothari
Elisabetta Barone

Financial Accounting

An International Approach

FT Prentice Hall
FINANCIAL TIMES

An imprint of **Pearson Education**

Harlow, England • London • New York • Boston • San Francisco • Toronto • Sydney • Singapore • Hong Kong
Tokyo • Seoul • Taipei • New Delhi • Cape Town • Madrid • Mexico City • Amsterdam • Munich • Paris • Milan

Pearson Education Limited
Edinburgh Gate
Harlow
Essex CM20 2JE
England

and Associated Companies throughout the world

Visit us on the World Wide Web at:
www.pearsoned.co.uk

First published 2006

ISBN: 978-0-27369-319-2

British Library Cataloguing-in-Publication Data
A catalogue record for this book is available from the British Library

Library of Congress Cataloging-in-Publication Data
A catalog record for this book is available from the Library of Congress

10 9 8 7 6 5
14 13

Typeset in 9.25/12pt Stone Serif by 35
Printed by Ashford Colour Press Ltd., Gosport

The publisher's policy is to use paper manufactured from sustainable forests.

Contents

Part Four Analysis and interpretation of financial statements

List of figures

List of tables

Foreword

In 2000, the European Commission committed itself to making international accounting standards mandatory from 2005 for listed companies within the European Union. It has happened and this year has seen the greatest revolution in financial reporting for a generation. A set of International Financial Reporting Standards (IFRSs), promulgated by the International Accounting Standards Board (IASB), has come into force for listed companies in all member countries of the European Union and in many other countries around the world.

This accounting reform is more than bookkeeping exercises. It will influence the way companies do business, improve market efficiencies and lower risk premiums. Harmonising global accounting standards will also stimulate more cross-border transactions.

The free flow of capital across borders will contribute to the wealth of nations by allocating capital more effectively and so lowering its cost to companies, institutions and individuals. Yet today's markets are far from global.

One reason for this situation is related to the incompatibility of the world's various accounting standards. This matters because disjunctive standards prevent market participants from efficiently comparing investment opportunities across borders. For companies, different accounting standards represent a burden that prevents them from having access to international funding. There is a clear need for global accounting standards which provide that businesses undertaking similar activities should be subject to broadly the same accounting treatment wherever they are.

After a period of transition, mutually acceptable and compatible accounting standards across borders will deliver tangible benefits. Comparable and transparent corporate reports and accounts will foster deeper and more liquid financial markets and will bolster investor confidence and hence global financial stability.

The IASB and the Financial Accounting Standards Board (FASB), the US standard-setting body, are aiming to achieve convergence between their two systems by 2007, removing the reconciliation between US generally accepted accounting principles and international standards. Once this convergence is achieved the harmonisation process will be complete and the resultant benefits for investors all over the world will be enormous.

This book, aimed at those students who wish to pursue careers as managers, focuses on the use of financial information rather than technical procedures. Recent scandals have clearly underlined the fact that managers today need to have a basic understanding of the concepts and principles of financial accounting. This book addresses these recent scandals and enables students to understand why they arose and how such scandals can be avoided in the future.

The book has a strong European focus, addressing the needs of students across Europe; and it is also aimed at students whose first language is not English.

It is based on the lectures given by the authors in the course of Accounting and Financial Statements Analysis for the Degree in International Economics and Management at Bocconi University, which is committed to providing internationally recognised education to its students from all over the world.

Prof Angelo Provasoli
Dean of Università Commerciale Luigi Bocconi
Milan, October 2005

Preface

Why this book?

The introduction of International Financial Reporting Standards (IFRSs) formerly known as International Accounting Standards (IASs) has globally happened!

In the European Union and its applicant member countries, listed companies from 1 January 2005 are required to adopt IASs/IFRSs. Some 7,000 companies in the European Union are affected. Australia, the Russian Federation, Japan and other countries have introduced IASs/IFRSs. Many countries around the world also require/encourage foreign listed companies to apply IASs/IFRSs with or without reconciliation to national accounting standards.

This book is written to reflect this new situation and its implications. A basic understanding of the requirements of the IASs/IFRSs is now essential for anyone studying financial accounting and reporting.

The style of this book is practical and interactive, as one of the authors has considerable experience of business and accounting practices of multinationals. Thus, we illustrate the importance of concepts such as net operating cash flows, core earnings or EBITDA, trade or operating working capital, etc. which are widely discussed and used today by the financial community.

We adopt a user approach that focuses on the use of financial information rather than on bookkeeping and its mechanics. We illustrate some of the fundamental accounting issues through examples of recent accounting failures in well-known listed companies.

This book is for non-accountants. It is intended primarily for students who are required to study accounting as part of a non-accounting degree or professional studies course. This book is therefore suitable for undergraduate and postgraduate students who are undertaking courses in accounting with an aim to pursue careers as non-financial managers and thus need a sound understanding of the role of financial accounting in their organisations. The book is particularly appropriate for required core courses in financial accounting, in which many of the students are not planning to take further elective accounting courses. It should also be of practical use to those working in commerce, industry, legal practices and government agencies that deal with financial information in their work.

Accounting books written specifically for non-accountants are often extremely demanding. The subject needs to be covered in such a way that non-accounting students do not become confused by too much technical information. They do not require the same detailed analysis that is essential for professional accountants. Some accounting books specially written for non-accountants go to the opposite extreme. They outline the subject so superficially that they are of little practical help.

The aim of this book is to offer a sound introduction to the study of financial accounting. We adopt a gradual progression in the level of rigour. We begin with a conceptual framework. The ground rules of double-entry bookkeeping (i.e. debits and credits) come later in the book in order not to distract the readers from the underlying concepts. This approach should help students to develop a proper understanding of these concepts. What we emphasise is the importance of understanding as opposed to the rote memorisation of procedures and terminology. This sequence provides a framework whereby readers can assimilate and appraise financial accounting, which is so critical for the proper functioning of the market economy. Only with such an overall understanding will the reader be able to follow and play an active part in the managerial role in whichever organisation they are employed.

Accounting textbooks are often not easily comprehensible to those from non-English-speaking backgrounds, because of the complexity of the language used. Many of the examples and questions in typical accounting books rely on strong knowledge of the nuances of the English language to interpret the questions, before students can attempt to answer them. This book adopts a plain English style that addresses the needs of students studying in a non-Anglo-Saxon environment.

Structure and pedagogy

The book is arranged in five parts. Part one investigates the fundamental principles and conventions that form the basics of accounting thought and practice. Part two outlines the primary financial statements and basic valuation issues. Part three provides tools for the preparation of financial reports both for a single entity and for a group of enterprises. Part four outlines the techniques of financial statement analysis. In Part five, issues relating to corporate reporting and corporate governance practices are presented and discussed, as we consider that readers should be aware of the importance of reliable and timely financial information for the smooth functioning of capital markets.

Guided tour of the book

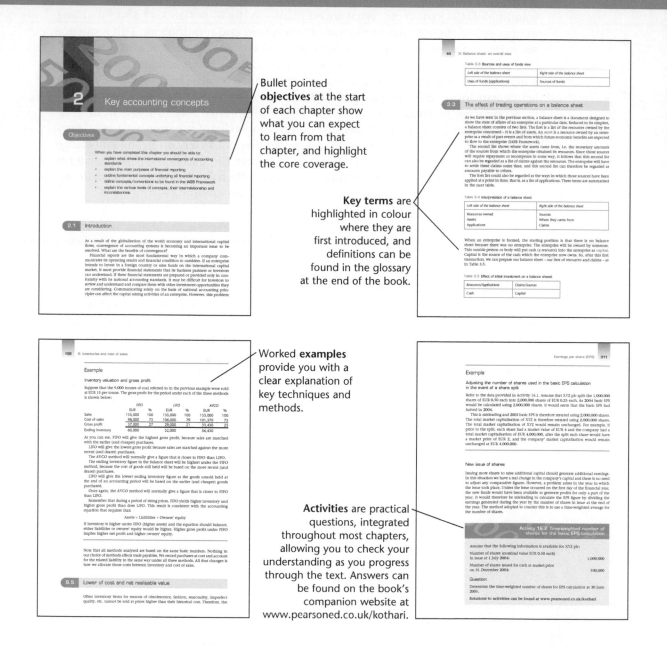

Bullet pointed **objectives** at the start of each chapter show what you can expect to learn from that chapter, and highlight the core coverage.

Key terms are highlighted in colour where they are first introduced, and definitions can be found in the glossary at the end of the book.

Worked **examples** provide you with a clear explanation of key techniques and methods.

Activities are practical questions, integrated throughout most chapters, allowing you to check your understanding as you progress through the text. Answers can be found on the book's companion website at www.pearsoned.co.uk/kothari.

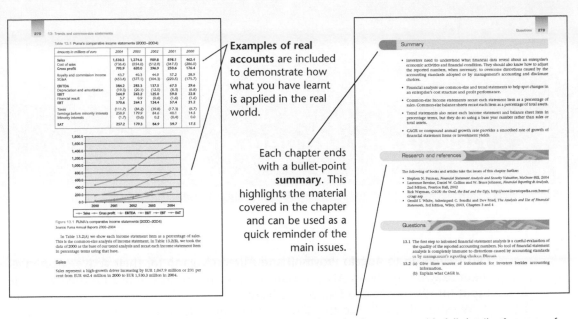

Examples of real accounts are included to demonstrate how what you have learnt is applied in the real world.

Each chapter ends with a bullet-point **summary**. This highlights the material covered in the chapter and can be used as a quick reminder of the main issues.

Research and references provide full details of sources of information referred to in the chapter, and suggestions for further reading, in order to pursue a topic in more depth or gain an alternative perspective.

Each chapter concludes with a **case study** based on a real example, and includes questions to test your application of accounting skills and techniques. Solutions are available for lecturers only on the companion website.

There are approximately six **questions** at the end of each chapter. These are designed to test your understanding of the chapter and to help you practice for exams. Solutions to selected questions are available for lecturers only on the companion website.

Acknowledgements

Our thanks go to Angelo Provasoli and Alfredo Viganò for their active encouragement to write this book. Also, to Paul De Sury and Andrea Nappa for their valuable input into Parts one and four respectively.

We should also like to thank our editors, Justinia Seaman, Matthew Smith and Sarah Wild, and their colleagues at Pearson Education for all the hard work that they have put into producing this book. It has been tough going for everyone involved in the process. We can only hope that the results will prove that it was all worthwhile.

Finally there is a personal acknowledgement we would like to make to Mary Kothari. Thank you for your encouragement and your help with the review of the manuscript: this book is dedicated to you.

Publisher's acknowledgements

We are grateful to the following for permission to reproduce copyright material:

Table 1.1 adapted from Alexander and Nobes (2004) *Financial Accounting: An International Approach*, 2nd edition, with permission from Pearson Education Ltd.; Figures 1.1a, 5.2, 9.1, 14.1 and Tables 3.1, 4.3 from *adidas-Salomon Annual Report 2004*, with permission of Adidas-Salomon AG, Herzogenaurach, Germany; Figures 1.2, 18.7 and 18.8 from Novo *Nordisk Annual Report 2004*, with permission from Novo Nordisk; Figure 2.2 from McLaney and Atrill (2005) *Accounting: An Introduction*, 3rd edition, with permission from Pearson Education Ltd; Figures 6.2, 7.2, 13.3, 13.4, 13.5, 13.6, 13.7, 18.5 and 18.6, and Tables 3.8, 3.9, 4.4, 12.1, 12.2 and Table in Activity 5.3 from *Puma 2004 Annual Report*, with permission of Puma AG, Herzenogaurach, Germany; Figure 3.6 from *Austrian Airlines Group Annual Report 2004*, with permission of Austrian Airlines, Vienna, Austria; Figure 5.1 and Figure 17.1 from *2004 Review of Financial Reporting Matters, March 2005*. © Huron Consulting Services LLC, 2005, all rights reserved; Figure 6.1 and Tables 6.1, 6.2 and 6.3 from Horngren Charles T., Sundem Gary L. and Elliot John A., *Introduction to Financial Accounting*, 8th edn. © 2002. Adapted by permission of Pearson Education Inc., Upper Saddle River, NJ, USA; Table 9.2 from the *Henkel Annual Report 2004*,

Henkel KgaA, Dusseldorf, Germany, with permission; Figures 4.1, 12.1, 12.2, 12.3, 12.4, 12.7, 12.8, 12.9, 12.10, 12.12, 15.4, 15.5, Table 15.1 and Figures on pp. 237, 243 and 244 adapted from Walsh (2002) *Key Management Ratios: Master the Management Metrics that Drive and Control your Business*, 3rd edition, with permission from Pearson Education Ltd.; Income statement on p. 280 from Deutsche Post Annual Report 2004, with permission of Deutsche Post; Tables 15.2 and 15.3 from *Kerry Group plc Annual Report 2004*, Kerry Group, Tralee, Ireland, with permission.

We are also grateful to the following for permission to reproduce textual material:

John Wiley and Sons Inc for an extract from *International Accounting and Multinational Enterprises* by Radebaugh and Gray; Sagalyn Literary Agency for an extract from *What Management Is, How it Works, and Why It's Everyone's Business* by Joan Magretta; and The Economist for 'Badly In Need of Repair' published in *The Economist* 2nd May 2002, and 'The Lessons of the Parmelat Scandal' published in *The Economist* 15th January 2004.

Part of the text of Chapter 17 is an extract from '*Rebuilding Public Confidence in Financial Reporting: An International Perspective*' of the Task Force on Rebuilding Public Confidence in Financial Reporting, published by the International Federation of Accountants (IFAC) in July 2003 and is used with permission.

Parts of the text in Chapter 18 have been reproduced from PricewaterhouseCoopers publications and are used with permission.

Some material has been drawn from publications by the International Accounting Standards Board (IASB) and is reproduced with permission. Copyright © 2004 International Accounting Standards Committee Foundation. All rights reserved. No permission granted to reproduce or distribute. The specific material is listed here:

Chapter 1 includes material drawn from IASB's *Framework for the Preparation and Presentation of Financial Statements*: paragraphs 9, 10 and 11.

Chapter 2 includes material drawn from IASB's *Framework for the Preparation and Presentation of Financial Statement*: paragraphs 12, 13, 14, 22, 23, 25, 26, 27, 28, 29, 30, 31, 32, 33, 34, 35, 36, 37, 38, 39, 40, 41, 42, 43, 44, 45; and IAS 1.

Chapter 3 includes material drawn from IASB's *Framework for the Preparation and Presentation of Financial Statement*: paragraph 49(b).

Chapter 4 includes Table from IAS 1.

Chapter 5 includes material drawn from IASB's IAS 18: paragraphs 14, 15, 16, 17, 18 and 19.

Chapter 7 includes material drawn from IASB's IAS 16: paragraphs 6, 16, 17; IAS 38: paragraphs 8, 9, 11, 13, 19, 20, 22, 24, 25, 26, 27, 44, 45, 46, 47, 79, 80, 88.

Chapter 8 includes material drawn from IASB's *Framework for the Preparation and Presentation of Financial Statement*: paragraph 49(b); Figure 8.2 from IAS 37.

Chapter 9 includes Table 9.1 from IAS 1.

Chapter 11 includes material drawn from IASB's IAS 28: paragraph 7; IAS 31: paragraph 10.

Chapter 12 includes material drawn from IASB's IAS 7: paragraphs 14, 16, 17, 19, 20(a), 20(b), 20(c).

Glossary includes some definitions from IASB's Glossary.

We are grateful to the Financial Times Limited for permission to reprint the following material:

Case Study Chapter 11 Branding – the bean counters get into creative accounting, © *Financial Times*, 31 August 2004; Case Study Chapter 16 A very secretive success story, © *Financial Times*, 17 August 2004; Case Study Chapter 18 Good ethics means more than ticking boxes, © *Financial Times*, 23 August 2005; Extract on p. 337 from We have to prove our own quality, © *Financial Times*, 21 July 2005.

We are grateful to the following for permission to use copyright material:

Extract on p. 23 from Sir David Tweedie – Standard bearer-in-chief from *The Financial Times Limited*, 14 November 2003, © Rod Newing; Extract on p. 329 from Accounts harmony is too big a prize to let go from *The Financial Times Limited*, 12 February 2004; © Jon Symonds; Extract on p. 337 from The best safeguard against financial scandal from *The Financial Times Limited*, 12 March 2004, © Thomas Healey; Extract on p. 348 from Sarbanes-Oxley has let fresh air into boardroom from *The Financial Times Limited*, 29 July 2005, © Thomas Healey and Robert Steel.

In some instances we have been unable to trace the owners of copyright material, and we would appreciate any information that would enable us to do so.

Part One The framework of financial reporting

1 Introduction to financial accounting

Objectives

When you have completed this chapter you should be able to:

- explain why financial accounting is important
- identify the main forms of business enterprise
- identify and discuss the main objectives of an enterprise
- identify the main users of financial information and their needs.

1.1 Introduction

What is 'accounting'? And what is it for?

Before answering these questions, we should look at the history and development of accounting, as this is fundamental to our understanding of present practices. Much of the regulatory and legal framework that we have today has resulted from past events. We will also see that the objectives of enterprises in society and the needs of users of financial information may influence that framework.

1.2 History of accounting

1.2.1 The origins of accounting

The precise origins of accountancy are difficult to trace. However, there is certainly evidence of some sort of record-keeping in many civilisations such as the Babylonian,

Assyrian and Egyptian. The Sumerian, an early Mesopotamian civilisation, recorded commercial transactions on stone dating back to 3600 BC and on clay tablets beginning about 3200 BC.

In ancient Egypt, accountants were scribes who also practised law. In the Pharaoh's central finance department, scribes prepared records of receipts and disbursements of silver, corn and other commodities. One recorded on papyrus the amount brought to the warehouse and another checked the emptying of the containers on the roof as the contents were poured into the storage building. Audit was performed by a third scribe who compared these two records. An official order was required for withdrawals, and the scribe in charge of the storehouse recorded the disbursements and retained the order. His records of receipts, disbursements and inventory balances were periodically audited by another scribe or his superior.

In 1939, archaeological excavation at Pylos, Greece (the possible site of the palace of Nestor of Trojan War fame) recovered hundreds of clay tablets written in Minoan script. Scholars have concluded that a Cretan scribe had been carried off by Mycenaean raiders and set to work keeping the accounting records of the Grecian king (circa 1400 BC). Perhaps from this beginning, it became customary to use slaves as scribes and auditors in Greece. With the growth of governmental revenues, particularly in Athens, accounting and auditing became more important. In the golden age of Pericles (461–429 BC), each citizen became an auditor through the custom of requiring contractors of public buildings to report their receipts and expenditures on tablets chiselled in stone on the walls of the building. One such tablet indicates that the Parthenon cost 469 talents of silver.

Roman civilisation was forward-thinking enough to have laws requiring taxpayers to prepare statements of their financial position. In fact, the Roman Empire made effective use of accounting and auditing to control the generals of conquered territories. The quaestors, who came into being about 200 BC, were financial officers responsible to Rome, who had custody of the treasury, supervised the scribes in their duties of recording treasury receipts and disbursements, and examined the accounts of the governors of subjugated countries. The quaestors were required to report periodically to Rome and have their records 'heard' by an examiner. The word 'auditor' came into use through this practice.

In the Middle Ages accounting suffered a decline because of the general disorganised condition of government and the economy throughout Europe. Gradually, however, accounting was re-established:

> *The complicated operations of the bankers, the papacy, and the monarchies required a careful system of bookkeeping. Archives and account books swelled with records of rents, tax, receipts, expenditures, audits and debits. The accounting methods of imperial Rome, lost in Western Europe in the seventh century, continued in Constantinople, were adopted by the Arabs and were revived in Italy during the Crusades. A fully developed system of double-entry bookkeeping appears in the communal accounts of Genoa in 1340.*
> (Durant 1950)

Several prerequisites have been identified as contributing towards the emergence of accounting as we know it today. These include:

- a system of writing, necessary to keep records

- arithmetic, necessary for simple computations

- money within the economy, as all transactions are denoted in this denominator

- the existence of credit (if all transactions are immediately completed there is little need to record them)
- commerce, as trade on a very small scale would be unlikely to result in the innovative development of complicated systems
- capital, the availability of which ensures that trade expands beyond a very small scale.

1.2.2 Luca Pacioli and the development of modern accounting practice

Double-entry bookkeeping (a system which records two aspects of every transaction) progressed in Italy around the thirteenth and fourteenth centuries as a result of the growth of maritime trade and banking institutions. Merchants required details of voyages to be kept, in order to calculate and share profits from overseas trading. The first bank with customer facilities opened in Venice in 1149. Balance sheets were evident from around 1400 and the Medici family had accounting records of 'cloth manufactured and sold'. Regular audits of the records of the Medici Bank were performed during the period 1397 to 1494. The main office in Florence required that an annual balance sheet be submitted by each branch. The general manager and his assistants audited these statements which are still found in the archives of Florence.

Luca Pacioli, a Franciscan monk, is widely believed to be the inventor of double-entry bookkeeping. However, a rudimentary system of double-entry bookkeeping was used in Genoa around 1340. In 1494, Pacioli documented the double-entry system being practised at the time by merchants in Venice in his famous book *Summa de arithmetica, geometria, proportioni et proportionalita* (The Collected Knowledge of Arithmetic, Geometry, Proportion and Proportionality). The *Summa* made Pacioli 'The Father of Accounting'.

During the 1550s the rise of nation states and the need to manage public finances underpinned the importance of good accounting practice:

> As commercial traffic shifted from the ports of Venice to the Atlantic shipping routes, Italy slipped in importance and relatively few new developments took place in accounting. . . . The French Revolution in the late 1700s marked the beginning of a great social upheaval that affected governments, finances, laws, and customs. Italy came under the influence of the French and then the Austrians, and their system of double-entry accounting was also influenced. It is interesting to note that Napoleon was surprised at how efficient the Italian system of accounting was.
>
> (Radebaugh and Gray 2002)

Development of accounting theory also began in this period and has continued to the present day. However, the influence of Pacioli's *Summa* continues to be felt in the double-entry bookkeeping we use today. Even the British, who acquired their knowledge of double-entry accounting soon after Pacioli's *Summa* was published, did not begin adopting the double-entry system until the Industrial Revolution (1760–1830). At that point, the importance of accounting grew substantially. As the scale of enterprise was increased by technological breakthroughs such as mass production, and fixed costs grew in importance compared to the variable costs, it became necessary to account for depreciation, the allocation of overheads, and inventory:

Since the early 1900s, the rapidity of change and the increasing complexity of the world's industrial economies necessitated still more changes in accounting. Mergers, acquisitions, and the growth of multinational corporations fostered new internal and external reporting and control systems. With widespread ownership of modern corporations came new audit and reporting procedures and new agencies became involved in promulgating accounting standards: namely, stock exchanges, securities regulation commissions, internal revenue agencies, and so on. Finally, with the dramatic increase in foreign investment and world trade and the formation of regional economic groups such as the European Union, problems arose concerning the international activities for business. This phenomenon remains particularly complex, for it involves reconciling the accounting practices of different nations in which each multinational operates, as well as dealing with accounting problems unique to international business. . . . Furthermore, there is growing public concern about the impact of corporations, especially in relation to so-called externalities (e.g., pollution of the environment and the influence of large corporations on national economic and social policies).

(Radebaugh and Gray 2002)

1.3   Accounting, accountability and the accounts

There are several definitions of accounting.

The Accounting Principles Board defines accounting as a service activity, the function of which is:

to provide quantitative information, primarily financial in nature, about economic entities that is intended to be useful in making economic decisions, in making resolved choice among alternative courses of action.

(Accounting Principles Board, Statement No. 4, 'Basic Concepts and Accounting Principles Underlying Financial Statements or Business Enterprises', New York, American Institute of Certified Public Accountants (AICPA) 1970, paragraph 40)

Accounting is the art of recording, classifying and summarizing in a significant manner and in terms of money, transactions and events which are, in part at least, of a financial character, and interpreting the results thereof.

('Review and Resume', Accounting Terminology Bulletin No. 1, American Institute of Certified Public Accountants (AICPA))

The American Accounting Association defines accounting as 'the process of identifying, measuring and communicating information to permit informed judgements and decisions by users of the information' (A Statement of Basic Accounting Theory 1996).

Compared with the previous two definitions, this is a more precise definition, for the reasons set out as follows:

- It recognises that accounting is a process: that process is concerned with representing business events, recording their financial effect, summarising and reporting the result of those effects, and interpreting those results.

- It is concerned with economic information: while this is predominantly financial, it also allows for non-financial information.

- Its purpose is to support 'informed judgements and decisions by users': this emphasises the usefulness of financial information in the decision-making process and the broad spectrum of 'users' of that information.[1]

As we illustrate in section 1.5, this book takes a stakeholder perspective in that users of financial information should include all those who may have an interest in the survival, profitability and growth of a business: shareholders, employees, customers, business trading partners, suppliers, government agencies, tax authorities, sell-side analysts, accounting standard setters, rating agencies, market regulators, banks, investment banks, large and small investors, and society as a whole.

Accounting for a narrow (shareholders) or a broad (societal) group of users is an important philosophical debate to which we will return in section 1.5. This debate derives from questions of accountability: to whom is the business accountable and for what, and what is the role of accounting and accountability?

Accountability is the capacity and willingness to give explanations for conduct, stating how one has discharged one's responsibilities, an explanation of conduct with a credible story of what happened, and a calculation and balancing of competing obligations, including moral ones (Boland and Schultze 1996). Accountability means explaining what happened and its financial consequences, as in the original meaning of the word account. According to this view, accounting is a collection of systems and processes used to record, report and interpret business transactions. Accounting provides an account – an explanation or report in financial terms – about the transactions of an organisation. It enables managers to satisfy the stakeholders in the organisation that they have acted in the best interests of stakeholders rather than for themselves. This is the notion of accountability to others, a result of the stewardship function of managers that takes place through the process of accounting. Stewardship is an important concept because in all but very small businesses, the owners of businesses are different individuals from the managers. This separation of ownership from control makes accounting particularly influential because of the emphasis given to increasing shareholder wealth. Accountability results in the production of financial statements, primarily for those interested parties who are external to the business. This function is called **financial accounting**.

1.4   Forms of business units

This book refers to businesses as 'enterprises', which is the definition used by the International Accounting Standards Board (IASB). This word is designed to cover all forms of business operations.

Sole tradership (or sole proprietorship)

At one extreme, an enterprise can be run by a single person with no partners. This enterprise is called sole tradership or sole proprietorship. This form of business tends to be adopted by small retail establishments or shops and individual enterprises such as those run by dentists, physicians and attorneys or lawyers.

The sole trader has an unlimited liability for the debts of the enterprise and pays personal income tax on the profits. If the enterprise is to be sold, then the trader must sell the (net) assets because there is no legal entity to sell. From an accounting viewpoint, each sole proprietorship is a separate entity that is distinct from the proprietor. Nevertheless, the proprietor keeps the accounts for the enterprise separate from other personal activities, in accordance with the business entity convention discussed in section 2.4.

Partnerships

As the enterprise becomes larger, it may be useful to have some joint owners (partners) who can contribute skills and money. The enterprise then becomes a partnership, which is formalised by a contract between the partners that states their rights and duties. In common law countries, a partnership does not have separate legal existence for most purposes. The partners are legally responsible for the enterprise's assets and liabilities, and they pay tax on their share of the profits.

Nevertheless, it is possible to set up a 'limited liability partnership' (LLP). This is the legal form many accountancy firms have chosen today. The purpose of this is to seek to protect the partners from some part of the liabilities of the enterprise if there are large legal claims.

Companies

The complete separation of owners from their enterprise is achieved by setting up a company, usually with limited liability for the owners. The ownership of the company is denoted by shares, which can be transferred from one owner (shareholder or stockholder) to another without affecting the company's existence. A company is a separate legal entity from its owners. The company can buy and sell assets and pays tax on its own profit.

In EU and other developed countries, companies can be either private or public. A private company does not have its shares listed on the stock exchange, so they can only be exchanged by private agreement between the owner and the buyer, whereas public companies have their shares freely traded on markets. Public companies are required to comply with rules fixed by the stock exchanges, regulators of stock exchanges or other bodies.

Groups

As an enterprise continues to increase in size and complexity, it normally finds it useful to arrange its activities as a group comprising a large number of legally separate entities. The reasons for such complex structures are:

- The combination of two enterprises may result in economies of scale and scope, that is to say the cost of producing the combined output will be less than the sum of the costs of producing the separate outputs or, alternatively, the combined output will be greater for the same total cost. Such economies may exist not only in production but also in administration, marketing, research and development, and financing.

- Combining with another enterprise may be one means of eliminating or reducing competition. Although integration may occur for many reasons, one reason may be that it is possible to reduce competition both by vertical integration, that is by combining with an enterprise at an earlier or later stage of the production cycle, or by horizontal integration, that is by combining with a firm at the same stage in the production cycle.

- By combining with another entity which makes different products, an enterprise is often able to reduce risk. Thus one reason for a combination involving businesses in different industries may be a desire to generate an earnings stream which is less variable and/or volatile than the separate earnings streams of the two individual businesses.

- The various entities in the group need to be legally separate when they operate in several countries under several different laws.

- Sometimes there are tax advantages in being separate or there may be tax disadvantages in combining formerly separate entities.

- The legal structures may partially reflect a hierarchical organisational structure.

- The (financial and non-financial) performances may improve thanks to a better integration of different activities carried out by the various enterprises forming the group.

1.5   Objectives of enterprises in society

An important question which is being debated concerns the role of enterprises in society. On one side of this long-running debate are those who argue that 'the business of business is business' (to borrow Milton Friedman's phrase) and, therefore, its goal is primarily and exclusively to enhance shareholder value. On the other side, there are those who argue that enterprises have a broader purpose: to create value by taking into account the interests of employees, customers, suppliers and the communities in which they operate.

Should enterprises seek only to maximise shareholder value or strive to serve the, often conflicting, interests of all stakeholders? In addition to this question, we may ask what is the managers' duty. An answer can be found in exploring two visions of the enterprise. The first one, known as the shareholder theory, is based on the primacy of the shareholders, while the second one, the stakeholder theory, claims that other stakeholders deserve consideration, too. According to the former, the managers primarily have a duty to maximise shareholder returns, while the latter claims that a manager's duty is to balance the shareholders' financial interests against the interest of other stakeholders such as employees, customers and the local community, even if it reduces shareholder returns.

The shareholder theory asserts that shareholders provide capital to a company's managers, who are supposed to use corporate funds only in ways that have been authorised by the shareholders. As Milton Friedman wrote in 1962:

> There is one and only one social responsibility of business – to use its resources and engage in activities designed to increase its profits so long as it . . . engages in open and free competition, without deception or fraud.

On the other hand, the stakeholder theory asserts that managers have a duty to both the corporation's shareholders and 'individuals and constituencies that contribute, either voluntarily or involuntarily, to a company's wealth-creating capacity and activities, and who are therefore its potential beneficiaries and/or risk bearers' (Post, Preston and Sachs 2002), such as its customers, employees, suppliers and the local community. According to the stakeholder theory, managers are agents of all stakeholders and have two main responsibilities:

- to ensure that the ethical rights of no stakeholder are violated
- to balance the legitimate interests of the stakeholders when making decisions.

The objective of a corporation is, thus, to balance profit maximisation with the long-term ability of the corporation to remain a going concern.

The fundamental distinction between the two approaches is that the stakeholder theory demands that interests of all stakeholders be considered even if it does not always maximise profits or wealth of the company or if it sometimes reduces the company profitability. In other words, under the shareholder theory, non-shareholders can be viewed as 'means' to the 'ends' of profitability; under the stakeholder theory, the interests of all stakeholders (i.e. shareholders and non-shareholders) are viewed as 'ends'.

In recent years we have witnessed a good deal of corporate executive behaviour that was at best disruptive to the free flow of commerce and, at worst, illegal. Few would dispute that such behaviour should be discouraged rather than rewarded. The real question, of course, is whether a corporation should prescribe, and therefore reward, behaviours that are actually detrimental to society. Many of the more strident critics of the shareholder theory seem to claim that as executives are charged with maximising shareholder value and are given large incentives to do so through stock options or other arrangements, they will respond by embracing whatever manipulations are necessary to achieve that goal.

This argument relies, however, on an incomplete and somewhat misrepresentative interpretation of the shareholder theory.

In fact, while the mantra of maximising shareholder value was indeed chanted by many in the economic and financial communities in the late 1990s until the scandals hit in 2002, it is not at all clear that such a goal is completely consistent with the intent of the shareholder theory. Management should worry about increasing dividends through profitability rather than increasing share price in the stock market with manipulation or fraudulent behaviours.

Moreover, the pursuit of profit should be done legally and without deception, and there is little room for the kinds of overtly illegal behaviour alleged in many recent financial scandals. The executives who broke the law were not operating according to the shareholder theory.

Finally, it must be remembered that many of the executives undertook actions that were more for their own benefit than for that of the shareholders. For example, Enron CFO (Chief Financial Officer) Andrew Fastow, who created a partnership that was bankrolled with Enron stock and invested in a portfolio of highly risky ventures, 'stood to make millions quickly, in fees and profits, even if Enron lost money on the deal,' according to the *Washington Post* (28 July 2002). Actually Enron lost more than $500 million from these initiatives and filed bankruptcy. Similarly, several other executives, including Kenneth Lay of Enron, Garry Winninck of Global Crossing

Holdings and Scott Sullivan of WorldCom, also benefited from bonuses and stock options at the same time that their companies' shareholders were suffering losses. Such behaviour is inexcusable, since theoretically executives should act only in the shareholders' interests and not in their own.

Yet business leaders in the past have been too short-term in their orientation, with great damage to shareholder culture. They need to think longer term. Yes, they should focus on shareholders; that's not in question. But how they do that, how they create long-term sustainable value, is the issue. And to do that, they have to take more account of their employees, their customers, their suppliers, and the health of their communities – and yes, the global economy, too.

(Jeffrey Garten, *The Economist*, 4 January 2003)

What we wish to emphasise is that profits are a result of satisfying the needs of these stakeholders. As David Packard, the co-founder of Hewlett-Packard said, 'Profit is not the proper end and aim of management – it is what makes all of the proper ends and aims possible.' According to his vision, the real purpose of an enterprise is to create value for its customers and to generate profit as a result (Magretta 2002).

---

adidas-Salomon
strives to be the global leader in the sporting goods industry with sports brands built on a passion for sports and a sporting lifestyle.

→

We are consumer focused.
That means we continuously improve the quality, look, feel and image of our products and our organizational structures to match and exceed consumer expectations and to provide them with the highest value.

→

We are innovation and design leaders
who seek to help athletes of all skill levels achieve peak performance with every product we bring to the market.

→

We are a global organization
that is socially and environmentally responsible, creative and financially rewarding for our employees and shareholders.

→

We are committed
to continuously strengthening our brands and products to improve our competitive position and financial performance.

→

In the medium term
we will extend our leading marketing position in Europe, expand our share of the US footwear market and be the fastest growing major sporting goods supplier in Asia and Latin America.

The resulting top-line growth, together with strict cost control and working capital improvements, will drive overproportionate earnings growth.

Figure 1.1 Examples of corporate purposes of leading multinationals
Source: adidas-Salomon Annual Report 2004

Our corporate purpose

Unilever's mission is to add Vitality to life. We meet everyday needs for nutrition, hygiene and personal care with brands that help people feel good, look good and get more out of life.

Our deep roots in local cultures and markets around the world give us our strong relationship with consumers and are the foundation for our future growth. We will bring our wealth of knowledge and international expertise to the service of local consumers – a truly multi-local multinational.

Our long-term success requires a total commitment to exceptional standards of performance and productivity, to working together effectively, and to a willingness to embrace new ideas and learn continuously.

To succeed also requires, we believe, the highest standards of corporate behaviour towards everyone we work with, the communities we touch, and the environment on which we have an impact.

This is our road to sustainable, profitable growth, creating long-term value for our shareholders, our people, and our business partners.

Figure 1.1 (*Cont'd*)
Source: Unilever Annual Report and Accounts 2004

Coloplast's Mission

Throughout the world we wish, within our selected business areas, to be the preferred source of medical devices and associated services, contributing to a better quality of life.

By being close to customers we fulfil their needs with innovative, high quality solutions. Through empathy, responsiveness and dependability we seek to earn their loyalty.

Our culture attracts and nourishes individuals who are energetic, committed and have a passion for our business.

We respect differences and pledge to act responsibly in social, environmental and business contexts.

By striving to be best in our business we achieve growth and increased value for our customers, employees and shareholders.

Figure 1.1 (*Cont'd*)
Source: Coloplast Annual Report 2003/04

Novo Nordisk explains its own view of stakeholder theory in its annual report as shown in Figure 1.2.

This model illustrates Novo Nordisk and its economic stakeholders and the interactions that drive economic growth in well-developed societies. When, for instance, investors provide risk capital so that Novo Nordisk can develop new products, it will benefit customers, employees and suppliers. For customers, in turn, the products from Novo Nordisk improve their ability to contribute to society. When employees, suppliers and investors spend their income to buy goods and services and make investments, they too contribute to wealth generation in society. And in their capacity as citizens in the local and global community, all economic actors pay taxes to the public sector in return for services. Our sustainable business practices are mechanisms that improve the outcome of the market economy model. The interactions and multiplier effects are illustrated by the blue circle linking the stakeholders.

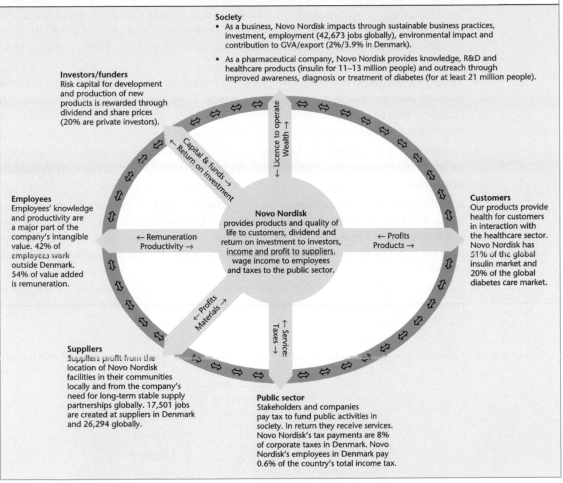

Society
- As a business, Novo Nordisk impacts through sustainable business practices, investment, employment (42,673 jobs globally), environmental impact and contribution to GVA/export (2%/3.9% in Denmark).
- As a pharmaceutical company, Novo Nordisk provides knowledge, R&D and healthcare products (insulin for 11–13 million people) and outreach through improved awareness, diagnosis or treatment of diabetes (for at least 21 million people).

Investors/funders
Risk capital for development and production of new products is rewarded through dividend and share prices (20% are private investors).

Employees
Employees' knowledge and productivity are a major part of the company's intangible value. 42% of employees work outside Denmark. 54% of value added is remuneration.

Novo Nordisk
provides products and quality of life to customers, dividend and return on investment to investors, income and profit to suppliers, wage income to employees and taxes to the public sector.

Customers
Our products provide health for customers in interaction with the healthcare sector. Novo Nordisk has 51% of the global insulin market and 20% of the global diabetes care market.

Suppliers
Suppliers profit from the location of Novo Nordisk facilities in their communities locally and from the company's need for long-term stable supply partnerships globally. 17,501 jobs are created at suppliers in Denmark and 26,294 globally.

Public sector
Stakeholders and companies pay tax to fund public activities in society. In return they receive services. Novo Nordisk's tax payments are 8% of corporate taxes in Denmark. Novo Nordisk's employees in Denmark pay 0.6% of the country's total income tax.

Figure 1.2 Novo Nordisk's economic stakeholder model
Source: Novo Nordisk Annual Report 2004

1.6   Main users of financial information of an enterprise

Information on an enterprise and in particular that contained in the annual report is used by a wide range of operators. Let us look closely at these users of financial information and, in particular, at the reasons why they need financial information relating to an enterprise.

The terminology we use is closely based on a document called *Framework for the Preparation and Presentation of Financial Statements* issued by the IASB.

The users of financial statements include present and potential investors, employees, lenders, suppliers and other trade creditors, customers, governments and their agencies and the public. They use financial statements in order to satisfy some of their different needs for information. These needs include the following:

- *Owners (or investors)* need financial information relating to the enterprise to assess how effectively the managers are running it and to make judgements about likely levels of risk and return in the future. Shareholders need information to assess the ability of the enterprise to pay them a return (dividend). The same applies to potential shareholders.

- *Employees and their representative groups* are interested in information about the stability and profitability of their employers. They too need information which enables them to assess the ability of the enterprise to provide remuneration, retirement benefits and employment opportunities.

- *Lenders* (such as banks) need financial information about an enterprise in order to assess its ability to meet its obligations, to pay interest and to repay the amount borrowed.

- *Suppliers* and other trade creditors need information that enables them to determine whether amounts owed to them will be paid when due. Trade creditors are likely to be interested in an enterprise over a shorter period than lenders unless they are dependent upon the continuation of the enterprise as a major customer.

- *Customers* have an interest in information about the continuance of an enterprise, especially when they have a long-term involvement with, or are dependent on, the enterprise.

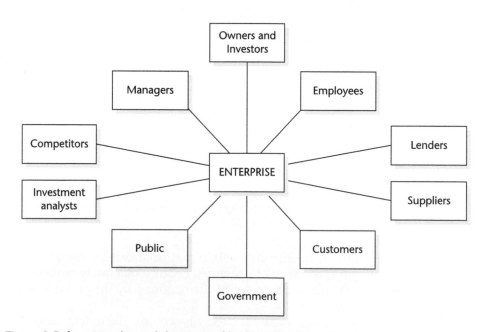

Figure 1.3 An enterprise and the users of its financial information

- *Governments and their agencies* need information in order to regulate the activities of enterprises, to assess whether they comply with agreed pricing policies, whether financial support is needed, and how much tax they should pay. They also require information in order to determine taxation policies and as the basis for national income and statistics.

- *Members of the public* are affected by enterprises in a variety of ways. For example, enterprises may make a substantial contribution to the local economy in many ways including the number of people they employ and their patronage of local suppliers. Financial statements may assist the public by providing information about the trends and recent developments in the prosperity of the enterprise and the range of its activities.

- *Investment analysts* need financial information relating to an enterprise to assess the likely risks and returns associated with the enterprise in order to determine its investment potential and to advise clients accordingly.

- *Competitors* need financial information relating to an enterprise to assess the threat to sales and profits posed by those businesses and to provide a benchmark against which the competitor's performance can be measured.

- *Managers* need financial information relating to an enterprise to help make decisions and plans for the business and to exercise control so that the plans come to fruition.

While all the information needs of these users cannot be met by financial statements, there are needs which are common to all users. As investors are providers of risk capital to the enterprise, the publication of financial statements that meet their needs will also meet most of the needs of other users.

It should however, be noted that some user groups (such as suppliers, customers, competitors, public) use financial information, but they have no right to claim this information as other user groups have.

The management of an enterprise has the primary responsibility for the preparation and presentation of its financial statements. Management is also interested in the information contained in the financial statements even though it has access to additional management and financial information that helps it carry out its planning, decision-making and control responsibilities.

1.7   Management accounting and financial accounting

The needs described in the previous section lead to an important distinction between two branches of accounting, namely that between management accounting and financial accounting. Although this book focuses on the latter, it is useful to highlight the differences between these two branches.

The former is concerned with the provision of information intended to be useful to management within the enterprise, while financial accounting is intended for users outside the enterprise itself.

The differences between the two types of accounting reflect the different user groups that they address and, to some extent, the differences in access to financial information. Management accounting should provide timely and accurate information to facilitate budgetary control over revenues and costs, to measure and improve productivity, and to devise improved production processes. In addition to that, management accounting must report accurate product costs so that pricing decisions, introduction of new products, abandonment of obsolete products, and response to rival products can be made.

The Chartered Institute of Management Accountants' definition of the core activities of management accounting includes:

- participation in the planning process at both strategic and operational levels, involving the establishment of policies and the formulation of budgets
- the initiation of any provision of guidance for management decisions, involving the generation, analysis, presentation and interpretation of relevant information
- contributing to the monitoring and control of performance through the provision of reports including comparisons of actual with budgeted performance, and their analysis and interpretation.

The major differences between management and financial accounting in terms of nature of the reports produced, level of detail, regulations, reporting interval, time horizon, range and quality of information are described in the following paragraphs:

- *Nature of the reports produced.* Financial accounting reports tend to be general purpose reports. That is, they contain financial information that will be useful for a broad range of users and decisions rather than being specifically designed for the needs of a particular group or set of decisions. Management accounting reports, on the other hand, are often specific purpose reports. They are designed either with a particular decision in mind or for a particular manager.
- *Level of detail.* Financial accounting reports provide users with a broad overview of the position and performance of an enterprise for a period. As a result, information is aggregated. On the contrary, management accounting reports provide managers with considerable detail to help them with particular operational decisions.
- *Regulations.* Financial reports, for many enterprises, are subject to accounting regulations that exist to ensure that they are produced according to a standardised format. These regulations are imposed by law and the accounting profession. Because management accounting reports are for internal use only, there is no regulation from external sources concerning their form and content: they can be designed to meet the needs of particular managers.
- *Reporting interval.* For most enterprises, financial accounting reports are produced on a yearly basis. However, larger companies may produce semi-annual reports and some produce quarterly reports. Management accounting reports may be produced as frequently as required by managers. In many enterprises, managers are provided with certain reports on a daily, weekly or monthly basis, which allows them to check progress on a need basis.
- *Time horizon.* Financial accounting reports reflect the performance and position of the business for the past period, whilst management accounting reports provide information concerning future performance as well as past performance. However, it is an oversimplification to suggest that financial accounting reports

never incorporate expectations concerning the future: occasionally, enterprises will release forecast information to other users in order to raise capital or to fight off unwanted takeover bids. Although differences undoubtedly exist, there is also a good deal of overlap between the needs of managers and the needs of other users with reference to the time horizon. For example, managers will, at times, be interested in receiving an historic overview of the enterprise's operations of the sort provided to other users. Equally, the other users would be interested in receiving information relating to the future, such as the forecast level of profits, and non-financial information such as the state of the order book and product innovations.

- *Range and quality of information.* Financial accounting concentrates on information that can be quantified in monetary terms, while management accounting in addition to such reports, produces reports that contain information of a non-financial nature, such as measures of physical quantities of inventories and output.

1.8 Notes on terminology

Many readers of this book will aim not only to master a subject new to them but also do so in a language that is not their first. One added difficulty is that for accounting issues, UK terms and US terms are considerably different.[2] The IASB issues its standards in English using a mixture of UK and US terms, while UK terms tend to be used by the fourth and seventh EU directives. On the whole, this book uses IASB terms.

Table 1.1 Examples of the UK, US and IASB terms

UK	US	IASB
Stock	Inventory	Inventory
Shares	Stock	Shares
Own shares	Treasury stock	Treasury shares
Debtors	Accounts receivable	Trade and other receivables
Creditors	Accounts payable	Trade and other payables
Finance lease	Capital lease	Finance lease
Turnover	Sales (or revenue)	Sales (or revenue)
Acquisition	Purchase	Acquisition
Fixed assets	Property, plant and equipment	Property, plant and equipment
Profit and loss account	Income statement	Income statement
Reducing balance depreciation method	Declining-balance depreciation method	Diminishing balance depreciation method

Source: adapted from Alexander and Nobes (2004)

Summary

- There is evidence of some sort of accounting in ancient civilisations dating back to around 3600 BC.

- Luca Pacioli, an Italian Franciscan monk, is widely considered to be the inventor of double-entry bookkeeping, which is the basis of current financial accounting.

- 'Accounting' is the process of identifying, measuring and communicating information to permit informed judgements and decisions by users of the information.

- The IASB refers to all forms of businesses as 'enterprises'.

- Throughout this book we consider that an enterprise's objective is not simply the maximisation of profit or dividends for shareholders, but to create value by also enriching employees, customers, suppliers and the community in which it operates.

- Financial accounting is designed to give financial information to particular groups of users. Different users have different needs.

- This book focuses on the reporting by business enterprises to shareholders and stakeholders.

- Accounting terms differ considerably between the UK and US practices. In the book we have opted for the accounting terms used by the IASB.

References and research

The IASB document relevant for this chapter is the *Framework for the Preparation and Presentation of Financial Statements*.

The following are examples of research papers and books that take the issues of this chapter further:

- David Alexander and Christopher Nobes, *Financial Accounting: An International Introduction*, 2nd Edition, Financial Times Prentice Hall, 2004, Chapter 1
- R.J. Boland and U. Schultze, 'Narrating Accountability', *Accountability: Power, Ethos and the Technologies of Managing*, R. Murno and J. Mouritsen (eds), Thompson Press: London, 1996
- Raymond de Roover, *The Rise and Decline of the Medici Bank, 1397–1494*, Harvard University Press, 1963
- Will Durant, *The History of Civilization: Our Oriental Heritage*, Vol. I, Simon and Schuster, 1935
- Will Durant, *The History of Civilization: The Age of Faith*, Vol. IV, Simon and Schuster, 1950
- M. Friedman, *Capitalism and Freedom*, University of Chicago Press, 1962
- Paul Jackson, David Tinius and William Weis, *Luca Pacioli: Unsung Hero of the Renaissance*, South-Western Publishing Company, 1990
- Joan Magretta, *What Management is: How it Works and Why it's Everyone's Business*, Free Press, 2002, page 131
- Kenneth S. Most, 'Accounting by the Ancients', *The Accountant*, May 1959

- J.E. Post, L.E. Preston and S. Sachs, *Redefining the Corporation: Stakeholder Management and Organizational Wealth*, 2002
- Lee H. Radebaugh and Sidney J. Gray, *International Accounting and Multinational Enterprises*, Wiley, 2002
- H. Jeff Smith, 'The shareholders vs. stakeholders debate', *MIT Sloan Management Review*, Vol. 44, No. 4, Summer 2003
- Williard E. Stone, 'Antecedents of the accounting profession', *The Accounting Review*, Vol. 44, No. 2, April 1969 (http://uk.jstor.org/)
- 'The good company. A survey of corporate social responsibility', *The Economist*, 22 January 2005

Questions

1.1 Why does financial accounting matter?

1.2 Think of the various groups of users of financial information. Suggest the information that each is likely to need from accounting statements and reports. Are there likely to be difficulties in satisfying the needs of all the groups you have considered with one common set of information?

1.3 Outline the relative benefits to users of financial reports relating to:

(a) information about the past
(b) information about the present
(c) information about the future.

1.4 In the context of your own national background, rank the nine 'external' user groups suggested in the text (i.e. omitting managers) according to the priority that you think should be given to their needs. Explain your reasons.

1.5 Compare your answer to the previous question with the answers of students of different national backgrounds to yours. Explore the likely causes of any major differences that emerge, in terms of legal, economic and cultural environments.

1.6 Read the mission statements reported in Figure 1.1. Explain how the objectives of enterprises described in section 1.5 are linked to those mission statements.

Case study   Ford and Dell

Read the following short case histories of Ford and Dell drawn from Joan Magretta's book. What messages can be inferred? How did these two enterprises link their objectives to their (financial and non-financial) performance measures and results? Can you see the difference between corporate purposes or objectives and results? Explain how these enterprises' objectives determined what results were meaningful and what measures were appropriate.

Case studies by Joan Magretta (excerpted with permission of the author from *What management is, how it works, and why it's everyones' business*, 2002, Free Press)

When Henry Ford started his company in 1903, his partners wanted him to make high-priced cars with high margins. Ford's co-owners were typical of early investors in the auto industry in thinking that profit per car was the best measure of performance. Ford balked at this. His purpose, his overriding goal was to 'build a car for the great multitude,' to democratize the auto. Ford wanted to create a car so affordable that it would displace the horse; he wanted cars to be so common that one day, hard as it must have been to imagine at the time, they would be 'taken for granted.'

By 1907, Ford had bought up enough shares in the company to assume a majority position. He used his new control to shift the company's direction. For him, the measure of success was the number of cars sold. Selling a lot of cars, at a 'reasonably small profit' would allow him to satisfy his two chief aims in life: more people could buy and enjoy cars, and more men could have good jobs at good wages. Ford created the 'people's car' by reducing prices by 58 percent from 1908 to 1916, at a time when he had more orders than he could fill, and could easily have raised them. Ford's shareholders responded by slapping him with a suit against the practice. At the same time, he instituted the five-dollar day for workers, double the industry's standard wage. The Wall Street Journal *condemned Ford for injecting 'spiritual principles into a field where they don't belong.'*

With 20–20 hindsight (and a better understanding of value creation), we can understand why Ford's measure was the right one, the one that fitted his purpose, his business model and, for a time, the competitive realities of the nascent auto industry. It led Ford to make the right pricing decision, that is, the one that supported his overriding purpose. At a time when turnover in the industry was astronomically high and, therefore, a real threat to Ford's ability to churn out its unprecedented volume of cars, it also led him to make the right decision about wages, which was the key people decision of the day. (The five-dollar-per-day wage also turned workers into customers who could afford cars.)

Dell Computer's measures for translating its mission into performance are equally fine grained and altogether different. When Michael Dell founded his company in 1984, his purpose was simple: give customers a better deal by selling to them directly instead of going through a middleman, as the rest of the industry then did. Working as a one-man operation from his college dorm room, Michael Dell had no need to articulate this purpose or to explain how the business worked. To become the industry giant Dell is today, however, he had to make the organization's purpose concrete. This meant defining results and specifying measures of performance that would keep a large organization focused on the right things.

In Dell's case, one of the keys to success is speed. More specifically, 'speed' refers to the elapsed time between the moment a computer's components are manufactured and the moment a fully assembled computer reaches the customer's desktop. Why does speed matter? In the computer business, new products are introduced so rapidly that if you have old components, even if they are just several months old, chances are those machines will be obsolete before they get to market. When that happens, the computer maker simply has to sell them at a deep discount and swallow the loss. The expense of obsolete inventory is a fact of life in any business where the product life cycle is short – whether the business is computers or fashion.

Very early on, Dell made the connection between its business model and its performance measures. Dell and his managers were able to translate what they were trying to do – give customers the best available technology at the lowest possible cost – into concrete metrics. For example, Dell discovered that the more often a component, a monitor, say, was touched by a Dell worker, the longer the assembly process took and the more likely it was that the final computer would have a quality problem. So, Dell began to measure 'touches,' and set about systematically to reduce the number. For its monitors, Dell ultimately drove this number to zero. Working with its supplier, Sony, whose quality rates are high, Dell was able to put its name on the monitors without ever taking them out of the box. As Michael Dell explains, 'What's the point in having a monitor put on a truck to Austin, Texas and taken off the truck and sent on a little tour around the warehouse, only to be put back on another truck?'

The imperative of speed was translated into Dell's financial strategy as well. One problem that plagues most growing companies, even profitable ones, is that, if they're not careful, they can run out of cash. (This is why start-ups often worry about burn rates, which is a measure of how fast a company is using up its seed money.) Thomas J. Meredith, Dell's former CFO, was an architect of the company's effort to solve the problem of financing rapid growth. The question is simple: How do you balance rapid growth with profitability and liquidity? Gross margin, which is revenue minus the cost of goods sold, is a traditional measure of profitability. It doesn't include, however, all the funds that have to be invested in growth (advertising to build your market, for example, and money invested in facilities and inventory). Meredith shifted Dell's financial focus from gross margin to return on invested capital, a measure that includes those funds, paving the way for Dell's focus on low-inventory manufacturing. In fact, his car's license plate was ROIC, which may seem silly, but is very telling. If you want thousands of people to march in the same direction, some symbolism and theatrics are usually required.

Dell wanted to grow fast and to do so without taking on a lot of debt to fund its working capital. To this end, one of the things they did was measure days inventory, a ratio that tells you how long it would take to draw the inventory you have. (It's the number of units on hand divided by the number of units sold per day.) Dell focused everyone in the organization on coming up with ideas to get that number lower and lower. Why? The less inventory a company has, the less money it ties up carrying it.

Notes

[1] According to the Accounting Standards Board (ASB) in the UK, 'the objective of financial statements is to provide information about the reporting entity's financial performance and fiancial position that is useful to a wide range of users for assessing the stewardship of the entity's management and for making economic decisions. The objective of financial statements can usually be met by focusing exclusively on the needs of present and potential investors. Such investors need information (. . .) that is useful to them in evaluating the reporting ability to generate cash (. . .). Financial statements do not provide all the information needed by users; they do, however, provide a frame of reference against which users can evaluate the more specific information they obtain from other sources.' ('Statement of Principles for Financial Reporting', ASB, 1999).

[2] More extensive references to these differences are provided in the Glossary.

2 Key accounting concepts

When you have completed this chapter you should be able to:

- explain what drives the international convergence of accounting standards
- explain the main purposes of financial reporting
- outline fundamental concepts underlying all financial reporting
- define concepts/conventions to be found in the IASB Framework
- explain the various levels of concepts, their interrelationship and inconsistencies.

2.1 Introduction

As a result of the globalisation of the world economy and international capital flows, convergence of accounting systems is becoming an important issue to be resolved. What are the benefits of convergence?

Financial reports are the most fundamental way in which a company communicates its operating results and financial condition to outsiders. If an enterprise intends to invest in a foreign country or raise funds on the international capital market, it must provide financial statements that its business partners or investors can understand. If these financial statements are prepared or provided only in conformity with its national accounting standards, it may be difficult for investors to review and understand and compare them with other investment opportunities they are considering. Communicating solely on the basis of national accounting principles can affect the capital raising activities of an enterprise. However, this problem can be avoided if an enterprise provides accounting information in accordance with a set of accounting standards that is accepted by most countries.

The need for a set of high-quality international standards is no longer confined to the conceptual level. There is a practical dimension to it. These standards will unify accounting practices around the world, simplify listings across national boundaries, and address the needs of national and international markets. If markets are to function properly and capital is to be allocated efficiently, investors require transparency and must have confidence that financial information accurately reflects economic performance. Investors should also be able to make comparisons between companies in order to make rational investment decisions, particularly in a rapidly globalising world.

The need for international convergence in accounting standards has emerged even more strongly in view of the recent high-profile corporate failures. There are a number of lessons to be learnt on how to avoid a repeat of these failures. The failures have highlighted again the critical importance of corporate governance, putting under the limelight issues such as the accountability of the board of directors and the audit committee, independence of auditors, quality of their audits in relation to a listed company, and not least the quality of accounting standards. We wish to emphasise the importance of high-quality accounting standards and their application and enforcement of them for instilling investor confidence in our increasingly globalised financial community.

It is therefore encouraging to note the decision by IASB and FASB in the United States to work together towards greater convergence between the US GAAP and IASs, now IFRSs. A successful outcome of this convergence would dramatically improve the efficiency of global capital markets: costs would decrease, comparability would improve and corporate governance would be enhanced.

As Sir David Tweedie, chairman of the IASB, states:

> *Global accounting standards bring massive transparency and open up new markets. Financial information is the cornerstone of the markets, and standards remove a major area of doubt for investors and reduce a major cause of market risk. You will get a better spread of investment, which makes things a bit safer, and which could shave several points off the cost of capital. We are not talking about arcane bookkeeping, we are talking about world growth, trade, investment and employment.*
>
> (from 'Standard bearer-in-chief', Rod Newing, *Financial Times*, 14 November 2003)

2.2 The accounting harmonisation process in the EU

As we have seen in the previous section, accountancy is becoming increasingly globalised, as enterprises become more multinational in nature, and the volume of trade and investment between enterprises in different countries increases. These factors have underlined the need for financial statements that are internationally comparable and consistent.

There has been considerable debate over the years as to which set of accounting standards enterprises should follow. In July 2002 the European Commission announced that all EU listed companies should use IASs for their published consolidated financial statements for the year ending 31 December 2005 (with comparative data for 2004). The International Organisation of Securities Commission (IOSCO) has actively encouraged the use and quality of IASs over the past 15 years.

IASs were issued by the International Accounting Standards Committee (IASC) that was established in 1973. In April 2001 IASC was restructured and is now known as IASB. The board is committed to developing, in the public interest, a single set of high-quality, understandable and enforceable global accounting standards that require transparent and comparable information in general purpose financial statements. In addition, the board cooperates with national accounting standard bodies to achieve convergence in accounting standards around the world. The standards issued by IASB are known as International Financial Reporting Standards (IFRSs). The 34 IASs will remain in force until amended or withdrawn by IASB.

IASB is based in London and is currently headed by Sir David Tweedie. There are 14 members of the board. Seven of the members have the responsibility for liaising with different countries' national accounting setters. IASB is funded by business organisations including major accounting firms, banking institutions and stock exchanges. In addition it generates revenue through the sale of its publications.

At present IASB has no authority to enforce the use of IFRSs by companies. This is why the EU requirement for the EU listed companies to adopt IFRSs for their consolidated financial statements by 1 January 2005, and IOSCO's recommendation to its members to use IFRSs are so important.

2.3   The objective of financial statements

According to the IASC Framework, the **objective** of financial statements is:

(a) to provide a fair presentation of information about the financial position, performance and changes in financial position of an entity. Financial statements prepared for this purpose meet the common needs of most users. However, financial statements do not provide all the information that users may need to make economic decisions since they largely portray the financial effects of past events and do not necessarily provide non-financial information.

(b) to show the results of management's stewardship (i.e. accountability for resources entrusted to it). Those users who wish to assess the stewardship or accountability of management do so in order that they may make economic decisions; these decisions may include, for example, whether to hold or sell their investment in the enterprise or whether to reappoint or replace the management.

A complete set of financial statements includes the following components:

- balance sheet
- income statement
- statement of changes in equity
- cash flow statement
- explanatory notes.

We will analyse the elements of the primary financial statements and how to prepare them in Parts two and three.

2.4   Underlying assumptions

These are the accrual basis and the going concern conventions. However, there are two more conventions which although not specifically covered by the IASB Framework are nevertheless important: business entity and accounting period conventions:

- *Accrual basis*. Financial statements of an enterprise are prepared on an accrual basis of accounting. Under this basis, the effects of transactions and other events are recognised when they occur (and not when cash or its equivalent is received or paid) and they are recorded in the accounting records and reported in the financial statements of the periods to which they relate. Financial statements prepared on an accrual basis inform users not only of past transactions involving the payment and receipt of cash but also of obligations to pay cash in the future and of resources that represent cash to be received in the future. Hence, they provide the type of information about past transactions and other events that is most useful to users in making economic decisions.

- *Going concern*. The financial statements are normally prepared on the assumption that an enterprise will continue in operation for the foreseeable future. Hence, it is assumed that an enterprise has neither the intention nor the need to liquidate or curtail materially the scale of its operations; if such an intention or need exists, the financial statements should be prepared on a different basis and the basis used should be disclosed.

- *Business entity*. This convention holds that an enterprise has an identity and existence distinct from its owners. From an accounting point of view, whatever the legal position, the business and the owner(s) are considered totally separately. Thus the owner can have claims against the enterprise.

- *Accounting period*. This convention recognises that profit occurs over time, and we cannot usefully speak of profit until we define the length of the period. The maximum length normally used is one year. This does not, of course, preclude the preparation of financial statements for shorter periods, although a formal period for published statements is normally one year. Increasingly, large enterprises report externally on a half-yearly or quarterly interim basis, and they normally report internally on a monthly basis.

2.5   Qualitative characteristics of financial information

Qualitative characteristics are the attributes that make the information provided in financial statements useful to users. The four principal qualitative characteristics are understandability, relevance, reliability and comparability.

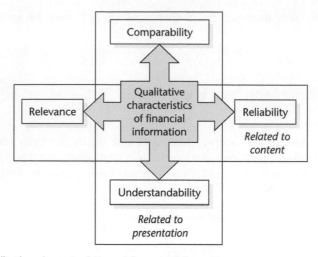

Figure 2.1 Qualitative characteristics of financial information

2.5.1 Understandability

An essential quality of the information provided in financial statements is that it should be readily understandable by users. For this purpose, users are assumed to have a reasonable knowledge of business and economic activities and accounting, and a willingness to study the information diligently. However, information about complex matters that should be included in the financial statements because of its relevance to the economic decision-making needs of users should not be excluded merely on the grounds that it may be too difficult for certain users to understand.

2.5.2 Comparability

Users must be able to compare the financial statements of an enterprise through time in order to identify trends in its financial position and performance. Users must also be able to compare the financial statements of different enterprises in order to evaluate their relative financial position, performance and changes in financial position. Hence, the measurement and display of the financial effect of similar transactions and other events must be carried out in a consistent way throughout an enterprise and over time for that enterprise and in a consistent way for different enterprises.

An important implication of the qualitative characteristic of comparability is that users should be informed of the accounting policies employed in the preparation of the financial statements, any changes in those policies and the effects of such changes. Users need to be able to identify differences between the accounting policies for like transactions and other events used by the same enterprise from period to period and by different enterprises.

The need for comparability should not be confused with mere uniformity and should not be allowed to become an impediment to the introduction of improved accounting standards. It is not appropriate for an enterprise to continue accounting in the same manner for a transaction or other event if the policy adopted is not in keeping with the qualitative characteristics of relevance and reliability. It is also inappropriate for an enterprise to leave its accounting policies unchanged when more relevant and reliable alternatives exist.

Because users wish to compare the financial position, performance and changes in financial position of an enterprise over time, it is important that the financial statements show corresponding information for the preceding periods.

2.5.3 Relevance

To be useful, information must be relevant to the decision-making needs of users. Information has the quality of relevance when it influences the economic decisions of users by helping them evaluate past, present or future events or confirming, or correcting, their past evaluations.

The predictive and confirmatory roles of information are interrelated. For example, information about the current level and structure of asset holdings has value to users when they endeavour to predict the ability of the enterprise to take advantage of opportunities and its ability to react to adverse situations. The same information plays a confirmatory role in respect of past predictions about, for example, the way in which the enterprise would be structured or the outcome of planned operations.

Information about financial position and past performance is frequently used as the basis for predicting future financial position and performance and other matters in which users are directly interested, such as dividend and wage payments, security price movements and the ability of the enterprise to meet its commitments as they fall due. To have predictive value, information need not be in the form of an explicit forecast. The ability to make predictions from financial statements is enhanced, however, by the manner in which information on past transactions and events is displayed. For example, the predictive value of the income statement is enhanced if unusual, abnormal and infrequent items of income or expense are separately disclosed.

Materiality

The relevance of information is affected by its nature and materiality. In some cases, the nature of information alone is sufficient to determine its relevance. For example, the reporting of diversification in a new segment of business may affect the assessment of the risks and opportunities facing the enterprise irrespective of the materiality of the results achieved by the new activity in the reporting period. In other cases, both the nature and materiality are important, for example the amounts of inventories held in each of the main categories that are appropriate to the business.

Information is material if its omission or misstatement could influence the economic decisions of users taken on the basis of the financial statements. Materiality depends on the size of the item or error judged in the particular circumstances of its omission or misstatement. Thus, materiality provides a threshold or cut-off point rather than being a primary qualitative characteristic which information must have if it is to be useful.

2.5.4 Reliability

To be useful, information must also be reliable. Information has the quality of reliability when it is free from material error and bias and can be depended upon by users to represent faithfully that which it either purports to represent or could reasonably be expected to represent.

Information may be relevant but so unreliable in nature or representation that its recognition may be potentially misleading. For example, if the validity and amount of a claim for damages under a legal action are disputed, it may be inappropriate for the enterprise to recognise the full amount of the claim in the balance sheet, although it may be appropriate to disclose the amount and circumstances of the claim.

Faithful representation

To be reliable, information must represent faithfully the transactions and other events it either purports to represent or could reasonably be expected to represent. Thus, for example, a balance sheet should represent faithfully the transactions and other events that result in assets, liabilities and equity of the enterprise at the reporting date.

Most financial information is subject to some risk of being less than a faithful representation of that which it purports to portray. This is not due to bias, but rather to inherent difficulties either in identifying the transactions and other events to be measured or in devising and applying measurement and presentation techniques that can convey messages that correspond with those transactions and events. In certain cases, the measurement of the financial effects of items could be so uncertain that enterprises generally would not recognise them in the financial statements: for example, although most enterprises generate goodwill internally over time, it is usually difficult to identify or measure that goodwill reliably.

Substance over form

If information is to represent faithfully the transactions and other events that it purports to represent, it is necessary that they are accounted for and presented in accordance with their substance and economic reality and not merely their legal form. The substance of transactions or other events is not always consistent with that which is apparent from their legal or contrived form. For example, an enterprise may dispose of an asset to another party in such a way that the documentation purports to pass legal ownership to that party; nevertheless, agreements may exist that ensure that the enterprise continues to enjoy the future economic benefits embodied in the asset. In such circumstances, the reporting of a sale would not represent faithfully the transaction entered into (if indeed there was a transaction).

Neutrality

To be reliable, the information contained in financial statements must be neutral, that is, free from bias. Financial statements are not neutral if, by the selection or presentation of information, they influence the making of a decision or judgement in order to achieve a predetermined result or outcome.

Prudence

When preparing financial statements, we do, however, have to contend with the uncertainties that inevitably surround many events and circumstances, such as the collectability of doubtful receivables, the probable useful life of plant and equipment and the number of warranty claims that may occur. Such uncertainties are recognised by the disclosure of their nature and extent and by the exercise of prudence in the preparation of the financial statements. Prudence is the inclusion of a degree of caution in the exercise of the judgements needed in making the estimates required under conditions of uncertainty, such that assets or income are not overstated and liabilities or expenses are not understated. However, the exercise of prudence does not allow, for example, the creation of hidden reserves or excessive provisions, the deliberate understatement of assets or income, or the deliberate overstatement of liabilities or expenses, because the financial statements would not be neutral and, therefore, not have the quality of reliability.

Completeness

To be reliable, the information in financial statements must be complete within the bounds of materiality and cost. An omission can cause information to be false or misleading and thus unreliable and deficient in terms of its relevance.

2.6 Constraints on relevant and reliable information

Timeliness

If there is undue delay in the reporting of information it may lose its relevance. Management may need to balance the relative merits of timely reporting and the provision of reliable information. To provide information on a timely basis it may often be necessary to report before all aspects of a transaction or other events are known, thus impairing reliability. Conversely, if reporting is delayed until all aspects are known, the information may be highly reliable but of little use to users who have had to make decisions in the interim. In achieving a balance between relevance and reliability, the overriding consideration is how best to satisfy the economic decision-making needs of users.

Balance between benefit and cost

The balance between benefit and cost is a pervasive constraint rather than a qualitative characteristic. The benefits derived from information should exceed the cost of providing it. The evaluation of benefits and costs is, however, largely a judgemental issue. Furthermore, the costs do not necessarily fall on those users who enjoy the benefits. Benefits may also be enjoyed by users other than those for whom the information is prepared: for example, the provision of further information to lenders may reduce the borrowing costs of an enterprise. For these reasons, it is difficult to apply a cost-benefit test in any particular case. Nevertheless, standard setters, as well as the preparers and users of financial statements, should be aware of this constraint.

Balance between qualitative characteristics

In practice a balancing, or trade-off, between qualitative characteristics is often necessary. Generally the aim is to achieve an appropriate balance among the

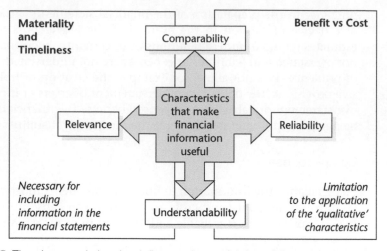

Figure 2.2 The characteristics that influence the usefulness of financial information. The figure shows that there are four qualitative characteristics that influence the usefulness of financial information. In addition, however, financial information should be material or significant, and timely, and the benefits of providing the information should outweigh the costs.

Source: McLaney and Atrill (2005)

characteristics in order to meet the objective of financial statements. The relative importance of the characteristics in different cases is a matter of professional judgement. For example:

- Information will not be relevant if there is undue delay in its preparation – there is therefore a trade-off between the requirements for timely reporting and the provision of reliable information.

- The cost of providing information (usually borne by the reporting entity) should not exceed the benefit obtained from it. Benefits are not only more difficult to quantify, but they also accrue to different users.

2.7   Hierarchy of concepts

The concepts we have analysed can be divided into different groups at different levels as shown in Figure 2.3.

The guiding principle which drives all IASs/IFRSs is the purpose of accounting, which is to provide a fair presentation of information about the financial position, performance and changes in financial position of an entity that is useful to a wide range of users in making economic decisions.

In order to provide a fair presentation of an enterprise, we need a series of concepts and conventions; and these need to be transformed into detailed technical rules regarding the recognition, measurement and presentation of assets, liabilities, equity, revenues, expenses, cash flows and various related disclosures. One of the examples of these rules is that inventories should be valued at the lower of their cost and net realisable value as we will see in Chapter 6.

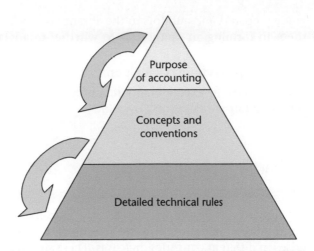

Figure 2.3 The pyramid of accounting concepts and rules in the IASs/IFRSs

What follows is a suggestion that pairs of conventions discussed above are, or may be, contradictory or in opposition to each other and an illustration of the possible conflicts between them (adapted from Alexander and Nobes 2004):

- *Prudence and going concern.* The going concern convention argues that the firm will keep going, e.g. that it will not be forced out of business by competition or bankruptcy. This may be a likely and rational assumption, but it is not necessarily prudent – in certain circumstances it could be decidedly risky.

- *Prudence and matching.* The matching convention, building on the going concern convention, allows us to carry forward assets into future periods on the grounds that they will be used profitably later. This obviously makes major assumptions about the future that may not be at all prudent. The contradiction between these two conventions is one of the major problems of accounting practice. Which one of these two conventions should be emphasised when in doubt?

- *Prudence and neutrality.* Neutrality implies certainty and precision. It implies freedom from personal opinion, freedom from bias. Prudence implies that we choose to report certain information based on judgement and therefore it is biased and not neutral. If accounting information could be genuinely neutral, then prudence would be irrelevant by definition, because any bias would be impossible. In practice, of course, since accounting always has to make assumptions about future events, neutrality can never be completely achieved.

- *Prudence and reliability/relevance.* We will use an example to explain the trade-off between these two concepts. The cost convention is supported by neutrality (not on the grounds that it is objective, but on the grounds that it usually has a greater objective element than alternative valuation concepts) and is often regarded as being supported by prudence. However, the valuation of property, plant and equipment according to the historical cost convention although prudent may be not relevant or reliable in times of rising prices.

To summarise, as the purpose of financial statements is to give a true and fair view of the state of the affairs of an enterprise, this general objective should be used to:

- guide preparers and auditors in the absence of a relevant technical rule and assist them in forming an opinion as to whether financial statements conform with IASs/IFRSs
- require preparers to make additional disclosures or
- require them, in exceptional circumstances, to depart from a rule in order to achieve a fair presentation ('override').

Summary

- Accountancy is becoming increasingly globalised, as enterprises become more multinational in nature, and the volume of trade and investment between enterprises in different countries increases. These situations have resulted in a need for financial statements that are internationally comparable and consistent.

- In July 2002 the European Commission announced that all EU listed companies should use International Accounting Standards (IASs) and International Financial Reporting Standards (IFRSs) for their published consolidated financial statements for the periods beginning January 2005 (with comparative data for 2004).

- Financial statements include: balance sheet, income statement, statement of changes in equity, cash flow statement and explanatory notes.

- The objectives of financial statements are to provide information about the financial position, performance and changes in financial position of an entity that is useful to a wide range of users in making economic decisions; and to show the results of management's stewardship (i.e. accountability for resources entrusted to it).

- The underlying assumptions when preparing the financial statements are: accrual basis, going concern, business entity, and accounting period.

- The four main qualitative characteristics of accounting information are: understandability, relevance, reliability and comparability.

- There are certain accounting conventions/assumptions and rules that can be contradictory or in opposition to each other.

References and research

The IASB documents relevant for this chapter are the *Framework for the Preparation and Presentation of Financial Statements* and IAS 1 – *Presentation of Financial Statements*.

The following are examples of research papers and books that take the issues of this chapter further:

- David Alexander and Christopher Nobes, *Financial Accounting, An International Introduction*, 2nd Edition, Financial Times-Prentice Hall, 2004, Chapter 3
- David Alexander, 'A benchmark for the adequacy of published financial statements', *Accounting and Business Research*, Vol. 29, No. 3, 1999

- Barry Elliott and Jamie Elliott, *Financial Accounting and Reporting*, 9th Edition, Financial Times-Prentice Hall, 2005, Chapter 7
- Eddie McLaney and Peter Atrill, *Accounting: An Introduction*, 3rd edition, Financial Times-Prentice Hall, 2005
- Hervé Stolowy and Michel J. Lebas, *Corporate Financial Reporting: A Global Perspective*, Thomson Learning, 2002, Chapter 1
- Hennie Van Greuning, *International Financial Reporting Standards: A Practical Guide*, The World Bank, 2005, Part I

Questions

2.1 (a) Which accounting conventions/concepts do you regard as most important in helping preparers and auditors of financial statements to do their work, and why?

(b) Which accounting conventions do you regard as most useful from the viewpoint of the readers of financial statements, and why?

(c) Explain any difference between your answers to a) and b) above.

2.2 'Substance over form is a recipe for failing to achieve comparability between accounting statements for different businesses.' Discuss.

2.3 What various purposes might there be for accounting? Which purpose does the IASB particularly focus on?

2.4 'Neutrality is about freedom from bias. Prudence is a bias. It is not possible to embrace both conventions in one coherent framework.' Discuss.

2.5 To what extent is the search for relevance of financial information hampered by the need for reliability?

2.6 'Accounting information should be understandable. As some users of accounting information have a poor knowledge of accounting, we should produce simplified financial reports to help them.' To what extent do you agree with this view?

Case study   Badly in need of repair

Read this extract from 'Badly in need of repair' (*The Economist*, 2 May 2002). Which accounting conventions/concepts does it refer to? Think of examples of these conventions which are bypassed thanks to some legal loopholes. Base your discussion on examples from your own country.

Off-balance-sheet holes

Accounts certainly rely too heavily on historic costs. But what concerns investors far more is the stuff that lurks beyond the balance sheet. Although numbers recorded on the balance sheet are often misleading, investors can adjust them by using information that companies are obliged to disclose elsewhere. The worrying thing about so-called 'off-balance-sheet' items is that they can appear suddenly out of nowhere, without warning. There may be clues in the footnotes, but few people pay close attention to these impenetrable bits of legalese.

Special-purpose entities (SPEs) are a sort of non-consolidated, off-balance-sheet vehicle that have some legitimate uses, such as, for example, the financing of a research and development partnership with another company. They can, however, also be used to shove nasty liabilities and risks into corners where, with luck, nobody will see them. At the moment, investors are assuming that they are being used mostly for the latter purpose.

In November 2000, Enron restated its financial statements, reducing its profits by $591m over four years and increasing its debts by $628m. Most of the restatement came from the consolidation of two SPEs. America's standard-setter, the Financial Accounting Standards Board (FASB), points to Enron's restatement as evidence that it was the energy trader's disobedience that was the problem, not the rules on special-purpose entities.

Another of Enron's special-purpose vehicles, however, called LJM2, stayed off its balance sheet in accordance with FASB standards. And there are many more SPEs out there, notably off the balance sheets of companies which securitise (ie, repackage and sell on to investors) large chunks of their assets.

Another example of off-balance-sheet deceit is the dry-sounding yet potentially dangerous phenomenon of commitments, a variety of contingent liability. A company commits itself to a future contingent payment but does not account for the liability. Telecoms-hardware manufacturers, for example, often guarantee bank loans to important customers in return for buying their products. That is fine so long as the business is healthy, but if a company enters into such a transaction purely to lubricate its own cashflow, the commitment can become a risk. At the moment, according to American, British and international accounting rules, many varieties of commitments are mentioned only in footnotes since there is, in theory, only a low probability that they will crystallise.

Operating leases, through which a company agrees to rent an asset over a substantial period of time, make up most off-balance-sheet financing. Airlines use them to clear their accounts of large numbers of aircraft. The practice helps to avoid tax, but it also results in a drastic understatement of the airlines' debt, according to Trevor Harris, an accounting analyst at Morgan Stanley Dean Witter. In 1997, one-third of the aircraft of the five biggest American airlines were treated as operating leases rather than as assets.

Needless to say, this is all done in accordance with accounting rules. Standard-setters have come up with hundreds of pages of rules on operating leases, but they have failed to get companies to admit what any analyst knows: that airlines reap the economic risks and rewards of their aeroplanes and ought to treat them as assets.

Unlike off-balance-sheet financing methods, most of which date from the last 15 years or so, the trick of recognising revenue too early (or booking sales that never materialise) is an old one. Global Crossing, a bankrupt telecoms-equipment company now under investigation by the Federal Bureau of Investigation and the Securities and Exchange Commission (SEC), is accused of swapping fibre-optic capacity with a competitor as a way to manufacture revenue. And according to the SEC, Xerox, a photocopier company, wrongly accelerated the recognition of equipment revenue by over $3 billion. Standard-setters admit that no country has adequate rules on the recognition of revenues. A solution in the meantime may be to look at cash, which is far harder to disguise or invent. Comroad duped its auditor about its revenues, but it could not conceal the fact that its cashflow was negative.

'Badly in need of repair', *The Economist*, 2 May 2002

Part Two Financial position and financial performance

3 Balance sheet: an overall view

Objectives

When you have completed this chapter you should be able to:

- explain the nature and purpose of financial statements
- understand the relationships between these statements
- prepare a balance sheet and interpret the information it contains
- discuss the accounting conventions underpinning a balance sheet
- calculate some ratios relating to a balance sheet.

3.1 Introduction

Financial statements are a structured financial representation of the financial position of, and the results of transactions undertaken by, an enterprise (IAS 1). The objective of general purpose financial statements is to provide information about the financial position, performance and cash flows of an enterprise that is useful to a wide range of users in making economic decisions. Financial statements also depict the results of management's stewardship of the resources entrusted to it. To meet this objective, financial statements provide information about an enterprise's:

(a) assets
(b) liabilities
(c) equity
(d) income and expenses
(e) cash flows.

This information along with other disclosures in the notes to financial statements, assists users in understanding the past performance and predicting an enterprise's future cash flows and in particular the timing and certainty of the generation of cash and cash equivalents.

Financial statements, balance sheet, income statement and cash flow statement, provide a picture of the overall financial position and performance of an enterprise. They are concerned with answering the following:

1. What cash movements took place over a particular period?
2. How much wealth was generated by the business over a particular period?
3. What is the accumulated wealth of the business at the end of a particular period?

These questions are addressed respectively by the following financial statements:

- Cash flow statement;
- Income statement; and
- Balance sheet.

All listed companies publish, at least annually, these three financial statements together with notes explaining the principal amounts and underlying transactions, segmental information and changes in equity.

Example

Financial statements

Filippo decided to embark on a business venture. He decided to buy kites from a local supplier and sell them in a park. Filippo begins his enterprise with EUR 40 in cash.

On the first day of trading, he purchased kites for EUR 40 and sold 75% of his inventory for EUR 45 cash.

Let us answer those three initial questions relating to Filippo's first day of trading:

1. What cash movements took place on the first day of trading?
2. How much wealth (profit) was generated by the enterprise on the first day of trading?
3. What is the accumulated wealth at the end of the first day?

Question 1: what cash movements took place on the first day of trading?

	EUR
Opening balance (cash introduced)	40
Proceeds from the sale of kites	45
	85
Cash paid to purchase kites	(40)
Closing balance	45

Filippo started with EUR 40 and ended the day with EUR 45 in his pocket.

Question 2: how much wealth (profit) was generated by the enterprise on the first day of trading?

Income statement for day 1

	EUR
Sales	45
Cost of sales (3/4 of EUR 40)	(30)
Profit	**15**

Filippo made a profit of EUR 15 at the end of his first day of trading.

Question 3: what is the accumulated wealth at the end of the first day?

Balance sheet at the end of day 1

	EUR
Cash (closing balance)	45
Kites left for resale (i.e. inventory)	
(1/4 of EUR 40)	10
Total enterprise wealth	**55**

Filippo's assets (cash and kites) at the end of day one are represented by the capital of EUR 40 and the profit of EUR 15.

On the second day of trading Filippo purchased more kites for EUR 20 cash.

He managed to sell all of the new kites and half of the kites in inventory for a total of EUR 38.

Once again, let us answer those three questions this time, relating to Filippo's second day of trading.

1. What cash movements took place on the second day of trading?
2. How much wealth (profit) was generated by the enterprise on the second day of trading?
3. What is the accumulated wealth at the end of the second day?

Question 1: what cash movements took place on the second day of trading?

Cash flow statement for day 2

	EUR
Opening balance (from day 1)	45
Proceeds from the sale of kites	38
	83
Cash paid to purchase kites	(20)
Closing balance	**63**

Question 2: how much wealth (profit) was generated by the enterprise on the second day of trading?

Income statement for day 2

	EUR
Sales	38
Cost of sales (EUR 20 + 1/2 of EUR 10)	(25)
Profit	**13**

Question 3: what is the accumulated wealth at the end of the second day?

Balance sheet at the end of day 2

	EUR
Cash (closing balance)	63
Kites left for resale (i.e. inventory) (1/2 of EUR 10)	5
Total enterprise wealth	68

On the third day of trading Filippo purchased more kites for EUR 46 cash. However, as it was raining, sales were slow. After he had sold for EUR 32 the kites which had cost EUR 23, he decided to stop trading until the following day.

Now, let us draw up the financial statements for the third day of Filippo's trading.

Cash flow statement for day 3

	EUR
Opening balance (from day 2)	63
Proceeds from the sale of kites	32
	95
Cash paid to purchase kites	(46)
Closing balance	49

Income statement for day 3

	EUR
Sales	32
Cost of sales	(23)
Profit	9

Balance sheet at the end of day 3

	EUR
Cash (closing balance)	49
Inventory (EUR 5 + 46 − 23)	28
Total enterprise wealth	77

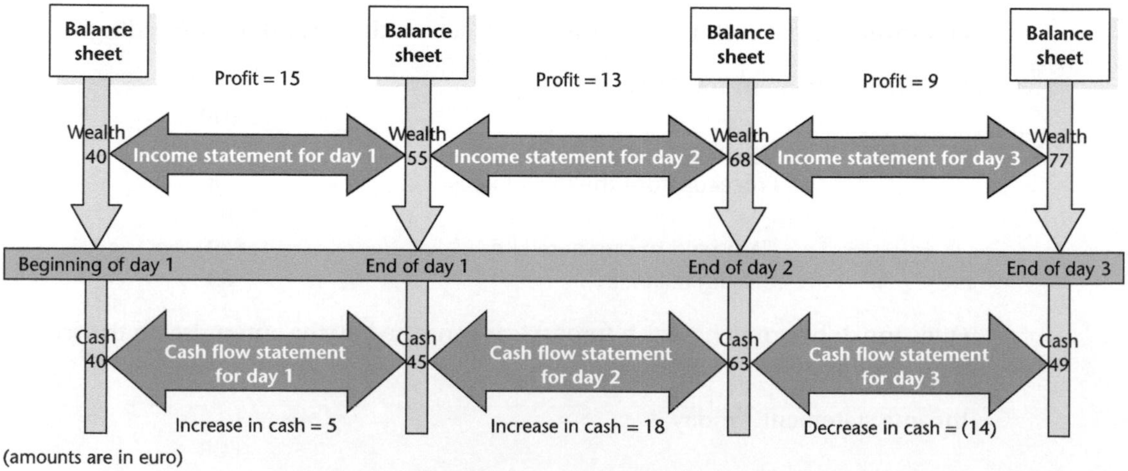

(amounts are in euro)

Figure 3.1 Relationship between the balance sheet, income statement and cash flow statement. This figure shows how the income statement and cash flow statement present flows of wealth over time. The balance sheet, however, presents the amount of wealth at a particular moment in time.

3.2   Purpose of a balance sheet

The purpose of the balance sheet is to set out the financial position of an enterprise at a given date. More specifically, the balance sheet reports the assets and claims (liabilities and owners' equity) of an enterprise at a specified moment in time. Because the balance sheet is a snapshot of a moment in time, it is a status report rather than a flow report.

Table 3.1 Consolidated balance sheet of adidas-Salomon as at 31 December 2004 (amounts in thousands of euro)

	Dec. 31 2004	Dec. 31 2003	Change in %
Cash and cash equivalents	195,997	189,503	3.4
Short-term financial assets	258,950	89,411	189.6
Accounts receivable	1,046,322	1,075,092	(2.7)
Inventories	1,155,374	1,163,518	(0.7)
Other current assets	378,303	259,427	45.8
Total current assets	**3,034,946**	2,776,951	9.3
Property, plant and equipment, net	367,928	344,554	6.8
Goodwill, net	572,426	591,045	(3.2)
Other intangible assets, net	96,312	103,797	(7.2)
Long-term financial assets	93,134	88,408	5.3
Deferred tax assets	160,135	178,484	(10.3)
Other non-current assets	102,599	104,569	(1.9)
Total non-current assets	**1,392,534**	1,410,857	(1.3)
Total assets	**4,427,480**	4,187,808	5.7
Short-term borrowings	185,837	–	–
Accounts payable	591,689	592,273	(0.1)
Income taxes	167,334	157,764	6.1
Accrued liabilities and provisions	558,121	454,573	22.8
Other current liabilities	184,332	139,095	32.5
Total current liabilities	**1,687,313**	1,343,705	25.6
Long-term borrowings	862,845	1,225,385	(29.6)
Pensions and similar obligations	111,321	105,264	5.8
Deferred tax liabilities	77,915	65,807	18.4
Other non-current liabilities	30,784	35,278	(12.7)
Total non-current liabilities	**1,082,865**	1,431,734	(24.4)
Minority interests	28,850	56,579	(49.0)
Shareholders' equity	1,628,452	1,355,790	20.1
Total liabilities, minority interests and shareholders' equity	**4,427,480**	4,187,808	5.7

Source: adidas-Salomon Annual Report 2004

A balance sheet for adidas-Salomon is shown in Table 3.1. Before considering its details, first examine this balance sheet for the basic accounting concepts we have already discussed in Chapter 2.

Note that the amounts are expressed in money and reflect only those matters that can be measured in monetary terms. The enterprise is adidas-Salomon, and the balance sheet refers to that enterprise rather than to any of the individuals associated with it. The statement assumes that adidas-Salomon is a going concern. The dual-aspect concept is evident from the fact that the assets listed on the top of the balance sheet are equal in total to the liabilities and shareholders' equity listed at the bottom.

Because of the dual-aspect concept, the two sections necessarily add up to the same total (EUR 4,187,808,000 in 2003 and EUR 4,427,480,000 in 2004). This balancing does not tell anything about the company's financial health. Since all of the assets of an enterprise are claimed by someone (either by its owners or by its creditors) and since the total of these claims cannot exceed the amount of assets to be claimed, it follows that:

$$Assets = Liabilities + Owners' \ equity$$

We will see how each transaction has a dual impact on the accounting records.

3.2.1 Resources and claims view

A balance sheet is the fundamental accounting statement in the sense that every accounting transaction can be analysed in terms of its dual impact on the balance sheet. To understand the information a balance sheet conveys and how economic events affect the balance sheet, the reader must be absolutely clear as to the meaning of its two sides. They can be interpreted in either of two ways, both of which are correct:

- resources and claims view
- sources and uses of funds view.

According to one interpretation, the resources and claims view, the items listed on the asset side are the economic resources of an enterprise as at the date of the balance sheet. Liabilities and owners' equity are claims against an enterprise at the same date. Liabilities are the claims of third parties – amounts that the enterprise owes to banks, suppliers, employees and other creditors. Owners' equity represents the claims of the owners for the money invested in the business when the enterprise was set up and for all profits earned by the enterprise which have not been paid out to the owners and are reinvested in the enterprise.

However, an enterprise's owners do not have a claim in the same sense that the creditors do. With reference to adidas-Salomon, it can be said with certainty that tax authorities had a claim of EUR 167,334,000 as at 31 December 2004 – that the company owed them EUR 167,334,000, neither more nor less. It is more difficult to interpret as a claim the amount shown as shareholders' equity, EUR 1,628,452,000. *If* the company were liquidated as at 31 December 2004, *if* the assets were sold for their book values, and *if* the creditors and minority interests were paid EUR 2,770,178,000 (total current liabilities EUR 1,687,313,000 plus total non-current liabilities EUR 1,082,865,000) and EUR 28,850,000 respectively owed to them, then the shareholders would get what was left which would be EUR 1,628,452,000.

However, these 'if' conditions are unrealistic. Based on the going concern concept, the company is not going to be liquidated; and therefore, the non-monetary assets are not shown at their liquidation values.

The **shareholders' equity** in terms of liquidation values might be worth considerably more or less than EUR 1,628,452,000. The shareholders' equity of a healthy, growing company is usually worth considerably more than its 'book value' – the amount shown on the balance sheet. On the other hand, if a company is not saleable as a going concern and is liquidated with the assets being sold piecemeal, the owners' proceeds are often only a small fraction of the amounts stated on the balance sheet. Often when a bankrupt company's assets are liquidated, the proceeds are insufficient to satisfy 100 per cent of the creditors' claims, in which case the owners receive little or nothing.

Table 3.2 Resources and claims view

Left side of the balance sheet	Right side of the balance sheet
Resources owned	Claims: • Owners • Third parties

3.2.2 Sources and uses of funds view

In this alternative view, the left-hand side of the balance sheet is considered to show the ways in which an enterprise has used, or invested, the funds provided to it as at the balance sheet date. These investments have been made in order to enable the enterprise achieve its objectives, which primarily consist of earning a satisfactory profit. The right-hand side shows the sources of the funds that are invested in the assets – it shows how the assets were financed. The liabilities describe how much of that financing was obtained from trade creditors ('accounts payable'), from lenders ('long-term borrowings'), and from other creditors ('accrued liabilities and provisions', 'pensions and similar obligations' and so on). The owners' equity section shows the finance provided by the owners. (The two ways in which the owners of an enterprise company provide it with funds – capital and accumulated profit – will be explained later in the chapter.)

Thus, with the sources and uses of funds view, the fundamental accounting equation:

$$\text{Assets (A)} = \text{Liabilities (L)} + \text{Owners' equity (E)}$$

has this interpretation: every euro invested in an enterprise's assets is supplied either by the enterprise's creditors or by its owners; and every euro thus is invested in some asset.

Both ways of interpreting a balance sheet are correct. In certain circumstances, the resources and claims view is easier to understand. In analysing a balance sheet of a going concern, however, the sources and uses of funds view usually provides a more meaningful interpretation.

Table 3.3 Sources and uses of funds view

Left side of the balance sheet	Right side of the balance sheet
Uses of funds (applications)	Sources of funds

3.3 The effect of trading operations on a balance sheet

As we have seen in the previous section, a balance sheet is a document designed to show the state of affairs of an enterprise at a particular date. Reduced to its simplest, a balance sheet consists of two lists. The first is a list of the resources owned by the enterprise concerned – it is a list of assets. An asset is a resource owned by an enterprise as a result of past events and from which future economic benefits are expected to flow to the enterprise (IASB *Framework*).

The second list shows where the assets came from, i.e. the monetary amounts of the sources from which the enterprise obtained its resources. Since those sources will require repayment or recompense in some way, it follows that this second list can also be regarded as a list of claims against the resources. The enterprise will have to settle these claims some time, and this second list can therefore be regarded as amounts payable to others.

The first list could also be regarded as the ways in which those sources have been applied at a point in time, that is, as a list of applications. These terms are summarised in the next table.

Table 3.4 Interpretation of a balance sheet

Left side of the balance sheet	Right side of the balance sheet
Resources owned	Sources
Assets	Where they came from
Applications	Claims

When an enterprise is formed, the starting position is that there is no balance sheet because there was no enterprise. The enterprise will be owned by someone. This outside person or body will put cash (a resource) into the enterprise as capital. Capital is the source of the cash which the enterprise now owns. So, after this first transaction, we can prepare our balance sheet – our lists of resources and claims – as in Table 3.5.

Table 3.5 Effect of initial investment on a balance sheeet

Resources/Applications	Claims/Sources
Cash	Capital

If we refer to our accounting equation we have:

$$A \quad = L \; + \quad E$$
$$Cash \quad = \qquad Capital$$

The separation of the enterprise from the owner is implied by showing the owner's contribution as a claim/source. Without a record of this separation, the affairs of the owner and the business would be mixed up, and measuring performance would be difficult.

On the day an enterprise begins, its financial status can be recorded on a balance sheet. From that day on, all transactions, which change the numbers on this first balance sheet, are recorded in accordance with the concepts described in Chapter 2 and in section 3.5 of this chapter. Accounting systems accumulate and summarise these changes as a basis for preparing new balance sheets at prescribed intervals, such as the end of a month, or a quarter, or a year. Each balance sheet shows the financial condition of the enterprise at the date it was prepared, after giving effect to all of these changes.

Although in practice a balance sheet is prepared only at prescribed intervals, in learning the accounting process it is useful to consider the changes one by one. This makes it possible to appreciate the effect of individual transactions without getting entangled with the mechanisms used to record these transactions. The following example shows the effects of certain transactions on a balance sheet. For the sake of simplicity they are assumed to occur on successive days.

Example

Transaction 1 – Initial investment

1 January   Paolo starts a retail shop called Funny Sun. He does this by depositing EUR 200,000 of his own funds in a bank account that he has opened in the name of the business enterprise, Funny Sun. He is thus the sole owner of the enterprise. The cash in bank is an asset, i.e. a resource, whereas the capital is a claim on the enterprise by the owner. In a sense, the capital is 'owed' by the enterprise to the owner.

The impact of this transaction on our accounting equation is as follows:

$$A \qquad\qquad = L \; + \qquad E$$

	Cash and cash equivalents		Capital
(1)	+ 200,000	=	+ 200,000

This transaction increases both the assets, specifically cash and cash equivalents, and the owners' equity. Liabilities are unaffected. Why? Because Funny Sun has no obligation to an outside party arising from this transaction.

We have called the account 'cash and cash equivalents' which is the term used by IAS/IFRS. In practice, we can find 'cash at bank' in the published balance sheet. As we will see in Chapter 12, cash equivalents are short-term, highly liquid investments that are readily convertible to known amounts of cash and which are subject to an insignificant risk of change in value. In other words, we consider cash at bank as cash equivalent. When the bank has a negative balance, it is called bank over-draft and we subtract it from the total amount of cash and cash equivalents. Therefore, unlike 'cash' which can never be a negative amount, cash and cash equivalents may be negative, and in that case we will find 'bank overdraft' in the current liabilities.

The balance sheet of Funny Sun will then be as follows:

Funny Sun
Balance sheet
as at 1 January

Assets	EUR	Owner's equity and liabilities	EUR
Cash and cash equivalents	200,000	Capital	200,000
Total assets	200,000	Total equity and liabilities	200,000

Transaction 2 – Loan from bank

2 January   Paolo borrows EUR 100,000 from his bank. This transaction provides an additional source, and therefore a claim, of EUR 100,000 in the form of a loan from the bank. In return, the business has cash or a resource of an extra EUR 100,000.

Let us look at the impact of this transaction on our accounting equation.

	A	=	L	+	E
	Cash and cash equivalents		Bank loan		Capital
(1)	+ 200,000	=			+ 200,000
(2)	+ 100,000	=	+ 100,000		
Bal.	300,000	=	100,000		200,000
	⎣___ 300,000 ___⎦		⎣___ 300,000 ___⎦		

The loan increases the asset, cash and cash equivalents, and increases the liability, bank loan, by the same amount, EUR 100,000. After the trans-action is completed, Funny Sun has assets of EUR 300,000, liabilities of EUR 100,000, and owners' equity of EUR 200,000. The totals of indi-vidual balances (abbreviated Bal.) on each side of the equation are equal as they always should be.

After this transaction, the balance sheet looks as follows (under IASs/IFRSs, long-term items are shown first in the balance sheet):

Funny Sun
Balance sheet
as at 2 January

Assets	EUR	Owner's equity and liabilities	EUR
Cash and cash equivalents	300,000	Capital	200,000
		Bank loan	100,000
Total assets	300,000	Total equity and liabilities	300,000

Transaction 3 – Acquisition of non-current assets

3 January Paolo buys fixed assets for EUR 100,000 which are classified under property, plant and equipment (PPE). This transaction involves using some of the cash to buy long-lived assets with which to operate the business. One resource (part of the cash) is turned into another resource (PPE), so that the total resources and claims remain the same. This implies that only one side of our accounting equation will be affected by this transaction. If we look at the balance sheet drawn after this transaction, the total assets and total liabilities will not change compared to the previous balance sheet. What has changed is only the composition of the resources held by Paolo.

	PPE	A Cash and cash equivalents	=	L Bank loan	+	E Capital
Bal.		300,000	=	100,000		200,000
(3)	+ 100,000	– 100,000	=			
Bal.	100,000	200,000	=	100,000		200,000

300,000   300,000

Funny Sun
Balance sheet
as at 3 January

Assets	EUR	Owner's equity and liabilities	EUR
Property, plant and equipment	100,000	Capital	200,000
Cash and cash equivalents	200,000	Bank loan	100,000
Total assets	300,000	Total equity and liabilities	300,000

Transaction 4 – Purchase of inventory on credit

4 January Paolo buys goods for resale costing EUR 90,000, on credit (i.e. the supplier agrees to be paid later).

This transaction involves a purchase of a new or additional resource (i.e. inventory) for EUR 90,000 and an increase in claims of third parties (i.e. trade and other payables) for the same amount.

	PPE	A Inventory	Cash and cash equivalents	=	Bank loan	L Trade and other payables	+	E Capital
Bal.	100,000		200,000	=	100,000			200,000
(4)		+ 90,000		=		+ 90,000		
Bal.	100,000	90,000	200,000	=	100,000	90,000		200,000

390,000   390,000

Funny Sun
Balance sheet
as at 4 January

Assets	EUR	Owner's equity and liabilities	EUR
Property, plant and equipment	100,000	Capital	200,000
Inventory	90,000	Bank loan	100,000
Cash and cash equivalents	200,000	Trade and other payables	90,000
Total assets	390,000	Total equity and liabilities	390,000

Transaction 5 – Disposal of PPE bought earlier on credit

5 January   Paolo sells an equipment for EUR 40,000, on credit. The selling price happens to equal its cost. This transaction involves a change in the application of resources: EUR 40,000, which had previously been part of the fixed assets has now changed to a different application, i.e. 'trade and other receivables'. As the equipment has been sold at cost, neither profit nor loss arises.

We are purposely avoiding transactions that result in profit or loss in the balance sheet equation. In this case, the transaction affects assets only; liabilities and owners' equity remain unchanged.

	PPE	Inventory	A Trade and other receivables	Cash and cash equivalents	=	L Bank loan	Trade and other payables	+	E Capital
Bal.	100,000	90,000		200,000	=	100,000	90,000		200,000
(5)	– 40,000		+ 40,000		=				
Bal.	100,000	90,000	400,000	200,000	=	100,000	90,000		200,000

390,000   390,000

Funny Sun
Balance sheet
as at 5 January

Assets	EUR	Owner's equity and liabilities	EUR
Property, plant and equipment	60,000	Capital	200,000
Inventory	90,000	Bank loan	100,000
Trade and other receivables	40,000	Trade and other payables	90,000
Cash and cash equivalents	200,000		
Total assets	390,000	Total equity and liabilities	390,000

Transaction 6 – Return of inventory to supplier

6 January   Paolo returns half of the inventory acquired on 4 January for EUR 90,000 to the supplier who agrees to credit Paolo for the amount of inventory returned, i.e. EUR 45,000.

When an enterprise returns goods to its suppliers, both the inventory and liability accounts are reduced. In this case, the amount of the decrease on each side of the equation is EUR 45,000.

	PPE	Inventory	A Trade and other receivables	Cash and cash equivalents	=	L Bank loan	Trade and other payables	+	E Capital
Bal.	60,000	90,000	40,000	200,000	=	100,000	90,000		200,000
(6)		– 45,000			=		– 45,000		
Bal.	60,000	45,000	40,000	200,000	=	100,000	45,000		200,000

345,000   345,000

Funny Sun
Balance sheet
as at 6 January

Assets	EUR	Owner's equity and liabilities	EUR
Property, plant and equipment	60,000	Capital	200,000
Inventory	45,000	Bank loan	100,000
Trade and other receivables	40,000	Trade and other payables	45,000
Cash and cash equivalents	200,000		
Total assets	345,000	Total equity and liabilities	345,000

Transaction 7 – Collection of trade receivables

7 January   Paolo receives from the customer EUR 30,000 against the receivable of EUR 40,000. Here the starting position is that there was a receivable – an asset, an amount owed to the enterprise. A part of this receivable is now collected by the enterprise. This tells us two things:

- First, the cash figure has increased by the amount of the cash received, i.e. EUR 30,000.
- Second, the enterprise is no longer owed EUR 40,000 because it has received a part of it. The receivable therefore is reduced by EUR 30,000, to EUR 10,000.

In summary, we have an increase in the asset 'cash and cash equivalents' and a decrease in the asset 'trade and other receivables', both by the same amount. Total assets remain the same, and therefore total claims also remain the same. All that has happened is that an earlier transaction has moved further towards completion – a part of the receivable has been turned into cash.

		A		=	L	+	E
PPE	Inventory	Trade and other receivables	Cash and cash equivalents		Bank loan	Trade and other receivables	Capital
Bal. 60,000	45,000	40,000	200,000	= 100,000	45,000		200,000
(7)		– 30,000	+ 30,000	=			
Bal. 60,000	45,000	10,000	230,000	= 100,000	45,000		200,000

345,000   345,000

Funny Sun
Balance sheet
as at 7 January

Assets	EUR	Owner's equity and liabilities	EUR
Property, plant and equipment	60,000	Capital	200,000
Inventory	45,000	Bank loan	100,000
Trade and other receivables	10,000	Trade and other payables	45,000
Cash and cash equivalents	230,000		
Total assets	345,000	Total equity and liabilities	345,000

Transaction 8 – Purchase of goods for cash and credit

8 January   Paolo buys goods costing EUR 50,000. A cash payment of EUR 10,000 is made on the same day. The remaining EUR 40,000 should be paid in 60 days. This transaction results in the inventory figure (i.e. the asset or resource) in the balance sheet increasing by the total amount of goods bought, regardless of whether payment is made in full now or later, or partially now and the balance later. Therefore, Funny Sun's inventory is increased by EUR 50,000, cash and cash equivalents is decreased by EUR 10,000, and trade and other payables is increased by the difference, EUR 40,000.

		A		=	L	+	E
PPE	Inventory	Trade and other receivables	Cash and cash equivalents		Bank loan	Trade and other payables	Capital
Bal. 60,000	45,000	10,000	230,000	= 100,000	45,000		200,000
(8)	+ 50,000		– 10,000	=		+ 40,000	
Bal. 60,000	95,000	10,000	220,000	= 100,000	85,000		200,000

385,000   385,000

Funny Sun
Balance sheet
as at 8 January

Assets	EUR	Owner's equity and liabilities	EUR
Property, plant and equipment	60,000	Capital	200,000
Inventory	95,000	Bank loan	100,000
Trade and other receivables	10,000	Trade and other payables	85,000
Cash and cash equivalents	220,000		
Total assets	385,000	Total equity and liabilities	385,000

The transactions just illustrated are summarised in Table 3.6 on page 52.

This example has been explored at considerable length because it is useful to keep thinking in terms of resource and claim. Does a transaction change one resource into another? Or does it represent more resources from somewhere and therefore does it increase both lists, namely both sides of the balance sheet? And if the total claims increase, is it through operating successfully and making a profit, or is it through borrowing money or simply deferring payment of resources acquired at a later date?

We will be able to answer these questions confidently after having studied Chapter 4.

3.4 Balance sheet layouts

A balance sheet normally consists of five basic building blocks; however, in the case of a consolidated balance sheet there are six building blocks if there is a minority interest. These appear in the balance sheet of any company, irrespective of the nature of the business or the country or countries within which it operates. The way in which the five or six building blocks are set out may depend partly on what is common practice or legally required within the particular business sector or country.

3.4.1 Formats of the horizontal and vertical balance sheet

For most companies the balance sheet format is as follows:

Non-current assets	Capital and reserves, including minority interests
Current assets	Non-current liabilities
	Current liabilities
Total assets	**Total equity and liabilities**

Table 3.6 Transaction analysis: summary (amounts in thousands of euro)

		RESOURCES/ASSETS						CLAIMS/SOURCES		
Date	Description of transaction	PPE	Inventory	Trade and other receivables	Cash and cash equivalents	=	Trade and other payables	Bank loan	Capital
1 Jan.	Invested cash in business				+200	=			+200
2 Jan.	Obtained bank loan				+100	=		+100	
3 Jan.	Bought PPE	+100			–100	=			
4 Jan.	Bought goods on credit		+90			=	+90		
5 Jan.	Disposal of equipment	–40		+40		=			
6 Jan.	Returned inventory		–45			=	–45		
7 Jan.	Collected cash from the customer			–30	+30	=			
8 Jan.	Bought goods on credit and for cash		+50		–10	=	+40		
	TOTALS	**+60**	**+95**	**+10**	**+220**	**=**	**+85**	**+100**	**+200**
			385					385	

This two-sided horizontal presentation of the balance sheet with total assets on one side and total equity and liabilities on the other is standard for most countries. The horizontal balance sheet for adidas-Salomon is set out in Figure 3.2.

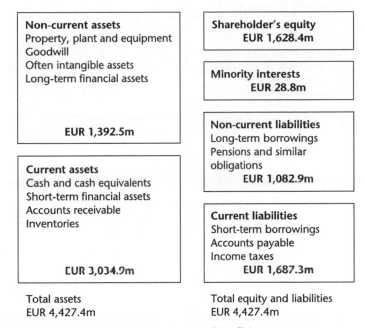

Non-current assets
Property, plant and equipment
Goodwill
Often intangible assets
Long-term financial assets

EUR 1,392.5m

Current assets
Cash and cash equivalents
Short-term financial assets
Accounts receivable
Inventories

EUR 3,034.9m

Shareholder's equity
EUR 1,628.4m

Minority interests
EUR 28.8m

Non-current liabilities
Long-term borrowings
Pensions and similar
obligations
EUR 1,082.9m

Current liabilities
Short-term borrowings
Accounts payable
Income taxes
EUR 1,687.3m

Total assets
EUR 4,427.4m

Total equity and liabilities
EUR 4,427.4m

Figure 3.2 Format of a horizontal balance sheet: adidas-Salomon

On one side of the balance sheet, non-current assets added to current assets give the total assets employed at the year-end. There are only three possible sources of funds that may be applied to finance total assets. These are set out on the other side of the balance sheet:

- Equity (both owners' equity and minority interest)
- Non-current (or long-term) liabilities
- Current liabilities.

How these three sources are combined to finance total assets employed is central to the understanding of the financial structure – the gearing or leverage – of a company. In particular we are interested in the proportion of finance provided by the shareholders or owners compared with that obtained from other sources, third party borrowings, loans or debt.

Instead of using the horizontal presentation of a balance sheet, we can use a vertical one as shown in Figure 3.3.

We can also use a vertical format that links current assets and current liabilities to highlight the net current assets and net assets employed as shown respectively in Figure 3.4 and Figure 3.5.

Net current assets are defined as current assets less current liabilities. This aggregate is more popularly known as working capital (abbreviated as WC). Changes in the components of the working capital of an enterprise can be important indicators of its performance and position. As an enterprise is managed there is a continual

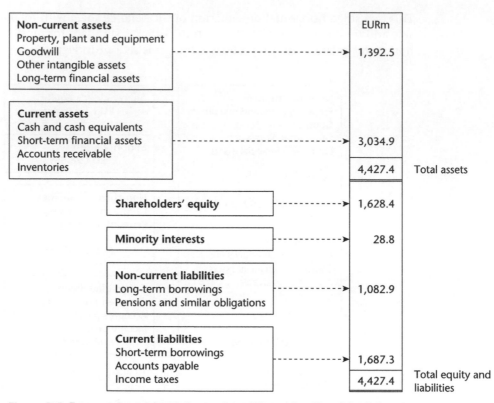

Figure 3.3 Format of a vertical balance sheet (Alternative 1): adidas-Salomon

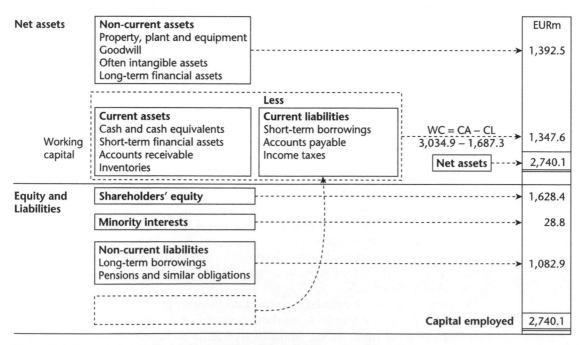

Figure 3.4 Format of a vertical balance sheet (Alternative 2): adidas-Salomon

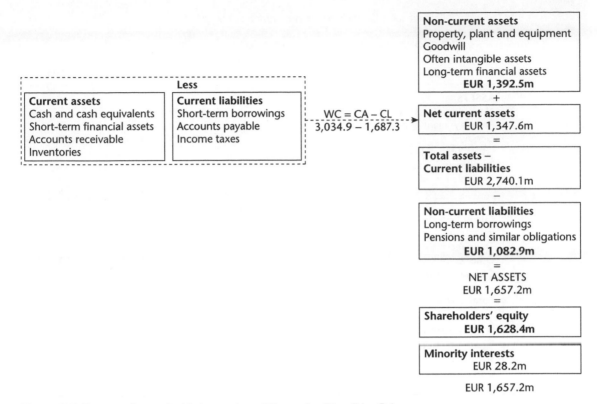

Figure 3.5 Format of a vertical balance sheet (Alternative 3): adidas-Salomon

movement of financial resources or funds including cash, as we will see in the next chapter (Figure 4.1). In a typical enterprise, inventory is produced or purchased, suppliers deliver raw materials, operating expenses are incurred and customers buy the products. All these transactions are completed either in cash or on credit terms.

The balance sheet layout in Figure 3.4 shows the net assets as follows:

Net assets = Non-current assets + Net current assets, or
           = Total assets – Current liabilities, or
           = Capital and reserves (including minority interests) + Non-current liabilities
           = Capital employed

The balance sheet shown in Figure 3.5 presents the net assets as follows:

Net assets = Capital and reserves (including minority interests), or
           = (Non-current assets + Net current assets) – Non-current liabilities

3.4.2 Format of the balance sheet recommended by IAS 1

Table 3.7 shows a balance sheet in the layout suggested by IAS 1.

Let us have a look at the five building blocks: non-current assets, current assets, capital and reserves (owners' funds), non-current liabilities and current liabilities. For the sake of simplicity we ignore the minority interest. We will deal with this item in Chapter 11.

Table 3.7 Format for a balance sheet recommended by IAS 1

XYZ GROUP – BALANCE SHEET AS AT 31 DECEMBER 2004 (in thousands of euro)		
	2004	*2003*
ASSETS		
Non-current assets		
Property, plant and equipment	X	X
Goodwill	X	X
Other intangible assets	X	X
Investments in associates	X	X
Available-for-sale investments	X	X
	X	X
Current assets		
Inventories	X	X
Trade receivables	X	X
Other current assets	X	X
Cash and cash equivalents	X	X
	X	X
Total assets	X	X
EQUITY AND LIABILITIES		
Equity attributable to equity holders of the parent		
Share capital	X	X
Other reserves	X	X
Retained earnings	X	X
	X	X
Minority interest	X	X
Total equity	X	X
Non-current liabilities		
Long-term borrowings	X	X
Deferred tax	X	X
Long-term provisions	X	X
Total non-current liabilities	X	X
Current liabilities		
Trade and other payables	X	X
Short-term borrowings	X	X
Current portion of long-term borrowings	X	X
Current tax payable	X	X
Short-term provisions	X	X
Total current liabilities	X	X
Total liabilities	X	X
Total equity and liabilities	X	X

Current and non-current assets

Assets are economic resources that are controlled by an enterprise and whose cost (or fair value) at the time of acquisition can be objectively measured. The four key points in this definition are:

1. An asset is acquired in a transaction.
2. An asset is an economic resource. A resource is an economic resource if it provides future benefits to the enterprise.
3. The resource is controlled by the enterprise.
4. Its cost (or fair value) at the time of acquisition is objectively measurable.

Activity 3.1 Definition of assets

Questions:

State which of the following items should appear on the balance sheet of ABC Ltd as an asset. Explain your reasoning in each case:

1. EUR 2,000 owing to ABC Ltd by a customer who will never be able to pay.
2. Acquisition of a licence from Red Ferrari SpA giving ABC Ltd a right to produce cars designed by Red Ferrari. Production of the new car under licence is expected to increase profits over the duration of the licence.
3. The hiring of a new production director by ABC Ltd who is confidently expected to reduce production costs by over 40 per cent over the next three years.
4. Acquisition of a machine which will save ABC Ltd EUR 20,000 per annum. It is currently being used by ABC but has been acquired on credit and is not yet paid for.

Solutions to activities can be found at www.pearsoned.co.uk/kothari

From this, it can be deduced that the sorts of items which normally appear as assets in the balance sheet of an enterprise include:

- buildings
- plant and machinery
- fixtures and fittings
- patents and trademarks
- trade and other receivables
- inventories
- investments
- cash at bank/in hand.

Assets are divided into current and non-current. The former are not held on a continuing basis: they are expected to be converted into cash at some future point in the normal course of trading. The latter are held for use in generating wealth rather than for resale.

It is worth noting that the classification of an asset as current or non-current may vary according to the purpose for which a particular asset is owned or held. For example, a van manufacturer will normally hold vans produced for resale and would therefore classify them as current assets (under the heading 'inventories'). On the other hand, the same van manufacturer will use vans for delivery of its products, say spare parts, and would classify them as fixed assets which are non-current assets.

Current and non-current liabilities

Liabilities result from past transactions or other past events. Thus, for example, the purchase of goods by Paolo on 8 January gave rise to a trade payable – as goods costing EUR 40,000 were neither paid in advance nor on delivery – and the bank loan obtained on 2 January resulted in an obligation to repay the loan. IASB defines a liability as:

> *A present obligation of the enterprise arising from past events, the settlement of which is expected to result in an outflow from the enterprise of resources embodying economic benefits.*

As for assets, we should distinguish between current and non-current liabilities. Current liabilities represent amounts due for repayment to third parties within 12 months of the balance sheet date (i.e. bank overdraft, short-term borrowing, trade payables, tax payables, etc.), while non-current liabilities represent those amounts due to other parties that are not liable for repayment in the 12 months following the balance sheet date (i.e. long-term borrowings).

Equity

One of the building blocks in the balance sheet indicates the amount of finance owners have provided to the enterprise. A variety of captions are used: capital and reserves, shareholders' funds or equity, owners' funds, net worth, and so on. Owners' equity is also described as net assets, since the amount of owners' equity is equal to the assets net of the liabilities, i.e. total assets less total liabilities.

The equity section of the balance sheet of a single enterprise normally contains three main headings:

- Issued capital
- Reserves
- Retained earnings.

The first category is the amount the owners have invested directly in the enterprise by subscribing for the shares issued by the company.

One of the reserves is usually represented by a share premium reserve. Each share has a stated or 'par' or 'nominal' value. Issued capital represents this value per share, times the number of shares outstanding. If investors actually paid more to the company than the stated value (as is often the case) for their shares, the excess is shown separately as a share premium.

The last category of the equity is labelled retained earnings. It is also known as accumulated profit/losses. The owners' equity increases through earnings (i.e. the results of profitable operations) and decreases when earnings are paid out in the form of dividends, or losses are made. Retained earnings generally represent the difference between the total profits of the enterprise from its formation and the total amount of losses incurred and dividends paid out to its shareholders over its entire life. That is, the difference represents that part of the total profits that have been retained or reinvested in the enterprise. If the difference is negative it represents accumulated deficit and it is subtracted from the owners' equity.

Note that the amount of accumulated profits at a given date is the cumulative amount that has been retained in the business from the beginning of the enterprise's existence. The amount of EUR 414.6 million of Puma's accumulated profits (see Table 3.8) represents the total amount retained in the business since Puma began operations. This amount does not indicate the ways in which the retained earnings have been reinvested. They may have been invested in any of the resources that appear in the current and non-current asset boxes.

Table 3.8 Consolidated balance sheet of Puma as at 31 December 2004

	Dec. 31, 2004	Dec. 31, 2003
	EURm	EURm
ASSETS		
Cash and cash equivalents	369.3	190.6
Inventories	201.1	196.2
Trade receivables and other receivables	189.6	175.6
Other short-term financial assets	0.3	1.9
Total current assets	760.3	564.3
Deferred income taxes	51.6	36.5
Property, plant and equipment	84.7	66.5
Goodwill	20.0	22.3
Other intangible assets	7.2	5.9
Other long-term financial assets	5.3	4.1
Investment in associated companies	0.6	0.6
Total assets	929.6	700.1
LIABILITIES AND EQUITY		
Financial liabilities	12.9	16.8
Trade payables	136.9	132.6
Other liabilities	123.3	69.0
Total current liabilities	273.1	218.5
Pension	21.2	18.5
Tax provisions	33.7	27.1
Other provisions	53.8	49.0
Total provisions	108.7	94.6
Long-term interest bearing liabilities	0.0	0.0
Deferred income taxes	9.6	3.2
Minority interest	2.4	0.8
Subscribed capital Puma AG	42.7	41.6
Group reserves	178.8	84.0
Accumulated profits	414.6	278.5
Treasury stock	−100.2	−20.9
Shareholders' equity	535.8	383.0
Total liabilities and shareholders' equity	929.6	700.1

Source: Puma Annual Report 2004

There is a common misconception that there is some connection between the amount of a company's retained earnings and the amount of cash it holds. There is no such connection. This should be apparent from the fact that the Puma balance sheet shows EUR 414.6 million of accumulated profits but a lower amount of cash and cash equivalents, EUR 369.3 million.

3.5   Accounting conventions and the balance sheet

In Chapter 2 we introduced business entity and going concern conventions. In section 3.2, we mentioned other conventions referring to the balance sheet of adidas-Salomon. Now we will examine money measurement and historic cost conventions.

Money measurement convention

In financial accounting, a record is made only of information that can be expressed in monetary terms. (A rule of thumb for accountants is 'if you can't measure it ignore it'.) The advantage of such a record is that money provides a common denominator by means of which heterogeneous facts about an enterprise can be expressed as numbers that can be added and subtracted.

Although it may be a fact that an enterprise owns EUR 50,000 of cash; 20,000 kilos of raw material; six vans; 30,000 square metres of building space, and so on, these numbers cannot be added together to produce a meaningful total of what that enterprise owns. Expressing these items in monetary terms – cash for EUR 50,000; raw material for EUR 30,000; trucks for EUR 120,000; and buildings for EUR 1,800,000 – makes such an addition possible.

Despite its advantage, the money measurement concept imposes a severe limitation on the scope of an accounting report. A major problem arises when the measurement unit, say the euro, dollar or sterling, changes in value over time. If, as occurs with inflation, the unit of measurement used in the accounts is worth more at the beginning of the period than at the end, the traditional accounting and reporting systems run into difficulties. Under conditions of continuous high inflation traditional accounting methods and reports are of little use. For example, what value should appear in the balance sheet when an enterprise purchases an asset at the beginning of the accounting period for EUR 5,000 and another identical asset at the end of the year that, owing to inflation, costs EUR 10,000? Ignoring depreciation, is it practical or useful to add the two figures together and show assets 'valued' at EUR 15,000? The answer must be no, and some adjustment is required to provide a more meaningful guide to the value to the enterprise of the assets employed at the end of the year.

There are several solutions to overcome the problems of inflation in company reports, such as current purchasing power accounting (CPP) and current cost accounting (CCA), but we will not deal with them, as they go beyond the scope of this book.

Historic cost convention

Assets are shown on the balance sheet at a value based on their historic cost (that is, acquisition cost). A fundamental concept of accounting, closely related to the going concern concept, is that an asset is ordinarily recorded initially in the accounting records at the price paid for its acquisition (i.e. its cost). In the case of non-current assets, the cost concept extends to their accounting subsequent to acquisition: cost continues to be the basis for all subsequent accounting for the asset. This is not true for most current assets. Subsequent to acquisition they are accounted for at their fair value. Fair value is the amount at which an asset could be exchanged in a current transaction between willing parties in an arm's length transaction, other than in a forced or liquidation sale.

Since, for a variety of reasons, the real worth of an asset may change with the passage of time, the accounting measurement of non-current assets does not necessarily reflect what assets are worth, except at the moment they are acquired.

The historic cost convention provides an excellent illustration of the trade-off between different accounting concepts (see section 2.7), namely prudence, relevance, neutrality and reliability. Cost is neutral not on the grounds that it is objective, but on the grounds that it usually has a greater objective element than the alternative of attempting to estimate fair values. However, when reading a company's annual report, we must recognise that it is based in part on the cost convention, and that current values can be estimated partly by analysing the information in the report and partly by using non-accounting information.

The cost convention does not mean that all non-current assets remain on the accounting records at their original acquisition price for as long as the enterprise owns them. The cost of a non-current asset that has a long but nevertheless limited life is systematically reduced over that life for depreciation and for any impairment loss, as we will discuss in Chapter 7.

3.6   Balance sheet structure and ratio analysis

In this chapter we have learnt to construct a balance sheet but in order to get as much information as we can, it is useful to analyse it using several techniques. These are horizontal analysis, trend analysis, vertical analysis and ratio analysis. We will discuss these techniques more thoroughly in Part four. However, we will address certain issues at appropriate places throughout the book, which will then be summarised in Part four.

With reference to a balance sheet we can apply vertical analysis. It consists in expressing all single assets or groups of them as a percentage of total assets. The same applies to the other side of the balance sheet. For example, for Puma (see Table 3.9), inventories represent 21.6 per cent and 28 per cent of the total assets as at 31 December 2004 and 2003, respectively.

If we look at Figure 3.6, from the Austrian Airlines Annual Report, we see that current assets represent a small part of the total assets both in 2004 and 2003. This means that Austrian Airlines has heavily invested in fixed assets. This is obvious as it belongs to the airline industry.

Table 3.9 Puma consolidated balance sheet

	2004		2003		+/– %
	EURm	%	EURm	%	
Cash and cash equivalents	369.3	39.7	190.6	27.2	93.8
Inventories	201.1	21.6	196.2	28.0	2.5
Accounts receivables	189.6	20.4	175.6	25.1	8.0
Other short-term assets	0.3	0.0	1.9	0.3	–85.6
Total current assets	**760.3**	**81.8**	**564.3**	80.6	34.7
Deferred income taxes	**51.6**	5.6	**36.5**	5.2	41.6
Long-term assets	**117.7**	12.7	**99.4**	14.2	18.4
Total assets	929.6	100.0	700.1	100.0	32.8
Bank borrowings	12.9	1.4	16.8	2.4	–23.0
Other liabilities	269.8	29.0	204.8	29.3	31.8
Total current liabilities	**282.8**	30.4	**221.6**	31.7	27.6
Pension	21.2	2.3	18.5	2.6	14.2
Tax provision	33.7	3.6	27.1	3.9	24.5
Other provisions	53.8	5.8	49.0	7.0	9.8
Provisions	**108.7**	11.7	**94.6**	13.5	14.9
Long-term interest bearing borrowings and minorities	**2.4**	0.3	**0.8**	0.1	196.0
Shareholders' equity	**535.8**	57.6	**383.0**	54.7	39.9
Total liabilities and shareholders' equity	929.6	100.0	700.1	100.0	32.8

Source: Puma Annual Report 2004

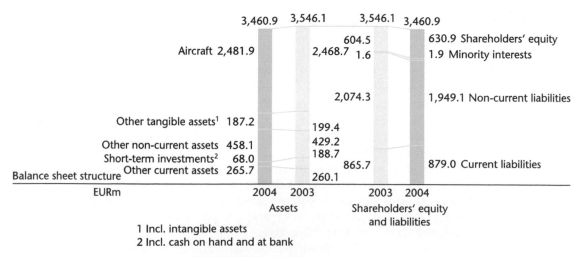

Figure 3.6 Austrian Airlines' consolidated balance sheet

Source: Austrian Airlines' Group Annual Report 2004

3.6.1 Ratios relating to the balance sheet

At this stage we can calculate some ratios with the data of the balance sheets of adidas-Salomon and Puma. A ratio is simply one number expressed in terms of another. It is found by dividing one number, the base, into the other.

The ratio of current assets to current liabilities is called the current ratio. It is an important indication of an enterprise's ability to meet its current obligations because if current assets do not exceed current liabilities by a comfortable margin, the enterprise may be unable to pay its current bills. This is because current assets are expected to be converted into cash within a year or less and, at the same time, current liabilities are obligations expected to be settled in cash within a year or less.

In most circumstances we can expect that current assets will exceed current liabilities. The current ratio will then be at least 1:1:

$$\text{Current ratio} = \frac{\text{Current assets}}{\text{Current liabilities}}$$

	2004	**2003**
Puma	$\frac{760.3}{273.1} = 2.78$	$\frac{564.3}{218.5} = 2.58$
adidas-Salomon	$\frac{3,034.9}{1,687.3} = 1.80$	$\frac{2,776.9}{1,343.7} = 2.07$

Note: Amounts in millions of euro. Ratios in units.

We should be careful in assuming that a factor of, say, 1:2 or a ratio of 0.50 would suggest that an enterprise will face an immediate liquidation. For example, tax and dividends may not have to be paid for some months after the year-end. In the meantime, the company may regularly collect cash from its customers and other debtors and it may be able to balance these against what it has to pay to its creditors. In some cases, however, a current ratio of less than 1 may signify a serious financial condition, especially if the current assets consist of a very high proportion of inventories. This leads us on to another ratio:

$$\text{Acid-test ratio (or quick ratio)} = \frac{\text{Current assets} - \text{Inventory}}{\text{Current liabilities}}$$

	2004	**2003**
Puma	$\frac{760.3 - 201.1}{273.1} = 2.05$	$\frac{564.3 - 196.2}{218.5} = 1.68$
adidas-Salomon	$\frac{3,034.9 - 1,155.4}{1,687.3} = 1.11$	$\frac{2,776.9 - 1,163.5}{1,343.7} = 1.2$

Note: Amounts in millions of euro. Ratios in units.

In terms of liquidity, inventories are less liquid than trade receivables, as you need to sell inventories to turn them into trade receivables and then into cash. So it is sensible to measure the current ratio by excluding the inventories. This ratio is called acid test or quick ratio.

Puma's current and quick ratio appear to be more robust or healthy than those of adidas-Salomon.

Summary

- The objective of general purpose financial statements is to provide information about the financial position, performance and cash flows of an enterprise that is useful to a wide range of users in making economic decisions. Such information is addressed respectively by the balance sheet, income statement and cash flow statement.

- A balance sheet shows the financial condition of an enterprise at a given date. It consists of five boxes: non-current and current assets represent the economic resources controlled by the entity that are expected to provide future benefits to it; owners' equity and non-current and current liabilities respectively represent the amount invested in the enterprise by the owners and the obligations of the enterprise towards third parties.

- The accounting conventions relating to financial statements are money measurement convention (only those facts that can be expressed in monetary terms are recorded); business entity (accounts for enterprises are separate from their owners); going concern (accounting assumes that an enterprise will continue to operate for an indefinitely long period in the future); historical cost (with few exceptions, assets are shown on the balance sheet at the amount paid to acquire them); and dual aspect (every transaction affects at least two items and maintains in balance the fundamental equation: $A = L + E$).

- Among the ratios relating to the balance sheet are current ratio (i.e. current assets divided by current liabilities) and acid test or quick ratio (i.e. current assets less inventories divided by current liabilities).

References and research

The IASB documents relevant for this chapter are the *Framework for the Preparation and Presentation of Financial Statements* and IAS1 – *Presentation of Financial Statements*.

The following are examples of books that take the issues of this chapter further:

- Robert N. Anthony, David F. Hawkins and Kenneth A. Merchant, *Accounting: Text and Cases*, McGraw-Hill, 1999, Chapter 2
- Barry Elliott and Jamie Elliott, *Financial Accounting and Reporting*, 9th Edition, Financial Times-Prentice Hall, 2005, Chapter 9
- Charles T. Horngren, Gary L. Sundem and John A. Elliott, *Introduction to Financial Accounting*, Pearson Education-Prentice Hall, 2002, Chapter 1

- Hennie Van Greuning, *International Financial Reporting Standards: A Practical Guide*, The World Bank, 2005, Part I
- Frank Wood and Alan Sangster, *Business Accounting*, Vol. 1, Financial Times-Prentice Hall, 9th Edition, March 2002, Part 2

Questions

3.1 Luca has just enrolled in the first year of a General Management degree programme. He has decided to sell his books used in high school. He thinks all his books are worth EUR 300.

On the first day, he sells two-thirds of the books for EUR 250. On the second day, he sells the rest for EUR 110.

(a) What cash movements took place on each day of trading?
(b) How much wealth (profit) was generated on each day of trading?
(c) What is the accumulated wealth at the end of each day?

3.2 XYZ's balance sheet as at 31 December 2004 had the following items (arranged here in random order):

	EUR		EUR
Trade payables	5,000	Financial assets	1,500
Trade receivables	7,000	Other current assets	3,500
Short-term borrowings	8,000	Property, plant and equipment	8,500
Cash and cash equivalents	2,000	Wages payable	1,500
Current portion of bonds payable	2,000		

(a) What is the current ratio at 31 December 2004?
(b) Explain what the current ratio indicates.

3.3 On 1 February 2005, Marco started a new business. During February he carried out the following transactions:

1 February:	deposited EUR 40,000 in a bank account
2 February:	purchased office furniture for EUR 12,000 cash, and inventory for EUR 16,000 on credit
3 February:	borrowed EUR 10,000 from a relative and deposited it in the bank
4 February:	purchased a van for EUR 14,000 cash
7 February:	purchased another van costing EUR 18,000. The van purchased on 4 February was given in part exchange at its cost (EUR 14,000). The balance of purchase price for the new van was paid in cash
8 February:	Marco won EUR 4,000 at Bingo and paid the amount into the enterprise's bank account. He also repaid EUR 2,000 of the loan.

Analyse each transaction using the accounting equation. Prepare a balance sheet for Marco's enterprise at the end of each day.

3.4 Lory & Co's balance sheet as at 31 December 2004 included the following accounts (arranged here in random order):

	EUR
Cash and cash equivalents	24,000
Short-term borrowings	20,000
Inventory	80,000
Issued capital	160,000
PPE	88,000
Trade and other receivables	28,000
Trade and other payables	16,000
Interest bearing borrowings	24,000

During January 2005, these transactions and events took place:

3 January:	purchased jackets for resale on credit for EUR 6,000
7 January:	sold at cost for EUR 2,000 store fixtures that were not needed
12 January:	issued new capital for EUR 24,000 to finance the acquisition of new equipment
20 January:	purchased a new shop for EUR 50,000, of which EUR 10,000 was paid in cash, the balance being settled by obtaining a bank loan.

Prepare a balance sheet as at 31 January 2005.

3.5   Ornella SpA's balance sheet as at 31 December 2004 included the following items:

	EUR million
PPE	634
Trade and other payables	926
Issued capital	6
Cash and cash equivalents	(A)
Total equity	(B)
Non-current liabilities	2,932
Total assets	4,942
Other assets	3,128
Reserves	(C)
Other liabilities	552

Prepare a balance sheet according to the format recommended by IAS 1 – *Presentation of Financial Statements*. Show your computation of:

(a) cash and cash equivalents
(b) total equity
(c) reserves.

3.6   The following is a list of the assets and claims of PB Ltd as at 31 December 2004:

	EUR
Trade and other payables	1,720
Delivery van	27,600
Bank loan	52,000
Machinery and equipment	21,400
Bank overdraft	23,200
Inventory	30,600
Building	64,000
Trade and other receivables	37,000

(a) Prepare a balance sheet of PB Ltd as at 31 December 2004 from the information listed using the vertical format. Bear in mind that there is a missing item which needs to be determined and inserted.

(b) Discuss the significant features revealed by this financial statement.

3.7   Refer to Table 3.8 – Consolidated balance sheet of Puma as at 31 December 2004.

Prepare an alternative presentation of the Puma balance sheet.

Case study   Diletta Ferrari enterprise (A)

Diletta made the following request to her boyfriend, 'My bookkeeper has quit, and I need to see the balance sheets of my company. He has left behind a book with the numbers already entered in it. Would you be willing to prepare balance sheets for me? Also, any comments you care to make about the numbers will be appreciated. The balance of cash and cash equivalents has almost doubled over one month, which is a good sign, and he has told me that the net income in July was EUR 19,635.'

The book contained a detailed record of transactions, and from it Diletta's boyfriend was able to extract the balances at the beginning of the month and at the end of the month as shown in Table 3.10.

Table 3.10 Data available

	1 July	31 July
	EUR	EUR
Trade payables	8,517	21,315
Trade receivables	21,798	16,505
Wages payable	1,974	2,202
Building (net)	429,000	427,050
Capital	390,000	390,000
Cash and cash equivalents	26,598	52,410
Equipment (net)	13,260	36,660
Land	89,700	89,700
Inventory	35,394	28,150
Other receivable (Diletta Ferrari)	11,700	0
Other non-current assets	4,857	5,265
Other non-current liabilities	2,451	2,451
Retained earnings	221,511	229,446
Taxes payable	5,700	7,224

Diletta is the only owner of Diletta Ferrari enterprise. At the end of July, Diletta paid herself a dividend of EUR 11,700 and used the money to repay her loan from the company.

Source: adapted from Anthony, Hawkins and Merchant (1999)

Questions:

1. Prepare the balance sheets as at 1 July and as at 31 July.
2. Comment on how the financial condition as at the end of July compared with that at the beginning of July.
3. Why do retained earnings not increase by the amount of July net profit?
4. At the end of July, do you consider that Diletta Ferrari enterprise is worth the amount of its owners' equity, EUR 619,446? Explain.

4 Income statement: an overall view

Objectives

When you have completed this chapter you should be able to:

- discuss the nature and purpose of an income statement
- discuss the main measurement issues that should be considered when preparing an income statement
- explain the main accounting conventions underpinning an income statement
- understand what gross profit margin and profit margin are.

4.1 Introduction

Chapter 3 described the balance sheet, which reports the financial condition of an enterprise at a given moment in time. This chapter will describe another financial statement, the income statement, which summarises the results of operations for a period of time. It is therefore a flow report, as contrasted with the balance sheet, which is a state of affairs report. These two financial statements illustrate two ways in which an enterprise can be described:

- in terms of flows over a period
- in terms of its position or state at a given moment in time.

Flows in an enterprise are continuous. Their essential nature, in most enterprises, is illustrated by the simplified diagram in Figure 4.1:

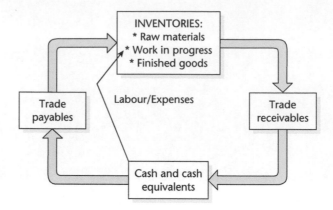

Figure 4.1 Operating cycle
Source: Walsh (2002)

- The enterprise has a pool of cash that it has obtained from investors and/or from past profitable transactions.
- It uses this cash to acquire inventories, either by purchasing goods from others or by producing them itself. It also incurs other expenses such as wages and salaries, advertising, freight, etc.
- Trade payables and various other assets and liabilities may intervene between the occurrence of these costs and the cash outflow to pay for them.
- The enterprise sells goods to customers, who either pay cash or agree to pay later, thus creating trade receivables.
- When the customers pay, the pool of cash is replenished.

4.2   Nature and purpose of an income statement

The purpose of an income statement is to measure and report the amount of wealth generated or destroyed over a period by an enterprise.

The amount of profit/loss generated during a period is of particular interest not only to owners, but also to managers, employees, suppliers and to other groups who may have an interest in the profit-making ability of the enterprise:

Profit (Loss) for the period = Total revenues − Total expenses incurred in generating the revenues

Revenues and expenses are the key components in measuring profit. These terms apply to the inflows and outflows of assets that occur during an enterprise's operating cycle. More specifically, revenues are gross increases in owners' equity arising from increases in assets received in exchange for the delivery of goods or services to customers. Expenses are decreases in owners' equity that arise as goods or services are delivered to customers. Together these items define the fundamental meaning of profit, which can simply be defined as the excess of revenues over expenses, as we can see from the next expanded accounting equation:

$$Assets = Liabilities + Owners' \ equity$$

$$Assets = Liabilities + Capital + Profit$$

$$Assets = Liabilities + Capital + Revenues - Expenses$$

The effect of trading operations on the income statement

Let us go back to the example presented in Chapter 3. The following equation summarises the first eight transactions of Paolo's enterprise in Table 3.6:

	RESOURCES/ASSETS			=	CLAIMS/SOURCES		
PPE	Inventory	Trade and other receivables	Cash and cash equivalents	=	Trade and other payables	Bank loan	Capital
+ 60,000	+ 95,000	+ 10,000	+ 220,000	=	+ 85,000	+ 100,000	+ 200,000

Now consider additional transactions.

Example

Transaction 9 – Sale on credit

9 January Paolo sells goods for EUR 70,000, on credit (i.e. the customer being allowed to pay later). The goods in question are those remaining after Transaction 6 (i.e. costing EUR 45,000). Two things happen simultaneously in the balance sheet equation:

- First, some of the inventory has been sold so the inventory figure reduces by EUR 45,000 (i.e. from EUR 95,000 to EUR 50,000).

- Second, the customer has contracted to pay the enterprise EUR 70,000 for the goods bought from Paolo. This does not mean that the enterprise has the cash; it does, however, own the contractual right to receive the cash. This is an additional resource of the business, an additional asset. EUR 70,000 represents the trade receivable.

The consequence of the transaction is that one resource has decreased by EUR 45,000 and another new resource has been acquired for EUR 70,000. This means that the total resources have increased by EUR 25,000. However, we cannot have a resource without a claim. What is the origin of this increase of EUR 25,000 in resources?

In intuitive terms it should be fairly clear what has happened. The enterprise has sold something for more than it had originally paid for it. It has turned an asset recorded for EUR 45,000 into another asset for EUR 70,000 (i.e. the receivable) through its trading operations. The difference of EUR 25,000 (EUR 70,000 of sales *less* EUR 45,000 of cost of sales) represents the profit earned by Paolo as the owner of the enterprise. On the balance sheet this profit is added to the owner's total claim (capital plus profit) against the enterprise. Thus the balance sheet balances.

			A		=	L		+	E
	PPE	Inventory	Trade and other receivables	Cash and cash equivalents		Bank loan	Trade and other payables	Capital	Profit
Bal.	60,000	95,000	10,000	220,000	=	100,000	85,000	200,000	
(9a)			+ 70,000		=				+ 70,000
(9b)		– 45,000			=				– 45,000
Bal.	60,000	50,000	80,000	220,000	=	100,000	85,000	200,000	25,000

410,000   410,000

Funny Sun
Balance sheet
as at 9 January

Assets	EUR	Owner's equity and liabilities	EUR
Property, plant and equipment	60,000	Capital	200,000
Inventory	50,000	Profit	25,000
Trade and other receivables	80,000	Owner's equity	225,000
Cash and cash equivalents	220,000		
		Bank loan	100,000
		Trade and other payables	85,000
Total assets	410,000	Total equity and liabilities	410,000

The profits earned by an enterprise are for the benefit of the owner and therefore they belong to the owner of the enterprise. Since these profits are held by the enterprise for the account of the owner, they are the owner's claim against the business.

It should be obvious by now that each transaction has at least two effects which are reflected in the balance sheet. This should also be clear from an analysis of the last transaction.

Example (continued)

Transaction 10 – Payment of wages

10 January   Paolo pays wages of EUR 10,000 for the period, in cash. Here two numerical alterations are needed to the balance sheet in order to incorporate the new event.

First, the amount of cash that the enterprise owns as an asset, reduces by EUR 10,000. This sum of money has actually been paid out by the enterprise so that the balance of cash will be EUR 10,000 less than it was before. The wages represent the reward given by the enterprise for labour hours that have been used. In other words, the wages represent services provided and used by the enterprise to generate profit in the trading period, which we had previously recorded at EUR 25,000. This therefore needs to be taken into account in calculating the overall profit made by the enterprise over the trading period.

Second, EUR 10,000 needs to be deducted from the profit figure of EUR 25,000 in order to show the appropriate profit earned by the enterprise for the benefit of the owner. The wages, which are an expense of the business, caused a reduction in assets (cash decreased) and resulted in a reduced claim of the owner (profit reduced).

		A		=	L		+	E	
PPE	Inventory	Trade and other receivables	Cash and cash equivalents		Bank loan	Trade and other payables		Capital	Profit
Bal. 60,000	50,000	80,000	220,000	= 100,000	85,000		200,000	+ 25,000
(10)			– 10,000	=					– 10,000
Bal. 60,000	50,000	80,000	210,000	= 100,000	85,000		200,000	15,000

$$\underbrace{\qquad\qquad\qquad}_{400,000} \qquad\qquad \underbrace{\qquad\qquad\qquad}_{400,000}$$

Funny Sun
Balance sheet
as at 10 January

Assets	EUR	Owner's equity and liabilities	EUR
Property, plant and equipment	60,000	Capital	200,000
Inventory	50,000	Profit	15,000
Trade and other receivables	80,000	Owner's equity	215,000
Cash and cash equivalents	210,000		
		Bank loan	100,000
		Trade and other payables	85,000
Total assets	400,000	Total equity and liabilities	400,000

Transaction 11 – Payment of rent, charges for depreciation, interest expense and income taxes

11 January Paolo pays rent of EUR 5,000 for the period 1–11 January, in cash. The amount of cash of the enterprise reduces by EUR 5,000. Therefore, the expense reduces the profit earned and the amount needs to be deducted from the profit figure of EUR 15,000.

The bank charged interest of EUR 500 on the loan for the first 11 days of January. Again, this amount reduces the profit earned and therefore it should be deducted from the profit and from the cash and cash equivalents.

As Paolo is keen to know how his enterprise is progressing, he wants to prepare an income statement for the period 1–11 January. Before doing that, he must account for depreciation, which in this case amounts to EUR 5,000. As we will see in Chapter 7, depreciation is a systematic allocation of the acquisition cost of non-current or long-lived assets to the income statement for a particular period (in this case 1–11 January) that benefits from the use of the assets.

In preparing the income statement, Paolo also takes into account the income taxes payable on the profit earned. Income taxes payable are determined at EUR 1,500. After the deduction of all expenses from the revenues earned, the remaining balance of profit is net profit or net income.

	PPE	Inventory	A Trade and other receivables	Cash and cash equivalents	=	Bank loan	L Trade and other payables	+	E Capital	Profit
Bal.	60,000	50,000	80,000	210,000	=	100,000	85,000		200,000	+ 15,000
(11a)				– 5,000	=					– 5,000
(11b)	– 5,000				=					– 5,000
(11c)				– 500	=					– 500
(11d)					=		+ 1,500			– 1,500
Bal.	55,000	50,000	80,000	204,500	=	100,000	86,500		200,000	3,000

389,500   389,500

Funny Sun
Balance sheet
as at 11 January

Assets	EUR	Owner's equity and liabilities	EUR
Property, plant and equipment	55,000	Capital	200,000
Inventory	50,000	Net profit	3,000
Trade and other receivables	80,000	Owner's equity	203,000
Cash and cash equivalents	204,500		
		Bank loan	100,000
		Trade and other payables	86,500
Total assets	389,500	Total equity and liabilities	389,500

This analysis of transactions enables us to obtain the net profit figure of EUR 3,000, which is part of the owner's equity. The income statement shows how the enterprise's operations for the period 1–11 January have increased the net assets through revenues and decreased the net assets by consuming resources (expenses). Table 4.1 shows how an income statement summarises these transactions.

If this net profit or income of EUR 3,000 is reinvested in the enterprise by Paolo to expand his business by acquiring, for instance, new equipment or new goods for resale, it will appear on the balance sheet as retained earnings, as we will see in Chapter 9.

Table 4.1 Paolo's income statement for the period 1–11 January

	EUR	EUR
Sales		70,000
Deduct Cost of sales		(45,000)
Gross profit (or gross margin)		25,000
Deduct: Operating expenses:		
Wages	10,000	
Rent	5,000	
Depreciation	5,000	
		(20,000)
Operating profit (or Operating income or earnings before interest and taxes, EBIT)		5,000
Deduct Interest expense		(500)
Profit (or income or earnings) before taxes (EBT)		4,500
Deduct Income taxes		(1,500)
Net profit (or income)		**3,000**

4.4 Income statement layouts

Two of the most common forms of presentation of an income statement start with the sales revenues for the year. Costs and expenses are then either subdivided by function (cost of sales, distribution, administration) or classified according to their nature or type (material, wages, etc.). The former classification is the most common and it is shown in Tables 4.2 and 4.3. As you can see, the income statement includes comparative figures for the previous year.

Table 4.2 Income statement for the year ended 31 December 2004 (illustrating the classification of expenses by function) (IAS 1)

(amounts in thousands of euro)	2004	2003
Revenues	X	X
Cost of sales	(X)	(X)
Gross profit	X	X
Other income	X	X
Distribution costs	(X)	(X)
Administrative expenses	(X)	(X)
Other expenses	(X)	(X)
Finance costs	(X)	(X)
Share of profit of associates	X	X
Profit before tax	X	X
Income tax expense	(X)	(X)
Profit for the year	X	X
Attributable to:		
Equity holders of the parent	X	X
Minority interest	X	X
	X	X

Source: After IAS 1

Table 4.3 adidas-Salomon income statement for 2004 (amounts in thousands of euro)

	2004	2003	Change in %
Net sales	6,478,072	6,266,800	3.4
Cost of sales	3,419,864	3,453,132	(1.0)
Gross profit	**3,058,208**	**2,813,668**	**8.7**
Selling, general and administrative expenses	2,376,266	2,228,135	6.6
Depreciation and amortization (excl. goodwill)	101,764	95,519	6.5
Operating profit	**580,178**	**490,014**	**18.4**
Goodwill amortization	46,352	44,809	3.4
Royalty and commission income	43,166	42,153	2.4
Financial expenses, net	56,832	49,170	15.6
Income before taxes and minority interests	**520,160**	**438,188**	**18.7**
Income taxes	196,691	166,712	18.0
Net income before minority interests	**323,469**	**271,476**	**19.2**
Minority interests	(9,221)	(11,391)	(19.0)
Net income	**314,248**	**260,085**	**20.8**

Source: adidas-Salomon Annual Report 2004

For management purposes we can present income statements following a different layout as shown in Table 4.4.

Table 4.4 Puma management income statement for 2004

	2004		2003		+/– %
	EURm	%	EURm	%	
Consolidated sales	**1,530.3**	100.0	**1,274.0**	100.0	**20.1**
Cost of material	736.4	48.1	654.0	51.3	12.6
Gross profit	**794.0**	51.9	**620.0**	48.7	**28.1**
Royalty and commission income	**43.7**	2.9	**40.3**	3.2	**8.3**
Selling, general and administrative expenses					
Marketing/Retail expenses	214.6	14.0	163.9	12.9	30.9
Research, design and development	36.9	2.4	29.9	2.3	23.3
Other expenses	202.0	13.2	183.3	14.4	10.2
Total	453.4	29.6	377.1	29.6	20.2
EBITDA	**384.2**	25.1	**283.3**	22.2	**35.6**
Depreciation	19.3	1.3	20.1	1.6	–4.1
EBIT	**365.0**	23.9	**263.2**	20.7	**38.7**
Financial result	**5.7**	0.4	**0.9**	0.1	**540.7**
EBT	**370.7**	24.2	**264.1**	20.7	**40.4**
Income taxes	**111.7**	7.3	**84.2**	6.6	**32.6**
Tax rate		30.1		31.9	
Minority interests	**–1.7**	–0.1	**–0.6**	–0.0	
Net earnings	**257.3**	16.8	**179.3**	14.1	**43.5**

Source: Puma Annual Report 2004

As you can see, terms such as EBITDA (earnings before interest, tax, depreciation and amortisation), EBIT (earnings before interest and tax) and EBT (earnings before tax) are today commonly used by management and analysts. We will explain them and calculate ratios using them, in Part four.

4.5   Accounting conventions and the income statement

4.5.1   Accounting period convention

Net profit for the entire life of an enterprise is relatively easy to measure. It is simply the difference between the money that has come in and the money that has gone out, excluding of course money invested by the owners or paid out to the owners.

Activity 4.1 Profit of an enterprise

Jonathan and Margaret Trevelyan operated a children's camp for one summer, renting all the necessary facilities and equipment. Before the camp opened, they invested EUR 70,000 for food, the initial rental payment, and certain other costs. The camp received EUR 150,000 in fees from parents. At the end of the summer, the Trevelyans paid the teachers EUR 50,000. After all affairs were wound up, Jonathan and Margaret were left with EUR 100,000, which included EUR 70,000 representing the original investment.

Question:

What is the profit realised by Jonathan and Margaret?

Solutions to activities can be found at www.pearsoned.co.uk/kothari

Relatively few enterprises have a life of only a few months, as was the case with the Trevelyans' summer camp. And therefore, it is unlikely that the net profit equals net cash inflows. Most enterprises operate for many years. Indeed, in accordance with the going concern convention, it is usually assumed that the life of an enterprise is virtually indefinite. Owners, management and other interested parties are unwilling to wait until the business has ended to obtain information on how much profit has been earned. They need to know at frequent intervals 'how things are going'. This need leads to the accounting period convention: accounting measures activities for a specified period of time, called the accounting period. For the purpose of reporting to outsiders, one year is the usual accounting period:

Books should be closed each year, especially in a partnership, because frequent accounting makes for long friendship.

(Luca Pacioli, *Summa de Arithmetica, Geometria, Proportioni et Proportionalita*, 1494, from the translation by John B. Geijsbeck)

4.5.2 Prudence convention

As we saw in Chapter 2, this concept can be stated informally as 'anticipate no profits but anticipate all losses'. More formally, we can state the two aspects of prudence convention as follows:

- recognise revenues only when they are realised (realisation convention). In Chapter 5 we will deal with revenue recognition more deeply.

- recognise expenses as soon as they are known even if they have not yet actually incurred (see the following example).

Example

Application of prudence concept to recognition of revenue and expenses

1. In December 2004, Shubber agrees to buy a car from Varauto srl, for delivery in January 2005. Although this is good news for Varauto srl, it is possible that something may go wrong and the sale may not take place. Therefore the prudence convention requires that the revenue should not be recorded or recognised until the car is actually delivered. Thus, Varauto srl will not recognise revenue from this transaction in 2004 because the revenue is not realised in 2004, even though it is reasonably probable. Rather, as the car is delivered in January 2005, the revenue is recognised in 2005.

2. An uninsured car disappears from Varauto srl premises in December 2004. Possibly it will be recovered; possibly it has been stolen and is gone for ever. In the latter case, Varauto srl's profit has decreased, as the enterprise has incurred an expense or loss. Suppose that Varauto srl is not certain that the car is gone forever until February 2005. Nevertheless, the prudence convention requires that the expense or loss be recognised in December 2004, when it became reasonably probable that an expense or loss was incurred and not in February 2005, when the expense became certain.

3. In late 2004 Varatuto srl learnt that the selling price of certain models in its inventory has declined to less than the cost of these cars. A loss (i.e. an expense) should be recognised in 2004 even though prices may rise again and the cars may even be sold in 2005 at a profit. (This 'lower of cost and net realisable value' rule, probably the most well-known application of the prudence concept, is described in Chapter 6.)

4.5.3 Matching convention

The matching convention states that the expenses to be charged to the current period income statement are those incurred to generate the revenues of the same period.

The conversion of cash received and cash paid to an accrual and prepayment basis at the end of an accounting period often involves a few simple arithmetical calculations. Account should be taken for accruals and prepayments at the end of the previous period (i.e. opening accruals and prepayments), as well as for accruals and prepayments at the end of the current period (i.e. closing accruals and prepayments).

Activities 4.2–4.4 and the following examples illustrate how to apply the matching convention:

Activity 4.2 Matching convention and cost of sales

In June 2004, Polar Trips Ltd buys 50 jackets for EUR 200 each from its supplier. Polar Trips sells 40 of the 50 jackets at EUR 350 each during the same month.

Question:

Determine the amount of profit made on the sale of the jackets in June, using the matching convention.

Solutions to activities can be found at www.pearsoned.co.uk/kothari

Example

Application of matching convention: prepayment

At the end of December, Lorenzo Srl pays in advance EUR 70 for a subscription for a magazine to be received in the next accounting period.

What happens here is that in the current year Lorenzo pays EUR 70 for a magazine he will receive in the subsequent year. The money paid is accounted for as a decrease in cash, not as an expense for the current period, and an offsetting asset is recorded on the balance sheet at the end of this year, because the subscriber has the right to receive the magazine. The asset, prepaid expense or prepayment, represents the subscriber's right to receive the future issues of the magazine for which he has already paid. The transaction cycle just discussed is illustrated as follows:

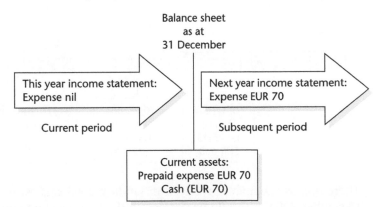

In terms of the accounting equation the transaction may be expressed as follows:

	A		= L +	E	
	Prepaid expense	Cash		Capital	Profit (loss)
In the current period:	+ EUR 70	– EUR 70	=		
In the subsequent period:	– EUR 70		=		– EUR 70

Activity 4.3 Matching convention and prepayments

At the end of September, Lollo SpA paid in advance EUR 12,000 for an insurance contract covering the period 1 October to 30 September.

Questions:

Assuming that Lollo SpA's financial year is 1 January–31 December, what is the insurance expense to be charged to the current period income statement? Illustrate the above transaction as an accounting equation.

Solutions to activities can be found at www.pearsoned.co.uk/kothari

Example

Application of matching convention and accrued expenses

User Ltd started trading on 1 January 2004 and incurs telephone charges of EUR 200 per month.

Its year-end date is 31 December and its next quarterly telephone bill is due on 10 January 2005.

By 31 December 2004 three telephone bills totalling EUR 1,800 were received, paid and charged to the income statement.

The telephone has been used from January to December and has helped to generate 12 months of sales revenue. The matching (accruals) concept says that we should match costs for 12 months against revenues for 12 months.

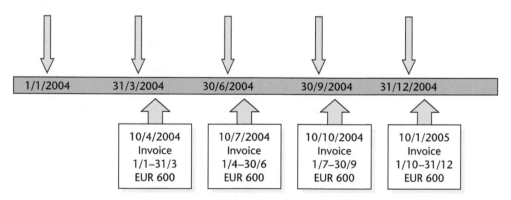

Therefore, as the invoice received in January 2005 relates to the period October to December 2004, it should be charged to the income statement for 2004.

Telephone expenses recorded and paid = EUR 600 × 3 invoices:	EUR 1,800
Add accrued expense (expense incurred but unpaid)	EUR 600
Total income statement charge	**EUR 2,400**

The charge to the income statement for 2004 now represents 12 months × EUR 200 per month.

Now let us illustrate the above transactions through the accounting equation:

	A	=	L	+	E	
	Cash and cash equivalents		Accrued expenses		Capital	Profit
10 April 2004:	– EUR 600	=				– EUR 600
10 July 2004:	– EUR 600	=				– EUR 600
10 October 2004:	– EUR 600	=				– EUR 600
31 December 2004:		=	+ EUR 600			– EUR 600
10 January 2005:	– EUR 600	=	– EUR 600			

Activity 4.4 Matching convention and accrued expenses

Fluff is in the business of making toys. He starts trading on 1 January 2003 and receives the following invoices in respect of light and heat:

Invoices received on:	Period covered by invoice:	Amount EUR
2 April 2003	1.1.2003–31.3.2003	3,000
9 July 2003	1.4.2003 30.6.2003	2,000
6 October 2003	1.7.2003–30.9.2003	2,000
10 January 2004	1.10.2003–31.12.2003	3,500
6 April 2004	1.1.2004–31.3.2004	2,200
7 July 2004	1.4.2004–30.6.2004	2,000
4 October 2004	1.7.2004–30.9.2004	2,000
9 January 2005	1.10.2004–31.12.2004	4,400

Questions:

1. Determine the light and heat expense to be charged to the income statements for the years ended 31 December 2003 and 2004.
2. Illustrate the above transactions through the accounting equation.

Solutions to activities can be found at www.pearsoned.co.uk/kothari

As you can see from the last example and Activity 4.4, accruals arise when an enterprise has received the benefit of a service or has received goods, but has not yet been invoiced for those goods or services. Moreover, cash is paid at a later date than the date of the receipt of goods or service.

In the balance sheet, accruals should be classified under current liabilities (amounts payable within the next 12 months).

The opposite effect results when an enterprise pays for or records an expense which relates to the following period.

In this case the current period's charge is unaffected and the expense is deferred to the next period.

Prepayments arise when an enterprise has paid cash in advance for services to be received in the future. Moreover, prepayments represent charges or expenses against future revenues. Prepayments are classified in the balance sheet as current assets.

4.6   Ratios relating to the income statement

In analysing an income statement, percentage relationships are normally calculated in terms of sales (vertical analysis). The net sales amount represents 100 per cent. Each income statement item is then expressed as a percentage of net sales as shown in the Puma management income statement (see Table 4.4).

Profit margin

In the income statement, the net profit margin can be used to analyse an enterprise's profitability. It is calculated by dividing net income (or net profit) by sales revenue and expressing the results as a percentage:

$$\text{Profit margin \%} = (\text{Profit} \div \text{Sales revenue}) \times 100$$

For Puma in 2004, this is 16.8 per cent (EUR 257.3 million ÷ EUR 1,530.3 million), while in 2003 it was 14.1 per cent (EUR 179.3 million ÷ EUR 1,274.0 million).

Gross profit margin

Working down the income statement, the first level of profit normally displayed is the gross profit (or gross margin), which is determined by deducting the cost of sales from sales revenue for the year:

$$\text{Gross profit margin \%} = (\text{Gross profit} \div \text{Sales revenue}) \times 100$$

The gross profit margin, or percentage, often simply referred to as the gross margin, offers an indication of the basic profitability of a business and is useful when comparing the performance of enterprises operating within the same industry. For Puma in 2004, this is 51.9 per cent: (EUR 794.0 million ÷ EUR 1,530.3 million) × 100. In 2003 it was 48.7 per cent: (EUR 620.0 million ÷ EUR 1,274.0 million) ÷ 100.

It indicates the average margin obtained on products (goods or services) sold before accounting for overheads. The gross profit margin is one of the most important ratios used by management and analysts in measuring and monitoring the performance of business operations.

Summary

- The purpose of an income statement is to measure and report the amount of wealth the enterprise has created or destroyed over a period.

- Profit or loss for a period represents the difference between total revenues and total expenses incurred in generating the revenues.

- Accounting measures activities for a specified period of time, called the accounting period. For the purpose of reporting to stakeholders, one year is the usual accounting period.

- Accruals arise where an enterprise has received the benefit of a service or has received goods, but has not yet been invoiced for those goods or services. In the balance sheet, accruals should be classified under current liabilities.

- When an enterprise pays for or records an expense which relates to the following period, this period's charge is reduced and the expense is deferred to the next period. Such amounts are classified in the balance sheet under current assets and are called prepayments.

- The gross profit margin offers an indication of the basic profitability of a business. It is calculated by dividing gross profit by sales revenue and expressing the results as a percentage.

- The net profit margin is determined by dividing net profit by sales revenue and expressing the result as a percentage.

- Gross profit margin and net profit margin are two most widely used key performance indicators (KPIs) by the financial community.

References and research

The IASB document relevant for this chapter is IAS 1 – *Presentation of Financial Statements*.

The following are examples of books that take the issues of this chapter further:

- Robert N. Anthony, David F. Hawkins and Kenneth A. Merchant, *Accounting: Text and Cases*, McGraw-Hill, 1999, Chapter 3
- Barry Elliott and Jamie Elliott, *Financial Accounting and Reporting*, 9th Edition, Financial Times-Prentice Hall, 2005, Chapter 9
- Charles T. Horngren, Gary L. Sundem and John A. Elliott, *Introduction to Financial Accounting*, Pearson Education-Prentice Hall, 2002, Chapter 2
- Hennie Van Greuning, *International Financial Reporting Standards: A Practical Guide*, The World Bank, 2005, Part I
- Frank Wood and Alan Sangster, *Business Accounting*, Vol. 1, Financial Times-Prentice Hall, 9th Edition, March 2002, Part 2

Questions

4.1 Analyse the following transactions incurred in 2004 and prepare an income statement for the period:

1. Capital was issued for EUR 100,000 cash.
2. Depreciation for plant and equipment amounted to EUR 8,500 for the year.
3. Inventory was purchased for EUR 15,900 cash.
4. EUR 9,400 worth of inventory was purchased on credit.
5. Inventory costing EUR 4,500 was sold for EUR 7,200 on credit.
6. EUR 3,500 in cash was received for merchandise sold on credit.
7. Dividends of EUR 3,000 were declared.
8. The declared dividends of EUR 3,000 were paid.
9. Income taxes payable in three months amounted to EUR 2,000.

4.2   The balance sheet of the Marvin Company as at 1 January follows:

Assets	EUR	Owner's equity and liabilities	EUR
Inventory	50,000	Capital	55,000
Cash	25,000	Short-term borrowings	20,000
Total	**75,000**	**Total**	**75,000**

The following transactions took place in January:

1. Goods, costing EUR 7,000, were sold for EUR 12,000 cash;
2. To increase inventory, Marvin placed an order to Star Company Merchandise for EUR 7,000;
3. Marvin received the goods ordered from Star and agreed to pay EUR 7,000 in 30 days;
4. Goods costing EUR 1,500 were sold for EUR 2,500 in cash;
5. Goods costing EUR 2,000 were sold for EUR 3,400 on credit;
6. Marvin paid the employees for January EUR 4,200 in cash;
7. Purchased land for EUR 20,000 in cash;
8. Marvin purchased a two-year insurance policy for EUR 2,800 in cash.

Illustrate the impact of each transaction on the accounting equation and prepare an income statement for the month of January and a new balance sheet as at 31 January.

4.3   Ziggy Ltd starts trading on 1 January 2003. Rent details are as follows:

Invoice paid	Period	EUR
02.04.2003	01.1.2003–31.3.2003	3,000
03.07.2003	01.4.2003–30.6.2003	4,000
04.10.2003	01.07.2003–30.09.2003	4,000
06.01.2004	01.10.2003–31.12.2003	5,000
03.04.2004	01.1.2004–31.3.2004	5,000
04.07.2004	01.4.2004–30.6.2004	5,000
06.10.2004	01.07.2004–30.09.2004	6,000
05.01.2005	01.10.2004–31.12.2004	7,000

Calculate the rent expense for the year ended:

(a) 31 December 2003
(b) 31 December 2004.

4.4   Tarla, the owner of a delicatessen shop, began trading on 28 February 2004. She provides you, her accountant, with the following information in respect of her business for the period ended 31 December 2004:

1. Rent
   Rents paid quarterly, in advance, on the following dates:

	EUR
28 February	3,250
31 May	3,250
31 August	3,250
30 November	3,250

2. Electricity

A bill was received and paid on 1 February 2005 for EUR 800. The bill covered the period 16 November 2004 to 15 January 2005. The charge for the rest of the period ended 31 December 2004 was EUR 3,200.

3. Bank interest

The bank statements for the delicatessen shop show that interest has been charged to the account as follows:

	EUR
1 March 2004 to 31 March 2004	206
1 April 2004 to 30 June 2004	789
1 July 2004 to 30 September 2004	696
1 October 2004 to 31 December 2004	764

(a) Calculate the total accruals and prepayments for the period ended 31 December 2004.

(b) Calculate the total amount of rent, electricity and bank interest expenses for the period ended 2004.

4.5 Luca & Lollo Srl, a wholesale distributor of home appliances, began business on July 2005. The following summarised transactions occurred during July:

1. On 1 July, two friends, Luca and Lorenzo, contributed EUR 120,000 in cash to the company.
2. On 1 July, a one-year rent contract for a warehouse was signed, paying EUR 30,000 in cash in advance for occupancy for 12 months.
3. On 1 July, warehouse equipment was acquired for EUR 50,000. A payment of EUR 20,000 was made the same day. EUR 30,000 was to be paid by the end of September.
4. On 1 July, EUR 12,000 was paid for a two-year insurance contract covering fire, casualty and related risks.
5. On 4 July, goods for EUR 112,500 were acquired, EUR 22,500 of which was paid in cash.
6. Total sales made in July amounted to EUR 100,000, of which EUR 15,000 was for cash.
7. Cost of inventory sold was EUR 80,000.
8. Depreciation expense of EUR 1,000 was recognised for July.
9. Collected EUR 20,000 from customers.
10. Paid EUR 40,000 to suppliers.

For simplicity, ignore all other possible expenses.

(a) Prepare an analysis of each transaction using the balance sheet equation. Show all amounts in thousands.

(b) Prepare an income statement for July on an accrual basis.

(c) Prepare a balance sheet as at 31 July 2005.

4.6 Refer to Table 4.3 adidas-Salomon income statement for 2004.

(a) Determine gross profit and net profit percentages.

(b) Determine EBITDA, EBIT and EBT.

(c) Compare gross profit and net profit percentages with those of Puma. Comment on the differences found.

Case study   Diletta Ferrari enterprise (B)

Diletta was grateful for the balance sheets that her boyfriend prepared (see Case study in Chapter 3). In going over the numbers, she remarked, 'It's surprising that cash increased by EUR 31,677, but net income was only EUR 19,635. Why was that?'

Her boyfriend replied, 'A partial answer to that question is to look at the income statement for July. I think I can find the data I need to prepare the income statement for you.'

In addition to the data given in Chapter 3, her boyfriend found a record of cash receipts and disbursements, which is summarised in Table 4.5. She also learned that all trade payables were to suppliers for purchase of goods and that cost of sales was EUR 39,345 in July.

Source: adapted from Anthony, Hawkins and Merchant (1999)

Questions:

1. Prepare an income statement for July according to IAS 1. Explain how you determined each item on this statement, including cost of sales.

2. Explain why the cash balance has increased more than the net profit.

3. Explain why the following amounts are incorrect cost of sales for July: (i) EUR 14,715 and (ii) EUR 36,030. Under what circumstances would these amounts be correct cost of sales amounts?

Table 4.5 Cash receipts and disbursements for July

Cash receipts	EUR	Cash disbursements	EUR
Cash sales	44,420	Equipment purchased	23,400
Credit customers	21,798	Other assets purchased	408
Diletta Ferrari	11,700	Payments of trade payables	8,517
Bank loan	20,865	Cash purchase of goods	14,715
Total receipts	98,783	Cash purchase of supplies	1,671
		Dividends	11,700
		Wages paid	5,660
		Utilities paid	900
		Miscellaneous payments	135
		Total disbursements	67,106

Reconciliation	EUR
Cash balance, 1 July	34,983
Receipts	98,783
Subtotal	133,766
Disbursements	(67,106)
Cash balance, 31 July	66,660

5 Revenues and trade receivables

Objectives

When you have completed this chapter you should be able to:

- define the basic principles of revenue recognition
- define deferred or unearned revenues
- account for cash and credit sales
- estimate and interpret uncollectible receivables
- determine construction contract revenue and expenses
- determine trade receivables turnover and days sales outstanding.

5.1 Introduction

This and the next four chapters discuss more thoroughly certain balance sheet and income statement items that were touched upon in Chapters 3 and 4. This chapter discusses two fundamental issues concerning revenue recognition:

1. *When* – in which accounting period – should revenue be recognised? i.e. when an order is taken or received, when it is shipped, or when payment is received?
2. *How much* revenue should be recognised?

A closely related matter, the measurement of trade receivables, is also discussed.

Revenue is typically the single largest item reported in an enterprise's financial statements. Investors place great importance on it in making investment decisions.

Revenue recognition has become a highly complex issue and is the main reason for restatements of financial statements for SEC registrants in the United States in recent years and this is also confirmed for 2004 as illustrated in Figure 5.1.

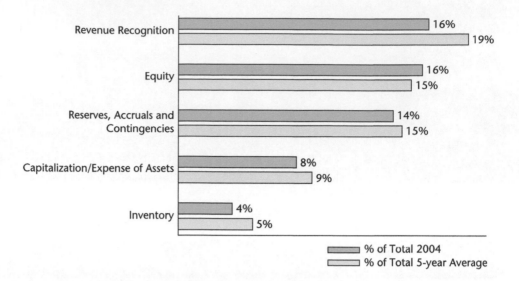

Accounting Issue	Explanation
Revenue Recognition	This category includes instances where a company has improperly recognised revenue on transactions.
Equity	This category includes errors involving stock option accounting, EPS accounting, and accounting for warrants and other equity instruments.
Reserves, Accruals and Contingencies	This category includes errors involved in accounts receivable and inventory reserves, restructuring reserves, accruals, and other loss contingencies.
Capitalization/ Expense of Assets	This category includes instances where a company has improperly capitalized an expenditure that should have been expensed under GAAP (or vice versa).
Inventory	This category includes inventory valuation issues, inventory quantity issues, as well as cost of sales adjustments.

Figure 5.1 Major accounting issues

Source: *2004 Annual Review of Financial Reporting Matters*, Huron Consulting Group

Enterprises may apply considerable discretion over when they book revenues. A common way of distorting accounts is by 'channel stuffing'. In order to meet quarterly targets, in the late 1990s, companies reported products as sold when they had merely been placed in a warehouse or on a retailer's shelf. Future sales were adversely affected and companies were often forced to write-down their inventories or restate their earlier sales and profits. This was the case with Sunbeam, Lucent and Xerox's Latin American division (*The Economist*, 7 February 2002).

Another example of discretion applied in revenue recognition is represented by Global Crossing, a bankrupted telecoms company, which leased capacity to other telecoms carriers and treated this as immediate revenue. At the same time, it leased capacity from other providers and treated this as a capital expense, amortising it over time.

5.2 Realisation convention

The realisation convention in accounting is designed to clarify the revenue recognition problem.

Revenue from the sale of goods should be recognised when all the following conditions have been satisfied:

- the enterprise has transferred to the buyer the significant risks and rewards of ownership of the goods
- the enterprise retains no control over the goods sold
- the amount of revenue can be measured reliably
- the costs incurred or to be incurred in respect of the transaction can be measured reliably.

The assessment of when an enterprise has transferred the significant risks and rewards of ownership to the buyer requires an examination of the circumstances of the transaction. In most cases, the transfer of the risks and rewards of ownership coincides with the transfer of the legal title or the passing of possession to the buyer. This is the case for most retail sales. In other cases, the transfer of risks and rewards of ownership occurs at a different time from the transfer of the legal title or the passing of possession.

If the enterprise retains significant risks of ownership, the transaction is not a sale, and revenue is not recognised. An enterprise may retain a significant risk of ownership in a number of ways. Examples of situations in which the enterprise may retain the significant risks and rewards of ownership are:

(a) when the enterprise retains an obligation for unsatisfactory performance not covered by normal warranty provisions

(b) when the receipt of the revenue from a particular sale is contingent on the derivation of revenue by the buyer from the enterprise's sale of the goods

(c) when the goods are shipped subject to installation and the installation is a significant part of the contract which has not yet been completed by the enterprise

(d) when the buyer has the right to rescind the purchase for a reason specified in the sales contract and the enterprise is uncertain about the probability of return.

If an enterprise retains only an insignificant risk of ownership, the transaction is a sale, and revenue is recognised. For example, a seller may retain the legal title to the goods solely to protect the collectability of the amount due. In such a case, if the enterprise has transferred the significant risks and rewards of ownership, the transaction is a sale, and revenue is recognised. Another example of an enterprise retaining only an insignificant risk of ownership may be a retail sale when a refund is offered if the customer is not satisfied. Revenue in such cases is recognised at the time of sale provided the seller can reliably estimate future returns and recognises a liability for returns, based on previous experience and other relevant factors.

Revenue and expenses that relate to the same transaction are recognised simultaneously: this process is commonly referred to as the matching of revenues and expenses. Expenses, including warranties and other costs to be incurred after the shipment of the goods can normally be measured reliably when the other conditions for the recognition of revenue have been satisfied. However, revenue should not be recognised when the expenses cannot be measured reliably: in such circumstances, any consideration already received for the sale of the goods is recognised as a liability (unearned revenue), as illustrated in the following examples.

Example

Application of realisation convention: deferred or unearned revenue

Publishing companies sell subscriptions for their magazines that the subscribers pay for in advance. If the subscription money, say EUR 70, is received this year for the magazine to be delivered next year, the revenue relates to the next year. The money received is recognised as an increase in cash, and deferred or unearned revenue. The cash received in advance for the magazines, which will be printed and delivered the following year represents a liability, which is recorded in the balance sheet at the end of this year, because legally the publisher is liable for the reimbursement of the subscription received when magazines are undelivered. The liability, deferred or unearned revenue, represents the enterprise's obligation to provide its subscribers the future issues of the magazine for which they have already paid. The transaction cycle just discussed is illustrated as follows:

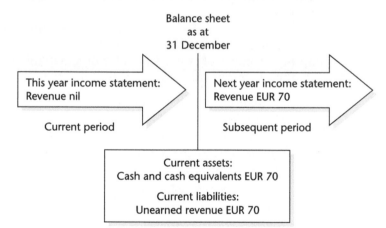

In terms of the accounting equation the transaction may be expressed as follows:

	A	=	L	+		E
	Cash and cash equivalents		Unearned revenue		Capital	Profit
In the current period:	+ EUR 70	=	+ EUR 70			
In the subsequent period:		=	− EUR 70			+ EUR 70

Note: We have illustrated this transaction from the subscriber's viewpoint in Chapter 4 (section 4.5.3 – first example).

To sum up, deferred or unearned revenues represent amounts invoiced and recorded by the enterprise, but not yet earned.

Activity 5.1 Realisation convention and deferred or unearned revenue

An insurance company, which has a calendar year as its financial year, receives insurance premium in advance from its clients. Suppose the contract covers the period October of this year until September of the next year and the client pays promptly in cash the annual premium of EUR 12,000.

Questions:

1. What is the revenue to be recognised by the insurance company in the current year. And in the next?
2. Illustrate the above described transactions through the accounting equation.

Solutions to activities can be found at www.pearsoned.co.uk/kothari

Example

Realisation convention and trade receivables

The converse of the situation described in the last example is illustrated by sales made on credit: the customer agrees to pay for the goods or services sometime after the date on which they are actually received. Suppose we sell and deliver goods at the end of December of the current period for EUR 5,000 and that our customer will pay at the end of February of the next period.

The revenue is recognised in the period in which the sale is made (i.e. when transfer of the legal title or the passing of possession to the buyer takes place), for example the current period illustrated in the chart below. If the payment is not due until the following period, an asset (trade and other receivables) is shown in the balance sheet as at the end of the current period. When cash is collected from the customer, the amount received does not represent revenue. Rather, the cash reduces the amount of trade receivables outstanding and increases cash and cash equivalents, leaving the net profit unchanged. The revenue needs to be recorded in the income statement of the year in which the sale took place. Collection of the trade receivables is the conversion of a non-cash asset into cash, which has no impact on the profit.

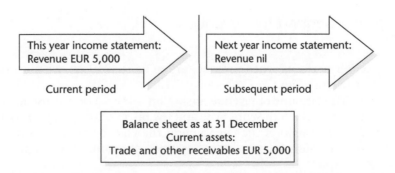

In terms of the accounting equation the transaction may be expressed as follows:

	A		= L +		E
	Cash and cash equivalents	Trade and other receivables		Capital	Profit
In the current period:		+ EUR 5,000 =			+ EUR 5,000
In the subsequent period:	+ EUR 5,000	− EUR 5,000 =			

Activity 5.2 Distinction between cash receipts and sales revenue

A number of sales transactions are shown below.

	Amount EUR	Current period	
		Cash receipts EUR	Sales revenue EUR
1. Cash sales made this year	1,000	_____	_____
2. Credit sales made last year; cash received this year	2,000	_____	_____
3. Credit sales made this year; cash received this year	2,500	_____	_____
4. Credit sales made this year; cash received next year	1,500	_____	_____
5. Credit sales made this year; 50% collected this year and 50% next year	4,000	_____	_____

Question:

Classify the effect of each transaction on cash receipts and sales revenue for the current period.

Solutions to activities can be found at www.pearsoned.co.uk/kothari

5.3 Accounting for revenues

After deciding when revenues are to be recognised, we must decide *how* we should measure them.

The amount of revenue arising on a transaction is usually determined by agreement between the enterprise and the buyer of the goods or user of a service (IAS 18). It is measured at the fair value of the consideration received or receivable, taking into account the amount of any trade discounts and volume rebates allowed by the enterprise.

A cash sale increases sales revenue in the income statement and increases cash and cash equivalents in the balance sheet as shown in the following accounting equation:

	A	=	L	+		E
					Capital	Profit
Cash sale:	Increase in					Increase in
	cash and cash	=				revenue
	equivalents					

A sale on credit has the same impact on the accounting equation as the previous one, except that the asset which is increased is trade and other receivables and not cash and cash equivalents.

	Assets	=	Liabilities	+		E
					Capital	Profit
Sale on credit:	Increase in					Increase in
	trade and other	=				revenue
	receivables					

Suppose revenue for a given sale is recognised at the point of that sale, but later the customer decides to return the goods because the product's colour, size, quality or style differs from the order. The supplier calls these sales returns, while the customer calls them purchase returns. Sometimes, instead of returning the goods, a customer may prefer to keep the goods and demand a reduction in the purchase price (from the customer's point of view) which he previously agreed on. These reductions are known as sales allowances (for the customer they represent purchase allowances).

Suppose a local outlet of Baby Bimbo has EUR 500,000 gross sales on credit and EUR 50,000 sales returns and allowances. An analysis of transactions would show:

	A	=	L	+		E
					Capital	Profit
Sales on credit:	Increase in					Increase in
	trade and other	=				sales revenue
	receivables					
	+ EUR 500,000	=				+ EUR 500,000
Returns and	Decrease in					Increase in
allowances:	trade and other	=				sales returns
	receivables					and allowances
	– EUR 50,000	=				– EUR 50,000

The income statement extract would be as follows:

Income statement (extract)

	EUR
Gross sales	500,000
Deduct: Sales returns and allowances	(50,000)
Net sales	450,000

OR:

	EUR
Net sales	450,000

Returns and allowances are not the only factors that affect gross and net sales figures. Generally, trade discounts also affect the reported sales in the same way we have just seen. Trade discounts represent discounts for large-volume purchases and such discounts are accounted for as a reduction of sales. Other types of discounts, such as cash discounts, are accounted for as operating expenses.

5.4   Trade receivables and bad debt provisions

As we have already seen, sales on credit increase trade and other receivables, which are amounts owed to the company by its customers as a result of delivering goods or services. Trade receivables arise when an enterprise agrees to accept payment in the future for goods or services delivered today.

Granting credit entails advantages and disadvantages. In fact, on the one hand it boosts sales and profit: many potential customers would not buy if credit was unavailable or they would buy from a competitor that offered credit. On the other hand, due to the delay in receiving payment, the seller must finance activities in other ways while awaiting payment. Another cost of granting credit arises from bad debts (i.e. receivables that some credit customers are unable to pay) as bad debt expenses.

At the end of an accounting period, the enterprise may not know specifically which of its trade receivables will never be collected. An estimate of the amount of bad debts can nevertheless be made and the accounting records are adjusted at the end of each accounting period to reflect this estimate.

This adjustment can be made either:

- by writing off the specific trade receivables identified as uncollectible or
- by estimating the total amount of uncollectible receivables. The estimate of uncollectible receivables is usually based on the historical experience of bad debts or uncollectable receivables.

An example of how enterprises determine bad debt provisions is reported as follows:

> Receivables are stated at nominal amounts less allowances for doubtful accounts. These allowances are determined on the basis of individual risk assessment and past experience of losses.

Figure 5.2 Receivables

Source: Notes to Consolidated Financial Statements – adidas-Salomon Annual Report 2004

The impact on the accounting equation of such estimates, whatever method has been used, is as follows:

	A	=	L	+		E
					Capital	Profit
Provision for doubtful debts	Decrease in trade and other receivables – EUR 15,000	= –				Increase in expenses (*bad debt expenses* or *bad debt provision*) – EUR 15,000

| 5.5 | Construction contracts |

A construction contract is negotiated for the construction of an asset such as a bridge, building, dam, pipeline, road, ship or tunnel (IAS 11). It is in the nature of such a contract that it lasts over a long period of time – often over more than one accounting period. The problem which arises in this case is related to the revenue recognition and, in particular, how the total profit should be allocated over the various accounting periods during which the construction takes place. If a contract extends over three years, should the recognised profit be 0 per cent, 0 per cent and 100 per cent, respectively, for the three years? Can we record a profit on, say, a bridge, before we have finished it? According to the prudence convention this is not possible. However, the matching principle requires that when the profit arising from a construction contract can be estimated reliably, it should be recognised by reference to the stage of completion of the contract activity at the balance sheet date. Notwithstanding all this, an expected loss on the construction contract should be recognised as a loss immediately when the expected loss is known.

The following example illustrates one method of determining the stage of completion of a contract and the timing of the recognition of contract revenue and expenses.

Example

The determination of contract revenue and expenses

A construction contractor has a fixed price contract for EUR 9,000 to build a bridge. The contractor's initial estimate of contract costs is EUR 8,000. It will take three years to build the bridge (from 2003 to 2005).

By the end of 2003, the contractor's estimate of contract costs has increased to EUR 8,050.

In 2004, the customer approves a variation resulting in an increase in contract revenue of EUR 200 and estimated additional contract costs of EUR 150.

The contractor determines the stage of completion of the contract by calculating the proportion that contract costs incurred for work performed to date, bear to the latest estimated total contract costs. A summary of the financial data during the construction period is as follows:

	2003 EUR	2004 EUR	2005 EUR
Initial amount of revenue agreed in contract	9,000	9,000	9,000
Variation	–	200	200
Total contract revenue	*9,000*	*9,200*	*9,200*
Contract costs incurred to date	2,093	6,068	8,200
Contract costs to complete	5,957	2,132	–
Total estimated contract costs	*8,050*	*8,200*	*8,200*
Estimated profit	950	1,000	1,000
Stage of completion (contract cost invoiced to date divided by contract costs to complete)	26%	74%	100%

The amount of revenue, expenses and profit recognised in the income statement in the three years is as follows:

	To date EUR	Recognised in prior years EUR	Recognised in current year EUR
2003			
Revenue (EUR 9,000 * 26%)	2,340	–	2,340
Deduct: Expenses (EUR 8,050 * 26%)	2,093	–	2,093
Profit	*247*	–	*247*
2004			
Revenue (EUR 9,200 * 74%)	6,808	2,340	4,468
Deduct: Expenses (EUR 8,200 * 74%)	6,068	2,093	3,975
Profit	*740*	*247*	*493*
2005			
Revenue (EUR 9,200 * 100%)	9,200	6,808	2,392
Deduct: Expenses (EUR 8,200 * 100%)	8,200	6,068	2,132
Profit	*1,000*	*740*	*260*

The impact on the accounting equation is illustrated as follows:

	A	=	L	+	E
To record cost incurred	Inventory		Trade and other payables		
2003	+ EUR 2,093	=	+ EUR 2,093		
2004	+ EUR 3,975	=	+ EUR 3,975		
2005	+ EUR 2,132	=	+ EUR 2,132		

	A	=	L	+		E
					Capital	Profit
To record profit realised:	Inventory					Income on long-term construction contract
2003	+ EUR 247	=				+ EUR 247
2004	+ EUR 493	=				+ EUR 493
2005	+ EUR 260	=				+ EUR 260

5.6   Ratios relating to revenues and trade receivables

Trade receivables turnover

As we will illustrate better in Chapter 14, one measure used to monitor receivables is the trade receivables turnover, which is calculated by dividing the credit sales (or the total sales when we do not have any information about those) by the trade receivables at the end of the period during which the sales were made:

$$\text{Trade receivables turnover} = \frac{\text{Net sales}}{\text{Trade receivables (net of VAT)}}$$

This ratio indicates how promptly collections are made. If the turnover were 12, and the normal credit terms granted to the customers were one month, it would indicate that receivables are collected on average after one month, in line with the credit terms.

However, in practice customers do not always pay on time and delay payments so that the collection days are higher than the credit terms granted.

Days sales outstanding (DSO)

The days to collect trade receivables, or average collection period or days sales outstanding is calculated by dividing 365 by the trade receivables turnover:

$$\text{Days sales outstanding (DSO)} = \frac{365}{\text{Trade receivables turnover}}$$

This alternative to the turnover ratio has an appealing interpretation: how long does it take to collect cash after having made a credit note?

Activity 5.3 Trade receivables turnover and DSO calculation

The annual report of Puma for 2004 shows the following data:

	Dec. 31, 2004 € million	Dec. 31, 2003 € million
Trade receivables	188.2	171.4
Other receivables	16.0	16.1
Prepaid expenses	5.5	4.9
Receivables, gross	209.7	192.4
Value adjustments	−20.1	−16.8
Receivables, net	**189.6**	**175.6**

Question:

Determine the trade receivables turnover and the DSO for 2004 and 2003. Assume that VAT is 20 per cent.

Solutions to activities can be found at www.pearsoned.co.uk/kothari

Summary

- Revenue for the sale of goods or provision of services is generally recognised in the period in which goods are delivered or services performed.
- Deferred or unearned revenues represent amounts invoiced and recorded by an enterprise, but not yet earned. They are classified in the balance sheet under current liabilities.

- Sales on credit increase trade receivables. At the end of an accounting period an enterprise may not know which of its receivables will never be collected, so it should estimate the amount of uncollectible receivables or bad debts to reflect the trade receivables at their net realisable value.

- If the earning process takes place over several accounting periods, the percentage-of-completion method recognises revenue in each of these periods, provided that there is a reasonable assurance of the profit margin and its ultimate realisation.

- Trade receivables turnover, calculated as net credit sales divided by trade receivables (net of VAT), indicates how rapidly collection occurs. An alternative to this ratio is DSO, which indicates how many days it takes for our customers to pay. It is given by 365 days divided by the trade receivables turnover.

References and research

The IASB documents relevant for this chapter are IAS 18 – *Revenue* and IAS 11 – *Construction Contracts*.

The following are examples of research papers and books that take the issues of this chapter further:

- *2003 PricewaterhouseCoopers Securities Litigation Study*, available at http://www.10b5.com
- Robert N. Anthony, David F. Hawkins and Kenneth A. Merchant, *Accounting: Text and Cases*, McGraw-Hill, 1999, Chapter 5
- Barry Elliott and Jamie Elliott, *Financial Accounting and Reporting*, 9th Edition, Financial Times-Prentice Hall, 2005, Chapters 2 and 20
- Charles T. Horngren, Gary L. Sundem and John A. Elliott, *Introduction to Financial Accounting*, Pearson Education-Prentice Hall, 2002, Chapter 5
- Hennie Van Greuning, *International Financial Reporting Standards: A Practical Guide*, The World Bank, 2005, Chapters 13 and 17

Questions

5.1 (a) Why is the realisable value of a sale on credit sometimes lower than that of a cash sale?

   (b) What is the difference between a cash discount and a trade discount?

5.2 A bookshop ordered 1,000 copies of an introductory accounting textbook from a publisher on 7 January 2004. The books were delivered on 2 February at which time an invoice was sent requesting payment of EUR 32.50 per book. However, a 5 per cent discount was allowed if the publisher received payment by 16 February. The bookshop made the payment on 12 February and on 23 February, it returned 40 books to the publisher.

(a) Analyse the impact of the above transactions on the accounting equation from the point of view of the publisher.

(b) Suppose this was the only sales transaction in 2004. Prepare the revenue section of the publisher's income statement.

5.3 Tuck Ltd made gross sales of EUR 100,000 during February 2005. Sales returns and allowances were EUR 8,000. Cash discounts granted were EUR 4,000.

(a) Analyse the impact of these transactions on the accounting equation.

(b) Prepare the revenue section of the income statement.

5.4 In 2004, Diletta & Co had the following:

- net sales: EUR 500,000
- cash discounts on sales: EUR 40,000
- sales returns and allowances: EUR 50,000.

(a) Prepare the revenue section of the 2004 income statement;

(b) Using the accounting equation, prepare an analysis for:
  i)   the revenue recognition of 2004 sales
  ii) sales returns and allowances
  iii) collection of trade receivables. Assume that all sales were on credit and all trade receivables for the 2004 sales were collected in 2004.

5.5 In January 2002 Emanuele & Lollo Co undertakes a four-year project at a contracted price of EUR 100 million that will be billed in four equal annual instalments of EUR 25 million each year over the project's life. The project is expected to cost EUR 90 million. Over the life of the project, the billings, cash receipts and cash outlays related to the project are:

Amounts in thousands of euro	2002	2003	2004	2005
Billings	25,000	25,000	25,000	25,000
Cash received	20,000	27,000	25,000	28,000
Cash paid	18,000	36,000	27,000	9,000

(a) Show the cash flows from the project each year.

(b) Prepare the income statement for each year.

(c) Prepare the balance sheet at the end of each year.

(d) Calculate some key financial ratios.

5.6 Consider the following:

Income statement (extract)	2004	2003	2002
	EUR	EUR	EUR
Sales	20,000	25,000	24,000

Balance sheet (extract)	31 Dec. 2004	31 Dec. 2003	31 Dec. 2002
	EUR	EUR	EUR
Trade and other receivables	1,950	1,900	1,850

Of the total sales, 20 per cent are for cash.

Assuming that VAT is 20 per cent, determine the days to collect trade receivables for the years 2004 and 2003. Comment on the results.

Case study   Quiang and his accounting course (A)

'Your course unfortunately doesn't give me the answer to a great many real-life problems,' said Quiang to his accounting professor. 'I've read carefully the text and listened to you attentively, but every once in a while I run across something that doesn't seem to fit the rules.'

'Not all of life's complications can be covered in a first-year course,' the professor replied. 'As is the case with law, medicine or indeed any of the professions, many matters are dealt with in advanced courses, and others are not settled in any classroom. Nevertheless, some problems that are not specifically discussed can be solved satisfactorily by relating them to principles that you already have learned. Let's take revenue recognition as a particularly difficult case in point. If you write down some of the matters about which you are now uncomfortable, I will gladly discuss them with you – that is, after you have given some thought as to the most reasonable solution.'

A week later, Quiang returned with the following list:

1. **Electric utility bills**

   When an electric utility customer uses electricity, the electric company has earned revenues. It is obviously impossible, however, for the company to read all of its customers' meters on the evening of 31 December. How does the electric company know its revenue for a given year? Explain.

2. **Retainer fee**

   A law firm received a 'retainer' of EUR 20,000 on 1 February 2005 from a client. In return it agreed to provide him with general legal advice upon request for one year. In addition, the client would be billed for regular legal services such as representation in litigation. There was no way of knowing how often, or when, the client would request advice, and it was quite possible that no such advice would be requested. How much of the EUR 20,000 should be considered as revenue in 2005? Why?

3. **Cruise**

   Viaggimmagine srl, a travel agency based in Milan, chartered a cruise ship for two weeks beginning 12 March 2005 for EUR 400,000. In return the ship's owner agreed to pay all costs of the cruise. In 2004, Viaggimmagine sold all available space on the ship for EUR 520,000. It incurred EUR 80,000 in selling and other costs in doing so. The amount of EUR 520,000 was received in cash from passengers in 2004. Viaggimmagine paid EUR 100,000 as an advance payment to the ship owner in 2004. How much, if any, of EUR 520,000 should be recognised as revenue in 2004? Does the question of whether passengers were entitled to a refund in 2005 if they cancelled their reservations make any difference to the answer? Why?

4. **Accretion**

   A nursery owner had one plot of land containing Christmas trees that were four years old on 1 November 2004. The owner had incurred costs of EUR 6 per tree up to that time. A wholesaler offered to buy the trees for EUR 10 each and to pay in addition all costs of cutting and bundling, and transporting them to market. The nursery owner declined this offer, deciding that it would be more profitable to let the trees grow for one more year. Only a trivial amount of additional cost would be involved. The price of Christmas trees varies with their height. Should the nursery owner recognise any revenue from these trees in 2004?

5. 'Unbilled' receivables

The balance sheet of an architectural enterprise shows a significant asset labelled 'unbilled receivables'. The firm says this asset represents projects in progress, valued at the rates at which the customers will be charged for the architects' time. Why would an enterprise do this instead of valuing projects in progress at their cost, as a manufacturing firm would value its inventory in progress? Does it make any difference in the owners' equity for the architectural enterprise to report such work in progress as receivables rather than as inventory? Why?

6. Franchises

A national real estate brokerage enterprise has become highly successful by selling franchises to local real estate brokers. It charges EUR 30,000 for the initial franchise fee and a service fee of 5 per cent of the broker's revenue thereafter. For this it permits use of its well-known name, and provides a one-week initial training course, a nationwide referral system, and various marketing and management aids. Currently, the franchise fee accounts for 25 per cent of the European revenues, but the enterprise expects that the EU market will be saturated within the next three years, and thereafter the enterprise will have to depend on the service fee and new sources of revenue that it may develop. Should it recognise EUR 30,000 as revenues in the year in which the franchise agreement is signed? Why? If it does, what will happen to its profits after the market has become saturated? Why?

Source: adapted from Anthony, Hawkins and Merchant (1999)

6 Inventories and cost of sales

Objectives

When you have completed this chapter you should be able to:

- appreciate connection between cost of sales, inventory valuation and gross profit
- determine the value of inventory and cost of sales using different methods: FIFO, LIFO and average cost
- explain impact on profit resulting from different valuation methods
- determine the value of inventories held at the end of an accounting period by applying the lower of cost and NRV test
- show the effects of inventory errors on financial statements
- evaluate the gross profit percentage and inventory turnover.

6.1 Introduction

For all enterprises, gross profit is one of the principal measures of profitability, as illustrated in Chapter 4. Gross profit or gross margin is the difference between sales revenues and costs of goods sold. Gross profit or margin should be sufficient to cover all other costs – selling, general and administrative expenses (SGA), interest and income taxes – and have enough net profit to remunerate the shareholders and reinvest in the business. As illustrated in Figure 6.1, products held for sales are reported as inventory, a current asset in the balance sheet. When the goods are sold, their cost becomes an expense, 'cost of sales', in the income statement. This expense is deducted from 'net sales' to determine 'gross profit', and all other expenses are deducted from the gross profit to determine the 'net profit'.

In theory, the accounting for inventory and cost of sales is very simple, as shown in the following example.

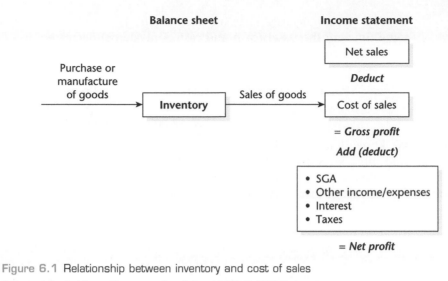

Figure 6.1 Relationship between inventory and cost of sales

Source: adapted from Horngren, Sundem and Elliott (2002)

Example

Inventory and cost of sales

Suppose John sells kites. Periodically, he buys kites of various colours. After a year, to evaluate his performance, John prepares financial statements. To calculate the value of inventory on hand, he counts all the inventory items remaining at year-end (known as a physical inventory count). He then values inventory by assigning a specific value from the historical cost records to each item in ending inventory. If the kites cost EUR 3.00 each and there are 100 kites remaining in inventory, John's total ending inventory is EUR 300. Suppose he had no kites at the beginning of the year, and total purchases for the year amounted to EUR 12,000. His cost of sales would thus be EUR 11,700 (EUR 12,000 of kite purchases less EUR 300 of unsold kites in stock). Note that the key to calculate the cost of sales is accounting for the ending inventory.

In practice, determining the cost of sales and accounting for inventory are, however, not so simple. In this chapter, we will deal with problems which arise in practice. As a future manager, you want to know how inventory accounting can affect reported earnings. Especially important is how economic events such as inflation or management decisions to increase or decrease inventory levels affect inventory values and thereby affect earnings.

6.2   Inventories, cost of sales and accounting equation

Look at Figure 6.1 and think of the transactions (relating to the purchases and sales of kites by John) in terms of the accounting equation.

When John purchased kites, an asset (inventory) increased by EUR 12,000; at the same time another asset (cash and cash equivalents) decreased or a liability (trade payables) increased by the same amount.

	A	=	L	+ E
Purchases of goods:	Increase inventory	=	Increase trade payables	
	+ EUR 12,000	=	+ EUR 12,000	

We know that John sold all the kites except for those costing EUR 300. Suppose he sold those kites (i.e. 3,900 kites) for EUR 15,000 cash. We must record not only an increase in cash on hand as a result of these sales, but also a decrease in inventory for the cost of inventory sold.

	A	= L +	E
			Profit
Sales of goods:	Increase in cash	=	Increase in revenue
	+ EUR 15,000	=	+ EUR 15,000
Cost of sales:	Decrease inventory (for the cost of inventory sold)	=	Increase cost of sales
	– EUR 11,700	=	– EUR 11,700

At the end of the year, John has inventory for EUR 300 (i.e. EUR 12,000 – EUR 11,700) and he would have made a gross profit of EUR 3,300 (for having sold at EUR 15,000 the kites which cost him EUR 11,700). His income statement and balance sheet will be as follows:

Income statement (extract)	EUR	Balance sheet (extract)	EUR
Sales	15,000	Current assets	
Cost of sales	(11,700)	Inventory	300
Gross profit	3,300	Cash	15,000
		Current liabilities	
		Trade and other payables	12,000

An alternative way to record the purchases and sales of goods is described as follows:

	A	=	L	+	E
					Profit
Purchases of goods:		=	Increase trade payables		Purchases
		=	+ EUR 12,000		– EUR 12,000
Sales of goods:	Increase cash	=			Sales revenue
	+ EUR 15,000	=			+ EUR 15,000
Ending inventory:	Increase current assets	=			Ending inventory
	+ EUR 300	=			+ EUR 300

At the end of the year, after a physical count of the goods unsold, we know that the ending inventory is worth EUR 300 which represents the cost. Now we can better define the cost of sales as:

Purchases – Ending inventory

If John had inventory at the beginning of the period, it should be added to purchases in order to determine the cost of sales. Therefore:

Cost of sales = Beginning inventory + Purchases − Ending inventory

We can restate John's income statement as follows:

Income statement (extract)

		EUR
Sales		15,000
Deduct Cost of sales:		
Beginning inventory	0	
Add Purchases	12,000	
Deduct Ending inventory	300	
Cost of sales		(11,700)
Gross profit		3,300

The amount of purchases shown in the income statement is net of purchases returns and purchases discounts or allowances. As we saw in section 5.3, from the seller's point of view, these are called sales returns and sales discounts or allowances.

6.3   Main valuation methods

The basic principles illustrated for John's business apply to any enterprise. An enterprise, in fact, must determine the cost of goods sold during a period and the cost of the goods remaining in stock at the end of a period.

To do this we can identify the actual physical units that we have bought and then sold. Each unit should be individually distinguishable, e.g. by serial number. In this instance we simply add up the recorded costs of those units sold to give cost of sales, and add up the cost of the units left to determine the inventory value. This method (specific identification method) is used for relatively expensive low-volume goods, such as custom artwork, diamond jewellery, and automobiles. However, most enterprises have numerous items in inventory to warrant such individual attention.

Most enterprises calculate the cost, of both the goods sold during the period and those remaining at the end of the period, as if they had been physically handled in a particular assumed manner, which has nothing to do with how the goods are *actually* handled.

The two most common assumptions are:

- FIFO (first in, first out) – goods bought or produced first are sold first
- LIFO (last in, first out) – goods bought or produced last are sold first.

Another way to determine the cost of ending inventory is to assume that goods entering the business lose their separate identity, and sales of goods reflect the average cost of the goods that are held. This is the weighted average cost (AVCO) method, where the weights used in determining the average cost figure are the quantities of each batch of goods purchased.

Because AVCO is closer to FIFO than LIFO, in practice many companies adopt AVCO as their inventory valuation policy.

Let us use an example to illustrate these methods.

Example

FIFO, LIFO and AVCO methods

An enterprise that supplies coal to factories has the following transactions during a period:

		Tonnes	Cost/tonne EUR
1 March	Beginning inventory	3,000	10
2 March	Purchases	4,000	11
3 March	Purchases	7,000	12
		14,000	
6 March	Sold	(9,000)	
	Ending inventory	5,000	

We will determine the cost of sales and value of ending inventory using:

(a) FIFO method;

(b) LIFO method; and

(c) AVCO method.

(a) Using the FIFO method, the first 9,000 tonnes of coal are assumed to be those that are sold and the balance represents the ending inventory.

	COST OF SALES			ENDING INVENTORY		
	Tonnes	Cost/tonne EUR	Total EUR	Tonnes	Cost/tonne EUR	Total EUR
1 March	3,000	10	30,000			
2 March	4,000	11	44,000			
3 March	2,000	12	24,000	5,000	12	60,000
Cost of sales			98,000	Ending inventory		60,000

(b) Using the LIFO method, the latest purchases are the first to be sold and the earlier purchases represent the ending inventory.

	COST OF SALES			ENDING INVENTORY		
	Tonnes	Cost/tonne EUR	Total EUR	Tonnes	Cost/tonne EUR	Total EUR
3 March	7,000	12	84,000			
2 March	2,000	11	22,000	2,000	11	22,000
1 March				3,000	10	30,000
Cost of sales			106,000	Ending inventory		52,000

(c) Using the AVCO method, a weighted cost will be determined that will be used to establish both the cost of sales and the cost of the ending inventory.

Purchases

	Tonnes	Cost/tonne	Total
		EUR	EUR
1 March	3,000	10	30,000
2 March	4,000	11	44,000
3 March	7,000	12	84,000
	14,000		158,000

AVCO = EUR 158,000/14,000 tonnes = EUR 11.29 per tonne

Therefore, using the AVCO method, the cost of sales and the cost of the ending inventory is as follows:

	COST OF SALES			ENDING INVENTORY		
	Tonnes	AVCO	Total	Tonnes	AVCO	Total
		EUR	EUR		EUR	EUR
	9,000	11.29	101,570	5,000	11.29	56,430
			101,570			56,430

According to IAS 2 – *Inventories*, the methods allowed are specific identification method (for items that are not ordinarily interchangeable), FIFO and AVCO methods. An enterprise should use the same cost formula for all inventories having a similar nature and usage for the enterprise. For inventories having a different nature or use, different cost formulas may be justified. IAS 2 does not permit the use of LIFO method to determine the cost of inventories. Figure 6.2 shows the inventory valuation method used by Puma in accordance with IAS 2.

Inventories

Inventories are valued at acquisition or manufacturing costs or at the lower net realizable values derived from the selling price at the balance sheet date. As a general rule, the acquisition cost of merchandise is determined using the average cost method. Value adjustments are determined in a uniform manner throughout the Group, depending on the age of the goods concerned. Risks due to fashion trends are adequately taken into account.

Figure 6.2 Inventory valuation method applied by Puma

Source: Puma Annual Report 2004

6.4   Gross profit resulting from different valuation methods

How does the gross profit change depending on the method used for the valuation of inventory?

Example

Inventory valuation and gross profit

Suppose that the 9,000 tonnes of coal referred to in the previous example were sold at EUR 15 per tonne. The gross profit for the period under each of the three methods is shown below:

	FIFO		LIFO		AVCO	
	EUR	%	EUR	%	EUR	%
Sales	135,000	100	135,000	100	135,000	100
Cost of sales	98,000	73	106,000	79	101,570	75
Gross profit	37,000	27	29,000	21	33,430	25
Ending inventory	60,000		52,000		56,430	

As you can see, FIFO will give the highest gross profit, because sales are matched with the earlier (and cheaper) purchases.

LIFO will give the lowest gross profit because sales are matched against the more recent (and dearer) purchases.

The AVCO method will normally give a figure that is closer to FIFO than LIFO.

The ending inventory figure in the balance sheet will be highest under the FIFO method, because the cost of goods still held will be based on the more recent (and dearer) purchases.

LIFO will give the lowest ending inventory figure as the goods unsold held at the end of an accounting period will be based on the earlier (and cheaper) goods purchased.

Once again, the AVCO method will normally give a figure that is closer to FIFO than LIFO.

Remember that during a period of rising prices, FIFO yields higher inventory and higher gross profit than does LIFO. This result is consistent with the accounting equation that requires that:

$$Assets = Liabilities + Owners'\ equity$$

If inventory is higher under FIFO (higher assets) and the equation should balance, either liabilities or owners' equity would be higher. Higher gross profit under FIFO implies higher net profit and higher owners' equity.

Note that all methods analysed are based on the same basic numbers. Nothing in our choice of methods affects trade payables. We record purchases at cost and account for the related liability in the same way under all three methods. All that changes is how we allocate those costs between inventory and cost of sales.

6.5   Lower of cost and net realisable value

Often inventory items for reasons of obsolescence, fashion, seasonality, imperfect quality, etc. cannot be sold at prices higher than their historical cost. Therefore, the net realisable value (NRV) is compared with historical cost determined under one of the three methods: AVCO, FIFO or LIFO.

If the cost is higher than the NRV, the inventory item is written down to its NRV.

NRV is defined as the estimated selling price in the ordinary course of business less the estimated cost to complete and to dispose of the inventory.

Net realisable value estimates should be based on the most reliable information available. Estimates should exclude temporary price or cost fluctuations.

The rule just described is an example of conservatism or prudence. Conservatism or prudence means selecting methods of measurement that yield profit only when realised and account for losses as soon as they are known. So assets should be accounted for at cost but never higher than their NRV.

Let us illustrate the lower of cost and NRV principle by way of an example.

Example

Lower of cost and NRV test

Suppose that the 5,000 tonnes of coal (i.e. ending inventory) referred to in the Example on page 106 had an NRV of EUR 11.10 per tonne.

What value would the ending inventory have in the financial statements as at 7 March using AVCO, LIFO or FIFO method? The illustration below answers this question.

	Cost	NRV	Lower of cost and NRV
AVCO	EUR 60,000	EUR 55,500	**EUR 55,500**
LIFO	52,000	55,500	**52,000**
FIFO	56,430	55,500	**55,500**

Activity 6.1 Lower of cost and NRV

The inventory of BBB Ltd on 31 March shows 450 tonnes at EUR 10 per tonne. A physical count on 30 April shows a total of 700 tonnes on hand. Revenue for sales of goods for April totals EUR 44,000.

The following purchases were made during April:

Date	Quantity purchased	Cost per tonne
10 April	2,000 tonnes	EUR 11
17 April	500 tonnes	EUR 12
30 April	650 tonnes	EUR 13

Questions:

1. Assuming that on 30 April the NRV is EUR 11.50 per tonne net of selling expenses, at which value would the ending inventory be reflected in the balance sheet as at 30 April using AVCO, LIFO and FIFO methods?

2. Determine the gross profit, using AVCO, LIFO and FIFO methods.

Solutions to activities can be found at www.pearsoned.co.uk/kothari

6.6   Characteristics and consequences of LIFO

According to IAS 2, LIFO is not allowed. However, in certain countries it is allowed for financial reporting and tax purposes.

When LIFO method is used, reported LIFO inventory values may be far below the true market value or NRV. A company's LIFO reserve is defined as the difference between inventories valued at LIFO and what they would be under FIFO or NRV.

Example

LIFO reserve

Assume that Harbor Electronics has purchases and sales in 1999–2004 as shown in Table 6.1.

Table 6.1 Purchases and sales of Harbor Electronics

Year	Units purchased	Purchase price per unit EUR	Units sold	Selling price per unit EUR
1999	100	10	0	0
2000	100	12	100	15
2001	100	14	100	17
2002	100	16	100	19
2003	100	18	100	21
2004	0	0	100	23

Source: Horngren, Sundem and Elliott (2002)

Its LIFO reserve can be obtained by looking at Table 6.2.

Table 6.2 Cost of sales, gross profit and ending inventory using FIFO and LIFO

Year	Purchase price per unit EUR	Selling price per unit EUR	Revenue EUR	FIFO Cost of sales EUR	FIFO Gross profit EUR	FIFO Ending inventory EUR	LIFO Cost of sales EUR	LIFO Gross profit EUR	LIFO Ending inventory EUR
1999	10	–	–	–	–	1,000	–	–	1,000
2000	12	15	1,500	1,000	500	1,200	1,200	300	1,000
2001	14	17	1,700	1,200	500	1,400	1,400	300	1,000
2002	16	19	1,900	1,400	500	1,600	1,600	300	1,000
2003	18	21	2,100	1,600	500	1,800	1,800	300	1,000
2004	–	23	2,300	1,800	500	0	1,000	1,300	0
Total			9,500	7,000	2,500		7,000	2,500	

Source: Horngren, Sundem and Elliott (2002)

What is the LIFO reserve at the end of 2000? It is EUR 200 (= EUR 1,200 – EUR 1,000), the difference between the FIFO and LIFO ending inventory. Note that the difference in gross profit is also EUR 200.

What about year 2001? The LIFO reserve is EUR 400 (FIFO ending inventory of EUR 1,400 less LIFO ending inventory of EUR 1,000). This difference represents the cumulative effect on gross profit over the first two years the company was in business. The effect on earnings in 2001 is the change in the LIFO reserve or EUR 200.

From Table 6.3 you will note that the annual difference between gross profit using FIFO and that using LIFO is the yearly change in the LIFO reserve.

Table 6.3 Annual and cumulative effects of LIFO reserve

Year	Ending inventory		LIFO reserve	Change in LIFO reserve	Gross profit effect	
	FIFO EUR	LIFO EUR	EUR	EUR	Current EUR	Cumulative EUR
1999	1,000	1,000	0	0	0	0
2000	1,200	1,000	200	200	200	200
2001	1,400	1,000	400	200	200	400
2002	1,600	1,000	600	200	200	600
2003	1,800	1,000	800	200	200	800
2004	0	0	0	(800)	(800)	0

Source: Horngren, Sundem and Elliott (2002)

Finally, when all inventory is sold in 2004, the liquidation of the LIFO inventory leads to recognition of higher earnings than under FIFO by the amount of the LIFO reserve.

Under LIFO higher profits are recognised when inventory levels are reduced. The LIFO reserve indicates the cumulative gross profit effect over all prior years.

What is the significance of using LIFO rather than FIFO? Over time, lower earnings are reported and taxes are deferred, particularly when prices are rising.

6.7   Effects of inventory misstatements

Inventory errors can arise from many sources. For example, incorrect physical counts might be taken because goods that were in receiving or shipping areas instead of in the inventory stockroom were not counted. A clerk might type a 5 on the keyboard instead of a 6.

An undiscovered inventory error usually affects two reporting periods. Amounts will be misstated in the period in which the error occurred, and in the following period. Consider the income statement extracts in Table 6.4, which assume that

Table 6.4 Ending inventory understated

Incorrect reporting

	Year 1	Year 2	Total
Sales	EUR 50,000	EUR 100,000	
Deduct Cost of sales:			
Beginning inventory	5,000	2,000	
Add: Purchases	35,000	70,000	
Deduct: Ending inventory	(2,000)	(15,000)	
(Understated in Year 1)	38,000	EUR 57,000	
Gross profit	**EUR 12,000**	**EUR 43,000**	**EUR 55,000**

Correct reporting

	Year 1	Year 2	Total
Sales	EUR 50,000	EUR 100,000	
Deduct Cost of sales:			
Beginning inventory	5,000	7,000	
Add: Purchases	35,000	70,000	
Deduct: Ending inventory	(7,000)	(15,000)	
	33,000	EUR 62,000	
Gross profit	**EUR 17,000**	**EUR 38,000**	**EUR 55,000**

year 1 ending inventory is undervalued by EUR 5,000 but, the year 2 ending inventory is correctly valued.

Think about the effect of the error on the following year's gross profit. The beginning inventory will be EUR 2,000 instead of the correct EUR 7,000. Therefore the error in year 1 will be offset by the counterbalancing error in year 2. Thus the total gross profit at the end of year 2 would show a cumulative effect of zero. Why? Because the gross profit in year 1 would be understated by EUR 5,000, but the gross profit in year 2 would be overstated by EUR 5,000.

The point here is that the ending inventory of one period is also the beginning inventory of the following period.

If you look at Table 6.5, where the ending inventory of year 1 is overstated, you can have a handy rule of thumb. If ending inventory is understated, then gross profit is understated. If ending inventory is overstated, gross profit is overstated. These relations are clear from the accounting equation. Why?

Understated inventory implies overstated cost of sales and therefore lower current year gross profit. The accounting equation follows:

$$
\begin{array}{lcccl}
\text{A} & = & \text{L} & + & \text{E} \\
\text{Inventory} & = & & + & \text{Profit} \\
\text{Effect of error:} \quad \text{EUR 5,000} & = & & + & \text{EUR 5,000} \\
\text{understated} & & & & \text{understated}
\end{array}
$$

If there are no other errors, then this understatement of inventory would have the same effect on net profit.

Table 6.5 Ending inventory overstated

Incorrect reporting

	Year 1	Year 2	Total
Sales	EUR 50,000	EUR 100,000	
Deduct Cost of sales:			
Beginning inventory	5,000	10,000	
Add: Purchases	35,000	70,000	
Deduct: Ending inventory	(10,000)	(15,000)	
(Overstated in Year 1)	30,000	EUR 65,000	
Gross profit	**EUR 20,000**	**EUR 35,000**	**EUR 55,000**

Correct reporting

	Year 1	Year 2	Total
Sales	EUR 50,000	EUR 100,000	
Deduct Cost of sales:			
Beginning inventory	5,000	7,000	
Add: Purchases	35,000	70,000	
Deduct: Ending inventory	(7,000)	(15,000)	
	33,000	EUR 62,000	
Gross profit	**EUR 17,000**	**EUR 38,000**	**EUR 55,000**

6.8   Ratios relating to inventory

We began this chapter by discussing gross profit, which is the result of sales revenue less the cost of sales. Gross profit is one of the key performance indicators. In comparing the gross profit of two enterprises, it is important to examine which inventory valuation method they have used to calculate the gross profit.

Inventory turnover

A first ratio relating to inventory is inventory turnover, which is defined as cost of sales divided by inventory:

$$\text{Inventory turnover} = \frac{\text{Cost of sales}}{\text{Inventory}}$$

Some enterprises calculate this ratio on the basis of the ending inventory, others on the basis of the average inventory. However, what is important is consistency in the way the ratio is calculated.

Refer to Table 3.8 – Consolidated balance sheet of Puma as at 31 December 2004 and to Table 4.4 – Puma management income statement for 2004. In 2004, Puma had an inventory turnover of 3.66 (EUR 736.4 million ÷ EUR 201.1 million), while in 2003 it was 3.33 (EUR 654.0 million ÷ EUR 196.2).

Inventory turnover

Inventory turnover varies greatly depending on the nature of the business. It should be high for a store that sells fresh products (fruits, meat, etc.). A supermarket may have an inventory turnover close to 50, while a jewellery store with a wide selection of expensive and unusual items may not turn its inventory as often as twice a year, and most art galleries have a turnover much lower than 1.

We must also consider the seasonality or sales. For example, college book stores have high inventory before the start of each new term, with lower inventories in between. In such enterprises an annual calculation of inventory turnover has little meaning, and inventory measured at various seasonal high and low points is more relevant.

Inventory turnover indicates the velocity with which merchandise moves through an enterprise. Turnover may fall either because of inventory build-up in anticipation of increased sales or because sales volume has declined, leaving excess merchandise on hand. The first is a favourable event; the second is unfavourable. The turnover ratio by itself does not indicate which is the cause.

Days inventory outstanding (DIO)

The same relationship can be expressed as the number of days inventory on hand. Once we have calculated inventory turnover, days inventory outstanding are simply:

$$\text{Days inventory outstanding (DIO)} = \frac{365}{\text{Inventory turnover}}$$

For Puma in 2004 DIO was 100 (365 ÷ 3.66). This means that Puma in 2004 sold all its inventory on average every 100 days, while in 2003 every 110 days (365 ÷ 3.33). There was an improvement in inventory management in 2004.

Summary

- The objectives of inventory accounting are (1) to match cost of sales, an expense, with the revenue earned in an accounting period and (2) to measure the value of inventory, an asset remaining unsold at the end of the period.

- The flow of costs can be measured by any of several methods. The most common are specific identification, average cost, first in first out, and last in first out.

- If the net realisable value (NRV) of an inventory item is below cost, the item is reported in the financial statements at its NRV.

- When analysing inventory, we use inventory turnover and days inventory outstanding to understand the velocity with which merchandise moves through an enterprise.

References and research

The IASB document relevant for this chapter is IAS 2 – *Inventories*.

The following are examples of research papers and books that take the issues of this chapter further:

- David Alexander and Christopher Nobes, *Financial Accounting: An International Introduction*, 2nd Edition, Chapter 10
- Robert N. Anthony, David F. Hawkins and Kenneth A. Merchant, *Accounting: Text and Cases*, McGraw-Hill, 1999, Chapter 6
- Barry Elliott and Jamie Elliott, *Financial Accounting and Reporting*, 9th Edition, Financial Times-Prentice Hall, 2005, Chapter 19
- Charles T. Horngren, Gary L. Sundem and John A. Elliott, *Introduction to Financial Accounting*, Pearson Education-Prentice Hall, 2002, Chapter 6
- Hennie Van Greuning, *International Financial Reporting Standards: A Practical Guide*, The World Bank, 2005, Chapter 12
- Hervé Stolowy and Michel J. Lebas, *Corporate Financial Reporting: A Global Perspective*, Thomson Learning, 2002, Chapter 9
- Frank Wood and Alan Sangster, *Business Accounting*, Vol. 1, 9th Edition, Financial Times-Prentice Hall, 2002, Part 4

Questions

6.1 IAS 2 – *Inventories* prescribes the accounting treatment for inventories under the historical cost system. Briefly explain how IAS 2 requires the following to be dealt with:

(a) The determination of the lower of cost and net realisable value.

(b) The identification of costs when there are large numbers of items which are ordinarily interchangeable.

6.2 (a) If sales are EUR 24,000 and cost of sales is EUR 18,000, then what is the gross profit margin?

(b) Sales are EUR 30,000 and gross profit margin is 20 per cent. What is cost of sales?

(c) BiBi SpA has beginning inventory of EUR 5,000 and ending inventory of EUR 20,000. The purchases of inventories during the period are EUR 1,282,000. Compute the 'cost of sales' amount for the income statement.

6.3 Naomi Ltd starts a business selling fake fur coats. The following purchases of fake fur are made during the first year:

Date	Quantity metres	Cost per metre EUR	Total cost EUR
10 January 2005	2,000	30.00	60,000
6 September 2005	5,000	31.50	157,500

At 31 October 2005 there are 1,500 metres of fake fur remaining in ending inventory. Their NRV is EUR 46,800. In applying the lower of cost and net realisable value rule, what value should be attributed to the ending fur?

6.4 At 30 September 2005 Ballata had the following inventories:

	Cost	Selling price	Estimated cost of realisation
	EUR	EUR	EUR
120 'Ping' irons No. 3	5,880	7,215	35
475 Doz golf balls	8,225	9,100	975
17 High-velocity shotguns	71,655	120,620	2,010
18 9mm Uzi	270,000	640,250	2,500
10 Terminator 2 videos	790	2,700	25
100 Return to the Blue Lagoon videos	7,999	6,250	240

Calculate the value of inventory as at 30 September 2005.

6.5 A retailer has the following purchases and sales of a particular product line:

	Units purchased	Purchase price per unit	Units sold	Selling price per unit
		EUR		EUR
2 December	100	500	60	530
16 December	60	503	80	528
30 December	70	506	50	526
14 January	50	509	70	524
28 January	80	512	50	522
11 February	40	515	40	520

On 28 February the inventory was 150 units. The cost of inventories is determined on a FIFO basis. Selling and distribution costs amount to 5 per cent of selling price and general administration expenses amount to 7 per cent of selling price.

(a) State three reasons why the net realisable value of inventory may be less than cost.
(b) Calculate to the nearest euro the value of inventory at 28 February:
   (i) at cost
   (ii) at net realisable value
   (iii) at the amount to be included in the financial statements in accordance with IAS 2 – *Inventories*.

6.6 Selim Plc began 2004 with inventory of EUR 320,000. Sales in 2004 were EUR 1,600,000, purchases of inventory totalled EUR 1,380,000, and ending inventory was EUR 440,000.

(a) Prepare a statement of gross profit for 2004
(b) Determine the inventory turnover and DIO.

Case study   Quiang and his accounting course (B)

Because an earlier discussion with the accounting professor (see Case study in Chapter 5) had cleared up some puzzling matters, Quiang decided to prepare a new list of problems as a basis for a second discussion. As before, he knew that the professor expected students to have worked out tentative answers to their questions prior to the meeting. The professor also required students to use whenever possible numerical examples to illustrate the issues they were raising. The list follows:

1. Evidently, there are two ways of handling purchase discounts. They can be either deducted from the cost of the purchased goods, or reported as other income. But is the effect on net profit not the same under all these methods? If so, why argue about which is preferable?

2. It is said that the LIFO method assumes that the goods purchased last are sold first. If this is so, the assumption is clearly unrealistic because companies ordinarily sell their oldest merchandise first. Can a method based on such an unrealistic assumption be supported, other than as a tax gimmick?

3. Are the following generalisations valid?

   (a) The difference between LIFO and FIFO is relatively small if inventory turnover is relatively high.

   (b) The AVCO method will result in net profit that is somewhere between that produced by the LIFO method and that produced by the FIFO method.

   (c) If prices rise in one year and fall by an equal amount the next year, the total income for the two years is the same under the FIFO method as under the LIFO method.

4. A distillery manufactured bourbon whiskey, which it aged in charred, white oak barrels for four years before bottling and selling it. Whiskey was carried in inventory at approximately EUR 3 per litre, which was the cost of ingredients, labour, and factory overhead of the manufacturing process. Barrels, which could not be reused, cost EUR 1 per litre. The distillery incurred EUR 0.50 of warehousing costs per litre per year, including costs involved in moving and testing the barrels. It also incurred EUR 0.30 per litre of interest costs per year. The costs of barrels, warehousing and interest were charged directly to the income statement. If the distillery had consistently earned pre-tax profit of EUR 1.5 million per year on annual production and sale of 1 million litres, what would happen to profit if it increased production to 1.2 million litres per year? At what amounts should it carry its whiskey in inventory?

Source: adapted from Anthony, Hawkins and Merchant (1999)

Give your answers to the issues just discussed, supporting them with calculations.

7

Tangible and intangible assets

Objectives

When you have completed this chapter you should be able to:

- distinguish between tangible and intangible assets, and explain how the costs of each are recognised
- compute depreciation for property, plant and equipment using various depreciation methods
- compute gains and losses on disposal of PPE
- distinguish between finance and operating lease
- describe accounting practice for various intangible assets
- account for impairment losses
- calculate ratios relating to tangible and intangible (non-current) assets.

7.1 Introduction

All resources an enterprise owns help it to produce its revenues and therefore are necessary for the day-to-day operations. When an enterprise incurs an expenditure to acquire such resources, the benefits deriving from them may be obtained either in the current period or are expected to be obtained in future periods. In the former case, that expenditure represents an expense and is therefore charged to the current period income statement; while in the latter case, that expenditure represents an asset and is thus recorded in the balance sheet.

As you can see from the example illustrated in Figure 7.1, the determination of whether an expenditure represents an asset (capital expenditure or CAPEX) or an

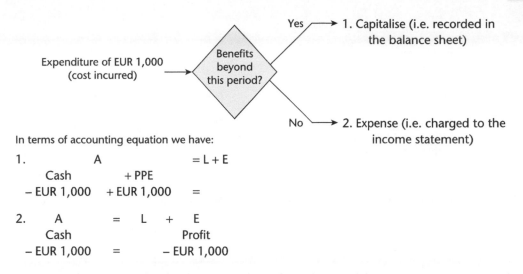

In terms of accounting equation we have:

1.   A   = L + E
     Cash   + PPE
   – EUR 1,000   + EUR 1,000   =

2.   A   =   L   +   E
       Cash   Profit
   – EUR 1,000   =   – EUR 1,000

If, without taking into account the above expenditure, the profit realised during the year is EUR 5,000, the different treatment of the expenditure above would give a different result of the net profit realised. Assuming that we can use the asset acquired for five years, we would have the following result:

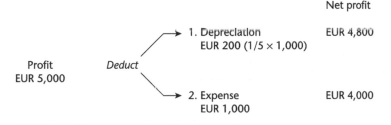

Figure 7.1 Expenditures: current and non current

expense can have a significant effect on an enterprise's net profit. The distinction between expenditures that are capitalised (i.e. recorded as an asset in the balance sheet) and expenditures that are expensed as period costs (i.e. recorded as an expense in the income statement) is not always clear-cut.

As we illustrated in Chapter 4, the cost of tangible and intangible, non-current, assets is first capitalised. Then a charge in the form of depreciation over the periods the asset is used is allocated to the income statement – thereby matching expenses with the revenues generated.

Table 7.1 lists principal types of non-current assets and the terminology used for the process of depreciating the cost of each type (see also Figure 7.2). The terms 'fixed assets' and 'long-lived assets' are also commonly used. The main distinction is between tangible assets and intangible assets. The former, such as land, natural resources, buildings and equipment, are physical items that can be seen and touched. Intangible assets such as patents, trademarks, copyrights and goodwill are rights or economic benefits that are not physical in nature.

It is important to highlight that non-current assets include also investments in equity securities of other enterprises and other financial assets. We will deal with investments in Chapter 11. Other financial assets go beyond the scope of this book and therefore will not be covered.

Table 7.1 Types of non-current assets

Type of assets	Terms used for allocating the cost of their use
Tangible assets:	
Land	Not depreciated (as it does not wear out or become obsolete)
Plant and equipment, Furniture and fixtures, Motor vehicles	Depreciation
Natural resources	Depletion
Intangible assets:	
Goodwill	Amortisation
Patents, copyrights, etc.	Amortisation
Leasehold improvements	Amortisation
Research	Expensed when incurred
Development	Amortisation

- **Property, Plant and Equipment**

  Property, plant and equipment are stated at acquisition cost net of accumulated depreciation. The depreciation period depends on the item's useful life. As a general rule, the straight-line method of depreciation is applied. The useful life depends on the type of assets involved:

	Depreciation period
Buildings	10 to 50 years
Machines, machine equipment and technical equipment, business and factory equipment	3 to 10 years

  Cost of maintenance and repair is recorded as expense at the time of origin. Significant improvements and renewals are capitalised. Interest on outside capital is reported as current expense.

  Leased items regarded as significant in terms of their amounts and qualifying as finance leasing are shown under property, plant and equipment; they are valued at the amount of the fair value or the lower present value of the minimum lease payments when recognised for the first time and net of accumulated depreciation in subsequent accounting periods.

- **Other Intangible Assets**

  Acquired intangible assets largely consist of concessions, industrial property rights and similar rights; they are valued at acquisition costs net of accumulated amortisation. The amortisation period is between three to five years, whereby the straight-line method is applied.

- **Extraordinary Depreciation and Amortisation**

  Property, plant and equipment, intangible assets and goodwill are subject to extraordinary depreciation or amortisation if there are indications of impairment in the value of the asset involved. In such a case, the recoverable amount (the higher amount from net realisable proceeds and utility value), is compared with the book value of the asset. If the recoverable value is lower than the book value, the asset is written down to the recoverable amount (IAS 36). If the reason for extraordinary depreciation or amortisation no longer exists, the asset is revalued; the revaluation amount may not exceed the amount of acquisition costs.

Figure 7.2 Accounting policies of long-lived assets of Puma
Source: Puma Annual Report 2004

7.2   Tangible assets – property, plant and equipment (PPE)

Tangible assets are usually listed in the balance sheet under the heading 'property, plant and equipment'.

Property, plant and equipment are tangible assets that:

(a) are held by an enterprise for use in the production or supply of goods or services, for rental to others or for administrative purposes

(b) are expected to be used during more than one period (IAS 16).

7.2.1   Initial measurement of PPE

An item of property, plant and equipment, such as machinery, motor vehicles, furniture and fixtures, office equipment, ships, aircraft, etc. should initially be measured at its cost. The cost of an item of PPE includes:

- the purchase price, including all non-refundable duties and taxes – any trade discount and rebates are deducted in arriving at the purchase price
- costs directly attributable to bringing the asset to working condition for its intended use. Directly attributable costs include:
  - ❐ site preparation; initial delivery and handling costs; installation and assembly costs
  - ❐ professional fees such as for architects and engineers
  - ❐ the initial estimate of the cost of dismantling and removing the item and site restoration costs, where the enterprise has an obligation to return the site to its original condition, for example the decommissioning of a nuclear power plant
  - ❐ the borrowing costs that are directly attributable to the acquisition, construction or production of an asset, in accordance with IAS 23.

Example

The calculation of the cost of an asset

Andrew Huskes Gmbh purchased a new motor car for its marketing director. The invoice received from the motor-car supplier showed the following:

	EUR	EUR
New DB7		26,350
Delivery charge	80	
Alloy wheels	660	
Sun-roof	200	
Petrol	30	
Number plates	130	
Road licence	155	
		1,255
Total amount payable		27,605

As you can see, the expenditure was for EUR 27,605 (the amount shown in the invoice), but only part of it, EUR 27,420, should be accounted for as Capital Expenditure (CAPEX) and capitalised (i.e. recognised as an asset):

	EUR	EUR
New DB7		26,350
Delivery charge	80	
Alloy wheels	660	
Sun-roof	200	
Number plates	130	
		1,070
CAPEX		27,420

The difference, EUR 185, represented by petrol and road licence, is an expense which should be charged to the current period income statement.

In terms of the accounting equation, we have the following:

A	=	L	+	E
				Profit
+ EUR 27,420	=	+ EUR 27,605		− EUR 185
(increase PPE for the new car acquired)		(increase trade payables)		(increase operating expenses)

7.2.2 Subsequent expenditure

Routine repairs and maintenance costs should normally be expensed in the income statement when costs are incurred. However, in circumstances where subsequent expenditure extends the useful life of an item of PPE, or increases its capacity, or achieves a substantial improvement in the quality of output, the additional expenditure should be recognised as part of the cost of the asset.

Activity 7.1 Accounting treatment of subsequent expenditure

Refer to the previous example. Suppose that after two years the car is resprayed at a cost of EUR 1,200. A new stereo system which costs EUR 800 is added to the car.

Questions:

1. Explain the accounting treatment of this expenditure.
2. Show its impact on the accounting equation.

Solutions to activities can be found at www.pearsoned.co.uk/kothari

7.2.3 Measurement subsequent to initial recognition

Subsequent to initial recognition as an asset, the carrying amount (or net book value, NBV) of an item of PPE is represented by its cost less any accumulated depreciation and any impairment losses (IAS 16). We will deal with impairment losses in section 7.5. In this section we will illustrate how to determine depreciation.

To calculate depreciation, four factors need to be considered:

- cost of the asset
- useful life of the asset
- residual value
- depreciation method.

Cost of the asset

As we have seen in section 7.2.1, this includes any directly attributable costs of bringing the asset to working condition for its intended use.

Useful life of the asset

This is either:

(a) the period of time over which an asset is expected to be used by the enterprise

or

(b) the number of production or similar units expected to be obtained from the asset by the enterprise.

When we talk about the useful life of an asset, we should take into account both its physical life and economic life:

- The *physical life of an asset* will be exhausted through the effects of wear and tear and/or the passage of time, although it is possible for the physical life to be extended considerably through careful maintenance, improvements, and so on.
- The *economic life of an asset* is determined by the effects of technological progress and changes in demand. After a while, in fact, the asset may be unable to compete with newer assets or may be no longer relevant to the needs of the enterprise.

Residual value

Also known as disposal value, terminal value, scrap value or salvage, this is the net amount which an enterprise expects to obtain for an asset at the end of its useful life after deducting the expected costs of disposal.

To calculate the total amount to be depreciated with regard to an asset, the residual value should be deducted from the cost of the asset. The likely amount to be received on disposal is often difficult to predict. So in practice, residual value which is hardly significant is ignored by enterprises:

$$\text{Depreciable amount} = \text{Cost} - \text{Residual value}$$

Depreciation methods

A variety of depreciation methods can be used to allocate the depreciable amount of an asset on a systematic basis over its useful life (IAS 16). These methods include:

- the straight-line method
- the diminishing-balance method
- the sum-of-the-units method.

Straight-line depreciation results in a constant charge over the useful life of the asset.

The diminishing-balance method results in a decreasing charge over the useful life of the asset. If the expected productivity or revenue-earning power of the asset is relatively greater during the earlier years of its life or where maintenance charges tend to increase during later years, this method may provide the most satisfactory allocation of cost.

The sum-of-the-units method results in a charge based on the expected use or output of the asset.

The method used for an asset is selected based on the expected pattern of economic benefits and is consistently applied from period to period unless there is a change in the expected pattern of economic benefits from the assets.

Tradition sometimes leads an enterprise to select the method used by other companies in its industry to enhance comparability. Sometimes one method provides far superior matching of expense and revenue. Sometimes the method is chosen to present the life-cycle cost of the asset. Moreover, enterprises do not necessarily use the same depreciation methods for all types of depreciable assets.

Example

Calculation of depreciation

We are given the following information:

Cost of a machine	EUR 40,000
Estimated residual value at the end of its useful life	EUR 1,024
Estimated useful life	4 years
Total units produced over four years	9,744
Units produced during year 1	2,260
Units produced during year 2	2,430
Units produced during year 3	2,550
Units produced during year 4	2,504

Now we will determine the depreciation charge for each year using:

- the straight-line method;
- the diminishing-balance method (use a depreciation percentage of 60 per cent[1]); and
- the sum-of-the-units method.

Straight-line Method

Amount to be depreciated = Cost – Residual Value

= EUR 40,000 – EUR 1,024 = EUR 38,976

Annual depreciation charge = EUR 38,976 ÷ 4 years = EUR 9,744

Diminishing-balance Method

Cost of a machine	EUR 40,000
Estimated residual value at the end of its useful life	EUR 1,024
Fixed percentage to be applied	60 per cent

	EUR
Cost of machine	40,000
Year 1 Depreciation charge (60 per cent of cost)	(24,000)
Carrying value or net book value (NBV) or written down value (WDV)	16,000
Year 2 Depreciation charge (60 per cent of NBV)	(9,600)
Carrying value	6,400
Year 3 Depreciation charge (60 per cent of NBV)	(3,840)
Carrying value	2,560
Year 4 Depreciation charge (60 per cent of NBV)	(1,536)
Residual value	**1,024**

Sum-of-the-units Method

Depreciation charge per unit produced = (Cost – Residual value) ÷ Number of units produced = EUR 38,976 ÷ 9,744 units = EUR 4

Depreciation charge for year 1 = EUR 4 * 2,260 = EUR 9,040
Depreciation charge for year 2 = EUR 4 * 2,430 = EUR 9,720
Depreciation charge for year 3 = EUR 4 * 2,550 = EUR 10,200
Depreciation charge for year 4 = EUR 4 * 2,504 = EUR 10,016

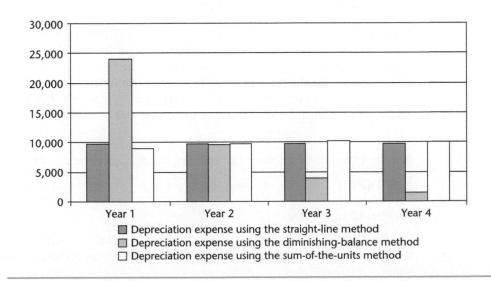

- Depreciation expense using the straight-line method
- Depreciation expense using the diminishing-balance method
- Depreciation expense using the sum-of-the-units method

Activity 7.2 Depreciation and the accounting equation

Use the data of the previous example.

Question:

Analyse the impact of the acquisition of PPE and calculation of depreciation expense on the accounting equation and on the presentation of financial statements. Use the amounts calculated under the straight-line method for your answer.

Solutions to activities can be found at www.pearsoned.co.uk/kothari

Activity 7.3 Net profit and depreciation methods

Use the data of the previous example. Assume that profit before depreciation for each of the four years in which the car was held is respectively EUR 20,000, EUR 18,000, EUR 22,000 and EUR 24,000.

Question:

Calculate the net profit for the enterprise for each year under each depreciation method and comment on your findings.

Solutions to activities can be found at www.pearsoned.co.uk/kothari

Review of useful life and depreciation policy

During the life of an asset, it may become apparent that the estimate of the useful life is inappropriate. For example, the useful life may be extended by a good repair and maintenance policy. Alternatively, technological changes or changes in the market for the products may reduce the useful life of the asset. In such cases, the depreciation rate is revised accordingly for the current and future periods to take into account the reduced useful life of the asset.

Example

Review of useful life

An asset which cost EUR 1,000 was estimated to have a useful life of 10 years and residual value EUR 200. After two years, useful life was revised to four remaining years.

The depreciation expense for the first four years is shown below:

	End of			
	Year 1	Year 2	Year 3	Year 4 ......
	EUR	EUR	EUR	EUR
Cost	1,000	1,000	1,000	1,000
Accumulated depreciation	(80)	(160)	(320)	(480)
Net book value	*920*	*840*	*680*	*520*

Depreciation expense for	Year 1	Year 2	Year 3	Year 4 ......
	$\dfrac{(1{,}000 - 200)}{10\ \text{years}}$	$\dfrac{(1{,}000 - 200)}{10\ \text{years}}$	$\dfrac{(840 - 200)}{4\ \text{years}}$	$\dfrac{(840 - 200)}{4\ \text{years}}$
	= EUR 80	= EUR 80	= EUR 160	= EUR 160

7.2.4 Retirements and disposals

The disposal of a non-current asset does not give rise to sales revenue. Disposals may give rise to gains or losses. Gains and losses for accounting purposes are the difference between the net book value of an asset and the cash received:

$$\text{Gain/Loss on disposal of PPE} = \text{Net disposal proceeds (i.e. cash received)}$$
$$- \text{Carrying value or NBV}$$

Example

Gain/Loss on disposal of PPE

Suppose we bought a truck at the beginning of 2003:

Cost of the truck	EUR 41,000
Estimated useful life	4 years
Estimated residual value at the end of its useful life	EUR 1,000

Applying the straight-line depreciation method:

	Balance sheet as at year-end (extract)			
	2003	2004	2005	2006
	EUR	EUR	EUR	EUR
Equipment (at historical cost)	41,000	41,000	41,000	41,000
Deduct accumulated depreciation	10,000	20,000	30,000	40,000
NBV	31,000	21,000	11,000	1,000

Now suppose the truck was sold on 31 December 2004 for EUR 27,000. The sale would have the following effect:

	A		= L +	E
Cash	PPE	Accumulated depreciation		Profit
+ EUR 27,000	– EUR 41,000	+ EUR 20,000 =		+ EUR 6,000 (Gain on disposal of equipment)

Note that the disposal of the truck requires the removal of its carrying value or NBV, which appears in two accounts, not one. Therefore, both the accumulated depreciation account and the equipment account are affected when disposals occur.

Now suppose the selling price was EUR 17,000 and not EUR 27,000. The effect on the accounting equation would be as follows:

	A		= L +	E
Cash	PPE	Accumulated depreciation		Profit
+ EUR 17,000	– EUR 41,000	+ EUR 20,000 =		– EUR 4,000 (Loss on disposal of equipment)

7.3   Leased assets

In a lease agreement, the owner of property, the lessor, conveys to another party, the lessee, the right to use property, plant or equipment for a stated period of time for a payment. For many leases this period of time is short relative to the total life of the asset. For example, agencies lease or rent automobiles for a few hours or days. Space in an office building may be leased on an annual basis. This lease is called an operating lease. In this case, the lease payments are expenses of the accounting period to which they refer and therefore charged to the income statement.

Other leases cover a period of time that is substantially equal to the estimated life of the asset, or they contain other provisions that give the lessee almost as many rights to the use of the asset as if the lessee owned it. Such a lease is called a finance lease (or capital lease).

Defining a lease contract as operating rather than as a finance lease has important implications on its accounting treatment and consequently on performance ratios (see Case study, Chapter 2).

7.3.1   Accounting for a finance lease

Finance leases are examples of transactions to which the principle of substance over form is applied to show a true and fair view of the financial statements. As we have seen in Chapter 2, the *Framework* identifies substance over form as an aspect of the qualitative characteristic of reliability. Under IAS 1, substance over form is a general consideration governing the selection of accounting policies.

Although the legal form of a lease agreement is such that the lessee may acquire no legal title to the leased asset, in the case of finance lease the substance and financial reality are such that the lessee acquires the economic benefits of the use of the leased asset for the major part of its economic life in return for entering into an obligation to pay for that right an amount approximating, at the inception of the lease, the fair value of the asset and the related finance charge. The lessee has also the option to purchase the asset at a price that is expected to be sufficiently lower than the fair value at the date the option becomes exercisable. The intention to exercise the bargain option price is an important condition for a lease to be considered as a finance lease.

If such lease transactions are not reflected in the lessee's balance sheet, the economic resources and the level of obligations of an entity are understated, thereby distorting underlying financial conditions. Therefore, it is appropriate for a finance lease to be recognised in the lessee's balance sheet both as an asset and as an obligation to pay future lease payments.

Example

'Substance over form' applied to a finance lease

Let us consider two enterprises, ABC and XYZ. The former borrowed EUR 20 million and bought PPE with this money. XYZ borrowed no money, but has leased PPE that would have cost EUR 20 million to buy. If XYZ accounts only for the legal form of the arrangement, its financial statements would look apparently better than ABC's. That is, XYZ will seem to have a better profitability in relation to asset used (because assets seem lower) and show lower liabilities (see the first two following balance sheets). As we will see key ratios significantly affected by this treatment are return on total assets and gearing.

ABC's balance sheet		XYZ's balance sheet (*form*)	
PPE			
+ EUR 20m	Loans + EUR 20m		

	XYZ's balance sheet (*substance*)	
PPE		
	+ EUR 20m	Lease liabilities + EUR 20m

Therefore, when a finance lease agreement exists, lessees should recognise finance leases as assets and liabilities in their balance sheets at amounts equal to the fair value of the leased property or, if lower, the present value of the minimum lease payments, each determined at the inception of the lease.

As illustrated in the following example, leased assets give rise to depreciation expense as if they are legally owned by the lessee. A finance lease gives rise also to interest expenses. In fact the lease payments shall be apportioned between the finance charges (i.e. interest expenses) and the fair value of the asset.

Example

Initial recognition and subsequent measurement of leased assets

ABC SpA leases an item of equipment whose useful life is 10 years. Lease payments are EUR 4,674 per year payable for the next 10 years at each year-end. The fair value of the equipment is EUR 30,000 (as is the present value of the lease payments).

As ABC SpA has the option to purchase this item at the end of the lease term for EUR 500, this agreement is considered and accounted for as a finance lease.

When the equipment is acquired, in terms of the accounting equation we have the following:

A	=	L	+	E
PPE		Lease obligation		
+ EUR 30,000	=	+ EUR 30,000		

Let us assume that the first annual lease payment of EUR 4,674 consists of EUR 2,700 for interest expense and EUR 1,974 to reduce the present value of the equipment leased. The impact on the accounting equation would be as follows:

A	=	L	+	E
Cash		Lease obligation		Profit
− EUR 4,674	=	− EUR 1,974		− EUR 2,700
				(Interest expense)

Depreciation on the asset would be charged as an expense each year, as if ABC SpA had bought and owned the asset. Assuming ABC SpA applies the straight-line method for such assets, the transaction in terms of the accounting equation would be as follows:

A	=	L	+	E
PPE				Profit
− EUR 3,000	=			− EUR 3,000
(Increase in				
Accumulated depreciation)				(Depreciation expense)

At the end of the 10 years, the 'cost' of EUR 30,000 would be allocated to the income statements of those years via the accounting for depreciation. Also the lease obligation would be reduced to zero, and the annual interest expense would be recognised in each of the 10 years as we have just shown.

As you can deduce from the accounting treatment for a finance lease just described, assets acquired by means of a finance lease are an exception to the general rule that assets shown in a balance sheet of an enterprise are legally owned by that entity. In our example, equipment is legally owned by the lessor, but they are accounted for as if they are owned by the lessee. In this way the lease obligation, which is in substance a long-term loan, is disclosed as a liability in the balance sheet.

7.3.2 Accounting for an operating lease

Lease payments (i.e. rental) under an operating lease should be recognised as an expense in the income statement as incurred over the lease term.

No balances appear in the balance sheet other than accruals and prepayments on rented rather than owned assets.

Activity 7.4 Operating lease

Under a lease agreement Williamson plc pays a non-returnable deposit of EUR 100,000 and then three years rental of EUR 100,000 per annum on the first day of each year. The asset has a life of six years.

Questions:

Show the effect of these transactions on the accounting equation.
Calculate the charge to the income statement for each year and any asset or liability on the balance sheet at the end of each year.

Solutions to activities can be found at www.pearsoned.co.uk/kothari

7.4 Intangible assets

Intangible assets are resources without physical substance such as scientific or technical knowledge, design and implementation of new processes or systems, licences, intellectual property, market knowledge and trademarks (including brand names and publishing titles). Common examples of items encompassed by these broad headings are:

- computer software
- patents
- copyrights
- motion picture films
- customer lists
- mortgage servicing rights
- fishing licences
- import quotas
- franchises
- customer or supplier relationships
- customer loyalty
- market share
- marketing rights.

Not all these items meet the definition of an intangible asset, which requires that an intangible asset be identifiable (or separable) and controlled (IAS 38).

An asset is separable if the enterprise could rent, sell, exchange or distribute the specific future economic benefits attributable to the asset without also disposing of future economic benefits that flow from other assets used in the same revenue earning activity.

An enterprise controls an asset if the enterprise has the power to obtain the future economic benefits flowing from the underlying resource and also can restrict the access of others to those benefits. The capacity of an enterprise to control the future economic benefits from an intangible asset would normally stem from legal rights that are enforceable in a court of law.

When we acquire a company with market and technical knowledge and/or with a particularly skilled staff and/or with a good portfolio of customers, the price we pay for it might be much higher than its equity. This is because we take into account those intangible items when defining the acquisition price (we will see the accounting treatment of this excess price in Chapter 11 on consolidated financial statements).

For example, suppose ABC SpA spent EUR 5 million to internally develop and patent a new drug. ABC SpA would charge EUR 5 million to expense; no asset would be recognised.

In contrast, if ABC SpA paid EUR 5 million to another company for its patent on an identical drug, it would record the amount paid as an intangible asset (at cost). The difference in treatment acknowledges that it is difficult for management to objectively value the results of its internal research and development efforts, while an independent transaction between separate companies realistically measures the value.

7.4.1 Recognition and initial measurement of an intangible asset

Once it is demonstrated that an item meets the definition of an intangible asset, it should be recognised if, and only if:

(a) it is probable that the future economic benefits that are attributable to the asset will flow to the enterprise

(b) the cost of the asset can be measured reliably.

An enterprise should assess the probability of future economic benefits using reasonable and supportable assumptions that represent management's best estimate of the set of economic conditions that will exist over the useful life of the asset.

An intangible asset should be measured initially at cost. This comprises its purchase price, including any non-refundable purchase taxes, and any directly attributable expenditure for preparing the asset for its intended use. Directly attributable expenditure includes, for example, professional fees for legal services.

7.4.2 Research and Development

Research is original and planned investigation undertaken with the prospect of gaining new scientific or technical knowledge and understanding.

Development is the application of research findings or other knowledge to a plan or design for the production of new or substantially improved materials, devices, products, processes, systems or services prior to the commencement of commercial production or use (IAS 38).

Examples of research activities are:

(a) activities aimed at obtaining new knowledge

(b) the search for, evaluation and final selection of, applications of research findings or other knowledge

(c) the search for alternatives for materials, devices, products, processes, systems or services

(d) the formulation, design, evaluation and final selection of possible alternatives for new or improved materials, devices, products, processes, systems or services.

Expenditure on research (or on the research phase of an internal project) should be recognised as an expense when it is incurred. This is because in the research phase of a project, an enterprise cannot demonstrate that an intangible asset exists that will generate probable future economic benefits.

Examples of development activities are:

(a) the design, construction and testing of pre-production or pre-use prototypes and models

(b) the design of tools, jigs, moulds and dies involving new technology

(c) the design, construction and operation of a pilot plant that is not of a scale economically feasible for commercial production

(d) the design, construction and testing of a chosen alternative for new or improved materials, devices, products, processes, systems or services.

An intangible asset arising from development (or from the development phase of an internal project) should be recognised if, and only if, an enterprise can demonstrate all of the following:

(a) the technical feasibility of completing the intangible asset so that it will be available for use or sale

(b) its intention to complete the intangible asset and use or sell it

(c) its ability to use or sell the intangible asset

(d) how the intangible asset will generate probable future economic benefits. Among other things, the enterprise should demonstrate the existence of a market for the output of the intangible asset or the intangible asset itself or, if it is to be used internally, the usefulness of the intangible asset

(e) the availability of adequate technical, financial and other resources to complete the development and to use or sell the intangible asset

(f) its ability to measure the expenditure attributable to the intangible asset during its development reliably.

In the development phase of a project, an enterprise can, in some instances, identify an intangible asset and demonstrate that the asset will generate probable future economic benefits. This is because the development phase of a project is further advanced than the research phase.

7.4.3 Subsequent expenditure

Subsequent expenditure for an intangible item should be, in general, recognised as an expense.

In fact, the nature of intangible assets is such that it is not possible to determine whether subsequent expenditure is likely to enhance or maintain the economic benefits that will flow to the enterprise from those assets.

As we have seen, expenditure for research is always recognised as an expense when it is incurred. Other examples of expenditure that is recognised as an expense when it is incurred include:

(a) expenditure for start-up activities (start-up costs), unless this expenditure is included in the cost of an item of property, plant and equipment. Start-up costs may consist of establishment costs such as legal and secretarial costs incurred in establishing a legal entity, expenditure to open a new facility or business (pre-opening costs) or expenditures for commencing new operations or launching new products or processes (pre-operating costs)

(b) expenditure for training activities

(c) expenditure for advertising and promotional activities

(d) expenditure for relocating or re-organising part or all of an enterprise.

7.4.4 Measurement subsequent to initial recognition

After initial recognition, an intangible asset should be carried at its cost less any accumulated amortisation and any accumulated impairment losses.

Amortisation period

The depreciable amount of an intangible asset should be allocated on a systematic basis over the best estimate of its useful or economic life. Amortisation should commence when the asset is available for use.

Many factors need to be considered in determining the useful life of an intangible asset including:

- the expected usage of the asset by the enterprise; typical product life cycles for similar assets

- the stability of the industry in which the enterprise operates, and the expected actions of competitors

- the speed of technological change and expected obsolescence

- the period of control over the asset and legal or similar limits on the use of the asset, such as the expiry dates of related leases. If control over the future economic benefits from an intangible asset is achieved through legal rights that have been granted for a finite period, the useful life of the intangible asset should not exceed the period of the legal rights.

Amortisation method

The amortisation method used should reflect the pattern in which the asset's economic benefits are consumed by the enterprise. If that pattern cannot be determined reliably, the straight-line method should be used.

Review of amortisation period and amortisation method

If during the life of an intangible asset, it becomes apparent that the estimate of its useful life is inappropriate, the amortisation charges for the current and future periods should be revised accordingly, as for tangible assets.

Activity 7.5 Amortisation of intangible assets

Questions:

1. On 29 December 2004, a publisher acquires the copyrights for a book by a South American author for EUR 2.4 million. The contractual duration is of six years. What is the amortisation for each year until 2010? Show this transaction also in terms of accounting equation for the years 2004 and 2005.

2. On 28 December 2004, Scholes Company purchased a patent for a calculator for EUR 360,000. The patent had 10 years of legal life. Technology changes fast, so Scholes expects the patent to be worthless in five years. What is the amortisation for each year until 2009?

Solutions to activities can be found at www.pearsoned.co.uk/kothari

---

7.5   Impairment losses

Depreciation/amortisation is aimed at allocating the cost of a non-current asset (tangible or intangible) against revenue over the asset's useful life. However, events such as a rapid economic obsolescence or physical damage of an asset, may make this systematic allocation inadequate. In these cases, the carrying value of the asset (i.e. its depreciated cost) may overstate what the asset is worth to the enterprise.

Once an impairment has been identified, we must measure its size. In order to do so, the enterprise must compare the asset's carrying value with its recoverable amount, as shown in Figure 7.3.

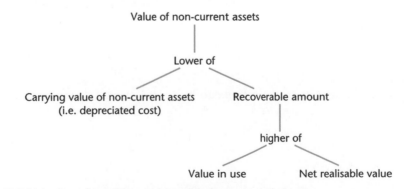

Figure 7.3 Valuation of tangible and intangible (non-current) assets

The asset's carrying value is in general its depreciated cost (i.e. historical cost less accumulated depreciation).

The recoverable amount is the higher of an asset's net realisable value and its value in use.

Value in use is the present value of estimated future cash inflows and outflows to be derived from continuing use of an asset and from its disposal at the end of its useful life. The determination of the value in use involves also considerable estimation of the appropriate discount rate to be applied to these future cash flows. Moreover, it may be impossible to make reasonable estimates for individual assets, and so impairment tests are carried out on groups of assets (called 'cash generating units') for which independent cash flows can be measured.

The net realisable value (NRV) is defined as the amount obtainable from the sale of an asset in an arm's length transaction between knowledgeable, willing parties, less the cost of disposal. Costs of disposal are incremental costs directly attributable to the disposal of an asset, such as legal costs, stamp duty, costs of removing the asset, and other direct incremental costs to bring an asset into condition for its sale.

If the recoverable amount of an asset is less than its carrying amount, then the carrying amount of the asset should be reduced to its recoverable amount. That reduction is an impairment loss.

An impairment loss should be recognised as an expense in the income statement immediately. After the recognition of an impairment loss, the depreciation (amortisation) charge for the asset should be adjusted in future periods to allocate the asset's revised carrying amount, less its residual value (if any), on a systematic basis over its remaining useful life.

Activity 7.6 Impairment test

In order to determine if an impairment loss has occurred, we should determine the recoverable amount and compare it with the carrying value or NBV. Assume that the carrying value of an asset was EUR 1,000.

Question:

Determine if an impairment loss occurred in the following three situations:

	Value in use	NRV
	EUR	EUR
(1)	900	1,050
(2)	900	980
(3)	960	925

Solutions to activities can be found at www.pearsoned.co.uk/kothari

7.6   Depletion of natural resources

Depletion is the accounting measure used to allocate the acquisition cost of natural resources such as minerals, oil and timber. Depletion differs from depreciation because depletion focuses specifically on the physical use and exhaustion of the natural resources, while depreciation focuses more broadly on any reduction of the economic value of non-current assets, including physical deterioration and obsolescence.

The costs of natural resources are usually classified as non-current assets. However, buying natural resources is actually like buying massive quantities of inventories under the ground (iron ore) or above the ground (timber). Depletion expense is the measure of that portion of this 'non-current' inventory that is used in a particular period. For example, a coal mine which cost EUR 40 million originally contained an estimated 2 million tonnes of usable coal. The depletion rate would be EUR 40 million ÷ 2 million tonnes = EUR 20 per tonne. If 100,000 tonnes were mined during the first year, the depletion would be 100,000 × EUR 20, or EUR 2 million for that year. Each year the amount of coal extracted would be measured, and the amount of depletion recorded would be based on that usage.

As this example shows, depletion is measured on a sum-of-the-units basis illustrated in section 7.2.3. The annual depletion may be accounted for as a direct reduction of the mining asset, or it may be accumulated in a separate account similar to accumulated depreciation:

	A	=	L	+		E
	PPE	=	Trade and other payables	+	Capital	Profit
Acquisition of coal mine	EUR 40m	=		EUR 40m		
Depletion for year 1	– EUR 2m	=				– EUR 2m

7.7   Ratios relating to tangible and intangible assets

A number of ratios may be determined to help the users of financial statements gain a better understanding of how effectively tangible and intangible assets are used to generate sales and profits.

Capital intensity ratios

There are two key ratios:

$$\text{Return on tangible assets} = \frac{\text{Net profit}}{\text{Tangible assets, net}}$$

$$\text{Tangible asset turnover} = \frac{\text{Sales revenue}}{\text{Tangible assets, net}}$$

They address the questions: 'how much profit the enterprise creates' and 'how much sales are generated for each euro invested in tangible assets'. These ratios are essential for extrapolating the consequences of investment strategies and their values are affected by the depreciation method chosen.

Average age and life of tangible assets

Actual and potential shareholders as well as financial analysts may need to evaluate the risk of obsolescence of the assets of an enterprise. Failing to have exact knowledge of the average age or life of the assets, we can estimate them by using the historical cost of the assets and the related accumulated depreciation:

$$\text{Average age} = \frac{\text{Accumulated depreciation at year-end}}{\text{Depreciation charge for the year}}$$

$$\text{Average life} = \frac{\text{Historical cost of depreciable assets at year-end}}{\text{Depreciation charge for the year}}$$

These two ratios suffer several limits since the depreciation charge and thus the accumulated depreciation vary depending on the depreciation method used. Furthermore, managers could manipulate tangible assets valuation by:

- increasing (or decreasing) an asset's useful life
- changing depreciation method
- deciding to capitalise or not certain acquisition costs.

Research and development ratios

We saw that under IAS 38 certain R&D expenditures are charged to the income statement and omitted from the balance sheet. As the global economy is increasingly moving into a knowledge-based, technology-intensive world, intangibles are becoming more and more important in the competitive strategy of an enterprise. However, as some intangibles are not reflected in the balance sheet, a loss of relevance of accounting information can be highlighted and one evidence of this phenomenon is the gap existing between the book value and the market value of most listed companies. Among intangibles, R&D has received special attention by analysts as it strengthens an enterprise's competitive position and ensures its future viability. Numerous academic studies have documented a positive relationship between a company's R&D investment and its market value in developed countries.

Two of the ratios often used for such an evaluation are:

$$\text{R\&D intensity} = \frac{\text{R\&D}}{\text{Sales revenue}}$$

$$\text{R\&D per employee} = \frac{\text{R\&D}}{\text{Number of employees}}$$

The first ratio is a function of the line of business of an enterprise. In industries with short product-life cycle or a pharmaceutical one, the need to invest in R&D is much greater than it is in industries where products and processes have a long life cycle and innovation is not essential.

Activity 7.7 Capital intensity ratios

Refer to Table 3.1 (on page 41) Consolidated balance sheet of adidas-Salomon as at 31 December 2004 and Table 4.3 (on page 76) adidas-Salomon income statement for 2004.

Question:

Determine the return on tangible assets and the tangible asset turnover for adidas-Salomon for 2003 and 2004.

Solutions to activities can be found at www.pearsoned.co.uk/kothari

Summary

- Tangible assets are listed in the balance sheet under the heading 'property, plant and equipment' and include land, buildings, machinery, motor vehicles, office equipment, etc.

- Intangible assets are resources without physical substance such as scientific or technical knowledge, design and implementation of new processes or systems, licences, intellectual property, market knowledge and trademarks (including brand names and publishing titles).

- *Depreciation* is the general term for the allocation of costs of non-current assets to the time periods that benefit from these assets. For natural resources the allocation is called depletion, while *amortisation* is typically used for the allocation of the costs of intangible assets.

- To calculate depreciation, four factors need to be considered: (i) cost of the asset (ii) useful life of the asset (iii) residual value (iv) depreciation method.

- Assets do not need to be owned: control of the resources is what matters. Consequently, certain leased assets are included in the balance sheet. This happens with leases covering a period of time that is substantially equal to the estimated life of the asset, or containing other provisions that give the lessee almost as many rights to the use of the asset as if the lessee owned it (finance lease or capital lease).

- Sometimes assets suffer impairments of value that are not captured by systematic depreciation/amortisation. Once an impairment has been identified, the assets must be written down to their *recoverable amounts* (i.e. the higher of an asset's net realisable value and its value in use).

- Capital intensity ratios (i.e. return on tangible assets and tangible asset turnover) and R&D intensity ratio are useful for understanding an enterprise's investment strategies.

References and research

The IASB documents relevant for this chapter are:

- IAS 8 – *Net Profit or Loss for the Period, Fundamental Errors and Changes in Accounting Policies*
- IAS 16 – *Property, Plant and Equipment*
- IAS 17 – *Leases*
- IAS 23 – *Borrowing Costs*
- IAS 36 – *Impairment of Assets*
- IAS 38 – *Intangible Assets*
- IAS 40 – *Investment Property*

The following are examples of books that take the issues of this chapter further:

- Robert N. Anthony, David F. Hawkins and Kenneth A. Merchant, *Accounting: Text and Cases*, McGraw-Hill, 1999, Chapter 7
- Barry Elliott and Jamie Elliott, *Financial Accounting and Reporting*, 9th Edition, Financial Times-Prentice Hall, 2005, Chapters 16, 17 and 18
- Charles T. Horngren, Gary L. Sundem and John A. Elliott, *Introduction to Financial Accounting*, Pearson Education-Prentice Hall, 2002, Chapter 7
- Hervé Stolowy and Michel J. Lebas, *Corporate Financial Reporting: A Global Perspective*, Thomson Learning 2002, Chapters 7 and 8
- Hennie Van Greuning, *International Financial Reporting Standards: A Practical Guide*, The World Bank, 2005, Chapters 15, 16, 21, 22, 24 and 26
- Frank Wood and Alan Sangster, *Business Accounting*, Vol. 1, 9th Edition, Financial Times-Prentice Hall, 2002, Part 4

Questions

7.1 (a) Define PPE and 'cost' in connection with PPE.

(b) Define depreciation. Explain what assets need not be depreciated and list the main methods of calculating depreciation.

(c) What is meant by 'useful life' and 'residual value'?

7.2 On 1 January 2005, Zetajane Inc acquired production equipment for EUR 250,000. The following further costs were incurred:

Delivery	EUR 18,000
Installation	EUR 24,000
General administration costs	EUR 3,000

The installation and setting-up period took three months, and a further amount of EUR 21,000 was spent on costs directly related to bringing the asset to its working condition. The equipment was ready for use on 1 April 2005.

Monthly managerial reports indicated that for the first five months, the production quantities from this equipment resulted in an initial operating loss of EUR 15,000 because of small quantities produced. The months thereafter show much more positive results.

The equipment has an estimated useful life of 14 years and a residual value of EUR 18,000. Estimated dismantling costs amount to EUR 12,500.

Determine the cost of the asset and the annual charge for the 2005 income statement related to the consumption of the economic benefits embodied in the assets.

7.3   At the beginning of 2002, Gadue Computer purchased a machine, used in the production of computers, for EUR 359,000. In addition to the price of the machine, Gadue paid insurance during shipment of EUR 2,500; transportation costs of EUR 3,500; installation costs of EUR 10,000; and training costs of EUR 7,000. Also repair costs incurred before the end of 2002 were EUR 2,000.

The machine was expected to last five years and has a residual value of EUR 25,000. Gadue uses straight-line depreciation on all machines of this type.

At the beginning of year 2005 the machine was sold for EUR 175,000.

(a) Determine the total capitalisable costs of the machine.
(b) Show the impact of the acquisition of this machine on the accounting equation.
(c) Determine the annual depreciation expense.
(d) Determine the gain (loss) on disposal of this machine.
(e) Use the accounting equation to analyse the disposal of the machine.

7.4   Laurensmani SpA's financial year is to 31 December. It uses the straight-line method of depreciation for machinery.

On 1 January 2004 the enterprise purchased a machine for EUR 10,000. The machine had an expected life of four years and an estimated residual value of EUR 2,000.

On 1 January 2005 the enterprise purchased another machine for EUR 15,000 giving in exchange the previous one plus the balance in cash.

Analyse these transactions using the accounting equation on the hypothesis that the difference paid in cash was:

(a) EUR 7,000
(b) EUR 6,000
(c) EUR 9,000.

7.5   On 1 January 2005 a manufacturing machine of EUR 330,000 is acquired by way of a finance lease agreement under the following terms:

• Lease term: three years
• Instalments of EUR 72,500 are payable half-yearly in arrears
• Deposit of EUR 30,000 immediately payable.

The amortisation table for this transaction is as follows (amounts in euro):

	Instalment	Interest	Capital	Balance
Cash price				330,000
Deposit	30,000	–	30,000	300,000
Instalment 1	72,500	35,320	37,180	262,820
Instalment 2	72,500	30,943	41,557	221,263
Subtotal	175,000	66,263	108,737	
Instalment 3	72,500	26,050	46,450	174,813
Instalment 4	72,500	20,581	51,919	122,894
Instalment 5	72,500	14,469	58,031	64,863
Instalment 6	72,500	7,637	64,863	–
TOTAL	**465,000**	**135,000**	**330,000**	

Present this finance lease in the lessee's financial statements for 2005.

7.6 *Expenditure on research costs should be recognized as an expense when it is incurred (. . .) An intangible asset arising from development should be recognized if, and only if, an enterprise can demonstrate all of the following . . .*   (IAS 38 – *Intangible Assets*)

(a) Explain why expenditure on research is treated differently from expenditure on development.

(b) State the criteria to be demonstrated for expenditure on development to be recognised as an intangible asset.

(c) An enterprise has incurred the following costs prior to commercial production of a new pollution filter for use on commercial vehicles:

Marketing awareness campaign	EUR 50,000
Patent royalty payable to inventor of filter	EUR 12,000
Salaries of staff testing filter prototypes	EUR 38,500

Which costs should be included in the internally generated intangible asset?

(d) Describe how and when development expenditure should be amortised.

7.7 Autocar Inc, a motor vehicle manufacturer, has a research division that worked on the following projects during 2004:

Project 1 – The design of a steering mechanism that does not operate like a conventional steering wheel, but reacts to the impulses from a driver's fingers.

Project 2 – The design of a welding apparatus that is controlled electronically rather than mechanically.

The following is a summary of the expenses of the particular department:

Amounts in thousands of euro	General	Project 1	Project 2
Material and services	128	935	620
Labour			
• Direct labour	–	620	320
• Department head salary	400	–	–
• Administrative personnel	725	–	–
Overhead			
• Direct	–	340	410
• Indirect	270	110	60

The departmental head spent 15 per cent of his time on Project 1 and 10 per cent of his time on Project 2.

Determine the costs to be capitalised.

Case study   Expenses *vs* capitalised costs

At the beginning of 2004 ABC SpA has assets of EUR 8,500, consisting of cash for EUR 500 and of plant and equipment for EUR 8,000. These assets are financed by EUR 200 of current liabilities, EUR 2,000 of 7 per cent long-term debt and EUR 6,300 of shareholders' equity.

During 2004, ABC has sales of EUR 10,000 and incurs EUR 7,000 of operating expenses, excluding depreciation; EUR 1,000 for new plant and equipment, and EUR 140 of interest expense. The enterprise depreciates its plant and equipment over 10 years (no residual value).

Questions:

1. Ignoring the effect of income taxes, prepare an income statement for 2004 and a balance sheet as at 1 January 2004 and 31 December 2004 assuming that:

   (i) ABC expenses EUR 1,000 in construction costs
   (ii) ABC capitalises these costs.

   Assume that construction costs will be depreciated over four years and that the resulting asset was ready for use on the 1st of July 2004.

2. Show the effects of decisions (i) and (ii) on shareholders' equity, profit before tax, pretax operating and investing cash flows, and on key financial ratios.

3. Summarise the results of decision (i) and decision (ii).

Note

[1] The depreciation percentage has been determined as follows:

$$\text{Rate of depreciation} = 1 - \sqrt[n]{\frac{\text{Residual value}}{\text{Cost of acquistion}}} = 1 - \sqrt[4]{\frac{\text{EUR 1,024}}{\text{EUR 40,000}}} = 1 - 0.4 = 0.6 = 60\%,$$

where 'n' is the number of years of useful life.

8 Liabilities

Objectives

When you have completed this chapter you should be able to:

- distinguish between current and non-current liabilities
- account for bonds and other borrowings
- understand the difference between liabilities, provisions and contingent liabilities
- explain why differences between accounting profit before taxes and taxable profit may give rise to deferred taxes
- determine deferred tax liabilities or assets
- use ratio analysis to assess an enterprise's debt level.

8.1 Introduction

We know that an balance sheet reports assets and claims of an enterprise at a specified moment in time. In Chapter 3 we saw that liabilities are the claims of third parties, while owners' equity represents the claims of the owners for the money invested in the business. These sources of funds can be tied to the enterprise for a short period of time (current liabilities) or for a longer or virtually indefinite period. In this case we talk about permanent capital which is represented by both non-current liabilities and owners' equity, as shown in Figure 8.1.

In Chapter 3, we defined liability as 'a present obligation of the enterprise arising from past events, the settlement of which is expected to result in an outflow from the enterprise of resources embodying economic benefits' (IASB *Framework*). We also distinguished between current and non-current liabilities.

A liability should be classified as current when it is due to be settled within 12 months after the balance sheet date.

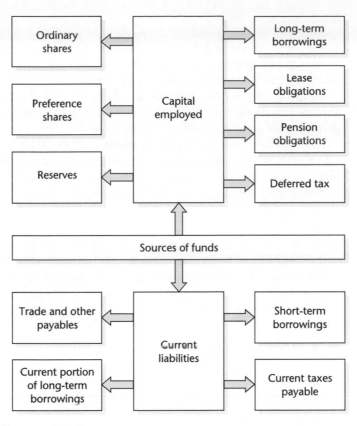

Figure 8.1 Sources of funds

The largest current liability for most enterprises is trade payables, i.e. amount owed to suppliers of goods and services. These amounts are recorded based on invoices from the suppliers of goods and/or services. Other current liabilities usually arise from wages payable, social expenses payable, interest payable and current taxes payable. Short-term borrowings and current portion of long-term borrowings are also classified among current liabilities as you can see from Figure 8.1.

We dealt with the accounting equation for current liabilities in Chapters 3, 4 and 6. So you should refer to those chapters.

Non-current liabilities normally consist of long-term borrowings, lease obligations, pension obligations and deferred taxes. In section 8.2, we deal with the issue and redemption of bonds. For lease obligations see Chapter 7, while for deferred taxes see section 8.4. Though pension obligations are becoming increasingly important, they go beyond the scope of this book and therefore we will not deal with them.

8.2 Accounting for long-term borrowings

Before starting we should discuss the main advantages and disadvantages of bond financing over share issue.

Advantages

By raising funds through bonds rather than issue of new share capital, shareholders' control is not affected. As bondholders do not have voting rights, current owners (shareholders) retain full control of the company and their rights are not diluted.

Bond interest is deductible for tax purposes; dividends on shares are not. This implies that bond interest lowers the taxable income and therefore there is the advantage of a reduction or saving in taxes.

Earnings per share (EPS) may be higher. Although bond interest expense reduces net income, EPS on ordinary share capital often is higher under bond financing because there is no dilution in the shareholders' equity (as we will see in Chapters 9 and 16).

Disadvantages

As interest must be paid on a periodic basis to bondholders and the principal amount of the bonds must be paid at maturity, a company with fluctuating earnings and a relatively weak cash position may face great difficulties in making interest payments on due dates. Bonds are normally subject to a number of covenants and they are required to be respected.

Issue of bonds at par value

We will now describe the impact on the accounting equation of:

- an issue of bond at par value
- an issue of bond at a discount
- an issue of bond at a premium
- bond interest expense
- bond redemption.

Assume Anacleto & Co issues 100 bonds having a nominal or face value of EUR 1,000 per bond. The bonds have a stated interest rate of 5 per cent. This means that the annual interest payment will be 5 per cent of the par value – in this case, EUR 50 per year for each bond. The bonds will mature at the end of the fifth year after their issuance. If Anacleto & Co receives EUR 100,000 for these bonds, the impact on the accounting equation would be as follows:

$$A \qquad = \qquad L \qquad + \quad E$$

A		L	+ E
Cash and cash equivalents		Bonds	
+ EUR 100,000	=	+ EUR 100,000	

Issue of bonds at a discount

For the bonds just referred to, assume that instead of receiving EUR 100,000 Anacleto & Co receives EUR 980,000. This may occur because the prevailing market rate is higher than 5 per cent or because an investment in Anacleto & Co represents a higher risk compared to, for example, government bonds. When bonds are issued for less than their par value, they are said to be issued at a discount. The issue of bonds at a discount has the following impact on the accounting equation:

	A		=	L	+ E
Discount on bonds	Cash and cash equivalents			Bonds	
+ EUR 2,000	+ EUR 98,000		=	+ EUR 100,000	

Bond discount is an asset, as it represents a 'prepaid expense' which will be charged against income over the duration of bonds; in the example the bonds will be redeemed at the end of five years.

Issue of bonds at a premium

If the prevailing rate of interest for similar bonds had been higher, Anacleto & Co would have issued its bonds at a premium. Assuming that Anacleto & Co received EUR 104,000, the analysis of the accounting equation would have been as follows:

	A	=	L		+ E
Cash and cash equivalents			Bonds	Premium on bonds	
+ EUR 104,000		=	+ EUR 100,000	+ EUR 4,000	

Bond premium is a liability, as it represents an 'unearned revenue' which will be credited to income over the duration of the bonds, i.e. up to the date of redemption.

Bond interest expenses

To the investor, the return on a bond is made up of two components:

1. the periodic cash interest payments
2. the difference between the bond's par value (received in cash at redemption) and the amount paid for the bond. The second component is an expense if the bond was issued at a discount, or a gain if issued at a premium.

From the standpoint of the bond issuer, the related interest also has two components. In fact, bond interest expense is made up of:

1. the periodic cash interest payments to the bondholder
2. the amortisation of the discount or premium on issue as bond discount or premium should be amortised over the life of the bonds.

These two components determine the effective rate of interest on the bond. The effective rate is higher than the nominal or coupon rate for bonds issued at a discount; the effective rate is lower than the nominal rate for bonds issued at a premium.

Assuming that the redemption takes place after five years, and the bond discount is EUR 2,000, a charge of EUR 400 (i.e. EUR 2,000 divided by five years) would be made against profit each year. Each year we also have to account for EUR 5,000 (i.e. EUR 100,000 $\times$ 5%) for interest.

	A		=	L +		E	
	Discount on bonds	Cash and cash equivalents		Bonds		Profit	
Op.bal.	+ EUR 2,000			+ EUR 100,000			
	– EUR 400	– EUR 5,000	=			– EUR 400 (Amortisation of discount on bonds)	– EUR 5,000 (Interest expense)
Clos.bal.	+ EUR 1,600			+ EUR 100,000			

The effective interest expense for Anacleto & Co each year is EUR 5,400 or 5.4 per cent (i.e. EUR 5,400 divided by EUR 100,000) and not the nominal rate of 5 per cent. Continuing this process for all five years the bond discount of EUR 2,000 will be completely amortised.

Keeping the assumption that the redemption takes place after five years, the bond premium of EUR 800 (i.e. EUR 4,000 divided by five years) would be credited to the income statement each year until the redemption at the end of the fifth year. Each year we also have to account for EUR 5,000 for interest expense.

	A	=	L		+	E
	Cash and cash equivalents		Bonds	Premium on bonds		Profit
Op.bal.			+ EUR 100,000	+ EUR 4,000		
	– EUR 5,000	=		– EUR 800		+ EUR 800
						– EUR 5,000
Clos.bal.			+ EUR 100,000	+ EUR 3,200		

In this case the effective interest expense for Anacleto & Co each year is EUR 4,200 or 4.2 per cent (i.e. EUR 4,200 divided by EUR 100,000) and not the nominal rate of 5 per cent.

8.3   Liabilities, provisions and contingent liabilities

An essential characteristic of a liability is that the enterprise has a present obligation arising from past events. An obligation is a duty or responsibility to act or perform in a certain way. Obligations may be legally enforceable as a consequence of a binding contract or statutory requirement. This is normally the case, for example, with amounts payable for goods and services received.

There are obligations for which either the triggering event may not come from a transaction with a third party, or the timing of the obligation may not be known, or the amount may not be well defined, or any combination of the three.

Thus liabilities (in strict sense) should be distinguished from:

- provisions
- accrued liabilities
- contingent liabilities.

Provision versus liability

IASB *Framework* explains that:

> Some liabilities can be measured only by using a substantial degree of estimation. Some enterprises describe these liabilities as provisions. In some countries, such provisions are not regarded as liabilities because the concept of a liability is defined narrowly so as to include only amounts that can be established without the need to make estimates. The definition of a liability . . . follows a broader approach. Thus, when a provision involves a present obligation and satisfies the rest of the definition, it is a liability even if the amount has to be estimated. Examples include provisions for payments to be made under existing warranties and provisions to cover pension obligations.

Therefore:

A provision should be recognised when [see Figure 8.2]:

(a) an enterprise has a present obligation (legal or constructive) as a result of a past event;

(b) it is probable that an outflow of resources embodying economic benefits will be required to settle the obligation; and

(c) a reliable estimate can be made of the amount of the obligation.

If these conditions are not met, no provision should be recognised.   (IAS 37)

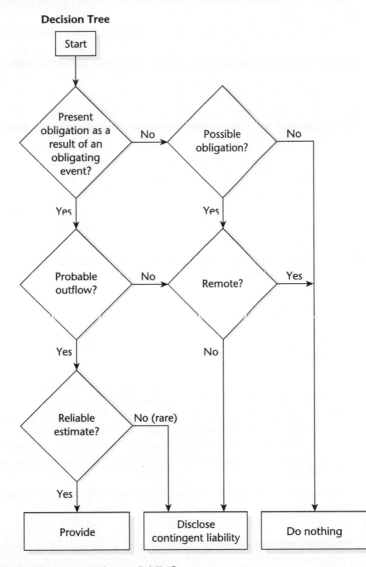

Figure 8.2 Provision or contingent liability?

Source: IAS 37

It is only those obligations arising from past events existing independently of an enterprise's future actions (i.e. the future conduct of its business) that are recognised as provisions. Common examples of provisions are doubtful debts, slow-moving and obsolete inventories, litigation, warranties on products, penalties or clean-up costs for unlawful environmental damage. Similarly, an enterprise recognises a provision for the decommissioning costs of an oil installation or a nuclear power station to the extent that the enterprise is obliged to rectify damage already caused. In contrast, because of commercial pressures or legal requirements, an enterprise may intend or need to carry out expenditure to operate in a particular way in the future (for example, by fitting smoke filters in a certain type of factory). Because the enterprise can avoid the future expenditure by its future actions, for example by changing its method of operation, it has no present obligation for that future expenditure and no provision is recognised.

An obligation always involves another party to whom the obligation is owed. It is not necessary, however, to know the identity of the party to whom the obligation is owed – indeed the obligation may be to the public at large. Because an obligation always involves a commitment to another party, it follows that a management or board decision does not give rise to a constructive obligation at the balance sheet date unless the decision has been communicated before the balance sheet date to those affected by it in a sufficiently specific manner to raise a valid expectation in them that the enterprise will discharge its responsibilities.

An event that does not give rise to an obligation immediately may do so at a later date, because of changes in the law or because an act (for example, a sufficiently specific public statement) by the enterprise gives rise to a constructive obligation. For example, when environmental damage is caused there may be no obligation to remedy the consequences. However, the causing of the damage will become an obligating event when a new law requires the existing damage to be rectified or when the enterprise publicly accepts responsibility for rectification in a way that creates a constructive obligation.

Provision versus accrued liabilities

Provisions can be distinguished from other liabilities such as trade payables and accruals because there is uncertainty about the timing or amount of the future expenditure required in settlement. By contrast:

(a) trade payables are liabilities to pay for goods or services that have been received or supplied and have been invoiced or formally agreed with the supplier; and

(b) accruals are liabilities to pay for goods or services that have been received or supplied but have not been paid, invoiced or formally agreed with the supplier, including amounts due to employees (for example, amounts relating to accrued vacation pay). Although it is sometimes necessary to estimate the amount or timing of accruals, the uncertainty is generally much less than for provisions.

Accruals are often reported as part of trade and other payables, whereas provisions are reported separately. (IAS 37)

Provision versus contingent liabilities

A contingent liability is a liability for which there is uncertainty simultaneously on causing principle, timing and amount. As the name implies, it is an obligation that is contingent (conditional) on events that are not entirely under the control of the enterprise. It is defined as:

(a) a possible obligation that arises from past events and whose existence will be confirmed only by an uncertain future event not wholly within the control of the enterprise; or

(b) *a present obligation that arises from past events but is not recognised because:*

     (i) *it is not probable that that obligation has to be settled; or*

     (ii) *the amount of the obligation cannot be measured with sufficient reliability.*   (IAS 37)

An enterprise should not recognise a contingent liability, but should only disclose it in the notes to financial statements (see Figure 8.2), unless the possibility of an outflow of resources embodying economic benefits is remote.

8.4   Accounting for income taxes

8.4.1   Differences between taxable profit and accounting profit

The first step in understanding how income taxes are accounted for in financial statements is to realise that taxable profit and accounting (or book) profit have different meanings. Taxable profit is computed in compliance with the tax legislation and is the basis upon which income taxes are paid. Accounting profit is computed using an enterprise's own accounting policies that comply with IAS/IFRS.

When determining taxable profit, an enterprise might be allowed or required by the tax code to use accounting methods that are different from those that comply with IAS/IFRS. The resulting differences might increase or decrease profits. For example, an enterprise might be allowed to use accelerated depreciation to compute taxable profit and so reduce its tax liability, while at the same time it uses straight-line depreciation in the determination of accounting profit in accordance with IAS/IFRS. Another example is tax rules often permit deduction of expenses (exchange losses, bad debts, losses on inventory) on a 'cash' basis and not on an accrual basis as required by IAS/IFRS.

The second step is to understand the difference between current taxes, deferred tax assets and liabilities, and income tax expense. Income tax expense is the expense reported in the income statement. Current taxes represent the income tax payable to tax authorities in accordance with the tax rules. The difference between the income tax expense and the amount currently payable to tax authorities represents deferred taxes as explained in the following example.

Example

Temporary and permanent differences between accounting profit and taxable profit

In the year just ended, GO.FRA.DE. SpA generated earnings from operations before depreciation and income taxes of EUR 6,000. In addition, it earned EUR 100 of tax-free municipal bond interest income. It has only two assets subject to depreciation: one machine that was purchased at the beginning of last year for EUR 5,000, and another one that was purchased at the beginning of this year for EUR 10,000. Both machines are being depreciated over 10 years. GO.FRA.DE. uses an accelerated method to compute depreciation for income tax purposes (worth EUR 3,000 this year) and the straight-line method to calculate depreciation for financial reporting purposes.

Based on the information provided, GO.FRA.DE.'s income tax return and income statement for the current year would be as follows (amounts in euros):

Income Tax Return		Income Statement	
Earnings from operations before depreciation and income taxes	6,000	Earnings from operations before depreciation and income taxes	6,000
Tax-free interest income[a]		Tax-free interest income	100
Depreciation	(3,000)	Depreciation[b]	(1,500)
Taxable profit	3,000	Pretax accounting profit	4,600
Income taxes payable to tax authorities (35% of 3,000)	1,050 →	Income tax expense * current 1,050 * deferred ????	????

a. Tax-free interest income is excluded from taxable profit.
b. (EUR 5,000 ÷ 10 years) + (EUR 10,000 ÷ 10 years) = EUR 1,500.

Based on the income tax return, the income tax that is owed to the government is EUR 1,050. The question is: what income tax expense should be reported in GO.FRA.DE.'s income statement? Is that EUR 1,610 (i.e. EUR 4,600 × 35%)?

Before answering let us look at the reasons why accounting profit and taxable profit are normally different:

- *Temporary differences* are those differences between accounting profit and taxable profit for an accounting period that arise whenever the measurement of assets and liabilities for income tax purposes differs from the measurement of assets and liabilities in accordance with IAS/IFRS. For example, if an enterprise uses the straight-line depreciation method for accounting purposes and accelerated depreciation for income tax purposes, the carrying value of the assets in the accounting records will differ from the tax carrying value of those assets. For income tax purposes, tax depreciation will be greater than book depreciation in the early years and lower than book depreciation in the later years.

- *Permanent differences* are those differences between accounting profit and taxable profit that arise when income is not taxed or expenses are not tax deductible. For example, tax-free interest income is not included in taxable income, even though it is part of the accounting profit. Fines paid for traffic offences are not a deductable expense for income tax purposes, although they are a business expense.

Permanent differences affect the current accounting period's effective income tax rate (the ratio of the reported income tax expense to pretax accounting profit), but do not have any impact on future income taxes. Temporary differences, on the other hand, affect the income taxes that will be paid in future years because they represent a deferral of taxable income from the current to subsequent accounting periods (or an acceleration of taxable income from the future into the current accounting period). Therefore, temporary differences do not affect an enterprise's effective income tax rate.

Now let us go back to the example of GO.FRA.DE and determine the deferred tax liability and income tax expense to be charged to the income statement.

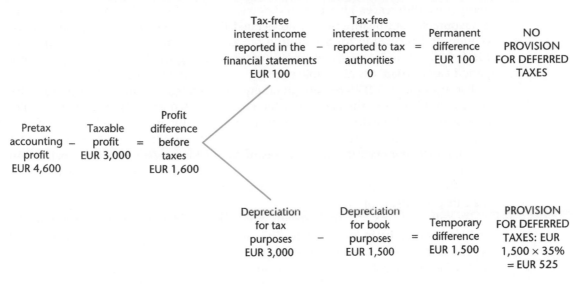

The difference of EUR 1,600 between pre-tax accounting profit and taxable profit consists of:

- EUR 100 of tax-free interest income that will never be taxed, but is included in the income statement. This is a permanent difference because this income is permanently excluded from taxation; the amount of tax that has to be paid now or in the future is zero.

- EUR 1,500. The difference between the accelerated depreciation (EUR 3,000) and the straight-line depreciation (EUR 1,500) is a temporary difference because the taxes that are saved in the current year are deferred to the future when the temporary differences reverse. Over the whole life of the equipment the total depreciation charge will be the same for income tax and book purposes. The amount of EUR 1,500 represents the difference in the amount of the total cost of the equipment that is allocated to this period by the two depreciation methods. The income statement has a lower depreciation cost than the tax return, which and will present a higher pretax income. This difference will reverse over time when the straight-line depreciation will be higher than the depreciation for tax purposes. To conclude, the income tax expense in the income statement would be EUR 1,575 (EUR 1,050 + EUR 525) and not EUR 1,610. Therefore the accounting equation would be affected as follows:

A	=	L	+	E
Cash – EUR 1,050	=	Deferred taxes liabilities + EUR 525		Profit – EUR 1,575 *(Current income tax expense: EUR 1,050 Deferred income tax expense: EUR 525)*

8.4.2 Deferred tax liabilities and deferred tax assets

Temporary differences give rise to deferred tax liabilities when they derive from a 'favourable' tax treatment (i.e. accelerated depreciation for tax purposes against economic depreciation for accounting purposes). A temporary difference will give rise to a deferred tax asset when an expense is recognised for book purposes in a period earlier than it is allowable or recognised for tax purposes.

For example, IAS/IFRS require an enterprise to charge estimated future warranty costs as an expense of the period in which the warranted goods are sold, but tax rules do not permit deducting such costs until they actually are incurred. So, a deferred tax asset would be recorded in an enterprise's financial statements. This means that an appliance manufacturer with increasing sales will show an increasing balance in a deferred tax asset account. This happens because (other things being equal) each period's lower warranty costs on its tax return will result in a taxable income higher than its accounting profit.

According to IAS 12, the carrying amount of a deferred tax asset should be reviewed at each balance sheet date. The carrying value of a deferred tax asset should be reduced to its net realisable value to the extent that it is no longer probable that sufficient taxable profit will be available to utilise the asset. Therefore, an asset should only be recognised when an enterprise expects to receive a benefit from its existence. The existence of deferred tax liability (to the same jurisdiction) is strong evidence that the asset will be recoverable.

Example

Deferred tax assets

Consider the following situations:

	Situation 1 EUR	Situation 2 EUR
Deferred tax liability	10,000	5,000
Deferred tax asset	(8,000)	(8,000)
Net position	**2,000**	**(3,000)**

- In situation 1 the existence of the liability ensures the recoverability of the asset, and the asset should be provided.
- In situation 2 the company would provide for EUR 5,000 of the asset but would need to consider carefully the recoverability of the remaining EUR 3,000.

Example

Deferred tax measurement

On 1 January 2000, Huskes Ltd purchased for EUR 1,200 a single depreciable asset. For tax purposes it is depreciated over three years while for financial reporting purposes it is depreciated over five years using a straight-line method with residual value of zero. There are no other differences between accounting and tax rules for this enterprise. Assume that its profit before depreciation and taxes is EUR 1 million each year and that the applicable tax rate is 40 per cent.

The next table shows how Huskes Ltd would calculate its income taxes to be paid to the tax authorities in each of the five years:

Year	Profit before depreciation and taxes	Depreciation charge	Taxable profit	Taxes due (at 40% rate)
1	EUR 1,000	EUR 400	EUR 600	EUR 240
2	EUR 1,000	EUR 400	EUR 600	EUR 240
3	EUR 1,000	EUR 400	EUR 600	EUR 240
4	EUR 1,000	-0-	EUR 1,000	EUR 400
5	EUR 1,000	-0-	EUR 1,000	EUR 400
	EUR 5,000	EUR 1,200	EUR 3,800	EUR 1,520

The next table shows the depreciation for tax purposes of the asset and its tax basis – balance of the asset account for tax purposes at the end of each year (amounts in thousands of euro):

Year	Original depreciable cost	Annual tax depreciation	Cumulative tax depreciation	Tax base
1	EUR 1,200	EUR 400	EUR 400	EUR 800
2	EUR 1,200	EUR 400	EUR 800	EUR 400
3	EUR 1,200	EUR 400	EUR 1,200	-0-
4	EUR 1,200	-0-	EUR 1,200	-0-
5	EUR 1,200	-0-	EUR 1,200	-0-

The next table presents the depreciation for accounting purposes and the net book value of the asset at the end of each year:

Year	Original accounting cost	Depreciation charge (straight-line depreciation method)	Accumulated depreciation	Net book value
1	EUR 1,200	EUR 240	EUR 240	EUR 960
2	EUR 1,200	EUR 240	EUR 480	EUR 720
3	EUR 1,200	EUR 240	EUR 720	EUR 480
4	EUR 1,200	EUR 240	EUR 960	EUR 240
5	EUR 1,200	EUR 240	EUR 1,200	-0-

The next table shows the calculation of the enterprise's deferred income taxes liability and deferred income tax expense using the balance sheet method:

Year	Net book value	Tax base	Net book value less tax base	Deferred tax liability (40%)	Deferred income taxes
1	EUR 960	EUR 800	EUR 160	EUR 64	EUR 64
2	EUR 720	EUR 400	EUR 320	EUR 128	EUR 64
3	EUR 480	-0-	EUR 480	EUR 192	EUR 64
4	EUR 240	-0-	EUR 240	EUR 96	EUR (96)
5	-0-	-0-	-0-	-0-	EUR (96)

In the next table, we show the impact of our calculations on the accounting equation for each of the five years (amounts in euro):

Year	A	=	L	+	E Profit
1	Cash: – 1,200 PPE: + 1,200	=	-0-		
	PPE: – 240	=			Depreciation: – 240
	Cash: – 240	=	Deferred tax liability: + 64		Deferred taxes: – 64 Current taxes: – 240
2	PPE: – 240	=			Depreciation: – 240
	Cash: – 240	=	Deferred tax liability: + 64		Deferred taxes: – 64 Current taxes: – 240
3	PPE: – 240	=			Depreciation: – 240
	Cash: – 240	=	Deferred tax liability: + 64		Deferred taxes: – 64 Current taxes: – 240
4	PPE: – 240	=			Depreciation: – 240
	Cash: – 400	=	Deferred tax liability: – 96		Deferred taxes: + 96 Current taxes: – 400
5	PPE: – 240	=			Depreciation: – 240
	Cash: – 400	=	Deferred tax liability: – 96		Deferred taxes: + 96 Current taxes: – 400

At the end of the life of the asset, the balance of the 'deferred tax liability' account is zero.

8.4.3 Tax rate changes

Up to now we have assumed that the tax rate would remain constant. What happens if income tax rates change? According to IAS 12, the balance in a deferred income tax account should be adjusted if a later change in the tax law changes the rates from those that were expected to apply. This adjustment affects accounting profit in the year in which the tax rate changes; the adjustment is a component of income tax expense as shown in the following example.

Example

Tax rate changes

	Carrying value EUR	Tax base EUR
PPE	460,000	320,000
Accrued interest:		
Receivable	18,000	-0-
Payable	(15,000)	-0-

The balance on the deferred tax account on 1 January 2004 was EUR 10,000. This was calculated at a tax rate of 30 per cent. During 2004 the government announced an unexpected increase in the level of corporate income tax up to 35 per cent.

Below, we illustrate the movement on the deferred tax account highlighting the charge to the income statement. In Note 1 we identify the part of the charge that is due to an increase in the rate of taxation.

	Deferred tax liability EUR	
Deferred tax liability as at 1 January 2004	10,000	
Income statement – rate change	1,667	
Opening balance restated ($10,000 \times 35/30$)	11,667	
Income statement – origination of temporary differences (balancing figure)	38,383	
Deferred tax liability as at 31 December 2004	50,050	**(See Note 1)**

(Note 1)	Carrying value EUR	Tax base EUR	Temporary difference EUR
PPE	460,000	320,000	140,000
Accrued interest:			
Receivable	18,000	-0-	18,000
Payable	(15,000)	-0-	(15,000)

Deferred tax liability [$35\% \times (140,000 + 18,000)$]	EUR 55,300
Deferred tax asset ($35\% \times 15,000$)	(EUR 5,250)
Deferred tax liability at 35%	EUR 50,050

Activity 8.1 Effect of a change in the tax rate

Lipreaders Company has a temporary difference of EUR 90 million, resulting in a deferred tax liability of EUR 30.6 million.

Question:

What is the impact of a decrease in the tax rate on deferred taxes and net profit? Choose the correct answer (A, B, C or D) and explain the reasons for your choice.

	Deferred taxes	Net profit
(A)	Increase	No effect
(B)	Decrease	Increase
(C)	No effect	No effect
(D)	No effect	Decrease

Solutions to activities can be found at www.pearsoned.co.uk/kothari

8.5   Ratios relating to liabilities

Debt ratios

An important aspect in the assessment of an enterprise's financial position is its capital structure and the way in which this is viewed by providers of finance.

Capital gearing or leverage is the relationship between borrowed capital and owners' equity.

The relationship between internal and external sources of finance (i.e. equity and liabilities) can be expressed as a percentage or a ratio: the debt to equity ratio:

$$\text{Debt-to-equity ratio} = \frac{\text{Liabilities}}{\text{Total owners' equity}}$$

The liabilities included in the numerator are non-current liabilities. Instead of using non-current liabilities, some companies use the net total borrowings (i.e. total liabilities *less* cash and cash equivalents *less* short-term financial assets).

This ratio has practical implications, as lending agreements usually include covenants which restrict maximum allowable debt-to-equity levels, where equity refers to the book value amount disclosed on the company's balance sheet.

An easier and perhaps more practical means of interpreting a company's gearing is provided by the debt ratio (also known as debt-to-total asset ratio):

$$\text{Debt ratio} = \frac{\text{Total liabilities}}{\text{Total assets}}$$

The higher the ratio the higher the gearing. A ratio of 50 per cent, commonly viewed as the limit for accepting without question a company's level of gearing, indicates that for every EUR 1 of assets EUR 0.50 has been financed by current and non-current liabilities.

Interest cover ratio

Interest paid on debt is charged as an expense before arriving at the profit for the year attributable to shareholders. An increase in external borrowings brings higher gearing and a higher interest charge in the income statement. Once a loan is taken, the interest payments must be made in cash, and the capital sum repaid on the agreed date. An enterprise not generating enough profit to cover interest payments or having insufficient cash available to repay the loan faces serious liquidity problems.

An effective ratio for combining profitability with the impact of gearing is interest cover. This measures the ability of an enterprise to generate sufficient profits to allow all interest on borrowings to be paid. It is calculated by dividing the EBIT (earnings before interest and tax) by the interest expense for the year:

$$\text{Interest cover ratio} = \frac{\text{EBIT}}{\text{Interest expenses}}$$

The higher the interest cover, the lower the risk that there will be insufficient profit available for payment of dividends to shareholders.

Activity 8.2 adidas-Salomon's leverage

Refer to Table 3.1 – Consolidated balance sheet of adidas-Salomon as at 31 December 2004 and Table 4.3 – adidas-Salomon income statement for 2004.

Questions:

1. Determine debt-to-equity ratio and debt ratio at the end of 2003 and 2004. Had they improved over the period considered?

2. Determine the interest cover ratio and explain its trend in comparison to debt-to-equity ratio.

Solutions to activities can be found at www.pearsoned.co.uk/kothari

Summary

- A liability is a present obligation of the enterprise arising from past events, the settlement of which is expected to result in an outflow from the enterprise of resources embodying economic benefits.

- Liabilities are distinguished between current and non-current. Among non-current liabilities, there are bonds. They may be issued at par value, at a discount and at a premium.

- Provisions can be distinguished from other liabilities because there is uncertainty about the timing or amount of the future expenditure required to be settled. Contingent liabilities are not recognised in the balance sheet because their existence will be confirmed only by the occurrence or non-occurrence of an uncertain future event. Contingent liabilities should be disclosed in the notes to the financial statements.

- There are some transactions that are reported differently for accounting and tax purposes. This causes a difference between accounting profit (before tax) and taxable profit. This difference can be permanent or temporary. Permanent differences do not require any provision for deferred income taxes; temporary differences require to account for deferred income taxes – liabilities or assets.

- The debt-to-equity ratio expresses the relationship between external and internal sources of finance. It is determined by dividing debt by equity. It is one of the critical ratios used by the business and financial community.

- Interest cover ratio is determined by dividing the EBIT by the interest expense for the year.

References and research

The IASB documents relevant for this chapter are:

- Framework for the preparation and presentation of financial statements
- IAS 1 – *Presentation of Financial Statements*
- IAS 12 – *Income Taxes*
- IAS 37 – *Provisions, Contingent Liabilities and Contingent Assets*

The following are examples of books that take the issues of this chapter further:

- Robert N. Anthony, David F. Hawkins and Kenneth A. Merchant, *Accounting: Text and Cases*, McGraw-Hill, 1999, Chapter 8
- Barry Elliott and Jamie Elliott, *Financial Accounting and Reporting*, 9th Edition, Financial Times-Prentice Hall, 2005, Chapters 12 and 15
- Charles T. Horngren, Gary L. Sundem and John A. Elliott, *Introduction to Financial Accounting*, Pearson Education-Prentice Hall, 2002, Chapter 8
- Hennie Van Greuning, *International Financial Reporting Standards: A Practical Guide*, The World Bank, 2005, Chapters 14 and 23

8.1 (a) Distinguish between current liabilities and non-current liabilities. Name and briefly describe three items belonging to each category.

(b) Why do the income taxes charged to an income statement not equal the profit multiplied by the current rate of income tax?

(c) At the balance sheet date, a private high school has lost a court case for an uninsured football injury. The amount of damages has not been set. A reasonable estimate is between EUR 500,000 (minimum) and EUR 900,000 (maximum). How should this information be presented or accounted for in the financial statements?

(d) Why would a lender want to add a covenant to a loan contract concerning a maximum debt-to-total assets ratio?

8.2 Suppose that on 1 October 2004 Viaggimmagine SpA, an Italian tour operator, issued bonds for EUR 1 million, at an interest rate of 5 per cent per annum, with semiannual interest payments, to be redeemed on 30 September 2015.

(a) Using the accounting equation, prepare a summary of the issuance of the bonds assuming that they were issued at:
- par value
- a discount of EUR 10,000
- a premium of EUR 50,000.

(b) Using the accounting equation, summarise the issuance of the first two semiannual interest payments.

(c) What should you account for at 31 December 2004? Why?

(d) How do you account for the redemption at 30 September 2015?

8.3 (a) The Mighty Mouse Trap Company has just started to export mouse traps to the US. The advertising slogan for the mouse traps is, 'A girl's best friend.' The Utopian Liberation Movement is claiming EUR 800,000 from the company because the advertising slogan allegedly compromises the dignity of women. The company's legal representatives are of the opinion that the success of the claim will depend on the judge, who presides over the case. They estimate, however, that there is a 70 per cent probability that the claim will be thrown out and a 30 per cent chance that it will succeed.

(b) Boss Ltd specialises in the design and manufacture of an exclusive sports car. During the current financial year, 90 sports cars were produced and sold. During the testing of the sports car, a serious defect was found in its steering mechanism.

All 90 customers were informed by way of a letter of the defect and were required to return their cars to have the defect repaired at no charge. The estimated cost of the recall amounts to EUR 900,000.

Would you make any provision in these two situations? Why?

8.4   The following information relates to Terril Co as at 31 December 2004:

	Carrying value EUR	Tax base EUR
Non-current assets		
Property, plant and equipment	200,000	175,000
Receivables		
Trade receivables (*)	50,000	
Interest receivable	1,000	
Payables		
Fine	10,000	
Interest payable	2,000	

(*) The trade receivables balance in the accounts is made up of the following amounts:

	EUR
Trade receivables	55,000
Doubtful debt provision	(5,000)
	50,000

Further information:

1. The deferred tax balance as at 1 January 2004 was EUR 1,200.
2. Interest is taxed on a cash basis.
3. Provisions for doubtful debts are not deductible for tax purposes.
4. Fines are not tax deductible.

Calculate the deferred tax provision which is required at 31 December 2004 and the charge for income taxes to the income statement for 2004.

8.5   Trevelyan was incorporated on 1 January 2004. On 10 January, equipment for EUR 48,000 and motor vehicles for EUR 12,000 were acquired. In the year ended 31 December 2004 the enterprise made a profit before taxation of EUR 121,000. This figure was after a depreciation charge of EUR 11,000. For tax purposes, the depreciation was EUR 15,000 (25 per cent of the original cost). Corporate tax rate was of 30 per cent.

(a) Calculate the income tax liability for the year ended 31 December 2004.
(b) Calculate the deferred tax balance to be recorded in the balance sheet as at 31 December 2004.
(c) Prepare a note showing the movement on the deferred tax account and thus calculate the deferred tax charge for the year ended 31 December 2004.
(d) Prepare the income statement note which shows the computation of the tax expense for the year ended 31 December 2004.
(e) Prepare a note which reconciles accounting profit multiplied by the applicable tax rate and the tax expense.
(f) Prepare a balance sheet note showing the movement on deferred tax in respect of each type of temporary differences.

8.6   Refer to Table 3.8 (on page 59) – Consolidated balance sheet of Puma as at 31 December 2004.

(a) Determine debt-to-equity ratio and debt ratio.

(b) Compare them with adidas-Salomon's (see Activity 8.2) and comment on the differences found.

Case study   Difir Inc and deferred taxes

Difir Inc owns the following property, plant and equipment at 1 January 2004 (amounts in thousands of euro):

	Cost	Accumulated depreciation	Carrying value	Tax base
Machinery	900	180	720	450
Land	500	–	500	–
Buildings	1,500	300	1,200	–

You are provided with further information in order to determine the deferred tax balance for 2004 and 2005:

- Machinery is depreciated on the straight-line basis over five years. It was acquired at the beginning of 2003.

- Land is not depreciated.

- Buildings are depreciated on the straight-line basis over 25 years.

- Depreciation of office buildings is not deductible for tax purposes. For machinery, tax depreciation is granted over a period of three years in the ratio of 50/30/20 (per cent) of cost, consecutively.

- The accounting profit before tax was EUR 300,000 for the 2004 financial year and EUR 400,000 for 2005. These figures include non-taxable revenue of EUR 80,000 in 2004 and EUR 100,000 in 2005.

- Difir Inc had a tax loss for the financial year ended 31 December 2003 of EUR 250,000.

- The tax rate for 2003 was 35 per cent, and for 2004 and 2005 it was 30 per cent.

9 Owners' equity

9.1 Introduction

In Part two we have described transactions affecting assets and liabilities. Now we will examine owners' equity in more detail.

Recall the basic accounting equation:

$$
\begin{aligned}
(1) \qquad \text{Assets} &= \text{Liabilities} + \text{Owners' equity} \\
\text{Capital deployed} &= \text{Capital sources}
\end{aligned}
$$

We can re-express this equation as follows:

$$
\begin{aligned}
(2) \qquad \text{Assets} - \text{Liabilities} &= \text{Owners' equity} \\
\text{Net capital deployed} &= \text{Owners' capital}
\end{aligned}
$$

Equation (1) focuses on an enterprise's assets. Capital sources (debt and shareholder financing) are lumped together. The enterprise's assets are considered to drive economic performance, so an enterprise is considered to represent the capital deployed

– the assets themselves. Who provided those assets (creditors versus shareholders) is of secondary importance.

The focus of the accounting equation (2) is on shareholders. In fact, this view isolates the capital provided by owners. In this perspective – known as proprietary view – the enterprise is considered to be the owners' equity investment. This view greatly influences income measurement. To see why, consider the basic accounting principle that income can be earned (or expenses incurred) only through transaction between an enterprise and outsiders. But who is inside an enterprise and who are the outsiders? Under the proprietary view, the enterprise and its owners are the same. Consequently, no income (or loss) can arise from transactions between the enterprise and its owners, because owners are not outsiders. This perspective explains why interest payments to banks or bondholders are expenses that reduce income, while dividend payments to ordinary and preferred shareholders represent distribution of profits and not expenses. Banks and bondholders are outsiders – hence, interest costs are expenses. Shareholders are not outsiders – thus, dividends are a distribution of profits to owners, not an expense of the company.

The proprietary view helps us understand why certain financing transactions generate income or losses, while other transactions do not.

9.2   Components of the owners' equity

In this section we will briefly discuss the characteristics of the several legal forms of enterprises, sole traderships, partnerships and companies (refer also to section 1.2), in order to describe the accounting treatment of owners' equity in each form.

9.2.1   Owners' equity in sole traderships

An enterprise owned by an individual is a sole tradership or sole proprietorship. This is a simple form of business organisation.

As regards the accounting for sole tradership not much more need be said than the comments made in Chapters 3 and 4 (see Paolo's enterprise). The following example illustrates the owners' equity accounts in a sole tradership with particular emphasis on the capital and drawing accounts.

Example

Owners' equity in a sole tradership

On 1 April 2004, Anthony Gold decided to set up in business as a jeweller. He introduced EUR 50,000 which was put in a bank account. He took an 18-month lease of a shop and employed a part time assistant, Anne Silver.

The business grew steadily over the first year, and in April 2005 Anthony Gold delivered his books and records to his accountant so that his accounts could be prepared.

The equity section of the balance sheet as at 31 March 2005 is as follows:

Capital introduced	50,000
Net profit for the year	307,920
	357,920
Deduct Drawings	(217,920)
	140,000

Capital introduced – Note that the money paid into the business bank account by Anthony Gold is shown in the balance sheet as capital introduced.

Capital introduced can also take the form of other assets introduced by the business owner, e.g. equipment already owned by the individual which is to be used in his business. In this case the asset should be stated at a value appropriate to its conditions when introduced to the business, i.e. its second-hand value.

Drawings – A sole trader will usually have to take money from his business bank account to enable him to pay his personal living costs. These are his personal drawings which reduce the amount of equity.

Profit – In a sole tradership, the profit (or loss) for the year belongs to the sole trader, or owner. In fact, this is shown as a part of the owners' capital account or owners' equity.

At the end of the financial year, Anthony Gold's capital account balance represents the original capital contributed by him plus accumulated profits not withdrawn by him, i.e. net profit less drawings.

9.2.2 Owners' equity in partnerships

Often several people may wish to combine and operate in business together. There are many reasons for wishing to do so, e.g. combining expertise or capital, or sharing the risks involved. The persons involved may well join forces in a partnership. (Alternatively they could form a limited company.) To operate as a partnership, a formal partnership agreement should be drawn up. This will include such matters as how partners will share profits and losses. In the absence of a specific agreement, in most jurisdictions the law assumes that net income is to be divided among the partners proportionally to the capital contributed.

Partnership agreements may also provide that the partners receive stated salaries and a stated share of residual profit after salaries, or a stated percentage of interest on the capital they have contributed and a stated share of residual profit, or a combination of salary and interest. Whatever the partnership arrangement, the law does not in general regard salaries or interest payments to the partners as different from any other type of drawings, as the partnership is not an entity legally separate from the individual partners.

A partnership operates in a very similar way to a sole tradership, the difference being that instead of one individual owning and running the business and earning the profits (losses), two or more people are involved. Therefore, accounting for the transactions of a partnership is similar to accounting for the transactions of a sole trader. However, instead of having only one capital account (as in a sole trader's accounts), each partner will have a capital account in the partnership accounts.

Example

Owners' equity in a partnership

On 1 April 2005, Anthony Gold and Anne Silver decided to go into partnership. Anthony Gold contributed a further EUR 60,000 to his original investment of EUR 140,000 and Anne Silver contributed EUR 50,000 to the enterprise.

As we now have two owners of the enterprise we must set up a capital account for Anne Silver, illustrated as follows:

	A	= L +		E
	Cash and		Anthony Gold	Anne Silver
	cash equivalents		Capital account	Capital account
Op.bal.			EUR 140,000	
	+ EUR 110,000	=	+ EUR 60,000	+ EUR 50,000

The total capital amounts to EUR 250,000. Anthony contributed EUR 200,000 (4/5 or 80 per cent of the total) and Anne EUR 50,000 (1/5 or 20 per cent). They will share the net profit (loss) according to these proportions.

As the year progresses each partner's drawings will be recorded in his/her drawings account. The partners' respective shares of profit will be added to their accounts at the year-end.

Considering that during the year ended 31 March 2006, the profit made was EUR 200,000 and that Anthony Gold and Anne Silver withdrew EUR 120,000 and 20,000 respectively, the equity section of the balance sheet as at 31 March 2006 will be as follows:

Anthony Gold – Capital account	EUR
Opening balance	140,000
Additional capital introduced	60,000
Net profit for the year (4/5 of 200,000)	160,000
	360,000
Deduct Drawings	(120,000)
	240,000
Anne Silver	
Capital introduced	50,000
Net profit for the year (1/5 of 200,000)	40,000
	90,000
Deduct Drawings	(20,000)
	70,000

9.2.3 Owners' equity in limited liability companies

Sole traders and partners are personally liable for the debts of the business. If there are insufficient assets available in the enterprise to pay the liabilities the creditors will have recourse to all the personal assets of the proprietors.

In the European Union countries, company law allows a business to be incorporated with the liability of the owners limited to the amounts they have contributed, or have subscribed or agreed to contribute, as share capital. If there are insufficient assets available in the company to pay its liabilities the owners' personal assets cannot be touched.

Companies vary considerably in size from the small private company where the owners (the shareholders) are those actually involved in running the business, to the large public company. Small private companies are generally run by the owners or shareholders of the company, whereas large public companies are usually run by professional managers called directors who may or may not own shares in the company.

The capital of a limited liability company is divided into a number of shares having a certain nominal (par) value. The owners of the shares (the shareholders) are therefore the owners of the company.

Example

Owners' equity in limited liability companies

Assume that ABC Ltd incorporates and issues 5,000 ordinary shares having a par value of EUR 50 each. The accounting equation would be as follows:

A	= L +	E
Cash and cash equivalents		Capital – ordinary shares
+ EUR 250,000	=	+ EUR 250,000

As the company starts trading, the money in the bank will be used to buy other assets and pay for expenses. Income will be generated and liabilities will be incurred. If at the end of the first year the company has generated EUR 75,000 profit, this will be reflected by an increase in the net assets, i.e. non-current assets (tangible and intangible fixed assets), and current assets (trade receivables, payables, inventory, cash and cash equivalents).

The balance sheet of ABC Ltd will now show:

Net assets	EUR	325,000
Capital – ordinary shares	EUR	250,000
Retained earnings	EUR	75,000
	EUR	325,000

The share capital of EUR 250,000 and the retained earnings are backed by the net assets of EUR 325,000. Thus each share of EUR 50 effectively represents net assets of EUR 65. If the company now issues more shares, it is unlikely to sell them for EUR 50 – they are now worth more. As a result of various other factors they may well be worth rather more than the book asset value of EUR 65.

Let us suppose that after five years, ABC Ltd, which in the meanwhile has been a successful business, asks its shareholders to pay in more capital. It issues 3,000 new shares (par value of EUR 50) at EUR 150. The EUR 50 par value per share bears no relationship to the market value of the shares. The difference between the issue price of EUR 150 and the par value of EUR 50 represents the premium on the shares.

Let us look at the effects of this transaction on the accounting equation.

	A	= L +		E
	Cash and		Capital –	Reserves
	cash equivalents		ordinary shares	(share premium)
	+ EUR 450,000	=	+ EUR 150,000	+ EUR 300,000

Suppose that seven years later ABC Ltd buys back 2,000 of these shares at a cost of EUR 60 each. When a company buys back its own shares, the repurchased shares are called treasury shares (or treasury stock) and represent a reduction of equity.

	A	= L +		E
	Cash and			Treasury
	cash equivalents			shares
	– EUR 120,000	=		– EUR 120,000

Notice that share repurchases do not involve accounting gains and losses as they are transactions between the company and its owners (the shareholders).

Now let us say ABC Ltd decides to raise more equity capital by reselling all 2,000 treasury shares several months later at EUR 65 per share.

	A	= L +		E	
	Cash and			Treasury	Reserves
	cash equivalents			shares	
	+ EUR 130,000	=		+ EUR 120,000	+ EUR 10,000

Companies are prompted to buy back their own shares when they are cash rich and share price remains low from the directors' point of view. The main arguments for purchasing their own shares are:

- to reduce the cost of capital when equity costs more than debt
- the shares are undervalued
- to return surplus cash to shareholders.

Ordinary shares, as the name implies, are the most basic and common type of shares. There is no fixed rate of dividend, and ordinary shareholders will receive a dividend only if profits available for distribution still remain after other investors (lenders and preference shareholders) have received their interest or dividend payments. If the business is closed down, the ordinary shareholders will receive any remaining proceeds from asset disposals only after lenders and creditors and, in some cases, after preference shareholders have received their entitlements.

Ordinary shareholders have voting rights, which give them the power to elect the directors and to remove them from office. They may enjoy/earn high returns (dividends) in proportion to the risk they take.

A company does not generally obtain any tax relief on dividends paid to shareholders, whereas interest on borrowings is tax deductible.

Preference shares offer investors a lower level of risk than ordinary shares. They offer owners different rights and preferential treatment. They do not usually have voting rights, but they do have a preferred claim on assets. In fact, provided that there are sufficient profits available, preference shares will normally be entitled to a fixed rate of dividend each year, and preference dividends will be paid before ordinary ones.

In summary, preference shareholders take a lower risk and their financial reward is in proportion to their risk.

Table 9.1 Illustration of the statement of changes in equity [IAS 1]

XYZ GROUP – STATEMENT OF CHANGES IN EQUITY FOR THE YEAR ENDED 31 DECEMBER 2004
(in thousands of currency units)

	Attributable to equity holders of the parent					Minority interest	Total equity
	Share capital	Other reserves	Translation reserve	Retained earnings	Total		
Balance at 31 December 2003	X	X	(X)	X	X	X	X
Changes in accounting policy				(X)	(X)	(X)	(X)
Restated balance	X	X	(X)	X	X	X	X
Changes in equity for 2004							
Gain on property revaluation		X			X	X	X
Available-for-sale investments:							
Valuation gains/(losses) taken to equity		(X)			(X)		(X)
Transferred to profit or loss on sale		(X)			(X)		(X)
Cash flow hedges:							
Gains/(losses) taken to equity		X			X	X	X
Transferred to profit or loss for the period		X			X	X	X
Transferred to initial carrying amount of hedged items		(X)			(X)		(X)
Exchange differences on translating foreign operations			(X)		(X)	(X)	(X)
Tax on items taken directly to or transferred from equity		(X)	X		(X)	(X)	(X)
Net income recognised directly in equity		(X)	(X)		(X)	(X)	(X)
Profit for the period				X	X	X	X
Total recognised income and expense for the period		(X)	(X)	X	X	X	X
Dividends		(X)	(X)	(X)	(X)	(X)	(X)
Issue of share capital	X				X		X
Balance at 31 December 2004	X	X	(X)	X	X	X	X

Source: After IAS 1

Preference shares are no longer an important source of finance.

A major reason for this is that dividends paid to preference shareholders are not allowable against taxable profits, whereas interest on loan capital is an allowable expense.

From the business's point of view, preference shares and loans are quite similar, and so the tax deductibility of loan interest is an important issue.

9.3   Statement of changes in shareholders' equity

A statement of changes in equity should be presented along with the other financial statements. The reason for including this statement in the annual report is that a number of gains and losses are either permitted or required by law or accounting standards to be dealt with directly through reserves. This means that financial statements would be incomplete if they stopped at the retained earnings figure without giving the shareholders information about other changes in their equity. As you can see from Table 9.1, the statement includes all gains and losses for the period and not just those that have passed through the income statement.

As you can see from Table 9.2 (on the following page) , in 2003 and 2004 neither ordinary nor preference shares were issued by Henkel. It is for this reason that ordinary shares and preferred shares accounts are unchanged, as well as capital reserve (also known as share premium reserve).

Revenue reserves include, among other things, the accumulated profits of previous years (Henkel calls them unappropriated profits). They also include changes due to the evaluation of investments in other enterprises with the equity method (as we will see in section 11.6) and may also include the effect of changes in accounting policies.

Other gains and losses such as the differences on translation of the annual financial statements of foreign subsidiaries and the effects of the revaluation of financial instruments (classified as non-current assets) are taken to equity without passing through the income statement, as we will explain in Chapter 11.

9.4   Ratios relating to equity

Earnings per share (EPS)

Shareholders use the reported EPS to estimate future growth which will affect the future share price. It is an important measure of growth over time. However, as we will better explain in Chapter 16, there are limitations in its use as a performance measure and for inter-company comparison:

$$EPS = \frac{Earnings}{Weighted\ number\ of\ ordinary\ shares}$$

IAS 33 requires two EPS figures for disclosure, namely:

- **basic EPS** based on ordinary shares currently in issue
- **diluted EPS** based on ordinary shares currently in issue *plus* potential ordinary shares.

Table 9.2 Statement of changes in equity: an example

in millions of euro	Ordinary shares	Preferred shares	Capital reserves	Revenue reserves	Unappro-priated profit	Gains and losses recognized in equity		Total
						Translation differences	Derivative financial instruments	
At January 1, 2003	**222**	**152**	**652**	**2,510**	**156**	**-405**	**-8**	**3,279**
Distributions				–	-156	–	–	-156
Earnings after minority interests				–	519	–	–	519
Allocations to reserves				352	-352	–	–	–
Foreign exchange effects				–	–	-268	–	-268
Derivative financial instruments				–	–	–	11	11
Other changes taken to equity				-74	–	–	–	-74
At Dec. 31, 2003/Jan. 1, 2004	**222**	**152**	**652**	**2,788**	**167**	**-673**	**3**	**3,311**
Distributions					-167			-167
Earnings after minority interests					1,735			1,735
Allocations to reserves				1,550	-1,550			
Foreign exchange effects						-322		-322
Derivative financial instruments							10	10
Other changes taken to equity				21				21
At December 31, 2004	**222**	**152**	**652**	**4,359**	**185**	**-995**	**13**	**4,588**

Source: Henkel Group Annual Report 2004

Example

Basic EPS calculation

Assume that XYZ plc had a net profit for 2004 of EUR 1,250,000 and an issued share capital of EUR 1,500,000 comprising 1,000,000 ordinary shares of EUR 0.50 each and 10 per cent 1,000,000 preference shares of EUR 1 each.

In order to determine the basic EPS for 2004 for XYZ plc, we need to deduct preference dividends (EUR 100,000) from net profit (EUR 1,250,000). The difference, EUR 1,150,000, represents the profit for the period attributable to ordinary shareholders. Therefore,

Basic EPS = EUR 1,150,000 ÷ 1,000,000 shares = **EUR 1.15**

In a modern corporate structure, a number of classes of persons such as the holders of convertible bonds, the holders of convertible preference shares, members of share option schemes and share warrant holders may be entitled as at the date of the balance sheet to become equity shareholders at a future date. If these people exercise their entitlements at a future date, the EPS would be reduced or diluted, as shown in the following example. The effect on future share price could be significant.

Example

Diluted EPS calculation

Assume that XYZ plc had a net profit for 2004 of EUR 1,250,000 and an issued share capital of EUR 1,500,000 comprising 1,000,000 ordinary shares of EUR 0.50 each and 1,000,000 convertible 8 per cent preference shares of EUR 1, convertible at one ordinary share for every five convertible preference shares in 2006.

Below, we illustrate how to determine the basic and diluted EPS for 2004 for XYZ plc.

	Earnings	Shares EUR	EPS EUR
Net profit for 2004	1,150,000		
Weighted average ordinary shares during 2004		1,000,000	
Basic EPS (EUR 1,150,000 ÷ 1,000,000)			1.15
Number of shares resulting from conversion		200,000	
Add back preference dividend paid in 2004	80,000		
Adjusted earnings and number of shares	1,230,000	1,200,000	
Diluted EPS (EUR 1,230,000 ÷ 1,200,000)			**1.025**

Return on equity (ROE)

This ratio is one of the most important in measuring the performance of an enterprise. It addresses the question: how effectively does the enterprise use the resources invested by its owners? It is given by:

$$ROE = \frac{\text{Net profit}}{\text{Owners' equity}}$$

Basic earnings per share are calculated by dividing the net income attributable to shareholders by the weighted average number of shares outstanding during the year.

Dilutive potential shares have arisen under the Management Share Option Plan (MSOP) of adidas-Salomon AG, which was implemented in 1999. As none of the required performance criteria for the exercise of the stock options of Tranche I (1999) of the share option plan have been fulfilled to date, this Tranche did not affect the calculation of dilutive earnings per share. However under Tranches II (2000), III (2001) and IV (2002) of the share option plan, dilutive potential shares impact the diluted earnings per share calculation.

It is necessary to include dilutive potential shares arising from the convertible bond issuance in October 2003 in the calculation of diluted earnings per share as at December 31, 2004 as the required conversion criteria were fulfilled at the balance sheet date. The convertible bond is assumed to have been converted into ordinary shares and the net income is adjusted to eliminate the interest expense less the tax effect.

Earnings Per Share

	Year ending 2004	December 31 2003
Net income (thousands of euro)	314,248	260,085
Weighted number of shares outstanding	45,649,560	45,452,361
Basic earnings per share (euro)	**6.88**	**5.72**
Net income (thousands of euro)	314,248	260,085
Interest expense on convertible bond (net of taxes) (thousands of euro)	10,464	0
Net income used to determine diluted earnings per share (thousands of euro)	**324,712**	**260,085**
Weighted number of shares outstanding	45,649,560	45,452,361
Weighted share options	98,217	17,005
Assumed conversion convertible bond	3,921,569	0
Weighted number of shares for diluted earnings per share	**49,669,346**	**45,469,366**
Diluted earnings per share (euro)	**6.54**	**5.72**

Figure 9.1 Earnings per share: an example
Source: adidas-Salomon Annual Report 2004

Activity 9.1 shows the calculation of ROE for adidas-Salomon for 1998–2004.

Activity 9.1 Changes in ROE

From the 2004 annual report of adidas-Salomon (summary of key financial data), we get the following information for 1998–2004 (amounts in millions of euro):

	1998	1999	2000	2001	2002	2003	2004
Net income (millions of euro)	205	228	182	208	229	260	314
Equity (millions of euro)	463	680	815	1,015	1,081	1,356	1,628
Net total borrowings (millions of euro)	1,655	1,591	1,791	1,679	1,498	946	594
Interest cover ratio	4.8	6.1	4.6	4.9	6.4	8.4	10.0
ROE	44.2%	33.5%	22.3%	20.5%	21.1%	19.2%	19.3%

Question:

Despite the increase of both net income and shareholders' equity over the period 1998–2004, ROE decreased. Explain the possible reasons for this.

Solutions to activities can be found at www.pearsoned.co.uk/kothari

Summary

- The names of the components of equity change according to the characteristics of the different legal forms of enterprises, sole tradership, partnership and companies.

- The issued capital of limited liability companies may be formed by several classes of shares. The main classes are ordinary shares and preference shares.

- The amount of equity changes over time due: (i) to profits not distributed (known as retained earnings) or losses made by the enterprise (ii) to payment of dividends to shareholders (iii) to the issue of new capital, etc. All these changes are shown in the statement of changes in shareholders' equity.

- EPS and ROE are two principal ratios relating to equity. EPS is determined by dividing earnings by the weighted number of ordinary shares, while ROE is determined by dividing net earnings by shareholders' equity.

References and research

The IASB documents relevant for this chapter are IAS 1 – *Presentation of Financial Statements* and IAS 33 – *Earnings per Share.*

The following are examples of books that take the issues of this chapter further:

- Robert N. Anthony, David F. Hawkins and Kenneth A. Merchant, *Accounting: Text and Cases,* McGraw-Hill, 1999, Chapter 9
- Barry Elliott and Jamie Elliott, *Financial Accounting and Reporting,* 9th Edition, Financial Times-Prentice Hall, 2005, Chapters 8 and 26
- Charles T. Horngren, Gary L. Sundem and John A. Elliott, *Introduction to Financial Accounting,* Pearson Education-Prentice Hall, 2002, Chapter 11
- Hennie Van Greuning, *International Financial Reporting Standards: A Practical Guide,* The World Bank, 2005, Chapters 1 and 36
- Frank Wood and Alan Sangster, *Business Accounting,* Vol. 2, 9th Edition, Financial Times-Prentice Hall, 2002, Part 2

Questions

9.1   (a)   Ordinary shareholders have limited liabilities. Explain.

(b)   'Treasury shares are unissued shares.' Do you agree?

(c)   In what way are preference shares similar to debt and to ordinary shares?

(d)   'A company's return on equity (ROE) indicates how much return an investor makes on the investment in the company's shares.' Do you agree? Why?

9.2   (a)   'When companies repurchase their own shares, the accounting depends on the purpose for which the shares are repurchased.' Explain.

(b) 'When a company retires shares, it must pay the shareholders an amount equal to the original par value and additional capital contributed for those shares plus the shareholders' fractional portion of retained earnings.' Do you agree? Why?

(c) Why might a company decide to buy back its own shares instead of paying additional cash dividends?

(d) Are treasury shares an asset? Explain.

(e) Gains and losses are not possible from a company's acquiring or selling its own shares. Do you agree? Why?

9.3 Two recent business school graduates, Alexander and Andrea, started a shop called Infinitum Exports on 1 January 2004. Their partnership agreement stipulated that each would receive 10 per cent interest on capital contributed and that they would share equally any net income in excess of this 10 per cent payment. Alexander had contributed EUR 50,000 and Andrea EUR 70,000. They also agreed that Alexander, who could devote only part time to the venture, would receive a salary of EUR 15,000 while Andrea would receive EUR 40,000. Net income for the first year (after deducting both partners' salaries) was EUR 66,000.

(a) What was each partner's total income (including salaries) from the enterprise?

(b) Analyse the impact of the transactions just mentioned, on the accounting equation.

9.4 On 31 December 2004, the shareholders' equity section of the balance sheet of XYZ was as follows:

Capital issued – ordinary shares 1,000,000 at EUR 5 par	EUR	5,000,000
Share premium reserve	EUR	20,000,000
Retained earnings	EUR	75,000,000
Total equity	*EUR*	*100,000,000*

At the shareholders' general meeting that took place in April 2005, dividends for EUR 10 million were declared. Moreover, it was decided to issue new shares for EUR 12 million by way of a bonus issue (i.e. by converting share premium reserve into share capital).

(a) How would the shareholders' equity section be affected?

(b) Show also the impact on the accounting equation of these transactions.

9.5 Refer to Table 3.8 – Consolidated balance sheet of Puma as at 31 December 2004 and Table 4.4 – Puma management income statement for 2004.

(a) Determine Puma's ROE for 2003 and 2004.

(b) Compare the ratios obtained with those of adidas-Salomon (refer to Activity 9.1) and comment on the differences found.

9.6   The equity of Net Facile, an Italian internet provider, as at 30 September 2005 and 2004 is as follows (amounts in millions of euro):

	2005	2004
Shareholders' equity		
Issued capital	1,000	800
Share premium reserve	10,000	5,000
Retained earnings	50	200
Total shareholders' equity	11,050	6,000

The net profit for the year ended 30 September 2005 was EUR 150 million. During the same year, Net Facile issued 4,000,000 new shares at a par value of EUR 50 each. The total amount received was EUR 5,200 million.

Prepare a statement of changes in equity for year ended 30 September 2005.

Case study   Genius Tech SpA

Genius Tech SpA is a high-tech company that was set up by three partners in early 1995. Their successful product designs led to rapid growth of the enterprise, with resulting needs for additional capital to support the growth.

This case describes the major financing transactions entered into by Genius Tech in its first years of existence. The enterprise's earnings history is also given.

You are required to analyse with the accounting equation each transaction as it is described. You should be explicit about what non-current liabilities and owners' equity – that is, capital employed – accounts are affected by the transactions; but effects on assets (including cash and cash equivalents) and current liabilities can be recorded in a single account, 'A&CL' (assets and current liabilities).

1995 – The firm began as a partnership on 9 January with the three equal partners, Alison, Betty and Carlotta, each contributing EUR 100,000 capital. The accountant set up a capital account for each of the three partners. On 3 April the partners arranged with a bank a loan of EUR 100,000, on which quarterly interest (8 per cent on an annual basis) was payable for five years, with the principal due in full as a lump sum at the end of the fifth year. The enterprise's net loss for 1995 was EUR 54,000. A salary for each partner was paid during the year and included in the calculation of net loss; no other payments were made to the partners.

1996 – To help the enterprise deal with a short-term liquidity problem, on 29 April Carlotta liquidated some personal securities and loaned the enterprise the proceeds of EUR 50,000. Carlotta expected to be repaid in no more than one year. In October, Betty's ownership interest in the enterprise was sold equally to Alison and Carlotta with Betty receiving a total of EUR 110,000 in cash and cash equivalents from Alison and Carlotta. The firm had EUR 12,000 net income for the year. Alison and Carlotta planned to incorporate the firm as at 1 January 1997 as a limited liability company. Prepare the equity section of the balance sheet of the partnership as at 31 December 1996.

1997 – The enterprise was incorporated on 1 January as planned. One hundred shares with a par value of EUR 100 were issued, 50 each to Alison and Carlotta. In March the bank agreed to increase the loan from EUR 100,000 to EUR 150,000; the proceeds of EUR 50,000 were used to repay Carlotta's EUR 50,000 loan. The net income for the year was EUR 26,000.

1998 – The net income was EUR 43,000. Calculate the EPS for 1998.

1999 – In January the company went public. One hundred thousand newly issued shares were sold at EUR 7.75 per share. The year's net income was EUR 68,000. Prepare a statement of invested capital as at 31 December 1999.

2000 – In January the company issued 500 20-year bonds with a face value of EUR 1,000 with an interest rate of 6 per cent. A part of the proceeds was used to repay the company's long-term debt. The year's net income was EUR 85,000.

2001 – In April Alison and Carlotta each sold 25,000 of their ordinary shares, receiving proceeds of EUR 11 per share. The company realised a net income of EUR 11,000. On 31 December, the company declared a dividend of EUR 0.15 per share, payable on 31 January 2002. Prepare the equity section of the balance sheet as at 31 December 2001.

2002 – Feeling that the market was undervaluing the company's shares, in June the management decided to purchase 20,000 on the open market. The purchase was made on 1 July at a price of EUR 10 per share. The shares were held as treasury shares, available for possible reissuance. The net income for 2002 was EUR 152,000. In December a dividend of EUR 0.20 per share was declared, payable the following month. Calculate the EPS for 2002.

2003 – In January the company issued 4,000 convertible preference shares with an annual dividend rate of EUR 5 per share. Proceeds of the issuance were EUR 200,000. Each share was convertible on demand into two ordinary shares. Net income before preferred dividends was EUR 186,000. In December a dividend of EUR 0.20 per ordinary share was declared, payable the following month. Calculate the basic and diluted EPS for 2003.

2004 – Net income before preference share dividends was EUR 252,000. On 31 December the company declared a dividend to be paid to ordinary shareholders of EUR 25,000. The market price of the ordinary shares on 31 December was EUR 17 per share. No preference shares were converted during the year. Calculate the basic and diluted EPS for 2004 and prepare the equity section of the balance sheet as at 31 December 2004. What is the company's debt-to-equity ratio at the end of 2004?

Source: adapted from Anthony, Hawkins and Merchant (1999)

Part Three Preparation of financial statements

How to record transactions and prepare financial statements for a single enterprise

When you have completed this chapter you should be able to:

- understand the basic principles of double-entry bookkeeping
- apply the principles of double-entry bookkeeping to transactions and balance the accounts
- extract a trial balance and explain its purpose
- prepare an income statement and a balance sheet from the underlying accounts.

10.1 Introduction

In Chapters 3 and 4, we saw how the accounting transactions of an enterprise may be recorded by making a series of entries on the balance sheet and/or income statement. Each of these entries had its corresponding 'double' so that the balance sheet always balanced once both sides of the transaction had been recorded. Adjusting the balance sheet in this way could be messy and confusing in the presence of a large number of transactions. For enterprises whose accounting system is on a computer, this problem is overcome because suitable software can deal with numerous 'plus' and 'minus' entries most reliably.

Methods of processing accounting data have changed dramatically in the last few decades as computerised systems have replaced manual ones. However, the steps for recording, storing and processing accounting data have not changed.

To be able to read and interpret financial statements, users should understand how these are prepared. Thus in this chapter we will focus on the methods used to record the data contained in those reports. In particular, we will explain the double-entry accounting system that is universally used to record and process an enterprise's transactions and how to prepare an income statement and a balance sheet from such records.

10.2   The basics of double-entry bookkeeping

> *What advantages a merchant derives from double entry bookkeeping! It is among the finest inventions of the human mind; and every good householder should introduce it into his economy*
> Johann Wolfgang von Goethe (1749–1832),
> *Wilhelm Meister's Apprenticeship, 1795–6*

Worldwide, the dominant recording process is a double-entry system, in which at least two accounts are affected by each transaction. Each transaction should be analysed to determine which accounts are involved, whether the accounts are increased or decreased, and how much each account balance will change.

Refer to the first three transactions carried out by Paolo in Chapter 3.

	PPE	A Cash and cash equivalents	=	L Bank loan	+	E Capital
(1)		+ 200,000	=			+ 200,000
(2)		+ 100,000	=	+ 100,000		
(3)	+ 100,000	– 100,000	=			

This accounting equation illustrates the basic concepts of the double-entry system showing two entries for each transaction. It also emphasises that the equation

$$\text{Assets} = \text{Liabilities} + \text{Owners' equity}$$

must always balance.

10.2.1   Ledger accounts

A ledger contains the records for a group of related accounts. The ledger may be in the form of a bound record book, a loose-leaf set of pages, or some kind of electronic storage element such as magnetic tape or disk, but it is always kept current in a systematic manner. For the sake of simplicity, we can think of a ledger as a book with one page for each account. When you hear about 'keeping the books' or 'auditing the books', the word 'books' refers to the ledgers. An enterprise's general ledger is a collection of accounts that accumulate the amounts reported in the enterprise's financial statements.

The ledger accounts used here are simplified versions of those used in practice. They are called T accounts because they take the form of the capital letter T. They capture the essence of the accounting process or double-entry bookkeeping you need to understand as non-specialists without burdening yourselves with too many details that accountants use. The vertical line in the T divides the account into left and right sides for recording increases and decreases in the account. The title of the account is on the horizontal line, as you can see in Figure 10.1.

Title of account	
Left or debit side	Right or credit side
Debit balance	Credit balance

Figure 10.1 A T account

The T accounts for the first three transactions effected by Paolo are as follows:

Assets	=	Liabilities	+	Owner's equity

Cash and cash equivalents   Bank loan   Owner's capital

Dr. +	Cr. −		Dr. −	Cr. +		Dr. −	Cr. +
(1) 200,000	100,000 (3)			100,000 (2)			200,000 (1)
(2) 100,000							

PPE

Dr. +	Cr. −
(3) 100,000	

Note: the numbers in brackets identify the transaction.

Note that two accounts are affected by each transaction, as is the rule under the double-entry system. In practice, accounts are created as needed. The process of creating a new T account for recording a transaction is called 'opening of an account'. For transaction 1, we opened *cash and cash equivalents* and *owners' capital* accounts. For transaction 2, we opened the account *bank loan* only, as the account *cash and cash equivalents* already existed, and for transaction 3, we opened the *PPE* account.

Each T account summarises the changes in a particular asset, liability, or owners' equity. Because the T accounts generally show only amounts and the minimum details, each transaction is keyed in some way, such as the numbering used in this illustration, or the date, or both. This keying helps the checking or verifying process for the tracing of entries in the ledger account to the original transactions, which are written down in the journal in chronological order as they occur.

Figure 10.1 indicates that a T account has a balance. A balance is the difference between the total amounts on the left side and right side of an account at any given date. Asset accounts have balances on the left side. The balances increase by entries on the left side and decrease by entries on the right side. This process is reversed for liabilities and owners' equity accounts that have balances on the right side. Such balances increase by entries on the right side and decrease by entries on the left side.

Example

Funny Sun and its first transactions

Take a look at the entries for each of Paolo's transactions. Notice that each transaction generates a left-side entry in one T account and a right-side entry for the same amount in another T account.

Transaction 1: Initial investment for EUR 200,000 in cash by Paolo in Funny Sun.
Entries: The asset, *Cash and cash equivalents*, increases.
The owner's equity, *Owner's capital*, also increases.

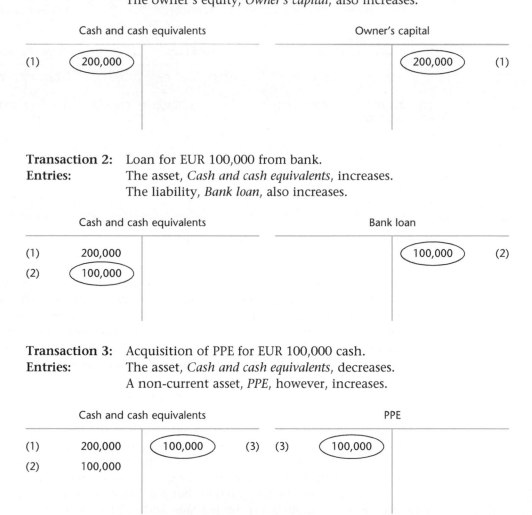

Transaction 2: Loan for EUR 100,000 from bank.
Entries: The asset, *Cash and cash equivalents*, increases.
The liability, *Bank loan*, also increases.

Transaction 3: Acquisition of PPE for EUR 100,000 cash.
Entries: The asset, *Cash and cash equivalents*, decreases.
A non-current asset, *PPE*, however, increases.

As we saw in Chapters 3 and 4, financial statements can be prepared at any given time. For example, the balance sheet of Paolo's Funny Sun after its first three transactions would include the following account balances:

Funny Sun
Balance sheet
as at 3 January

Assets	EUR	Owner's equity and liabilities	EUR
Property, plant and equipment	100,000	Owner's capital	200,000
Cash and cash equivalents	200,000	Bank loan	100,000
Total assets	300,000	Total equity and liabilities	300,000

When the accounts have only one transaction, it is easy to determine the balance. For *cash and cash equivalents*, the balance of EUR 200,000 is the difference between the total on the left side of EUR 300,000 (EUR 200,000 + EUR 100,000) and the total amount of EUR 100,000 on the right side.

10.2.2 Debits and credits

As shown in Figure 10.1, the term 'debit' (abbreviated dr) is used to denote an entry on the left side of any account, and the term 'credit' (abbreviated cr) denotes an entry on the right side of any account. Many people make the mistake of thinking that credit means increase and debit means decrease. 'Left' and 'right' terms would be much easier and more descriptive to use, but debit and credit are the standard terms for the double-entry system. The word 'charge' is often used instead of debit, but there is no synonym for credit. We must remember that debit is on the left side and credit is on the right side.

10.3   The recording process

In the previous section we entered Paolo's transactions 1, 2, and 3 directly in the ledger. However, in practice the recording process does not start with the ledger. The sequence of steps in recording transactions is as shown in Figure 10.2.

Transactions | Step 1 Documentation | Step 2 Journal | Step 3 Ledger | Step 4 Trial balance | Step 5 Financial statements

Figure 10.2 Steps for the recording process

Step 1: Documentation

The recording process begins with source documents. These are the original records of any transaction. Examples of source documents include sales slips or invoices, check stubs, purchase orders, receiving reports, cash receipt slips, minutes of the board of directors, and so on. As soon as a transaction occurs, it generates a source document. For example, when an enterprise sells for cash a product to a customer, a cash receipt is made for the sale. Source documents are kept on file so they can be used to verify the details of a transaction and the accuracy of subsequent records if necessary.

Step 2: Journal

In the second step of the recording process, a description of the transaction, based on the source documents, is noted or recorded in a book of original entry, which is a formal chronological listing of each transaction and how it affects the balances in particular accounts. The most common example of a book of original entry is the general journal. The general journal is basically a diary of all the events (transactions) in an enterprise's life. Each transaction is listed in its entirety in one place in the journal.

Step 3: Ledger

When transactions are entered into the ledger, which is the third step of the recording process, they are not entered in a single place. Instead, as we have seen, each component is entered into the left side or the right side of the appropriate account. The timing of the steps differs. Transactions occur constantly and source documents are prepared continuously. Depending on the size and nature of the enterprise, transaction listing may occur instantaneously (i.e. in real time), daily, weekly or monthly. Basically, the timing of the steps in the recording process should conform to the needs of the users of the data and to the legal requirements in a given country.

Step 4: Trial balance

The fourth step of the recording process is the preparation of the trial balance which is a simple listing of the accounts in the general ledger together with their balances. This listing aids in verifying clerical accuracy and in preparing financial statements. Thus, trial balances are prepared as needed, each month, each quarter or annually as an enterprise prepares its financial statements.

Step 5: Financial statements

The final step, the preparation of financial statements occurs at least once a year or once a quarter for external reporting. However, today all large and well-run enterprises prepare financial statements monthly for the benefit of management.

10.3.1 Journalising transactions

The process of entering transactions in the journal is called journalising. A journal entry is a classification of all the effects of a single transaction on the various accounts, usually accompanied by an explanation. For each transaction, this classification identifies the accounts to be debited and credited.

The top of Figure 10.3 (on page 188) shows how the first three transactions for Funny Sun are journalised.

The conventional form for recording in the general journal includes the following:

1. The date and identification number of the entry make up the first two columns.

2. The accounts affected are shown in the next column, accounts and explanation. The title of the account or accounts to be debited is placed on the left. The title of the account or accounts to be credited is placed on the right. The journal entry is followed by a narrative explanation of the transaction.

3. The Post ref. (posting reference) column includes the number that is assigned to each account and is used for cross-referencing to the ledger accounts.

4. The debit and credit columns are for recording the amounts that are to be debited (left) or credited (right) in each account.

10.3.2 Chart of accounts

To ensure consistent record keeping, enterprises specify a chart of accounts, which is normally a numbered or coded list of all account titles. This list specifies the accounts (or categories) that the enterprise uses in recording its activities. These account numbers are used as references in the Post ref. column of the journal, as Figure 10.3 demonstrates.

Table 10.1 (on page 189) shows the chart of accounts for Funny Sun.

The chart of accounts is usually more detailed than the one illustrated for Funny Sun. For example, for the account 101, we can have numerous sub accounts such as:

101.1   Trade receivable – Customer X

101.2   Trade receivable – Customer Y

101.3   Trade receivable – Customer Z

101.4   Trade receivable – Customer T

101.5   Other receivables

When you prepare financial statements you will group all these sub accounts in one account (trade and other receivables) according to the layout prescribed by IAS 1.

The same applies to other accounts. Let us consider expense accounts such as salaries and wages, insurance, telephone, lighting and power, repairs and mainten- ance, etc. When preparing the income statement each of these items will be allocated either to distribution, selling and marketing costs, or administrative expenses, or other operating expenses or apportioned if the expense relates to more than one of these classifications.

General Journal

Date	Entry No.	Accounts and explanations	Post Ref.	Debit	Credit
1/1	1	Cash and cash equivalents	100	200000	
		Owner's capital	500		200000
		Issued capital for EUR 200,000			
2/1	2	Cash and cash equivalents	100	100000	
		Bank loan	400		100000
		Obtained a loan from bank repayable in five years			
3/1	3	PPE	200	100000	
		Cash and cash equivalents	100		100000
		Acquired PPE for cash			

General Ledger

CASH AND CASH EQUIVALENTS   Account No. 100

Date	Explanation	Journ. Ref.	Debit	Date	Explanation	Journ. Ref.	Credit
1/1	(Often blank because			3/1		3	100000
	the explanation is						
	already in the journal)	1	200000				
2/1		2	100000				

PPE   Account No. 200

Date	Explanation	Journ. Ref.	Debit	Date	Explanation	Journ. Ref.	Credit
3/1		3	100000				

OWNER'S CAPITAL   Account No. 500

Date	Explanation	Journ. Ref.	Debit	Date	Explanation	Journ. Ref.	Credit
				1/1		1	200000

BANK LOAN   Account No. 400

Date	Explanation	Journ. Ref.	Debit	Date	Explanation	Journ. Ref.	Credit
				2/1		2	100000

Figure 10.3 Funny Sun's first three transactions recorded in general journal and posted to general ledger accounts

Table 10.1 Chart of accounts for Funny Sun

Account number	Account title
100	Cash and cash equivalents
101	Trade and other receivables
102	Inventory
103	Prepayments
104	Short-term financial assets
200	Property, plant and equipment
201	Accumulated depreciation
202	Goodwill
203	Licences
204	Long-term investments
205	Other financial assets (long term)
300	Trade and other payables
301	Short-term borrowings
400	Bank loan
401	Provisions
500	Owner's capital
501	Reserves
502	Retained earnings
503	Accumulated losses
600	Sales revenue
601	Purchases
602	Cost of sales
603	Wages (expense)
604	Depreciation (charge)
605	Amortisation (expense)
606	Rent expense
607	Interest expense
608	Income taxes
609	Net profit

10.3.3 Posting transactions to the ledger

Posting is the transferring of amounts from the journal to the debit or credit side of the appropriate accounts in the ledger. To illustrate, consider transaction 3 for Funny Sun. Figure 10.3 shows with arrows how the credit to *cash and cash equivalents* is posted using the information and amounts from the journal entry. Dates, explanations and journal references are provided for debits on the left side and for credits on the right side.

Note how cross-referencing is done between the journal and the ledger. The date is recorded in the journal and the ledger, and the journal entry number for each transaction is written in the reference column of the ledger. The process of numbering, dating, and/or using some other form of identification to relate each posting to the appropriate journal entry is known as cross-referencing. Transactions from the journal are often posted to several different accounts, but cross-referencing allows users to find all the components of the transactions in the ledger no matter where they start.

10.3.4 Classifying, journalising and posting transactions

The first three transactions of Funny Sun have been classified, recorded in a journal entry, and then posted to the general ledger where all transactions affecting an account are grouped together (see Figure 10.3). We can now apply this process to all other transactions of Paolo's enterprise. We have omitted explanations for the journal entries because they are already presented in the statement of the transactions. The posting of the elements of the transaction to the T accounts is indicated by encircling the new amount.

Transaction 4:   Purchase of inventory on credit for EUR 90,000.
Analysis: The asset, *Inventory*, increases.
The liability, *Trade and other payables*, also increases.
Journal entry: Inventory 90,000
Trade and other payables 90,000
Posting:

Inventory			Trade and other payables		
(4)	90,000			90,000	(4)

Transaction 5:   Disposal of equipment on credit at its cost for EUR 40,000.
Analysis: The asset, *Trade and other receivables*, increases.
The asset, *PPE*, decreases.
Journal entry: Trade and other receivables 40,000
PPE 40,000
Posting:

PPE			Trade and other receivables		
(3)	100,000	40,000 (5)	(5)	40,000	

Transaction 6:   Return of inventory to supplier for EUR 45,000.
Analysis: The liability, *Trade and other payables*, decreases.
The asset, *Inventory*, decreases.
Journal entry: Trade and other payables 45,000
Inventory 45,000
Posting:

Inventory			Trade and other payables		
(4)	90,000	45,000 (6)	(6)	45,000	90,000 (4)

Transaction 7:   Collection of cash from customers for EUR 30,000.
Analysis: The asset, *Cash and cash equivalents*, increases.
The asset, *Trade and other receivables,* decreases.
Journal entry: Cash and cash equivalents 30,000
Trade and other receivables 30,000
Posting:

Cash and cash equivalents			Trade and other receivables		
(1)	200,000	100,000 (3)	(5)	40,000	30,000 (7)
(2)	100,000				
(7)	30,000				

Transactions 1–7 represent simple entries in that only the two accounts shown in each transaction are affected by the same transaction.

Transaction 8: Purchase of goods for cash for EUR 10,000 and on credit for EUR 40,000.
Analysis: The asset, *Inventory*, increases.
The asset, *Cash and cash equivalents*, decreases.
The liability, *Trade and other payables*, increases.
Journal entry: Inventory 50,000
Cash and cash equivalents 10,000
Trade and other payables 40,000
Posting:

	Inventory				Trade and other payables		
(4)	90,000	45,000	(6)	(6)	45,000	90,000	(4)
(8)	50,000					40,000	(8)

	Cash and cash equivalents		
(1)	200,000	100,000	(3)
(2)	100,000	10,000	(8)
(7)	30,000		

Transaction 8 represents a compound entry, which means that more than two accounts are affected by a single transaction. Whether transactions are simple (such as transactions 1–7) or compound, the total of all left-side entries must always equal the total of all right-side entries in order to keep the accounting equation in balance. In transaction 8, we have:

$$\text{Assets} = \text{Liabilities} + \text{Owners' equity}$$
$$+\text{ EUR } 50,000 - \text{EUR } 10,000 = + \text{EUR } 40,000$$

10.3.5 Revenue and expense transactions

Revenue and expense transactions deserve special attention because their connection to the balance sheet equation is less obvious. To understand this connection, the balance sheet equation can be broken down as follows:

$$\text{Assets} = \text{Liabilities} + \text{Owners' equity}$$

$$\text{Assets} = \text{Liabilities} + (\text{Owners' capital} + \text{Retained earnings})$$

If we ignore dividends, retained earnings are merely total revenues less expenses. Therefore, the T accounts can be grouped as shown in Figure 10.4 (on page 192).

As you can see in Figure 10.4, because an enterprise incurs various categories of expenses, such as cost of sales, selling and distribution expenses, general and administrative expenses, interest expenses, income taxes, etc., it is easier, simpler

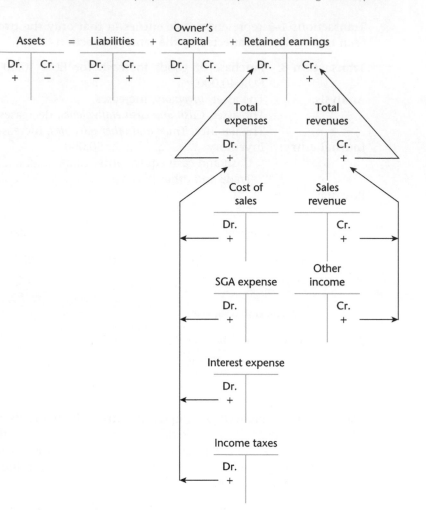

Figure 10.4 Connection between retained earnings, total expenses and total revenues

and more meaningful to prepare a separate income statement to determine the net profit (or loss) earned by the enterprise during a period or year.

We will now examine two transactions involving revenues and expenses. Consider Paolo's transactions 9(a) and 9(b):

Transaction 9(a):	Sales on credit for EUR 70,000.
Analysis:	The asset, *Trade and other receivables*, increases.
	The owners' equity, *Sales revenue*, increases.
Journal entry:	Trade and other receivables 70,000
	Sales revenue 70,000
Posting:	

	Trade and other receivables				Sales revenue	
(5)	40,000	30,000	(7)		70,000	(9a)
(9a)	70,000					

The *sales revenue* account is increased by a credit, or an entry on the right side: this increase represents an increase in the owner's equity account, *retained earnings*. In this transaction, the expense account, *cost of sales*, is increased by a debit, or an entry on the left side. The result is a decrease in the owner's equity account, *retained earnings*.

Transaction 9(b):	Cost of inventory sold, EUR 45,000.
Analysis:	The asset, *Inventory*, decreases.
	Owner's equity is decreased by creating an expense account, *Cost of sales*, which is a debit or charge against the owner's equity account.
Journal entry:	Cost of sales 45,000
	Inventory 45,000
Posting:	

Inventory				Cost of sales	
(4)	90,000	45,000	(6)	(9b)	45,000
(8)	50,000	45,000	(9b)		

Funny Sun's transactions 10 and 11 illustrate journal entries and posting of various expenses.

Transaction 10:	Paid wages of EUR 10,000.
Analysis:	The asset, *Cash and cash equivalents*, decreases.
	Owner's equity is decreased through an expense account, *Wages*.
Journal entry:	Wages 10,000
	Cash and cash equivalents 10,000
Posting:	

Cash and cash equivalents				Wages	
(1)	200,000	100,000	(3)	(10)	10,000
(2)	100,000	10,000	(8)		
(7)	30,000	10,000	(10)		

Transaction 11(a):	Paid rent in cash for EUR 5,000.
Analysis:	The asset, *Cash and cash equivalents*, decreases.
	Owner's equity is decreased through an expense account, *Rent expense*.
Journal entry:	Rent expense 5,000
	Cash and cash equivalents 5,000
Posting:	

Cash and cash equivalents				Rent expense	
(1)	200,000	100,000	(3)	(11a)	5,000
(2)	100,000	10,000	(8)		
(7)	30,000	10,000	(10)		
		5,000	(11a)		

Transaction 11(b): Recognised depreciation charge for EUR 5,000.

Analysis: The asset-reduction account, *Accumulated depreciation*, increases. Owner's equity is decreased through an expense account, *Depreciation (charge)*.

Journal entry: Depreciation 5,000

Accumulated depreciation 5,000

Posting:

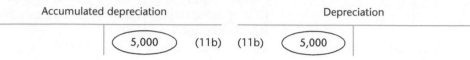

Accumulated depreciation			Depreciation	
	5,000 (11b)	(11b)	5,000	

In transaction 11(b), a new account, *Accumulated depreciation*, is opened. After this entry, the net book value, or carrying value as mentioned in Chapter 7, of PPE is given by:

PPE	EUR 60,000
Deduct: Accumulated depreciation	EUR (5,000)
PPE, net	EUR 55,000

Transaction 11(c): Interest on bank loan for EUR 500.

Analysis: Owner's equity is decreased through an expense account, *Interest expense*.

Cash and cash equivalents decreases.

Journal entry: Interest expense 500

Cash and cash equivalents 500

Posting:

Cash and cash equivalents				Interest expense	
(1)	200,000	100,000 (3)	(11c)	500	
(2)	100,000	10,000 (8)			
(7)	30,000	10,000 (10)			
		5,000 (11a)			
		500 (11c)			

Transaction 11(d): Recognised income taxes payable for EUR 1,500.

Analysis: Owner's equity is decreased through an expense account, *Income taxes*.

A liability, *Trade and other payables*, increases.

Journal entry: Income taxes 1,500

Trade and other payables 1,500

Posting:

Income taxes			Trade and other payables		
(11d)	1,500		(6)	45,000	90,000 (4)
					40,000 (8)
					1,500 (11d)

Figure 10.5 presents the rules for debit and credit and the side (left or right, debit or credit) on which the balance should normally appear.

Assets = Liabilities + Owner's equity

Assets = Liabilities + [Owner's capital – Owner's drawings + Retained earnings]

Assets = Liabilities + [Owner's capital – Owner's drawings + (Revenues – Expenses)]

Assets		=	Liabilities		+	Owner's capital		–	Owner's drawings		+	Revenues		–	Expenses	
Dr.	Cr.		Dr.	Cr.		Dr.	Cr.		Dr.	Cr.		Dr.	Cr.		Dr.	Cr.
+	–		–	+		–	+		+	–		–	+		+	–

Asset Accounts		Liability Accounts	
Debit Increase	Credit Decrease	Debit Decrease	Credit Increase
+	–	–	+
Normal balance			Normal balance

Owner's Drawings		Owner's Equity Accounts	
Debit Increase	Credit Increase	Debit Decrease	Credit Increase
Normal balance			Normal balance

Expense Accounts		Revenue Accounts	
Debit Increase	Credit Decrease	Debit Decrease	Credit Increase
+	–	–	+
Normal balance			Normal balance

Figure 10.5 Rules for debit and credit and balance of accounts

Figure 10.6 (on page 196) lists the journal entries for Paolo's transactions 4–11, just analysed. The posting reference (Post ref.) column uses the account numbers from the Funny Sun chart of accounts in Table 10.1. These account numbers also appear on each account in the Funny Sun's general ledger.

Figure 10.7 (on page 197) shows Funny Sun's general ledger.

Figure 10.8 (on page 198) shows the balances for the T accounts. C/F stands for a balance carried forward; B/F for a balance brought forward.

Date	Entry No.	Accounts and explanations	Post Ref.	Debit	Credit
4/1	4	Inventory	102	90000	
		Trade and other payables	300		90000
		Acquired inventory on credit			
5/1	5	Trade and other receivables	101	40000	
		PPE	200		40000
		Disposal of equipment on credit			
6/1	6	Trade and other payables	300	45000	
		Inventory	102		45000
		Returned inventory to supplier			
7/1	7	Cash and cash equivalents	100	30000	
		Trade and other receivables	101		30000
		Collected cash from customers			
8/1	8	Inventory	102	50000	
		Cash and cash equivalents	100		10000
		Trade and other payables	300		40000
		Purchased goods for cash and on credit			
9/1	9(a)	Trade and other receivables	101	70000	
		Sales revenue	600		70000
		Sold goods on credit			
	9(b)	Cost of sales	602	45000	
		Inventory	102		45000
		To record the cost of inventory sold			
10/1	10	Wages	603	10000	
		Cash and cash equivalents	100		10000
		Payment of wages			
11/1	11(a)	Rent expense	606	5000	
		Cash and cash equivalents	100		5000
		Payment of rent in advance			
	11(b)	Depreciation	604	5000	
		Accumulated depreciation	201		5000
		Recognise depreciation			
	11(c)	Interest expense	607	500	
		Cash and cash equivalents	100		500
		Interest on bank loan			
	11(d)	Income taxes	608	1500	
		Trade and other payables	300		1500
		Income tax expenses			

Figure 10.6 General journal of Funny Sun

Assets

PPE	Acc. N° 200		
(3)	100,000	40,000	(5)

Accumulated depreciation	201		
		5,000	(11b)

Inventory	102		
(4)	90,000	45,000	(6)
(8)	50,000	45,000	(9b)

Trade and other receivables	101		
(5)	40,000	30,000	(7)
(9a)	70,000		

Cash and cash equivalents	100		
(1)	200,000	100,000	(3)
(2)	100,000	10,000	(8)
(7)	30,000	10,000	(10)
		5,000	(11a)
		500	(11c)

=

Liabilities

Bank loan	Acc. N° 400		
		100,000	(2)

Trade and other payables	300		
(6)	45,000	90,000	(4)
		40,000	(8)
		1,500	(11d)

Cost of sales	602	
(9b)	45,000	

Wages	603	
(10)	10,000	

Rent expense	606	
(11a)	5,000	

Depreciation	604	
(11b)	5,000	

Interest expense	607	
(11c)	500	

Income taxes	608	
(11d)	1,500	

+

Owner's equity

Owner's capital	Acc. N° 500		
		200,000	(1)

Retained earnings	502		
		3,000(*)	Bal. 11/1

Sales revenue	600		
		70,000	(9a)

(*) The details of the revenue and expense accounts appear in the income statement. Their net result is then transferred to a single account, retained earnings, in the balance sheet. In this case, EUR 70,000 – EUR 45,000 – EUR 10,000 – EUR 5,000 – EUR 5,000 – EUR 500 – EUR 1,500 = EUR 3,000, which represents a net profit or net income and an increase in the owner's equity.

Figure 10.7 General ledger of Funny Sun

Assets

PPE — Acc. N° 200

(3)	100,000	(5)	40,000	
		Bal. c/f	60,000	
	100,000		100,000	
Bal. b/f	**60,000**			

Accumulated depreciation — 201

Bal. c/f	5,000	(11b)	5,000	
	5,000		5,000	
		Bal. b/f	**5,000**	

Inventory — 102

(4)	90,000	(6)	45,000	
(8)	50,000	(9b)	45,000	
		Bal. c/f	50,000	
	140,000		140,000	
Bal. b/f	**50,000**			

Trade and other receivables — 101

(5)	40,000	(7)	30,000	
(9a)	70,000	Bal. c/f	80,000	
	110,000		110,000	
Bal. b/f	**80,000**			

Cash and cash equivalents — 100

(1)	200,000	(3)	100,000	
(2)	100,000	(8)	10,000	
(7)	30,000	(10)	10,000	
		(11a)	5,000	
		(11c)	500	
			125,500	
		Bal. c/f	204,500	
	330,000		330,000	
Bal. b/f	**204,500**			

=

Liabilities

Bank loan — Acc. N° 400

Bal. c/f	100,000	(2)	100,000	
	100,000		100,000	
		Bal. b/f	**100,000**	

Trade and other payables — 300

(6)	45,000	(4)	90,000	
		(8)	40,000	
Bal. c/f	86,500	(11d)	1,500	
	131,500		131,500	
		Bal. b/f	**86,500**	

Cost of sales — 602

(9b)	45,000

Wages — 603

(10)	10,000

Rent expense — 606

(11a)	5,000

Depreciation expense — 604

(11b)	5,000

Interest expense — 607

(11c)	500

Income taxes — 608

(11d)	1,500

+

Owner's equity

Owner's capital — Acc. N° 500

Bal. c/f	200,000	(1)	200,000	
	200,000		200,000	
		Bal. b/f	**200,000**	

Retained earnings — 502

Bal. c/f	3,000	(9a)	3,000	
	3,000		3,000	
		Bal. b/f	**3,000**	

Sales revenue — 600

	(9a)	70,000

Figure 10.8 General ledger of Funny Sun with the balances for each account

10.4   Trial balance

Once journal entries have been posted to the ledger, the next step in the process of recording transactions is the preparation of a trial balance. A trial balance is a list of all the accounts which have balances. It is prepared as a check before proceeding further. Thus, the purpose of the trial balance is twofold:

1. to check the accuracy of posting by proving that the total debits equal total credits
2. to obtain a summary of balances for the preparation of the financial statements to ensure that no balance is missed out.

A trial balance may be drawn at any given date, provided that the accounts are up to date. For example, we may prepare a trial balance for Funny Sun on 3 January after its first three transactions as shown in Table 10.2.

Table 10.3 shows the trial balance of the general ledger in Figure 10.9. As shown, the trial balance normally lists the balance sheet accounts first, in the order of assets, liabilities and owners' equity. These are followed by the income statement accounts, revenues and expenses. Note that the account retained earnings has no balance because in our example it was zero at the beginning of the period. The revenues and

Table 10.2 Funny Sun, trial balance at 3 January (amounts in euro)

Account number	Account title	Balance	
		Debit	Credit
200	PPE	100,000	
100	Cash and cash equivalents	200,000	
500	Owner's capital		200,000
400	Bank loan		100,000
Total		300,000	300,000

Table 10.3 Funny Sun, trial balance at 11 January (amount in euro)

	Debit	Credit
Cash and cash equivalents	204,500	
Trade and other receivables	80,000	
Inventory	50,000	
Property, plant and equipment	60,000	
Accumulated depreciation		5,000
Trade and other payables		86,500
Bank loan		100,000
Owner's capital		200,000
Retained earnings		0
Sales revenue		70,000
Cost of sales	45,000	
Wages	10,000	
Depreciation	5,000	
Rent expense	5,000	
Interest expense	500	
Income taxes	1,500	
Total	461,500	461,500

expenses for the current period listed in the trial balance constitute the increase or decrease in retained earnings for the current period. When an accountant prepares financial statements, the revenue and expense accounts are listed in the income statement, and their difference is the net profit.

10.5   Trial balance and recording errors

Although the trial balance helps to find possible errors, a trial balance may balance even when there are *recording errors*. The following are examples of errors not disclosed by a trial balance which balances:

- a transaction could have been completely omitted from books (*omission*)
- a purchase for cash could have been entered in the account *cash and cash equivalents* as a debit and in the account *inventory* as a credit, when it should have been entered as a credit in the account *cash and cash equivalents* and as a debit in the account *inventory* (*reversal of entry*)
- a transaction may have been entered in the wrong type of account, e.g. the purchase of equipment is debited to an expense account, instead of the PPE account
- a transaction may have been entered in the correct category of account, but in the wrong sub account. For example, instead of trade receivable – customer X, trade receivable – customer Z is debited (*commission*)
- an error may have been made in adding the debit side of one account, and an identical error made in adding the credit side of another account: the two errors then cancel each other out (*compensating*)
- a transaction may be entered incorrectly in both accounts. For example, a clerk may misread EUR 10,000 cash receipt on account as EUR 1,000 and record the erroneous amount in both the *cash and cash equivalents* and *trade and other receivables* accounts. Both accounts are in error but the trial balance will balance.

Such errors may only be discovered if all the double-entry postings or entries are checked.

10.6   Preparation of financial statements from a trial balance

A trial balance shows that the debits equal credits. It is also the springboard for the preparation of the income statement and the balance sheet, as shown in Figure 10.9. The difference or net result of all the revenues and expenses listed in the income statement represents net income or net loss, which then becomes part of retained earnings in the balance sheet. You will notice that the amount for retained earnings in the balance sheet in Figure 10.9 is EUR 3,000, which is the balance of retained earnings at the end of the period, i.e. 11 January. The beginning balance for the next trial balance is the ending balance of the previous period. Hence, the beginning balance for the period starting 12 January for Funny Sun is EUR 3,000.

Funny Sun – Trial balance as at 11 January

	Debits	Credits
Cash and cash equivalents	204,500	
Trade and other receivables	80,000	
Inventory	50,000	
PPE	60,000	
Accumulated depreciation		5,000
Trade and other payables		86,500
Bank loan		100,000
Owner's capital		200,000
Retained earnings		0
Sales revenue		70,000
Cost of sales	45,000	
Wages	10,000	
Depreciation	5,000	
Rent expense	5,000	
Interest expense	500	
Income taxes	1,500	
Total	**461,500**	**461,500**

Funny Sun – Balance sheet as at 11 January

Assets		Owner's equity and liabilities	
Non-current assets		**Owner's equity**	
PPE, net	55,000	Owner's capital	200,000
Current assets		Retained earnings	3,000
Inventory	50,000		203,000
Trade and other receivables	80,000	**Non-current liabilities**	
Cash and cash equivalents	204,500	Bank loan	100,000
	334,500	**Current liabilities**	
		Trade and other payables	86,500
Total Assets	389,500	Total equity and liabilities	389,500

Funny Sun – Income statement for the period 1–11 January

Sales revenue		70,000
Deduct Cost of sales		(45,000)
Gross profit		25,000
Deduct Operating expenses:		
Wages	10,000	
Rent	5,000	
Depreciation	5,000	
		(20,000)
Operating profit (or EBIT)		5,000
Deduct Interest expense		(500)
Income before taxes (or EBIT)		4,500
Deduct Income taxes		(1,500)
Net profit (or EAT)		3,000

Figure 10.9 Trial balance, income statement and balance sheet (amounts in euro)

Note: The profit for the year is included in the balance sheet. This means the balance sheet is prepared once the transfer of profits to reserves (retained earnings) has taken place.

At the end of the accounting period, when the financial statements have been finalised all income statement accounts will have a zero or nil balance. Income statement accounts (e.g. sales revenue, interest expense, rent, etc.) will never have a balance carried forward from the previous year. Balance sheet accounts, on the other hand, will have brought forward balances at the balance sheet date.

Summary

- Methods of processing accounting data have changed dramatically in the last few decades as computerised systems have replaced manual ones. However, the steps for recording, storing and processing accounting data have not changed.
- Worldwide, the recording process is a double-entry system, in which at least two accounts are affected by each transaction.
- By convention, the left side of any account is called the debit side, and the right side is the credit side.
- Each accounting transaction has its origin in a source document. This document serves as the basis for making a descriptive entry in a journal.
- The journal provides a chronological list of the transactions. After journalising accounting entries, they are posted to the general ledger.
- A trial balance is a list of all the accounts with balances. It is prepared as a check before proceeding to prepare the income statement and balance sheet.

References and research

If you would like to explore the topics covered in this chapter in more depth, we recommend the following books:

- Robert N. Anthony, David F. Hawkins and Kenneth A. Merchant, *Accounting: Text and Cases*, McGraw-Hill, 1999
- Sidney J. Gray and Belverd E. Needles, *Financial Accounting: A Global Approach*, Houghton Mifflin Company, 1999, Chapter 2
- Charles T. Horngren, Gary L. Sundem and John A. Elliott, *Introduction to Financial Accounting*, Pearson Education-Prentice Hall, 2002
- Hervé Stolowy and Michel J. Lebas, *Corporate Financial Reporting: A Global Perspective*, Thomson Learning 2002, Chapter 4
- Frank Wood and Alan Sangster, *Business Accounting*, Vol. 1, 9th Edition, Financial Times-Prentice Hall, 2002, Parts 1, 3 and 4

Questions

10.1 For each of the following accounts, indicate whether it normally has a debit or a credit balance. Use dr. or cr:

1. Sales revenue
2. Trade and other payables
3. Trade and other receivables
4. Interest expense
5. Inventory
6. Interest income
7. Retained earnings
8. Depreciation expense
9. Dividends payable
10. Issued capital
11. Bad debt provision
12. Accumulated depreciation

10.2 Prepare journal entries and post to T accounts the following transactions of Edoardo Catering Company:

(a) Cash sales, EUR 10,000.
(b) Collection of trade receivables, EUR 6,000.
(c) Paid cash for wages, EUR 3,000.
(d) Acquired inventory on credit, EUR 5,000.
(e) Paid cash for cleaning services, EUR 600.

10.3 Reconstruct the journal entries (omit explanations) that would have resulted for the postings to the following T accounts of a consulting enterprise:

Cash and cash equivalents					PPE				Revenue fees	
a	120,000	2,000	b	c	30,000				160,000	d
		10,000	c							

Trade and other receivables			Bank loan			Supply expense	
d	160,000			20,000	c	e	600

Inventory				Issued capital	
b	2,000	600	e	120,000	a

10.4 Consider the following trial balance (amounts in euro):

Beppe & Brothers Auto Parts Store – trial balance as at 31 March 2005

	Debit	Credit
Cash and cash equivalents	32,000	
Trade and other receivables	28,000	
Inventory	258,000	
Prepaid rent		8,000
Prepaid insurance	2,000	
PPE	66,000	
Accumulated depreciation	30,000	
Trade and other payables	84,000	
Short-term borrowings	80,000	
Issued capital		24,000
Retained earnings		20,000
Sales		1,576,000
Cost of sales	1,000,000	
Wages	200,000	
Other operating expenses	160,000	
Administrative expenses		60,000
TOTAL	**1,940,000**	**1,688,000**

(a) List and describe all the errors made in the trial balance of Beppe & Brothers Auto Parts Store.
(b) Prepare a correct trial balance.

10.5 Sabrina Migliaccio owned and managed a franchise of Caffè Espresso srl. The trial balance on 1 January 2005, the beginning of its accounting period, is listed as follows:

Caffè Espresso srl – trial balance as at 1 January 2005 (amounts in euro)

	Debit	Credit
Cash and cash equivalents	7,800	
Trade and other receivables	75,600	
Inventory	233,400	
Prepaid rent	12,000	
PPE	63,000	
Accumulated depreciation		17,250
Trade and other payables		135,000
Issued capital		90,000
Retained earnings		149,550
TOTAL	**391,800**	**391,800**

Summarised transactions for January 2005 were:

- Purchase of goods on account, EUR 156,000.
- Sales for cash, EUR 117,750.
- Payments to creditors, EUR 87,000.
- Sales on credit, EUR 114,000.
- Advertising in newspapers, paid in cash, EUR 9,000.
- Cost of sales, EUR 120,000.
- Collections from customers, EUR 99,450.
- Miscellaneous expenses paid in cash, EUR 24,000.
- Wages paid in cash, EUR 27,000.
- Entry for rent expense. (Rent was paid quarterly in advance, EUR 18,000 per quarter. Payments were due on 1 March, 1 June, 1 September and 1 December.)
- Depreciation of PPE, EUR 750.

(a) Enter the 1 January 2005 balances in a general ledger.
(b) Prepare journal entries for each transaction.
(c) Post the journal entries to the general ledger.
(d) Prepare an income statement for the month ended 31 January 2005 and a balance sheet as at 31 January 2005.

10.6 La Campania SpA produced various types of pasta. The company had the following trial balance for the year ended 30 June 2005 (amounts in millions of euro):

	Debit	Credit
Current assets	4,173	
PPE, net	5,266	
Intangible assets, net	4,735	
Other assets	3,377	
Current liabilities		3,788
Long-term debt and other liabilities		6,882
Shareholders' equity*		5,609
Sales		20,367
Cost of sales	8,198	
Selling, general and administrative expenses	9,103	
Other expenses	2,217	
Other income		1,201
Cash dividends	778	
Total	*37,847*	*37,847*

* Includes beginning retained earnings.

(a) Prepare La Campania SpA's income statement for the year ended 30 June 2005.
(b) Prepare La Campania SpA's balance sheet as at 30 June 2005.

Case study   Anacleto SpA

The following data are available for Anacleto SpA for the year ended 30 September 2005:

Trial balance of Anacleto SpA as at 30 September 2005
(*amounts in thousands of euro*)

Interest expense on bank overdraft	2,300	
Bank overdraft		17,250
Cash in hand	9,200	
Long-term loans		126,500
Trade and other receivables	57,500	
Accumulated depreciation on equipment		6,900
Accumulated depreciation on motor vehicles		18,400
Directors' remuneration	2,300	
Dividends	3,450	
Equipment	29,900	
Audit fees	2,300	
Land	115,000	
Buildings	115,000	
Hire charges	600	
Interest on long-term loans	12,650	
Share capital		34,500
Lighting and power	1,840	
Miscellaneous expenses	550	
Motor expenses	18,400	
Motor vehicles	41,400	
Postage, telephone, courier	3,680	
Retained earnings		115,000
Provision for income taxes		11,500
Purchases	517,500	
Insurance	6,900	
Repairs and maintenance	5,520	
Salaries and wages	36,110	
Income tax	11,500	
Sales		690,000
Inventory at 1 October 2004	86,250	
Trade and other payables		59,800
	1,079,850	1,079,850

The following information has not yet been taken into account in the amounts shown in the trial balance:

- Inventory at cost at 30 September 2005 was EUR 45,750,000. Inventory of certain items at net realisable value (NRV) at 30 September 2005 was EUR 6,000,000. The cost of this inventory was EUR 8,000,000.

- Depreciation is to be provided as follows:
  - ❐ 2 per cent on buildings using the straight-line method
  - ❐ 10 per cent on equipment using the diminishing-balance method
  - ❐ 25 per cent on motor vehicles using the diminishing-balance method.
- EUR 4,600,000 was prepaid for repairs and EUR 10,350,000 has accrued for wages.

Help the financial controller to draw up an income statement and a balance sheet according to the layout prescribed by IAS 1.

When allocating expenses to distribution, selling and marketing costs or to administrative expenses, use the following assumptions:

	Distribution	Administrative
Directors' remuneration	–	100%
Audit fees	–	100%
Hire charges	50%	50%
Lighting and power	50%	50%
Miscellaneous expenses	50%	50%
Motor expenses	100%	–
Postage, telephone, courier	50%	50%
Insurance	50%	50%
Repairs and maintenance	50%	50%
Salaries and wages	50%	50%
Depreciation	70%	30%

11 Financial statements for a group of enterprises

11.1 Introduction

To grow or expand, enterprises can either form wholly owned domestic or foreign entities (organic growth) or invest in other enterprises by acquiring their equity. These investments are typically long-term investments; when they are large enough, they allow the investing enterprise varying degrees of control over the investee company.

A group exists when an enterprise (a parent or holding company) controls, either directly or indirectly, another enterprise (the subsidiary). Therefore a group consists of a parent and its subsidiary/ies. We explained the reasons for such complex structures in Chapter 1 (section 1.2).

Control is defined as the power to govern the financial and operating policies of an enterprise so as to obtain benefits derived from its activities. Control is assumed when one party in the combination owns more than half of the voting rights of

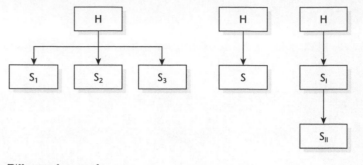

Figure 11.1 Different forms of groups

Note: H represents the parent or holding company; S_I represents a subsidiary directly controlled, while S_{II} represents a subsidiary controlled through another one.

the other either directly or through a subsidiary (see third group on the right in Figure 11.1).

However, even if the voting rights acquired are less than half, it may still be possible to have control if the parent acquires:

(a) power over more than one half of the voting rights of the other enterprise by virtue of an agreement with other investors

(b) power to govern the financial and operating policies of the other enterprise under a statute or an agreement

(c) power to appoint or remove the majority of the members of the board of directors or equivalent governing body of the other enterprise

(d) power to cast the majority of votes at a meeting of the board of directors or equivalent governing body of the other enterprise.

In most cases, a parent company is required to prepare consolidated financial statements. These show the accounts of a group as though that group was one enterprise. The net assets of the companies in a group will thus be combined and any inter-company profits and balances eliminated.

A parent company may not be required to prepare consolidated financial statements if it is itself a wholly owned or virtually wholly owned subsidiary. 'Virtually wholly owned' means 90 per cent in many countries.

The accounting for investments in other enterprises depends on the size of the ownership the investor has, as you can see from Figure 11.2.

11.2 Preparation of consolidated financial statements at the date of acquisition

When control exists, the parent and subsidiary are really one in an economic sense although not in legal sense. Consolidated financial statements are designed to cut across artificial corporate boundaries to portray the economic activities of the parent and subsidiary as if they were one entity. Let us see some examples of how this happens.

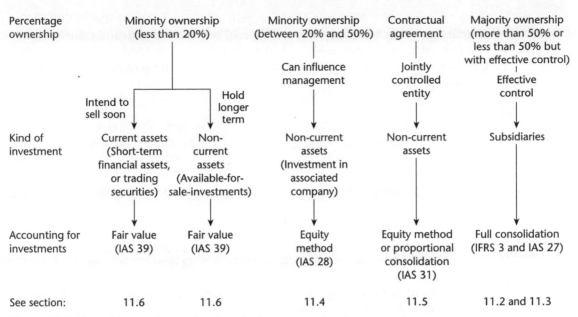

Figure 11.2 Financial reporting alternatives for investments in other enterprises

In the following example we illustrate consolidation of a subsidiary at the date of acquisition. In this instance the consideration paid for the acquisition of a subsidiary equals the parent company's share of the fair market value of the net assets or equity of the acquired enterprise:

$$
\begin{array}{l}
\text{Fair market value} \\
\text{(FMV) of acquired} \\
\text{enterprise's net assets} \\
\text{or equity}
\end{array}
=
\begin{array}{l}
\text{FMV of acquired} \\
\text{enterprise's assets}
\end{array}
-
\begin{array}{l}
\text{FMV of acquired} \\
\text{enterprise's} \\
\text{liabilities}
\end{array}
$$

Example

Consolidation at the date of acquisition

The balance sheet of Halbert SpA as at 31 December 2004 is shown below:

	Halbert EUR
Non-current assets	25,000
Net current assets	23,000
Total assets	**48,000**
Share capital	16,000
Retained earnings	27,000
Non-current liabilities	5,000
Shareholders' equity and liabilities	**48,000**

On 1 January 2005, Halbert SpA (H) acquired 100 per cent of the 10,000 EUR 1 ordinary shares in Settimo SpA (S) at EUR 1.50 per share in cash and gained control. The fair value of the net assets of S at that date was the same as the book value. The balance sheets of H and S on 1 January 2005 (i.e. the acquisition date) were as follows:

	H	S
	EUR	EUR
Non-current assets	25,000	12,000
Investment in S(*)	15,000	–
Net current assets	8,000(**)	5,000
Total assets	*48,000*	*17,000*
Share capital	16,000	10,000
Retained earnings	27,000	5,000
Non-current liabilities	5,000	2,000
Shareholders' equity and liabilities	*48,000*	*17,000*

(*) Investment in S is a component of non-current assets. However, for the purposes of illustration it is shown separately.

(**) EUR 23,000 before the investment in S *less* EUR 15,000 for the consideration paid in cash to acquire S.

When preparing the consolidated balance sheet at the date of acquisition, we should follow the steps described below:

Step (1) The investment in the subsidiary for EUR 15,000 is set off against the parent company's share of the subsidiary's capital and retained earnings of EUR 15,000, because the investment of EUR 15,000 represents the equity (i.e. share capital and retained earnings) of S. Thus, these inter-company balances are eliminated and do not appear in the consolidated balance sheet. The consolidated balance sheet only includes the share capital and retained earnings of the parent company, because the owners or shareholders of H wholly own S.

Step (2) Add the assets and liabilities of the two enterprises to obtain the con-solidated balance sheet after reflecting the elimination of intercompany balances, which are known as consolidation adjustments.

	H Balance sheet	S Balance sheet	Adjustments Dr	Adjustments Cr	Consolidated balance sheet
	EUR	EUR	EUR	EUR	EUR
Non-current assets	25,000	12,000			37,000
Investment in S	15,000	–		15,000	
Net current assets	8,000	5,000			13,000
Total assets	*48,000*	*17,000*			*50,000*
Share capital	16,000	10,000	10,000		16,000
Retained earnings	27,000	5,000	5,000		27,000
Non-current liabilities	5,000	2,000			7,000
Shareholders' equity and liabilities	*48,000*	*17,000*	*15,000*	*15,000*	*50,000*

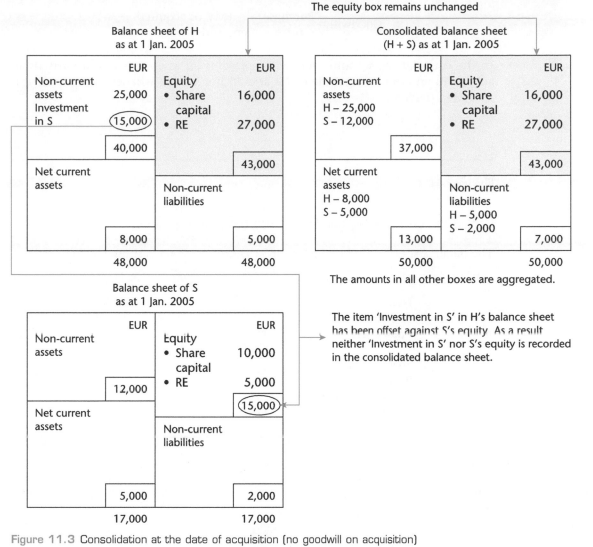

Figure 11.3 Consolidation at the date of acquisition (no goodwill on acquisition)

11.2.1 Accounting for goodwill arising on consolidation

In the following example we complicate matters slightly by assuming that to acquire the subsidiary, the parent company pays more than the fair value of the net assets. Why can this happen? A reason might be that the subsidiary has a higher earning power compared to other enterprises in the same industry. This can be due to its customer portfolio, technological and innovative skills represented by its management and employees, reputation for quality, sound financial management, etc.

From an accounting point of view, goodwill is the difference between the cost of the investment and the fair value of the assets and liabilities acquired at the date of the acquisition:

$$\text{Goodwill} = \frac{\text{Purchase}}{\text{price}} - \frac{\text{FMV of acquired}}{\text{enterprise's net assets}}$$

In the consolidated accounts goodwill represents an asset. It is not amortised but subject to an annual impairment test and ad hoc testing whenever impairment is indicated (IFRS 3).

Example

Consolidation including goodwill at the date of acquisition

The balance sheet of Halbert SpA as at 31 December 2004 is shown as follows:

	EUR
Non-current assets	25,000
Net current assets	23,000
Total assets	**48,000**
Share capital	16,000
Retained earnings	27,000
Non-current liabilities	5,000
Shareholders' equity and liabilities	**48,000**

On 1 January 2005, Halbert SpA (H) acquired 100 per cent of the 10,000 EUR 1 ordinary shares in Settimo SpA (S) for EUR 1.60 per share in cash and gained control. The fair value of the net assets of S at that date was the same as the book value. The balance sheets of H and S on 1 January 2005 or the acquisition date were as follows:

	H	S
	EUR	EUR
Non-current assets	25,000	12,000
Investment in S	16,000	–
Net current assets	7,000(*)	5,000
Total assets	**48,000**	**17,000**
Share capital	16,000	10,000
Retained earnings	27,000	5,000
Non-current liabilities	5,000	2,000
Shareholders' equity and liabilities	**48,000**	**17,000**

(*) EUR 23,000 before the acquisition of S *less* EUR 16,000 for the consideration paid in cash to acquire S.

Step (1)   Determine the goodwill for inclusion in the consolidated balance sheet:

	EUR	EUR
Investment in S		16,000
Deduct: H's share of the subsidiary's equity (*)		
(100% × EUR 10,000)	10,000	
(100% × EUR 5,000)	5,000	
		(15,000)
Goodwill		**1,000**

(*) In this example S's fair value of the net assets equals S's equity or capital and retained earnings

Step (2)   Add the assets and liabilities of the two enterprises to obtain the consolidated balance sheet:

	EUR
Non-current assets (25,000 + 12,000)	37,000
Goodwill (as just calculated)	1,000
Net current assets (7,000 + 5,000)	12,000
Total assets	50,000
Non-current liabilities (5,000 + 2,000)	*7,000*

Step (3)   Determine the share capital and retained earnings to obtain the consolidated balance sheet:

	H Balance sheet EUR	S Balance sheet EUR	Adjustments Dr EUR	Adjustments Cr EUR	Consolidated balance sheet EUR
Non-current assets	25,000	12,000			37,000
Investment in S	16,000	–		16,000	
Goodwill (*)			1,000		1,000
Net current assets	7,000	5,000			12,000
Total assets	*48,000*	*17,000*			*50,000*
Share capital	16,000	10,000	10,000		16,000
Retained earnings	27,000	5,000	5,000		27,000
Non-current liabilities	5,000	2,000			7,000
Shareholders' equity and liabilities	*48,000*	*17,000*	*16,000*	*16,000*	*50,000*

(*) Goodwill is a component of non-current assets. However, for the purposes of illustration it is shown separately.

In this example, the elimination of intercompany balances and the accounting for goodwill represent consolidation adjustments.

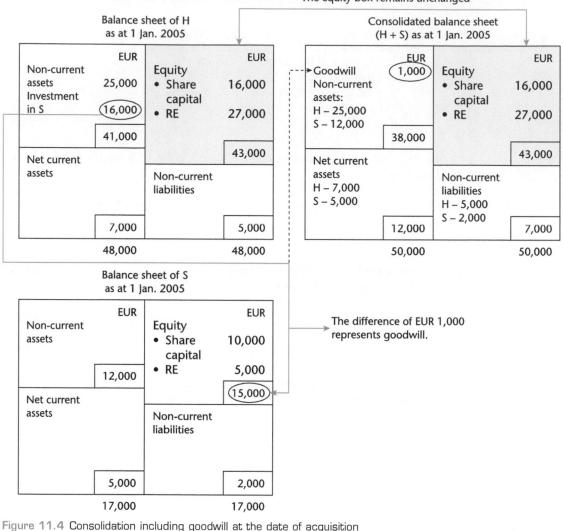

Figure 11.4 Consolidation including goodwill at the date of acquisition

11.2.2 Minority interest

A company does not need to purchase all the shares of another company to gain control. The holders of the remaining shares are collectively referred to as the minority shareholders, and the equity owned by them is known as minority interest. They are part owners of the subsidiary and, therefore, are part owners of the equity or net assets of the subsidiary. At the same time, although the parent does not own all the net assets of the acquired company it nevertheless controls them.

One of the purposes of preparing consolidated financial statements is to show the consequences of that control. Thus all the net assets of the subsidiary will be included in the group or consolidated balance sheet, and the minority interest will be shown as partly financing those net assets. In the consolidated income statement the total net profit earned by the subsidiary will be included, and the part attributable to the minority interest will be shown as a deduction from the total consolidated profit to show the net profit attributable to the shareholders of the parent company.

Example

Minority interest

The balance sheet of Halbert SpA as at 31 December 2004 is shown as follows:

	EUR
Non-current assets	25,000
Net current assets	23,000
Total assets	**48,000**
Share capital	16,000
Retained earnings	27,000
Non-currrent liabilities	5,000
Shareholders' equity and liabilities	**48,000**

On 1 January 2005, Halbert SpA (H) acquired 80 per cent of the 10,000 EUR 1 ordinary shares in Settimo SpA (S) for EUR 1.60 per share in cash and gained control. The fair value of the net assets of S at that date was the same as the book value. The balance sheets of H and S on 1 January 2005 (i.e. at the acquisition date) were as follows:

	H	S
	EUR	EUR
Non-current assets	25,000	12,000
Investment in S	12,800	–
Net current assets	10,200(*)	3,000
Total assets	**48,000**	**15,000**
Share capital	16,000	10,000
Retained earnings	27,000	5,000
Non-current liabilities	5,000	
Shareholders' equity and liabilities	**48,000**	**15,000**

(*) EUR 23,000 before the acquisition *less* EUR 12,800 for the consideration paid to acquire S

Step (1)   Determine the goodwill for inclusion in the consolidated balance sheet:

	EUR	EUR
The parent company's investment in S		12,800
Deduct: H's share of the subsidiary's equity		
(80% × EUR 10,000)	8,000	
(80% × EUR 5,000)	4,000	
		(12,000)
Goodwill		**800**

Step (2)   Determine the minority interest in the equity of S:

	EUR
(20% × EUR 10,000)	2,000
(20% × EUR 5,000)	1,000
	3,000

Step (3)   Add the assets and liabilities of the two companies to obtain the consolidated balance sheet:

	EUR
Non-current assets (25,000 + 12,000)	37,000
Goodwill (as just calculated)	800
Net current assets (10,200 + 3,000)	13,200
Total assets	*51,000*
Non-current liabilities	*5,000*

Step (4)   Determine the share capital and retained earnings for the consolidated balance sheet:

	H Balance sheet EUR	S Balance sheet EUR	Adjustments Dr EUR	Adjustments Cr EUR	Consolidated balance sheet EUR
Non-current assets	25,000	12,000			37,000
Investment in S	12,800	–		12,800	
Goodwill			800		800
Net current assets	10,200	3,000			13,200
Total assets	*48,000*	*15,000*			*51,000*
Share capital	16,000	10,000	8,000		16,000
			2,000		
Retained earnings	27,000	5,000	4,000		27,000
			1,000		
Minority interest				3,000	3,000
Non-currrent liabilities	5,000				5,000
Shareholders' equity and liabilities	*48,000*	*15,000*	*15,800*	*15,800*	*51,000*

Note that no goodwill is attributed (credited) to the minority interest and correspondingly only the goodwill relating to the 80 per cent interest of the parent appears in the balance sheet. The rationale for this treatment is that the consideration paid for an 80 per cent interest in S includes goodwill or a premium of EUR 800, whereas nothing has changed for the minority shareholders.

11.2.3 Accounting for differences between a subsidiary's fair values and book values

In the previous sections we have assumed that the book value of the net assets in the subsidiary is equal to their fair values. In practice, book value of the investment by the parent company rarely cquals fair values of the net assets of the subsidiary, and it is necessary to revalue the group's share of the assets and liabilities of the subsidiary prior to consolidation. Moreover, there may be intangible assets not accounted for in the subsidiary's balance sheet that should be separately recognised in the consolidated financial statements. All the identifiable intangible assets of the acquired enterprise should be recorded at their fair values. IFRS 3 includes a list of assets that are expected to be recognised separately from goodwill, such as trademarks, brands, patents, computer software, etc. The valuation of such assets is a complex process. An intangible asset with an indefinite useful life is not amortised but is subject to annual impairment testing. Intangible assets may have an indefinite life if there is no foreseeable limit on the period over which the asset will generate cash flows. The criteria for the intangible assets having indefinite lives are very strict, and relatively few assets are expected to meet them. Many will be considered long-lived assets instead.

The following example illustrates the same as the last one, but assumes that the fair value of Settimo SpA's non-current assets is equal to EUR 12,400 and not its book value of EUR 12,000.

Note that, when consolidating, the parent's company assets remain unchanged – it is only the subsidiary's assets that are adjusted for the purpose of the consolidated financial statements. Therefore, the non-current assets will be increased to the extent of Halbert's interest, i.e. by EUR 320 (80 per cent × EUR 400).

Example

Differences between a subsidiary's fair values and book values

	H Balance sheet EUR	S Balance sheet EUR	Adjustments Dr. EUR	Adjustments Cr. EUR	Consolidated balance sheet EUR	Notes
Non-current assets	25,000	12,000	320		37,320	(i)
Investment in S	12,800	–		12,800		
Goodwill			480		480	(ii)
Net current assets	10,200	3,000			13,200	
Total assets	48,000	15,000			51,000	
Share capital	16,000	10,000	8,000		16,000	
			2,000			
Retained earnings	27,000	5,000	4,000		27,000	
			1,000			
Minority interest				3,000	3,000	(iii)
Non current liabilities	5,000				5,000	
Shareholders' equity and liabilities	48,000	15,000	15,800	15,800	51,000	

Note (i):   **Non-current assets**
(EUR 25,000 + 12,000 + 80% × 400)   **EUR 37,320**

Note (ii): Goodwill

	EUR	EUR
The parent company's investment in S		12,800
Deduct:		
The parent's share of the subsidiary's equity	12,000	
The parent's share of the valuation of the assets to their fair values	320	
		(12,320)
Goodwill		**480**

Note (iii): Minority interest

(20% × EUR 10,000)	2,000
(20% × EUR 5,000)	1,000
	3,000

Only the parent's share has been accounted for at fair values. From the point of view of the minority shareholders nothing has changed.

11.3 Preparation of consolidated financial statements after the date of acquisition

11.3.1 Pre- and post-acquisition profits

Any profits or losses made before the date of acquisition are referred to as pre-acquisition profits or losses. This is because the consideration paid for acquiring the interest in the subsidiary includes a share in the retained earnings, proportionate to the interest acquired by the parent company.

Any profits or losses made after the date of acquisition are referred to as post-acquisition profits. Profits arising subsequent to the acquisition of the subsidiary will be accounted for in the consolidated income statement, and will be part of the retained earnings figure in the consolidated balance sheet. So it is important to distinguish between pre-acquisition and post-acquisition profits in retained earnings.

The following example illustrates the accounting for pre- and post-acquisition profits.

Example

Pre- and post-acquisition profits

On 1 January 2004 ABC SpA acquired 80 per cent of the 20,000 EUR 10 shares of XYZ SpA for EUR 15 per share in cash and gained control. The total cost of the investment in the subsidiary was EUR 240,000 (80 per cent × 20,000 shares × EUR 15). The retained earnings of XYZ at the date of acquisition amounted to EUR 80,000. The fair value of XYZ's PPE (land) was EUR 12,000 above the book value. An impairment test carried out at the end of 2004 revealed a loss of EUR 1,280 for goodwill. (Note: We made these hypotheses for didactic purposes. In fact this is most unlikely to happen in practice. Otherwise, it would mean that management made a mistake and overpaid when it acquired the subsidiary!)

The balance sheets of ABC and XYZ as at 31 December 2004 are as follows (amounts in thousands of euro):

	ABC EUR	XYZ EUR
Non-current assets		
Investment in XYZ	240,000	–
PPE	520,000	300,000
	760,000	300,000
Net current assets	380,000	80,000
Total assets	*1,140,000*	*380,000*
Shareholders' equity		
Issued capital	320,000	200,000
Retained earnings	700,000	120,000
	1,020,000	320,000
Non-current liabilities	120,000	60,000
Total shareholders' equity and liabilities	*1,140,000*	*380,000*

Step (1) Determine the fair value of PPE and goodwill as at 31 December 2004:

	EUR	EUR
The parent company's investment in XYZ		240,000
Deduct:		
• The parent's share of the subsidiary capital		
(80% × EUR 200,000)	160,000	
• The parent's share of the subsidiary's retained earnings as at 1 January 2004		
(80% × EUR 80,000)	64,000	
• The parent's share of fair value adjustment		
(80% of revaluation of PPE for EUR 12,000)	9,600	
		(233,600)
Goodwill at the date of acquisition, 1 January 2004		6,400
Impairment loss in 2004		(1,280)
Goodwill at 31 December 2004		**5,120**

Step (2) Determine minority interest as at 31 December 2004:

	EUR
• Minority interest in the issued capital of XYZ	
(20% × EUR 200,000)	40,000
• Minority interest in the total retained earnings of XYZ	
(20% × EUR 120,000)	24,000
Minority interest at 31 December 2004	**64,000**

Step (3)   Add the assets and liabilities of the parent and subsidiary for the consolidated balance sheet as at 31 December 2004:

	ABC	XYZ	Consolidated balance sheet
	EUR	EUR	EUR
PPE	520,000	(300,000 + 9,600*)	829,600
Goodwill		(as calculated in Step 1)	5,120
Net current assets	380,000	80,000	460,000
Total assets			**1,294,720**

* Fair value adjustment

Step (4)   Determine the consolidated share capital and retained earnings for the consolidated balance sheet as at 31 December 2004:

	EUR	EUR	EUR
ABC Issued capital			320,000
ABC Retained earnings		700,000	
ABC's share of the post-acquisition profit of XYZ			
80% × (EUR 120,000 – EUR 80,000)	32,000		
Impairment loss for goodwill (see Step 1)	(1,280)		
		30,720	
			730,720
Total shareholders' equity			**1,050,720**

Note that as the valuation of PPE refers to land it is not amortised.

	ABC	XYZ	Adjustments Dr	Adjustments Cr	Consolidated balance sheet
	EUR	EUR	EUR	EUR	EUR
Non-current assets					
Investment in XYZ	240,000	–		240,000	–
PPE	520,000	300,000	9,600		829,600
Goodwill			6,400	1,280	**5,120**
	760,000	300,000			834,720
Net current assets	380,000	80,000			460,000
Total assets	**1,140,000**	**380,000**			**1,294,720**
Shareholders' equity					
Issued capital	320,000	200,000	160,000		320,000
			40,000		
Retained earnings	700,000	120,000	64,000		730,720
			24,000		
			1,280		
Minority interest				64,000	**64,000**
Non-current liabilities	120,000	60,000			180,000
Total shareholders' equity and liabilities	**1,140,000**	**380,000**	**305,280**	**305,280**	**1,294,720**

11.3.2 Intercompany balances

Consolidation requires adjustments because of intercompany transactions. For example, the parent company may hold bonds issued by its subsidiaries, or may have trade receivables from its subsidiaries or vice versa. In the following example we show consolidation adjustments in order that consolidated balance sheet does not double count the assets and/or liabilities as a result of intercompany transactions.

Example

Intercompany balances

An extract of the balance sheets of Prose SpA (P) and Verse SpA (V) as at 31 December 2004 is presented as follows (amounts in thousands of euro):

	P	V
CURRENT ASSETS:		
Trade and other receivables	5,000	3,000
Bank	2,000	1,000
Total current assets	7,000	4,000
CURRENT LIABILITIES:		
Trade and other payables		1,000
Short-term borrowings	2,700	1,600
Total current liabilities	2,700	2,600

V owes P EUR 1,000,000 as at 31 December 2004 for sales made by P on credit during 2004.

When preparing the consolidated balance sheet, we need to eliminate EUR 1,000,000 which is currently in P's trade and other receivables and in V's trade and other payables. If we did not make this consolidation adjustment both trade and other receivables and trade and other payables would be overstated by EUR 1,000,000, thus distorting the consolidated amounts.

Amounts in thousands of euro	P	V	Adjustments Dr	Cr	Consolidated balance sheet
CURRENT ASSETS:					
Trade and other receivables	5,000	3,000		1,000	7,000
Bank	2,000	1,000			3,000
Total current assets	7,000	4,000			10,000
CURRENT LIABILITIES:					
Trade and other payables		1,000	1,000		
Short-term borrowings	2,700	1,600			4,300
Total current liabilities	2,700	2,600	1,000	1,000	6,300

Note: In practice intercompany balances will be disclosed separately in the balance sheets of the parent and subsidiary(ies) and not as just illustrated.

11.3.3 Unrealised profit on intercompany sales

When sales are made by one company to another within the group, there may be a profit that has not been realised by the group if the goods have not been sold to a third party before the year-end. As the aim of consolidation is to present the group as a single entity or enterprise, profits should be accounted for only on transactions with third parties only. What is important is substance over 'legal' form.

The parent company may sell goods to its subsidiary (or vice versa) at a profit. If the subsidiary re-sells all the goods to external customers before the end of the financial year, all the profit is then realised and there is no need for a consolidation adjustment. However, when at the year-end the subsidiary has in its warehouse part of the goods purchased from another subsidiary or a group company then we need to make a consolidation adjustment to account for the unrealised profit in the inventory, as shown in the following example. It should be borne in mind that the same principle applies when a subsidiary sells its goods to the parent.

Example

Intercompany profit

H sells goods to S for EUR 10,000 which cost H EUR 6,000.
S sells those goods to a third party (T) for EUR 13,000.
Tax rate is 40 per cent.

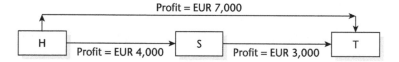

Therefore, the group has made a total profit of EUR 7,000, e.g. Sales – Cost of sales = EUR 13,000 – EUR 6,000.

But if some of the goods are unsold by the year-end (by S), then H's profits on these are unrealised from the group's point of view.

Suppose S sells to third parties only half of the goods bought from H. In this case, the balance sheet of S at 31 December 2004 shows inventory costing EUR 5,000. S determines its net profit taking into account a value of ending inventory of EUR 5,000. From the group's point of view, the cost of inventory is EUR 3,000 and not EUR 5,000. Therefore, the profit of EUR 2,000 made by H in its statutory or legal accounts should be eliminated from the consolidated profit and retained earnings as shown below:

Balance sheet extract (amounts in euro):

	H	S	Adjustments Dr	Adjustments Cr	Consolidated balance sheet
Inventory	–	5,000		2,000	3,000
Deferred tax assets			800		800
Retained earnings	12,000	–	1,200		10,800

Note: S paid more taxes than those due from the group's point of view. Therefore we should reduce retained earnings by EUR 1,200 (= EUR 2,000 *less* 40 per cent of EUR 2,000) as EUR 1,200 represents the profit net of tax recorded by H.

11.4   Accounting for associated companies (equity method)

An associate is an enterprise in which the investor has significant influence and which is neither a subsidiary nor a joint venture of the investor. Significant influence is the power to participate in the financial and operating policy decisions of the investee but the investor has no legal control over these policies.

Significant influence is assumed in situations where one company has 20 per cent or more of the voting power in another enterprise, unless it can be clearly demonstrated that there is no such influence.

The existence of significant influence by an investor is usually evidenced in one or more of the following ways:

(a) representation on the board of directors or equivalent governing body of the investee

(b) participation in policy-making processes, including participation in decisions about dividends or other distributions

(c) material transactions between the investor and the investee

(d) interchange of managerial personnel

(e) provision of essential technical information (IAS 28).

The account of the associated companies should be reflected in the consolidated financial statements under the equity method. Under the equity method the investment is initially recorded at its cost. Thereafter, the investment amount is increased (debited) to reflect the investing company's share in the investee's net profit (or loss); the offsetting credit is to the income statement account. If a dividend is received from the investee, the investment amount is decreased (credited) and the offsetting debit is to cash and cash equivalents or to dividends receivable. Moreover, consolidation adjustments are required for certain matters, such as the elimination of intercompany profits or conformation to the investor's accounting policies.

The following example illustrates the equity method:

Example

Equity method

On 1 January 2004, A purchased 30 per cent of the ordinary shares of B for EUR 9,000. The book value and fair value of B's net assets is EUR 30,000. During 2004 B earns a net profit of EUR 6,000 and declares a dividend of EUR 1,500. Using the equity method, the accounting entries made by A are:

Recording the acquisition
Dr Investment in B   EUR 9,000
   Cr Cash   EUR 9,000

Recording earnings
Dr Investment in B   EUR 1,800
   Cr Investment income   EUR 1,800

Recording dividends
Dr Dividends receivable from B   EUR   450
   Cr Investment in B   EUR   450

As the example shows, A's income statement is affected only by its pro rata share of B's net profit. The dividend declaration – and subsequent payment – by B has no effect on A's income. Under the equity method, the carrying value of the investment at 31 December 2004 is given by:

Original cost	EUR 9,000
Add: A's pro rata share of B's income	EUR 1,800
Deduct: A's pro rata share of dividends declared by B	(EUR 450)
Carrying value of investment in B	***EUR 11,250***

11.5   Accounting for joint ventures (proportionate consolidation)

A joint venture is a contractual arrangement whereby two or more parties undertake an economic activity that is subject to joint control.

The following are characteristics of all joint ventures:

- Two or more ventures are bound by a contractual arrangement.

- A joint venture establishes joint control; that is, the contractually agreed sharing of control over a joint venture is such that none of the parties on its own can exercise unilateral control.

- A venturer is a party to a joint venture and has joint control over that joint venture.

The existence of a contractual arrangement distinguishes joint ventures from associates. It is usually in writing and deals with such matters as:

- activity, duration and reporting
- appointment of a board of directors or equivalent body and voting rights
- capital contributions by venturers
- sharing by the venturers of the output, income, expenses or results of the joint venture (IAS 31).

An enterprise should account for its interest as a venturer in jointly controlled entities using either the equity method or proportionate consolidation. Procedures for proportionate consolidation are mostly similar to consolidation procedures already described.

The following example illustrates the accounting issues raised by joint control in an enterprise.

Example

Financial reporting of interests in joint ventures

Tecnocasa SpA was incorporated after three independent engineering companies decided to pool their knowledge to implement and market new technology. The three companies acquired the following interests in the equity of Tecnocasa SpA on the date of its incorporation:

- Elettrotecnica SpA   30%
- Officine Meccaniche SpA   40%
- Costruzioni Civili SpA   30%

The following information was taken from the financial statements of Tecnocasa SpA as well as one of the joint owners, Officine Meccaniche SpA.

Income statement for the year ended 30 June 2005 (amounts in thousands of euro):

	Officine Meccaniche SpA	Tecnocasa SpA
Revenue	3,100	980
Cost of sales	(1,800)	(610)
Gross profit	1,300	370
Other operating income	150	–
Operating costs	(850)	170
Profit before tax	600	200
Income tax expense	(250)	(90)
Net profit for the period	350	110

Officine Meccaniche SpA sold goods for EUR 600,000 to Tecnocasa SpA during the year. Included in Tecnocasa SpA's inventories as at 30 June 2005 is an amount of EUR 240,000, which represents goods purchased from Officine Meccaniche SpA at a profit mark-up of 20 per cent. The income tax rate is 30 per cent.

Tecnocasa SpA paid an administration fee of EUR 120,000 to Officine Meccaniche SpA during the year. This amount is included under the caption 'other operating income'.

In order to combine the results of Tecnocasa SpA with those of Officine Meccaniche SpA the following issues would need to be resolved:

1. Is Tecnocasa SpA an associate or joint venture for financial reporting purposes?

2. Which is the appropriate method for reporting the results of Tecnocasa in the financial statements of Officine Meccaniche?

3. How are the transactions between the two enterprises to be recorded and presented for financial reporting purposes in the consolidated income statement?

1. *First issue*: The existence of a contractual agreement, whereby the parties involved undertake an economic activity subject to joint control, distinguishes a joint venture from an associate. No one of the joint-venture partners is able to exercise unilateral control. However, in the event that no contractual agreement exists, the investment would be regarded as being an associate because the investor holds more than 20 per cent of the voting power and is therefore presumed to have significant influence over the investee.

2. *Second issue*: If Tecnocasa SpA is regarded as a joint venture, the proportionate consolidation method or the equity method must be used. However, if Tecnocasa SpA is regarded as an associate, the equity method would be used.

3. *Third issue*: It is assumed that Tecnocasa SpA is a joint venture for purposes of this illustration.

Consolidated income statement for the year ended 30 June 2005 (amounts in thousands of euro)

	(1) Off. Mecc.	(2) Tecn. 100%	(3) Tecn. 40%	(4) (1) + (3)	Consolidation adjustments	Consolidated income statement	Notes
Revenue	3,100	980	392	3,492	(240)	3,252	(a)
Cost of sales	(1,800)	(610)	(244)	(2,044)	224	(1,820)	(b)
Gross profit	1,300	370	148	1,448		1,432	
Other operating income	150	–	–	150	(48)	102	(c)
Operating costs	(850)	(170)	(68)	(918)	48	(870)	(d)
Profit before tax	600	200	80	680		664	
Income tax expense	(250)	(90)	(36)	(286)	5	(281)	(e)
Net profit	350	110	44	394		**383**	

The proportionate consolidation method is applied by adding 40 per cent of the income statement items of Tecnocasa SpA to those of Officine Meccaniche SpA.

The transactions between the two companies are then eliminated in the consolidation adjustments.

Calculations (amounts in thousands of euro):

(a) Sales

Officine Meccaniche	3,100
Intercompany sales (40% × 600)	(240)
Tecnocasa (40% × 980)	392
	3,252

(b) Cost of sales

Officine Meccaniche	1,800
Intercompany sales	(240)
Unrealised profit (40% × 20/120 × 240)	16
Tecnocasa (40% × 610)	244
	1,820

(c) Other operating income

Officine Meccaniche	150
Intercompany fee (40% × 120)	(48)
	102

(d) Operating costs

Officine Meccaniche	850
Tecnocasa (40% × 170)	68
Intercompany fee (40% × 120)	48
	870

Note: The administration fee is eliminated by reducing other operating income with Officine Meccaniche SpA's portion of the total fee, namely EUR 48,000, and reducing operating expenses accordingly. The net effect on the consolidated profit is nil.

(e) Income tax expense

Officine Meccaniche	250
Unrealised profit (30% × 16 rounded up)	(5)
Tecnocasa (40% × 90)	36
	281

Note: The income taxes payable on the unrealised profit (EUR 5) represent a deferred tax asset from the group's point of view.

11.6   Accounting for minority ownerships

As shown in Figure 11.2, investments that do not give effective control may represent either a short-term or long-term investment. In both cases they are accounted for at fair value (also known as mark-to-market) in accordance with IAS 39. The only difference is that any unrealised gain/loss on short-term investment is recognised in the income statement while any unrealised gain/loss on long-term investment represents a change in equity without passing through the income statement.

The following example illustrates how to account for trading securities.

Example

Mark-to-market and unrealised profit taken through the income statement

On 30 November 2004, a company buys 100 shares of Gamazon for EUR 90 per share and 100 shares of BMI for EUR 75 per share.

The securities are classified as trading securities (current assets) and are valued at fair value (market value).

This classification implies that any increase or decrease in the value of the security is included in net profit in the year in which it occurs. Also, any income received from the security is recorded in net profit.

To record the initial purchases, the entry is:

Dr Trading securities	EUR 16,500(*)	
Cr Cash		EUR 16,500

(*) This amount is given by: (100 shares of Gamazon × EUR 90) + (100 shares of BMI × EUR 75)

Let us assume that on 31 December 2004, Gamazon's share price was EUR 70 per share and BMI's was EUR 80 per share. Therefore when preparing its financial statements, our company should account for any unrealised gain/loss on its investments.

Its investments in Gamazon and BMI have fallen to EUR 15,000 (100 × EUR 70 + 100 × EUR 80). The short-term investments account is adjusted as follows:

Dr Unrealised loss on investments	EUR 1,500	
Cr Trading securities		EUR 1,500

Note that the loss on Gamazon and gain on BMI are netted. Thus, a net loss is recorded, which reduces the company's profit. This is an unrealised loss, as the shares have not been sold, so the company has not actually realised a loss, but this is still recorded in the income statement.

Suppose that in mid-January 2005, the company receives a dividend of EUR 0.16 for each BMI share. It accounts for the dividends as follows:

Dr Cash	EUR 16(*)	
Cr Investment income		EUR 16

(*) This amount is given by: (EUR 0.16 × 100 shares of BMI)

Now assume that on 23 January 2005, the enterprise sells both securities receiving EUR 85 per share for Gamazon and EUR 90 per share for the BMI. It will account for this transaction as shown below:

Dr Cash	EUR 17,500(*)	
Cr Trading securities		EUR 15,000
Cr Gain on investments		EUR 2,500

(*) This amount is given by: (100 shares of Gamazon × EUR 85) + (100 shares of BMI × EUR 90)

The amount of gain which is realised and recorded is equal to the proceeds of EUR 17,500 less the balance of the short-term investments account (which is EUR 15,000, after the entry made on 31 December 2004).

Summary

- Financial reporting for investments in other enterprises depends on the parent's ownership of such enterprises.

- When the ownership share is less than 20 per cent, it is presumed that the investor cannot exert influence on the decisions of the investee. These investments are shown at their fair values in the balance sheet.

- Ownership between 20 per cent and 50 per cent is presumed to give the ability to influence decisions of the investee. The equity method is used to account for such investments.

- Consolidation is required for subsidiaries, i.e. when ownership generally exceeds 50 per cent. Consolidated financial statements are designed to portray the economic activities of the parent and subsidiaries as if they were one entity.

- When consolidating a subsidiary, goodwill generally arises. Goodwill is the difference between the cost of the investment and the fair value of the assets and liabilities acquired. In the consolidated financial statements it represents an asset and is subject to annual impairment test.

- Where a subsidiary is not wholly owned by the parent, it is necessary to account for minority interest. Minority shareholders are part owners of the subsidiary and, therefore, part owners of the equity or net assets of the subsidiary. As all the net assets of the subsidiary will be included in the consolidated balance sheet, the minority interest will be shown as partly financing those net assets.

References and research

The IASB documents relevant for this chapter are:

- IAS 27 – *Consolidated and Separate Financial Statements*
- IAS 28 – *Accounting for Investments in Associates*
- IAS 31 – *Financial Reporting of Interests in Joint Ventures*
- IAS 39 – *Financial Instruments: Recognition and Measurement*
- IFRS 3 – *Business Combinations*
- SIC 12 – *Consolidation: Special Purpose Entities*

The following are examples of research papers and books that take the issues of this chapter further:

- L.T. Johnson and K.R. Petrone, 'Is goodwill an asset?', *Accounting Horizons*, September 1998
- C.W. Nobes, 'An analysis of the international development of the equity method', *Abacus*, February 2002
- PricewaterhouseCoopers, SIC-12 and FIN46R. The substance of control, 2000 (www.pwc.com/ifrs)
- Hennie Van Greuning, *International Financial Reporting Standards: A Practical Guide*, The World Bank, 2005, Part II
- Frank Wood and Alan Sangster, *Business Accounting*, Vol. 2, 9th Edition, Financial Times-Prentice Hall, 2002, Part 3

Questions

11.1 (a) What criterion is used to determine whether a parent–subsidiary relationship exists?

(b) Why have a subsidiary or subsidiaries?

(c) Suppose company A buys 100 per cent of the shares of B for cash. How does B record this transaction in its books?

(d) Distinguish between *control of* an enterprise and *significant influence over* an enterprise.

(e) What is the *equity method*? When do you apply it?

(f) How do you account for investments of less than 20 per cent in other enterprises?

11.2 (a) A consolidated income statement will show higher net profit than the parent-company-only income statement when both the parent and subsidiary have disclosed net profits in their respective income statements. Do you agree? Why?

(b) Goodwill is the excess of purchase price over the book values of the individual assets acquired. Do you agree? Why?

(c) What is a minority interest? Why do minority interests arise in connection with consolidated financial statements, but not with investments in associated companies?

11.3 La Vecchia Società (V) acquired for cash all shares of La Giovane Compagnia (G) on 31 March 2005 for EUR 87,000. The balance sheets of the two companies before the acquisition were as follows (amount in thousands of euro):

	V	G
Non-current assets	1,639	27
Current assets	3,281	54
Total assets	*4,920*	*81*
Share capital	2,000	58
Retained earnings	800	4
Non-current liabilities	1,760	15
Current liabilities	360	4
Total shareholders' equity and liabilities	*4,920*	*81*

An independent appraiser valued the assets of G as follows:

	Fair value EUR
Non-current assets	29
Current assets	56

Prepare a consolidated balance sheet as at the acquisition date.

11.4 Mini Company is a wholly owned subsidiary of Maxi Company. At the end of the present accounting period, the following items will affect the consolidated financial statements:

1. During the year, Mini Company sold goods to Maxi Company for EUR 337 million. The cost of these goods for Mini Company was EUR 285 million. Maxi Company sold all these goods to third parties.

2. Maxi Company owes Mini Company EUR 75 million (trade payables).
3. Mini has a payable to Maxi for a long-term loan from Maxi for EUR 400 million.
4. Maxi earned interest for EUR 20 million from this loan during the year.

Determine and comment on the consolidation adjustments that would be needed to prepare the consolidated financial statements.

11.5 On 1 February 2005 Diletta & Co paid EUR 620,000 to acquire all the issued shares of Lollo SpA. The recorded assets and liabilities of Lollo SpA on 1 February 2005 are (amounts in thousands of euro):

Cash and cash equivalents		60
Inventory		180
PPE		
Historical cost	540	
Accumulated depreciation	(220)	
Net book value		320
Intangible assets		100
Liabilities		(120)
Net assets		540

On 1 February 2005 Lollo's inventory had a fair value of EUR 150 and its PPE had a fair value of EUR 380.

What is the amount of goodwill resulting from the business combination?

11.6 ABC Company had the following transactions with XYZ Company over a two-year period:

Year 2003
1. On 1 January, ABC purchased a 35 per cent interest in XYZ for EUR 700,000 cash.
2. XYZ had net profit of EUR 70,000.
3. At year-end, XYZ paid its shareholders dividends of EUR 60,000.

Year 2004
1. ABC purchased on 1 January an additional 5 per cent of XYZ's shares for EUR 75,000 cash.
2. XYZ declared dividends of EUR 100,000.
3. XYZ had net profit of EUR 150,000 for the year.
4. At year-end, XYZ paid its shareholders the dividends declared.

Determine the carrying value of the investment in XYZ in the balance sheet of ABC as at 1 January 2003, 31 December 2003 and 2004.

11.7 Dolo Inc acquired a 40 per cent interest in the ordinary shares of Nutro Inc on the date of incorporation, 1 January 2000, for an amount of EUR 220,000. This enabled Dolo Inc to exercise significant influence over Nutro Inc. On 31 December 2003, the shareholders' equity of Nutro Inc was as follows:

	EUR
Ordinary issued share capital	550,000
Reserves	180,000
Retained earnings	650,000
	1,380,000

The following extracts were taken from the financial statements of Nutro Inc for the year ending 31 December 2004:

	EUR
Income statement (extract)	
Profit after tax	228,000
Extraordinary item	(12,000)
Net profit for the period	216,000
Statement of changes in equity (extract)	
Accumulated profits at beginning of the year	650,000
Net profit for the period	216,000
Dividends paid	(80,000)
Accumulated profits at end of the year	786,000

In November 2004, Dolo Inc sold inventories to Nutro Inc for the first time. The total sales amounted to EUR 50,000 and Dolo Inc earned a profit of EUR 10,000 on that transaction. None of the inventories had been sold by Nutro Inc by 31 December 2004. The income tax rate is 30 per cent.

Determine the carrying value of the investment in Nutro Inc as at 31 December 2004.

Case study — Intangible assets in the consolidated financial statements   FT

. . . The impetus is an accounting change that fundamentally alters the way listed companies in Europe account for acquisitions. Its impact will become apparent next year [2005] when these companies report results.

The new regime, which resembles one already implemented in the US, would require public companies to record the value of intangible assets – such as brands – on their balance sheets when they are acquired. When these assets are judged to have an indefinite life – which is often the case with a brand – they will be subject to annual review for impairment. The same test will be conducted on goodwill – the difference between the value of the assets acquired and the price paid.

The resulting writedowns which would follow any impairment are 'only' paper losses, as they do not affect a company's cashflow statement. But the US experience suggests that such exercises can produce stomach-churning moments for managements that have overpaid for intangible assets or managed them badly. In 2002, the company then known as AOL Time Warner took a staggering Dollars 54bn charge for the value lost when AOL acquired Time Warner during the waning days of the bull market in 2000. As a demonstration of management failure it could hardly have been more dramatic . . .

While all European companies will be required to comply with the new rules, the policies for unlisted companies vary by country. UK private companies have the option of adopting the new rules. Those in countries such as Spain or France are barred from the new regime.

The new rules, which are being implemented by the International Accounting Standards Board, seek to address one of the most glaring deficiencies in accounting – its lack of relevance to the way business is conducted in today's economy.

The concept of an asset dates back to the time when most assets were tangible. Things such as plant and equipment were assigned a market value and expected to wear out over time. In today's service economies, most assets would be intangible – such as the group accountants refer to as the 'assembled work force', the assets that famously ride up and down in the elevators every day.

'The accounting model is based on the economy of 120 years ago,' says Robert Willens, tax and accounting analyst at Lehman Brothers in New York. 'The model is geared to an economy that isn't in existence anymore.'

The new standards focus on the confusion that resulted as more and more acquisition activity involved companies that consisted largely of intangible assets – such as AOL. Under the old rules, the value of tangible assets was calculated and the difference between that amount and the purchase price was recorded as goodwill and written off over decades.

The deficiencies were obvious. Attributing massive amounts of value to goodwill raised more questions than it answered for investors in public companies. What specific assets accounted for the goodwill? How were managements valuing these assets? How were companies managing these assets over time?

Moreover, the practice of slowly writing off goodwill – as a charge against earnings – also had problems. Some brands, for example, increase in value over time and these values can be maintained for long periods. Consider Coca-Cola, IBM, Rolls-Royce or, to pick a more classical example, Stradivarius.

Under the new rules, companies will have to calculate values for a long list of assets.

Determining such values is tricky. The methods suggested by the regulators typically involve making use of estimates of future cashflows and economic conditions – never an easy task. A further option would involve comparing the prices fetched by recent sales of comparable assets.

Regardless of the method used, one complication will be figuring out which assets have definite lives – meaning their values will be written off over time – and which do not. In some cases, such as those involving contracts, the answers will be obvious. Other assets might give companies more wiggle room, which raises the possibility of abuses, Willens says.

The new accounting rules represent only a partial response to the question of how to better inform investors because they only govern intangible assets that are acquired. Companies are not being required to value intangible assets they create and build themselves. There is also no provision for giving intangible assets a higher value over time . . .

'Branding – the bean counters get into creative accounting', Gary Silverman, *Financial Times*, 31 August 2004

Discuss the implications of the new IAS/IFRS rules on the financial statements and share prices. Illustrate your comments based on actual examples of listed companies.

12 Measuring and reporting cash flows

Objectives

When you have completed this chapter you should be able to:

- understand corporate liquidity and the factors that drive it
- define 'cash and cash equivalents'
- classify activities affecting cash as operating, investing and financing activities
- use the indirect and direct methods to calculate cash flows from operations
- relate depreciation to cash flows provided by operating activities
- determine cash flows from financing and investing activities
- prepare a cash flow statement.

12.1 Introduction

Despite their usefulness, the income statement and the balance sheet do not stress the importance of liquidity.

The accruals-based nature of the income statement tends to obscure the question of how and where an enterprise is generating the cash it needs to continue its operations and thereby generate more cash.

People and organisations will not normally accept other than cash in settlement of their claims against an enterprise. If an enterprise wants to employ people, it must pay them in cash. If it wants to buy new equipment, the seller of the asset will normally insist on being paid in cash, probably after a short period of credit. When enterprises fail, it is their inability to find the cash to pay claimants that really drives them under.

These factors lead to cash being the pre-eminent business asset and, therefore, the one that analysts and others watch most carefully in trying to assess the ability of enterprises to survive and/or to take advantage of commercial opportunities as they arise.

The old business adage says: *cash is king*. This reflects the fact that it is possible to make a profit yet still run into cash flow problems. A successful enterprise is one which actively manages the cash flow.

12.2 Corporate liquidity and the cash flow cycle

12.2.1 Operating cash cycle

The flow chart presented in Figure 12.1 shows a part of the total cash cycle, the part that we refer to as the working capital cash flow.

Central to the system is a cash tank, or reservoir, through which cash flows constantly. It is crucial to the independent survival of an enterprise that this tank does not run dry.

Supporting the cash tank is a supplementary supply, representing overdrafts or unused short-term borrowings. These provide a first line of defence against a cash shortage. Day-to-day liquidity consists of these two separate cash reservoirs. The main flow of cash into the reservoir comes from 'trade receivables'. These are the customers who pay for the goods or services received from the enterprise.

The main cash outflows can be identified under two headings:

- payments of 'trade payables', that is, the suppliers of raw materials and services
- payments of staff salaries/wages, and payments of all other operating expenses.

As explained in section 4.1 (see Figure 4.1 on page 70), we can trace the steps in the cycle: 'trade payables' supply 'raw materials'. In time these pass through 'work in progress' and then into the 'finished goods' category. During this conversion, cash

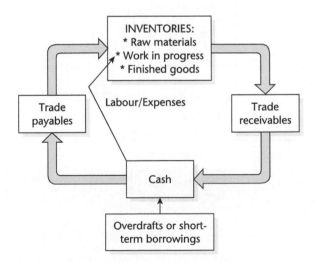

Figure 12.1 Working capital cash flow cycle
Source: Walsh (2002)

is absorbed in the form of labour expenses and payments to suppliers. In due course, these 'finished goods' are sold. Value passes down into the 'trade receivables' box, from which it flows back into the 'cash' reservoir to complete the cycle.

12.2.2 Operating cash cycle and the role of profit and depreciation and amortisation

In Figure 12.2, two further input values are shown that produce an increase in cash in circulation:

- profit
- depreciation and amortisation.

The input from profit is easy to understand. Normally goods are sold at a price that exceeds cost. For instance, if goods that cost EUR 100 are sold at a price of EUR 125, the profit of EUR 25 will quickly flow into the enterprise in the form of cash.

It is a little more difficult to understand the cash input from depreciation and amortisation. It will be easy to see when we understand that:

Operating cash flow = Operating profit + Depreciation and amortisation

For most enterprises, depreciation and amortisation are the only major cost items in the income statement that do not have a cash outflow attached to them. While referred to as a source of cash, it is really the retention of profit, and therefore cash. Even though depreciation and amortisation do not cause a cash outflow, they represent a cost nevertheless. The relevant cash outflow simply took place at an earlier time. At the time the related non-current assets are purchased, the cash representing the cost is not charged against profits. It is, instead, recorded in the balance sheet as a non-current asset.

As the asset is used or consumed, an appropriate amount of cost is charged to the income statement. This is called depreciation or amortisation depending on whether the non-current asset is tangible or intangible, as we saw in Chapter 7.

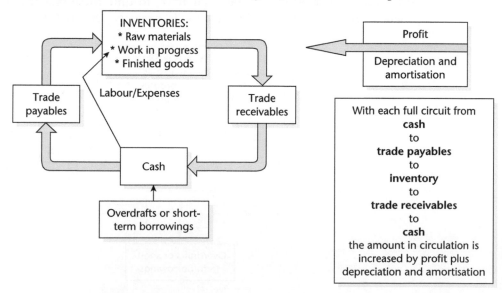

Figure 12.2 Operating cash cycle and the role of profit, depreciation and amortisation
Source: Walsh (2002)

Example

Depreciation and cash flow

Let us assume that a small haulage business has one single asset, namely a vehicle valued at EUR 40,000 that the owner uses to transport goods on a jobbing basis. The enterprise has no inventories or trade receivables. It has no bank overdraft or other loans and all its transactions are carried out for cash. The opening balance sheet, income statement and closing balance sheet follow.

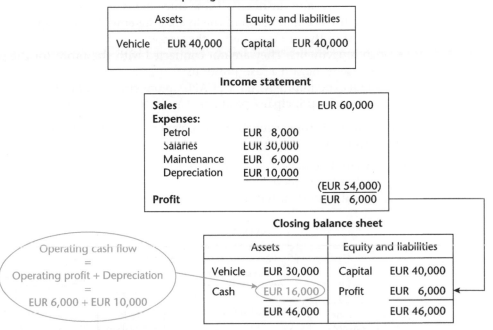

Opening balance sheet

Assets		Equity and liabilities	
Vehicle	EUR 40,000	Capital	EUR 40,000

Income statement

Sales		EUR 60,000
Expenses:		
Petrol	EUR 8,000	
Salaries	EUR 30,000	
Maintenance	EUR 6,000	
Depreciation	EUR 10,000	
		(EUR 54,000)
Profit		EUR 6,000

Closing balance sheet

Operating cash flow
=
Operating profit + Depreciation
=
EUR 6,000 + EUR 10,000

Assets		Equity and liabilities	
Vehicle	EUR 30,000	Capital	EUR 40,000
Cash	EUR 16,000	Profit	EUR 6,000
	EUR 46,000		EUR 46,000

Source: Walsh (2002)

The opening balance sheet is simple. It shows a single asset of EUR 40,000 that is represented by capital of the same amount.

The income statement for the period presents sales of EUR 60,000, total expenses of EUR 54,000 and a profit of EUR 6,000.

The closing balance sheet shows a cash figure of EUR 16,000. The enterprise started with no cash and ended up with EUR 16,000, but the profit was EUR 6,000.

How can this be? If we look at the expenses we note that the depreciation charge is EUR 10,000. No cash was paid for this expense. The operating cash receipts were EUR 60,000 and the operating cash expenses were EUR 44,000. Therefore the net cash from trading was EUR 16,000. However, from this net cash we must deduct depreciation to arrive at the profit of EUR 6,000.

Therefore, it is simply a convenient shortcut to arrive at the operating cash flow by adding back depreciation to profit.

An interesting aspect of the effect of depreciation and amortisation is that certain enterprises can suffer serious trading losses without suffering cash shortage. These are enterprises where depreciation and amortisation represent a big proportion of the total cost, e.g. transportation and utility companies on the one hand and pharmaceutical and telecommunications companies on the other. So long as losses are less than the depreciation/amortisation charged to the financial statements, operations are cash positive.

12.2.3 Non-operating cash flows

In Figure 12.3, additional outflows are added:

- interest, tax and dividends. These three items are deducted from EBIT (earnings before interest and taxes) in the income statement. They represent a distribution of most of the profit earned in the period;
- loan repayments. They are not connected with the profit for the period but can give rise to negative cash positions;
- capital expenditure (CAPEX). CAPEX represents cash outflows for the purchase of fixed assets, principally productive assets to generate future revenue streams.

In Figure 12.4, three sources of cash from external sources are shown feeding into the cash reservoir. These are:

- new equity capital
- new long-term loans
- disposal of non-current assets.

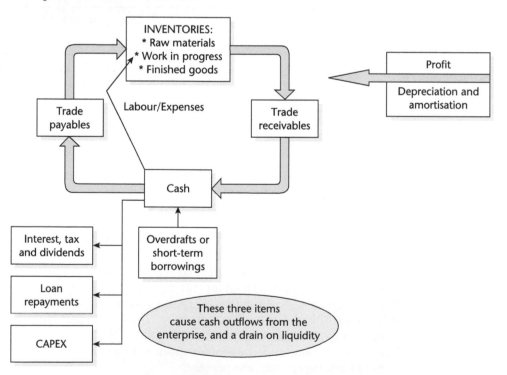

Figure 12.3 Non-operating cash outflows
Source: Walsh (2002)

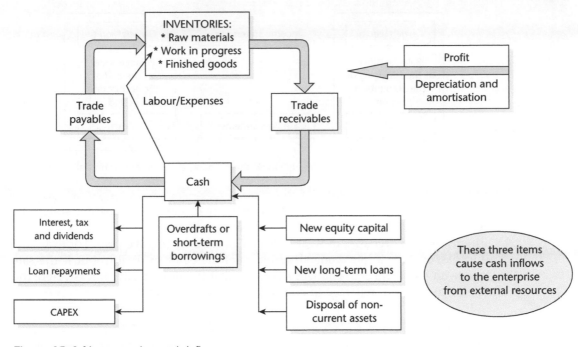

Figure 12.4 Non-operating cash inflows

Source: Walsh (2002)

12.3   Objectives of a cash flow statement and its relationship with the income statement and balance sheet

Information about the cash flows of an enterprise is useful in providing users of financial statements with a basis to assess the ability of the enterprise to generate cash and cash equivalents, and the uses the enterprise makes of those cash in-flows.

The economic decisions that are taken by users require an evaluation of the ability of an enterprise to generate cash and cash equivalents and the timing and certainty of their generation.

A cash flow statement, when used in conjunction with the rest of the financial statements, provides information that enables users to determine the following:

- the ability of an enterprise to generate cash from its operations
- the cash consequences of investing and financing decisions
- the sustainability of an enterprise's cash-generating capability
- how well operating cash flow correlates to net profit
- information about the liquidity and long-term solvency of an enterprise
- the ability of an enterprise to finance its growth from internally generated funds.

A statement of cash flow reports the cash receipts and cash payments of an enterprise during a given period.

It shows the relationship of net profit to changes in cash balances. Cash balances can decline despite positive profit and vice versa.

It explains where cash and cash equivalents came from during a period and where they went.

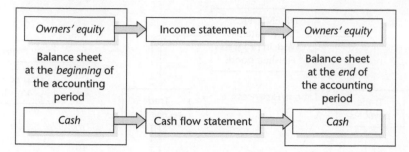

Figure 12.5 Relationship between the balance sheet, income statement and cash flow statement

Cash flow statement confines itself to cash movements, while income statement is concerned with movements in wealth (see Figure 12.5).

Increases and decreases in wealth do not necessarily involve cash. For example, a business making a sale (generating revenue) increases its wealth, but if the sale is made on credit, no cash changes hands – not at the time of sale, at least. Here the increase in wealth is reflected in another asset (trade receivables).

Activity 12.1 Effect of transactions on cash and profit

Question:

State the effect (increase, decrease or no effect) of the following business/accounting events on both cash and profit:

	Effect on	
	Cash	Profit
1. Repayment of a loan	_____	_____
2. Making a sale on credit	_____	_____
3. Buying a fixed asset for cash	_____	_____
4. Receiving cash from a customer	_____	_____
5. Depreciating a fixed asset	_____	_____
6. Buying goods for cash	_____	_____
7. Issue of shares for cash	_____	_____

Solutions to activities can be found at www. personed.co.ok/kothari

12.4 Cash and cash equivalents

Cash equivalents are held for the purpose of meeting short-term cash commitments rather than for investment or other purposes.

For an investment to qualify as a cash equivalent it must be readily convertible into cash and be subject to an insignificant risk of changes in value.

Thus, an investment normally qualifies as a cash equivalent only when it has a short maturity of, for example, three months or less from the date of acquisition (see Figure 12.6).

Cash and cash equivalents as of December 31, 2004 amounted to €3.6 billion
(2003: €2.7 billion). In accordance with IAS 7 (Cash Flow Statements), this item also
includes financial securities with original maturities of up to three months. The liquid assets
of €3.6 billion (2003: €2.9 billion) shown in the balance sheet also include marketable
securities and other instruments.

Figure 12.6 Cash and cash equivalents
Source: Bayer Annual Report 2004

Equity investments are excluded from cash equivalents unless they are, in substance,
cash equivalents.

Bank borrowings are generally considered to be financing activities.

However, bank overdrafts form an integral part of an enterprise's cash management. Thus, bank overdrafts are included as a negative component of cash and cash
equivalents. A characteristic of such banking arrangements is that the bank balance
often fluctuates from being positive to overdrawn.

Cash flows exclude movements between items that constitute cash or cash equivalents because these components are part of the cash management of an enterprise
rather than part of its operating, investing and financing activities.

Cash management includes the investment of excess cash in cash equivalents.

12.5   Activities affecting cash

Two primary areas of management of an enterprise affect cash:

- *operating management*, which is largely concerned with the major day-to-day
  activities that generate revenues and incur expenses (**operating activities**)
- *financial management*, which is largely concerned with where to get cash (**financing
  activities**) and how to use cash (**investing activities**).

12.5.1 Operating activities

Operating activities are generally activities or transactions that affect the income
statement. For example, sales are linked to collections from customers, and wage
expenses are closely tied to cash payments to employees. The amount of cash flows
arising from operating activities is a key indicator of the extent to which the operations
of the enterprise have generated sufficient cash flows to repay loans, pay dividends
and make new investments without recourse to external sources of financing. Information about the specific components of historical operating cash flows is useful, in
conjunction with other information, in forecasting future operating cash flows. Cash
flows from operating activities are primarily derived from the principal revenue-
producing activities of the enterprise. Therefore, they generally result from the
transactions and other events that enter into the determination of net profit or loss.

Examples of cash flows from operating activities are:

- cash receipts from the sale of goods and the rendering of services
- cash receipts from royalties, fees, commissions and other revenue

- cash payments to suppliers for goods and services
- cash payments to and on behalf of employees
- cash payments or refunds of income taxes
- cash receipts and payments from contracts held for dealing or trading purposes (IAS 7).

Transactions such as the sale of an item of plant may give rise to a gain or loss which is included in the determination of net profit or loss. However, the related cash flows are cash flows from investing activities.

12.5.2 Investing activities

Investing activities involve providing and collecting cash as a lender or as an owner of securities, and acquiring and disposing of plant and equipment, and other long-lived assets.

The separate disclosure of cash flows arising from investing activities is important because the cash flows represent the extent to which expenditures have been made for resources intended to generate future income and cash flows.

Examples of cash flows arising from investing activities are:

- cash payments to acquire property, plant and equipment, intangibles and other long-term assets
- cash receipts from sales of property, plant and equipment, intangibles and other long-term assets
- cash payments to acquire equity or debt instruments of other enterprises and interests in joint ventures
- cash receipts from sales of equity or debt instruments of other enterprises and interests in joint ventures
- cash advances and loans made to other parties
- cash receipts from the repayment of advances and loans made to other parties
- cash payments for futures contracts, forward contracts, option contracts and swap contracts except when the contracts are held for dealing or trading purposes, or the payments are classified as financing activities (IAS 7).

12.5.3 Financing activities

Financing activities involve obtaining resources as a borrower or issuer of securities and repaying creditors and owners.

The separate disclosure of cash flows arising from financing activities is important because it is useful in predicting claims on future cash flows by providers of capital to the enterprise.

Examples of cash flows arising from financing activities are:

- cash proceeds from issuing shares or other equity instruments
- cash payments to owners to acquire or redeem the enterprise's shares
- cash proceeds from issuing debentures, loans, notes, bonds, mortgages and other short- or long-term borrowings
- cash repayments of amounts borrowed
- cash payments by a lessee for the reduction of the outstanding liability relating to a finance lease (IAS 7).

12.6   How to prepare a cash flow statement

12.6.1 Sources and applications of funds

There are several methods that can be used to prepare a cash flow statement depending on the intended use. The following example, based on Walsh (2002), illustrates the sources and applications of funds method. When using this method, it can be difficult at first to distinguish sources from uses and it is easy to put items in the wrong place. You should remember a simple rule which makes the classification easy:

	Increase	**Decrease**
Asset	Application	Source
Liability	Source	Application

Example

Sources and applications of funds method

In the table below a simplified balance sheet is shown for 2003 and 2004. It has been laid out in vertical columns to facilitate comparison between the two years.

To the right of the balance sheet, two extra columns have been added – respectively 'source' and 'application'.

Balance sheets (thousand of euro)	2003	2004	Source	Application
Assets				
Non-current assets	45,000	65,000		20,000
Current assets				
Inventories	25,000	28,700		
Trade and other receivables	30,000	32,000		
Cash and cash equivalents	3,500	0		
Total Assets	103,500	125,700		
Owners' equity and liabilities				
Equity				
Issued capital	36,000	36,000		
Reserves	19,000	21,500		
Non-current liabilities	16,000	18,000		
Current liabilities				
Trade and other payables	27,500	34,000		
Bank overdraft	0	10,200		
Taxes payable	5,000	6,000	1,000	
Total Equity and Liabilities	103,500	125,700		

Increase in assets = Application of funds

Increase in liability = Source of funds

Source: Walsh (2002)

Two entries are illustrated:

- The logic of the first is fairly obvious. Non-current assets have increased from EUR 45,000 to EUR 65,000. The company paid by cheque or bank transfer EUR 20,000 (for the purpose of this example we ignore revaluation and depreciation). The company 'applied' EUR 20,000 to acquire a non-current asset.

- The second entry is less obvious. The amount shown under 'tax payable' has increased from EUR 5,000 to EUR 6,000. How can an increase of tax be a source of funds? The liability for tax of EUR 6,000 is unpaid. However, EUR 1,000 has been deducted from the profit for this liability and therefore we have additional 'cash'. The company now has the use of additional EUR 1,000 of government money than it had one year ago, so for the present it is a source of funds. This liability will need to be paid off in due course. It will then disappear from the balance sheet and it will decrease cash and cash equivalents.

Balance sheets (thousands of euro)	2003	2004	Source	Application
Assets				
Non-current assets	45,000	65,000		20,000
Current assets				
Inventories	25,000	28,700		3,700
Trade and other receivables	30,000	32,000		2,000
Cash and cash equivalents	3,500	0	3,500	
Total Assets	103,500	125,700		
Owners' equity and liabilities				
Equity				
Issued capital	36,000	36,000		
Reserves	19,000	21,500	2,500	
Non-current liabilities	16,000	18,000	2,000	
Current liabilities				
Trade and other payables	27,500	34000	6,500	
Bank overdraft	0	10200	10,200	
Taxes payable	5,000	6000	1,000	
Total Equity and Liabilities	103,500	125,700	25,700	25,700

Net movements
This figure gives the net change in non-current assets. It probably masks a depreciation charge offset by an even greater figure for CAPEX, e.g. if depreciation of EUR 5,000 had been charged in the period, then the total CAPEX is EUR 25,000.

Source: Walsh (2002)

As highlighted in the box on the right, the method just illustrated picks up only the net movements in balance sheet values. Of course, a net change can be the result of two opposing movements that partly cancel out.

A cash flow statement should identify such items. Even more importantly some movements in the balance sheet values do not give rise to cash flow – revaluation of fixed assets is an example. It may be necessary to get behind some of the numbers to find out if there are any offsetting or non-cash movements.

Once the sources and applications have been identified and reconciled, we can use various layouts of the cash flow statement to draw a conclusion on specific issues.

For instance, the company's cash position could deteriorate even though high profits have been achieved. To explain why, we could use a layout that would reconcile opening and closing cash. It would show:

- opening balance of cash and cash equivalents
- cash outflows
- cash inflows
- closing balance of cash and cash equivalents.

Figure 12.7 (on page 246) shows such a reconciliation. In the cash reconciliation statement all the entries are taken from the sources/applications statement shown in the last example. Cash-out items are taken from the application column and cash-in items from the source column. The movements in cash and cash equivalents and bank overdraft are not listed because they are included in the opening and closing cash positions.

The net cash outflow of EUR 13,700 is the difference between total cash outflows (EUR 25,700) and total cash inflows (EUR 12,000). Why do you think this enterprise experienced such a negative cash flow?

The answer lies in the fact that the enterprise acquired EUR 20,000 of non-current assets. This relatively large cash outflow has not been matched by any corresponding large cash inflow.

The information provided in Figure 12.7 adds considerably more to our knowledge of the company's affairs derived from the balance sheet and income statement. Alternative layouts of the cash flow data provide more insights.

In Figure 12.8 (on page 247), the same original data has been plotted into a grid that distinguishes between 'long' and 'short' sources on the one hand, and 'long' and 'short' applications on the other.

Each item in the 'source' column has been slotted into its appropriate 'long' or 'short' box. The same applies to all items in the 'application' column. The four totals in the four boxes provide a useful comparison.

As you can see, the main outflow of cash has taken place in the 'long-application' box, which is the acquisition of non-current assets for EUR 20,000 (*investing activities*). The corresponding 'long-source' box shows EUR 4,500. The total amount of cash received by way of non-current liabilities and reserves (*financing activities*) falls considerably short of the expenditure in non-current assets.

As 'sources' and 'applications' must balance, the deficit must be covered by the 'short-source' box. In fact, most of the money that has come into the enterprise has come from 'trade and other payables' and 'bank overdraft'. These are repayable within the next 12 months. So the enterprise has used short-term sources to finance long-term investments.

This layout of the cash flow highlights the fact that 'current liabilities' have increased by much more than 'current assets'.

Strategy for long- and short-term movements of funds

Figure 12.9 (on page 248) shows the total values in each section of the grid. Arrows show the movements of funds. The largest single movement of funds in the enterprise for the 2003–2004 period shows that EUR 15,500 is raised short-term and invested long-term.

The problem with this strategy is that short-term funds are generally required to be repaid quickly, but cash cannot easily be made available from the investment to meet this repayment. Therefore, a new source of funds must be found to meet the repayments. Conditions could deteriorate to the extent that the enterprise may be unable to raise new money and it would then face a financial crisis.

Balance sheets (thousands of euro)	2003	2004	Source	Application
Assets				
Non-current assets	45,000	65,000		20,000
Current assets				
Inventories	25,000	28,700		3,700
Trade and other receivables	30,000	32,000		2,000
Cash and cash equivalents	3,500	0	3,500	
Total Assets	103,500	125,700		
Owners' equity and liabilities				
Equity				
Issued capital	36,000	36,000		
Reserves	19,000	21,500	2,500	
Non-current liabilities	16,000	18,000	2,000	
Current liabilities				
Accounts payable	27,500	34,000	6,500	
Bank overdraft	0	10,200	10,200	
Taxes payable	5,000	6,000	1,000	
Total Equity and Liabilities	103,500	125,700	25,700	25,700

Cash reconciliation statement (thousands of euro)

(A) Opening cash position		3,500
Cash outflows (Applications)		
Non-current assets	20,000	
Inventories	3,700	
Trade and other receivables	2,000	
(B) Total cash outflows		25,700
Cash inflows (Sources)		
Reserves	2,500	
Non-current liabilities	2,000	
Trade and other payables	6,500	
Taxes payable	1,000	
(C) Total cash inflows		12,000
(D) Net cash outflow (C–B)		(13,700)
Closing cash position (A–D)		(10,200)

Figure 12.7 Sources and applications of funds and cash reconciliation statement

Note: A cash balance can be positive or negative. A positive balance is where there is a cash asset whereas a negative position represents a short-term bank loan or a bank overdraft.

Source: Walsh (2002)

Balance sheets (thousands of euro)	2003	2004	Source	Application
Assets				
Non-current assets	45,000	65,000		20,000
Current assets				
Inventories	25,000	28,700		3,700
Trade and other receivables	30,000	32,000		2,000
Cash and cash equivalents	3,500	0	3,500	
Total Assets	103,500	125,700		
Owners' equity and liabilities				
Equity				
Issued capital	36,000	36,000		
Reserves	19,000	21,500	2,500	
Non-current liabilities	16,000	18,000	2,000	
Current liabilities				
Accounts payable	27,500	34,000	6,500	
Bank overdraft	0	10,200	10,200	
Taxes payable	5,000	6,000	1,000	
Total Equity and Liabilities	103,500	125,700	25,700	25,700

		Source		Application
		EUR 000		EUR 000
Long	Reserves	2,500	Non-current assets	20,000
	Non-current liabilities	2,000		
		4,500		20,000
Short	Bank overdraft	10,200	Inventories	3,700
	Trade and other payables	6,500	Trade and other receivables	2,000
	Taxes payable	1,000		
	Cash and cash equivalents	3,500		
		21,200		5,700
		25,700		25,700

Figure 12.8 Long- and short-term sources and applications of funds

Source: Walsh (2002)

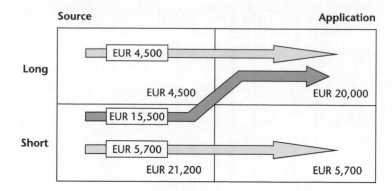

Figure 12.9 Pattern of cash flows (thousands of euro)

Note: The most significant movement of funds is that EUR 15,500 is raised in the short source box and invested in the long application box. When an enterprise raises funds short term and invests them long term, it increases the risk of a financial crisis.

Source: Walsh (2002)

Over a long period, the cash pattern should be as illustrated in Figure 12.10:

1. investments in non-current assets being funded by long-term sources
2. short-term investments being funded by short-term sources
3. some long-term funds being invested in short-term assets.

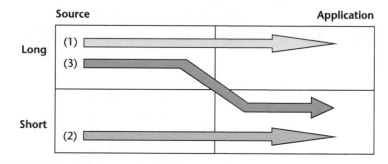

Figure 12.10 An ideal pattern of cash flows

Source: Walsh (2002)

12.6.2 How to report cash flows in accordance with IAS 7

According to IAS 7, the cash flow statement should be prepared by all enterprises. It should classify changes in cash and cash equivalents into:

- operating
- investing
- financing activities.

There are two methods to determine *cash flows from operating activities*:

- the direct method, which computes cash flow from operating activities as receipts less disbursements – this means that only the cash part of each item in the income statement is taken into account

- the indirect method, which computes cash flow from operating activities by adjusting the operating profit or loss on an accrual basis to reflect only cash receipts and outlays.

The *direct method* provides information which may be useful in estimating future cash flows and which is not available under the indirect method. Under the direct method, information about major classes of gross cash receipts and gross cash payments may be obtained either:

- from the accounting records of the enterprise or
- by adjusting sales, cost of sales and other items in the income statement for:
  - ❒ changes during the period in inventories and operating receivables and payables
  - ❒ other non-cash items
  - ❒ other items for which the cash effects are investing or financing cash flows (IAS 7).

Under the *indirect method*, the net cash flow from operating activities is determined, as shown in Figure 12.11, by adjusting operating profit or loss for the effects of:

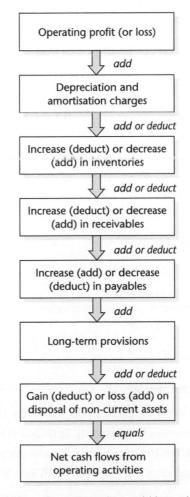

Figure 12.11 Reporting cash flows from operating activities – the indirect method

- changes during the period in inventories and operating receivables and payables
- non-cash items such as depreciation, amortisation, provisions, deferred taxes, etc.
- all other items for which the cash effects are investing or financing cash flows (IAS 7).

Depreciation/amortisation and cash flow from operating activities

The most crucial aspect of a statement of cash flows prepared using the indirect method is how depreciation/amortisation and other non-cash expenses relate to the cash flows generated by operating activities. Depreciation and amortisation are an allocation of historical cost to expense and *do not* entail a current outflow of cash. Therefore, depreciation and amortisation are added to the operating profit to compute cash flow simply to offset the original deduction in calculating the net profit in the income statement. As illustrated earlier, depreciation and amortisation are *not* a source of cash.

Example

Cash flows from operating activities

The income statement of Paolo & Francesca SpA is shown below:

Paolo & Francesca SpA
Income Statement
For the year ended 31 December 2004

(Amounts in thousands of euro)

Sales		8,200
Deduct Cost of sales:		
Opening inventory	2,100	
Add Purchases	4,600	
Deduct Ending inventory	1,700	
		(5,000)
Gross profit		3,200
Deduct Operating expenses:		
Selling expenses	900	
Administrative expenses	850	
		(1,750)
Operating profit		*1,450*

Additional information:

1. Trade and other receivables decreased by EUR 400,000 during 2004.
2. Prepaid expenses increased by EUR 200,000 during 2004.
3. Trade payables (to suppliers of goods) decreased by EUR 400,000 in 2004.
4. Accrued expenses decreased by EUR 200,000 during the year.

5. Administrative expenses include depreciation charge for EUR 80,000.

6. Taxation is ignored.

Now we illustrate the operating section of the cash flow statement for Paolo & Francesca SpA prepared using both the direct and indirect method. You should note that:

- Under the indirect method, cash flow from operations is determined by making adjustments to operating profit.
- Under the direct method, cash flow from operations is determined by subtracting cash paid for operating activities from cash received from operating activities.
- The investing and financing sections of the statement are the same under the direct and indirect methods
- Cash at the end of the period should be the same as the amount reported in the balance sheet.

(a) Indirect method

Paolo & Francesca SpA
Cash flows from operating activities
For the year ended 31 December 2004

(Amounts in thousands of euro)

Operating profit		1,450
Adjustments to reconcile operating profit		
to net cash provided by operating activities:		
Depreciation	80	
Decrease in trade and other receivables	400	
Decrease in inventory	400	
Increase in prepaid expenses	(200)	
Decrease in trade payables	(400)	
Decrease in accrued expenses	(200)	
		(80)
Net cash provided by operating activities		*1,530*

(b) Direct method

Paolo & Francesca SpA
Cash flows from operating activities
For the year ended 31 December 2004

(Amounts in thousands of euro)

Cash receipts from customers		8,600	Note 1
Cash payments:			
To trade suppliers	5,000		Note 2
For operating expenses	2,070		Note 3
		(7,070)	
Net cash provided by operating activities		*1,530*	

Note 1:

Cash receipts from customers:	
Sales	8,200
Add: Decrease in Trade and other receivables	400
	8,600

Note 2:

Cash payments to trade suppliers:	
Cost of sales	5,000
Deduct: Decrease in inventories	400
Cost of purchases	4,600
Add: Decrease in Trade and other payables	400
	5,000

Note 3:

Cash payments for operating expenses:	
Operating expenses, excluding depreciation	1,670
Add: Increase in prepaid expenses	200
Add: Decrease in accrued expenses	200
	2,070

Cash flows from investing activities primarily represent changes in non-current asset accounts and their effect on cash, as explained in section 12.5.2.

Example

Cash flows from investing activities

The balance sheet of Dante & Beatrice SpA shows PPE for EUR 90 million and EUR 100 million respectively at 31 December 2003 and 2004. Depreciation in 2004 was EUR 10 million and net book value of assets disposed of was EUR 1 million. The gain on disposal of PPE was of EUR 200,000.

During 2004 Dante & Beatrice SpA acquired a new subsidiary for EUR 25 million.

The cash flows from investing activities for Dante & Beatrice SpA in 2004 is shown below:

Dante & Beatrice SpA
Cash flows from investing activities
For the year ended 31 December 2004

(Amounts in thousands of euro)

Investments in PPE	(21,000)	Note 1
Proceeds from disposal of PPE	1,200	Note 2
Investment in subsidiary	(25,000)	
Net cash outflows from investing activities	*(44,800)*	

Note 1:

PPE as at 31 December 2003	90,000
Depreciation	(10,000)
Disposals (net book value of PPE disposed of)	(1,000)
Investing outflows (balancing figure)	*(21,000)*
PPE as at 31 December 2004	100,000

Note 2:

EUR 1 million (net book value of PPE disposed of) + EUR 200,000 (gain on disposal of PPE)

Cash flows from financing activities show the cash flows to/from providers of capital, which would include the related non-current liability and shareholders' equity accounts as explained in section 12.5.3.

Example

Cash flows from financing activities

Balance sheet extracts of Giulietta & Romeo SpA as at 31 December are shown below (amounts in thousands of euro):

	2004	2003
Share capital	150,000	100,000
Share premium	48,000	40,000
Retained earnings	17,000	20,000
Bank loan	50,000	80,000

During 2004 shares with a nominal value of EUR 50 million were issued for EUR 58 million.

The net profit for 2004 was of EUR 7 million.

Here we illustrate how to determine the cash flows from financing activities for Giulietta & Romeo SpA in 2004.

Giulietta & Romeo SpA
Cash flows from financing activities
For the year ended 31 December 2004

(Amounts in thousands of euro)

Repayment of bank loan	(30,000)	
Issue of new shares	58,000	
Dividends paid to shareholders	(10,000)	Note 1
Net cash inflows from financing activities	*18,000*	

Note 1:
Dividends paid to shareholders = Opening balance of retained earnings +/− Profit (loss) − Ending balance of retained earnings = EUR 20 million + EUR 7 million − EUR 17 million = EUR 10 million

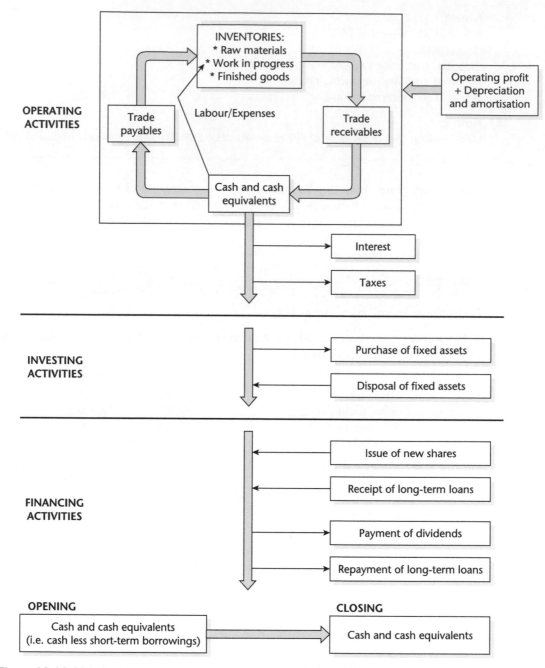

Figure 12.12 Main headings of a corporate cash flow statement under IAS 7
Source: Walsh (2002)

Classification of certain items

In the section 'Cash flow from operating activities', the cash flow statement pre-pared using the direct method would not include any gains (or losses) from the disposal of non-current assets. Whereas, under the indirect method, in order to avoid double counting gains or losses on disposals of non-current assets, the gains or losses are deducted from, or added to the net profit, respectively, in the cash flow statement.

In both the direct and indirect methods, the amount of the proceeds from the disposal of non-current assets would be listed in investing activities.

Dividends paid are classified as a financing cash flow because they represent a 'cost' of equity resources obtained.

Cash flows arising from interest and income taxes should be separately disclosed and should be classified as cash flows from operating activities unless they can be specifically identified with financing and investing activities.

Example

Preparation of a cash flow statement

The income statement for the year ended 31 March 2005 and balance sheets as at 31 March 2004 and 2005 (including the PPE schedule) for GIOIA SpA are shown below, and on the following page (all amounts are in thousands of euro). On page 257 we reproduce the income statement and balance sheet of GIOIA SpA adding on the right of these statements explanations on how the different items have been treated in the cash flow statements (all amounts are in thousands of euro).

GIOIA SpA
Income statement for the year ended 31 March 2005

Sales	18,000
Cost of sales	(12,000)
Gross profit	6,000
Net operating expenses	(2,958)
Gain on disposal of land	240
Loss on disposal of plant	(162)
Profit before interest and tax (EBIT)	3,120
Interest expense	(120)
Profit before tax (EBT)	3,000
Income taxes	(1,200)
Net profit (EAT)	1,800

GIOIA SpA
Balance sheets as at 31 March 2005 and 2004

	2005	2004
Non-current assets		
Intangible assets	1,080	2,520
PPE, net	13,788	12,408
Available-for-sale investments	90	
	14,958	*14,928*
Current assets		
Inventory	7,200	4,800
Trade and other receivables	5,400	4,080
Cash	90	60
	12,690	*8,940*
Total assets	**27,648**	**23,868**
Shareholders' equity		
Issued capital	12,000	10,800
Share premium	1,200	300
Other reserves	1,200	600
Retained earnings	3,900	2,100
	18,300	*13,800*
Non-current liabilities	*900*	*1,200*
Current liabilities		
Trade and other payables	4,080	3,240
Taxes payable	1,020	1,140
Dividends payable		420
Short-term borrowings	3,348	4,068
	8,448	*8,868*
Total shareholders' equity and liabilities	**27,648**	**23,868**

PPE schedule for GIOIA SpA as at 31 March 2005

	Land	Building	Plant	Equipment	TOTAL
At cost 1 April 2004	9,600	2,400	2,520	600	15,120
Additions	2,400	600	360		3,360
Revaluation	600				600
Deduct Disposals	1,800		720		2,520
At cost/valuation 31 March 2005	*10,800*	*3,000*	*2,160*	*600*	*16,560*
Accumulated depreciation at 1 April 2004		1,152	1,200	360	2,712
Depreciation charge for the year		60	432	120	612
Deduct Accumulated depreciation on assets disposed of			(552)		(552)
Accumulated depreciation at 31 March 2005		*1,212*	*1,080*	*480*	*2,772*
Net book value at 1 April 2004	9,600	1,248	1,320	240	12,408
Net book value at 31 March 2005	10,800	1,788	1,080	120	13,788

GIOIA SpA
Income statement for the year ended 31 March 2005

		How treated in cash flow statement	
Sales	18,000		
Cost of sales	(12,000)		
Gross profit	6,000		
Net operating expenses	(2,958)		
Gain on disposal of land	240		
Loss on disposal of plant	(162)		
Profit before interest and tax (EBIT)	3,120		
Interest expense	(120)	Operating activity	(120)
Profit before tax (EBT)	3,000	Operating activity	+ 3,000
Income taxes	(1,200)	Operating activity	(1,200)
Net profit (EAT)	1,800		

GIOIA SpA
Balance sheets as at 31 March 2005 and 2004

	2005	2004	Change	How treated in cash flow statement	
Non-current assets				Operating activities	
Intangible assets	1,080	2,520	(1,440)	(adjustment for amortisation)	+ 1,440
PPE, net	13,788	12,408	1,380	Investing activities (see notes 1 and 2)	
Available-for-sale investments	90		90	Investing activities	(90)
	14,958	14,928			
Current assets					
Inventory	7,200	4,800	2,400	Operating activities	(2,400)
Trade and other receivables	5,400	4,080	1,320	Operating activities	(1,320)
Cash	90	60	30	Cash and cash equivalents (see note 3)	
	12,690	8,940			
Total assets	27,648	23,868			
Shareholders' equity					
Issued capital	12,000	10,800	1,200	Financing activities	+ 1,200
Share premium	1,200	300	900	Financing activities	+ 900
Other reserves	1,200	600	600	Non-cash movement	
Retained earnings	3,900	2,100	1,800	Already included in operating activities	
	18,300	13,800			
Non-current liabilities	900	1,200	(300)	Financing activities	(300)
Current liabilities					
Trade and other payables	4,080	3,240	840	Operating activities	+ 840
Taxes payable	1,020	1,140	(120)	Operating activities	(120)
Dividends payable		420	(420)	Financing activities	(420)
Short-term borrowings	3,348	4,068	(720)	Cash and cash equivalents (see note 3)	
	8,448	8,868			
Total shareholders' equity and liabilities	27,648	23,868			

Note 1:

The non-cash items required for the reconciliation are calculated as follows:

- depreciation is given in the schedule of PPE.
- amortisation of intangible assets is obtained from change in the balance sheet figures: EUR 2,520 – EUR 1,080 = EUR 1,440.
- gain on disposal of land: EUR 240.
- loss on disposal of plant: EUR 162.

Note 2:

The sale proceeds from the disposals of land and plant are calculated for the investing activities section as follows:

- land: net book value EUR 1,800 (see PPE schedule) *plus* gain on disposal EUR 240 = EUR 2,040
- plant: net book value EUR 168 (see PPE schedule: EUR 720 – EUR 552) *less* loss on disposal EUR 162 = EUR 6.

Note 3:

Cash and cash equivalents at 1 April 2004:

Cash	60
Deduct Short-term borrowings	(4,068)
	(4,008)

Cash and cash equivalents at 31 March 2005:

Cash	90
Deduct Short-term borrowings	(3,348)
	(3,258)

Cash and cash equivalents have increased by EUR 750. The cash flow statement explains which activities caused this increase.

Cash flows from operating activities (indirect method)	EUR	EUR
Operating profit (EBIT)	3,120	
Adjustments for:		
Depreciation	612	
Amortisation	1,440	
Loss on disposal of plant	162	
Gain on disposal of land	(240)	
Operating profit before working capital change	5,094	
Increase in trade and other receivables	(1,320)	
Increase in inventories	(2,400)	
Increase in trade and other payables	840	
Cash generated from operations	2,214	
Interest paid	(120)	
Income taxes paid (1,140 + 1,200 − 1,020)	(1,320)	
Net cash from operating activities		774
Cash flow from investing activities		
Purchase of property, plant and equipment	(3,360)	
Proceeds from sale of land	2,040	
Proceeds from sale of plant	6	
Available-for-sale investments	(90)	
Net cash used in investing activities		(1,404)
Cash flows from financing activities		
Proceeds from issue of share capital	2,100	
Repayment of non-current liabilities	(300)	
Dividends paid	(420)	
Net cash used in financing activities		1,380
Net increase in cash and cash equivalents		750
Cash and cash equivalents at beginning of period		(4,008)
Cash and cash equivalents at end of period		(3,258)

You will note that in order to determine cash flows from operating activities, we started from operating profit and not net profit as we wished to highlight 'interest paid' and 'income taxes paid' as recommended by IAS 7. In practice, most published cash flow statements start with the net profit figure.

Summary

- Information about the cash flows of an enterprise is useful in providing users of financial statements with a basis to assess the ability of the enterprise to generate cash and cash equivalents and the needs of the enterprise to use those cash flows.

- Cash and cash equivalents comprise investments readily convertible into cash and subject to an insignificant risk of changes in value. Bank overdrafts are included as a negative component of cash and cash equivalents.

- Cash flow statement focuses on the change, i.e. increase or decrease in cash and cash equivalents and the activities that cause that increase or decrease, i.e. operating, investing and financing activities.

- Cash flows from operating activities may be calculated using either the direct or indirect methods. The former restates each income statement item to reflect the movement of cash. The latter starts with the operating profit and adjusts it for the effects of changes in inventories and other operating assets and non-cash items such as depreciation, amortisation, and long-term provisions.

- Cash flows from investing activities primarily represent changes in non-current assets and their effects on cash, such as the acquisition or disposal of PPE, equity and debt instruments of other enterprises, advances and loans made to, or repayments from, third parties.

- Cash flows from financing activities show the cash flows to/from providers of capital, such as receipts from an issue of share or other equity securities; payments made to redeem such securities; proceeds from the issue of debentures and repayments of such securities.

References and research

The IASB document relevant to this chapter is IAS 7 – *Cash Flow Statement*.

The following are examples of books that take the issues of this chapter further:

- Robert N. Anthony, David F. Hawkins and Kenneth A. Merchant, *Accounting: Text and Cases*, 10th Edition, McGraw-Hill, 1999, Chapter 11
- Charles T. Horngren, Gary L. Sundem and John A. Elliott, *Introduction to Financial Accounting*, 8th Edition, Prentice Hall, 2002, Chapter 10
- Hennie Van Greuning, *International Financial Reporting Standards: A Practical Guide*, Revised Edition, The World Bank, Washington, DC, 2005, Chapter 4
- Ciaran Walsh, *Key Management Ratios: Master the Management Metrics that Drive and Control your Business*, 3rd Edition, Financial Times-Prentice Hall, December 2002, Chapters 8 and 11

Questions

12.1 (a) List four operating activities included in a cash flow statement.

    (b) List three investing activities included in a cash flow statement.

    (c) List three financing activities included in a cash flow statement.

12.2 (a) Trevelyan Ltd sold equipment with a net book value of EUR 25,000 and recorded a gain of EUR 10,000 on disposal of non-current assets. How should this be reported in a statement of cash flows?

    (b) Diletta & Co earned an operating profit for the year, but the cash flow from operating activities was negative. How do you explain this? In which industries can this be a common occurrence?

    (c) Paolo & Co had an operating loss in an accounting period, but the cash flow from operations was positive. How can this happen? In which industries can this be a common occurrence?

12.3 Glocal Consulting SpA provides consulting services. During the year ended 31 March 2005 it had revenues for EUR 47,000 and expenses for EUR 28,500. The only non-cash expenses were depreciation for EUR 2,500 and amortisation for EUR 2,000. Glocal Consulting has no inventory. The opening balance of trade and other receivables was EUR 20,000 and the closing balance was EUR 25,000. Trade and other payables were unchanged.

Prepare the operating section of the cash flow statement. Use the direct method.

12.4 On 5 January 2004 Guidotti & Bruni SpA issued new shares for EUR 600,000. The company acquired PPE for EUR 280,000 and inventory for EUR 130,000. In December 2004 it sold equipment at its book value of EUR 40,000. Half of the inventory was sold for EUR 110,000 during the year. On 23 December 2004, excess cash of EUR 120,000 was used to purchase bonds issued by Baldi SpA, which Guidotti & Bruni regarded as a long-term investment.

Prepare the investing activities section of the cash flow statement for Guidotti & Bruni SpA for 2004.

12.5 In 2004 Guidotti & Bruni SpA refinanced its long-term debt. It spent EUR 80,000 to retire long-term debt due in two years and issued EUR 100,000 bonds repayable in 2019. It issued new shares for EUR 60,000 including share premium for EUR 10,000. Interest expense for 2004 was EUR 12,000 of which EUR 10,000 was paid. Dividends declared and paid during the year amounted to EUR 6,000.

Prepare the financing activities section of the cash flow statement for Guidotti & Bruni SpA for 2004.

12.6 ABC SpA has the following balance sheets as at 31 December 2003 and 2004, and income statement for 2004 (amounts in euro):

ABC SpA
Balance sheet as at 31 December 2004 and 2003

	2004	2003
ASSETS		
PPE, net	1,440,000	880,000
Cash and cash equivalents	176,000	116,000
Trade and other receivables	272,000	152,000
Inventories	256,000	216,000
Prepaid expense	16,000	-0-
Total assets	**2,160,000**	**1,364,000**
SHAREHOLDERS' EQUITY AND LIABILITIES		
Issued capital	708,000	508,000
Retained earnings	720,000	600,000
Non-current liabilities	500,000	104,000
Trade and other payables	120,000	76,000
Wages payable	12,000	16,000
Tax payable	100,000	60,000
Total shareholders' equity and liabilities	**2,160,000**	**1,364,000**

ABC SpA
Income statement for the year ended 31 December 2004

Sales		1,832,000
Cost of sales		(752,000)
Gross profit		1,080,000
Operating expenses:		
Administrative expenses	493,000	
Depreciation	80,000	
Wages	287,000	
		(860,000)
EBIT		220,000
Income taxes		(100,000)
EAT		120,000

Calculate the cash flows from operating, investing and financing activities for the year ended 31 December 2004. Use both the direct and indirect methods for reporting cash flows from operating activities.

Case study   Puma and cash flows

Table 12.1 shows the Puma cash flow statement as required by IAS 7.

Table 12.1 Puma consolidated cash flow statement for the years ended
31 December 2004 and 2003

	2004	2003
	EURm	EURm
Operating activities		
Profit before tax	370.7	264.1
Adjustments for:		
Depreciation	19.3	20.1
Non-realized currency gains/losses, net	3.4	−3.5
Interest received	−7.0	−2.3
Interest paid	1.3	1.4
Income from the sale of fixed assets	−4.7	0.2
Additions to pension accruals	2.6	0.6
Gross Cashflow	**385.6**	**280.6**
Increase in receivables and other current assets	−18.3	−40.7
Increase in inventories	−8.4	−17.9
Increase in trade payables and other current liabilities	27.2	33.8
Cash provided by operations	386.1	255.8
Interest paid	−1.3	−1.4
Income taxes paid	−99.0	−89.3
One time expenses paid	0.0	0.0
Net cash from operating activities	**285.7**	**165.0**
Cash flows from investment activities		
Payment for goodwill (previous year: purchase of participations)	0.0	−30.3
Purchase of property and equipment	−43.1	−27.0
Proceeds from sale of property and equipment	8.2	1.2
Increase/decrease in other long-term assets	−1.3	−3.7
Interest received	7.0	2.2
Net cash used in investing activities	**−29.2**	**−57.6**
Cash flows from financing activities		
Payments made regarding long-term liabilities, net	0.3	0.0
Payments received regarding short-term bank borrowing, net	−3.7	−3.0
Payments made regarding convertible bonds, net	0.0	0.0
Dividend payments	−11.2	−8.7
Capital increase	23.2	9.5
Purchase of treasury stock	−79.2	−20.9
Other changes	−0.1	−0.2
Net cash used in financing activities	**−70.8**	**−23.4**
Effect of exchange rates on cash	**−7.0**	**−7.0**
Increase in cash and cash equivalents	**178.8**	**77.0**
Cash and cash equivalents at beginning of financial year	190.6	113.6
Cash and cash equivalents at year end	**369.3**	**190.6**

Source: Puma Annual Report 2004

Table 12.2 Puma cash flow statement for the years ended 31 December 2004 and 2003 (Management Report)

	2004	2003	+/– %
	EURm	EURm	
Earnings before taxes on income	370.7	264.1	40.4
Non cash effected expenses and income	14.9	16.5	–10.0
Gross Cashflow	**385.6**	**280.6**	**37.4**
Change in current assets, net	0.5	–24.8	–102.1
taxes and other interest payments	–100.3	–90.8	–
Net cash from operating activities	**285.7**	**165.0**	**73.1**
Net cash used in investing activities	**–29.2**	**–57.6**	**–49.4**
Free Cashflow	256.6	107.4	138.9
Free Cashflow before acquisition cost	256.6	137.7	86.3
– in per cent of sales	16.8	10.8	–
Net cash used in financing activities	**–70.8**	**–23.4**	**202.9**
Effect on exchange rates on cash	–7.0	–7.0	–0.1
Change in cash and cash equivalents	178.8	77.0	132.2
Cash and cash equivalents at beginning of financial year	190.6	113.6	67.8
Cash and cash equivalents at year-end	**369.3**	**190.6**	**93.8**

Source: Puma Annual Report 2004

Table 12.2 shows the total value of each section of the cash flow statement and highlights the free cash flow (i.e. net cash from operating activities less net cash used in investing activities) and the free cash flow before acquisition cost.

Questions:

1. In 2004 Puma's gross cash flow increased by 37.4 per cent compared to the previous financial year. Explain why.

2. Net cash flow from operating activities was EUR 285.7 million in 2004 while the increase in cash and cash equivalents was only EUR 178.8 million. Explain what happened to cause the increase in cash and cash equivalents to reduce to EUR 178.8 million.

3. The Management Report highlights free cash flow. Why does Puma's management consider free cash flow to be important?

4. Puma has increased cash and cash equivalents from EUR 113.6 million on 1 January 2003 to EUR 369.3 million on 31 December 2004. How do you interpret Puma's management of cash?

Part Four Analysis and interpretation
of financial statements

13 Trends and common-size statements

Objectives

When you have completed this chapter you should be able to:

- locate and use different sources of information about an enterprise performance
- explain why analysts worry about the quality of financial information and how quality is determined
- analyse an enterprise using common-size and trend analysis
- determine the compound annual growth rate.

13.1 Introduction

In Part two and Part three, we concentrated on how to collect financial data and how to prepare financial statements.

In Chapter 2, we saw that the objective of financial statements is to provide useful, reliable, relevant, timely and comparable information to several groups of users. Financial statements analysis involves using that information to assess the performance of an enterprise.

Different people read financial statements for different reasons. Suppliers might want to see if a customer can afford a price hike and still respect payment terms. Customers might want to know if a company will still be around in a year to honour a warranty. Managers, creditors, investors, all have their purposes for reading the financial statements. Our focus is on investors. Investors read financial statements either to monitor their current investments or to plan their future ones. Investors analyse financial statements to determine whether their views about an enterprise have been borne out and what expectations they should have about the future.

How can you get the future out of financial statements? Throughout Part two we introduced certain ratios and other tools of analysis. Part four integrates the tools you have already seen and teaches you new ones. The sources of information about an enterprise take on many forms. Annual reports are important because of their completeness in terms of quantitative and qualitative information. In addition to the balance sheet, income statement and cash flow statement, annual reports contain footnotes to the financial statements, a management report, the auditor's report, comparative financial data and key performance indicators (KPIs) for either five or ten years, narrative information about the enterprise, etc.

On top of this information directors of an enterprise regularly make presentations to analysts about their current and future business performance in light of the prevailing economic conditions.

13.2   Objectives of financial analysis

Different types of investors expect different types of returns. Equity investors expect dividends and an increase in the value of the shares they hold. Lenders, however, expect to receive interest and the repayment of the capital lent. Although the types of returns they expect are different, equity investors and lenders both risk not receiving those returns. Therefore, both types of investors use financial statements analysis to:

- predict their expected returns
- assess the risks associated with those returns.

Creditors and lenders mainly want to know about short-term liquidity and long-term solvency. Short-term liquidity refers to how much cash an enterprise has on hand to meet current payments, such as purchase of goods and revenues, wages, interest, taxes, and so on, as they become due. Conversely, long-term solvency refers to an enterprise's ability to generate cash to repay long-term debts to lenders and other creditors as they mature.

In contrast, equity investors are more concerned with profitability and future share prices. This is because dividend payments depend on how profitable operations are, and share prices depend on the market assessment of an enterprise's future prospects. Investors gain when they receive dividends and when the value of their shares rises. Rising profits spur both events. Actually, lenders also want to know about profitability because the profitable operations that drive share prices to higher levels also provide the cash to repay loans and finance growth.

Lenders, creditors and equity investors are all interested in what will happen to an enterprise in the future. How can financial statements analysis help them since the financial statements deal solely with past events? Financial statement analysis helps creditors and equity investors because past performance is often a good indicator of future performance. Trends in past sales, operating expenses, and net profits often continue, so financial statements analysis of past performance gives clues to future returns.

13.3   Financial analysis tools

There are several ways of looking at financial statements information. We will provide you with an overview of three financial analysis tools:

- common-size statements
- trends statements
- financial ratios.

In this chapter (and the next three), we will show how each tool is used and explain how to interpret the results from each. But the important message is that all financial analysis tools are built around reported accounting data, and these tools cannot be better than the data from which they are derived. Which financial data an enterprise chooses to report and how the data are reported affect not only the financial statements themselves but also the ratios and other numbers used to analyse those statements.

Investors use financial statements and financial data in many ways and for many different purposes. Two ways to use financial statements are time-series analysis and cross-sectional analysis.

Time-series analysis helps identify financial trends over time for a single enterprise. The analysts might be interested in determining the rate of growth in sales for an enterprise, or the degree to which this enterprise's earnings have fluctuated historically with inflation, business cycles, foreign currency exchange rates, or changes in economic growth in domestic or foreign markets.

Cross-sectional analysis helps identify similarities and differences across enterprises at a given point in time. The analyst might compare the 2004 profitability of one enterprise in an industry to a competitor's profitability.

Analysts use a mixture of time-series and cross-sectional tools when evaluating a particular enterprise. Both can reveal meaningful details about the current profitability and financial condition, and also details about recent changes that might affect future profitability or financial condition. However, these comparisons make use of financial statements data and hence they are influenced by distortions of those data, if any.

13.4   Evaluation of trends: an illustration

Informed financial statements analysis begins with knowledge of the enterprise and its industry. In this section we will carry on with an evaluation of trends in Puma. You can get information on Puma and its industry from various sources. The Internet is a valuable source.

13.4.1   Analysis of income statement

Abbreviated comparative income statements for Puma are shown in Table 13.1. The layout is different from that required by IAS, but it highlights results relevant to our analysis. These are shown also in a graph format (Figure 13.1).

Table 13.1 Puma's comparative income statements (2000–2004)

Amounts in millions of euro	2004	2003	2002	2001	2000
Sales	**1,530.3**	**1,274.0**	**909.8**	**598.1**	**462.4**
Cost of sales	(736.4)	(654.0)	(512.9)	(347.5)	(286.0)
Gross profit	**793.9**	**620.0**	**396.9**	**250.6**	**176.4**
Royalty and commission income	43.7	40.3	44.9	37.2	28.9
SG&A	(453.4)	(377.1)	(304.3)	(220.5)	(175.7)
EBITDA	**384.2**	**283.3**	**137.5**	**67.3**	**29.6**
Depreciation and amortisation	(19.3)	(20.1)	(12.5)	(8.3)	(6.8)
EBIT	**364.9**	**263.2**	**125.0**	**59.0**	**22.8**
Financial result	5.7	0.9	(0.6)	(1.6)	(1.6)
EBT	**370.6**	**264.1**	**124.4**	**57.4**	**21.2**
Taxes	(111.7)	(84.2)	(39.8)	(17.3)	(6.7)
Earnings before minority interests	258.9	179.9	84.6	40.1	14.5
Minority interests	(1.7)	(0.6)	0.2	(0.4)	0.0
EAT	**257.2**	**179.3**	**84.9**	**39.7**	**17.5**

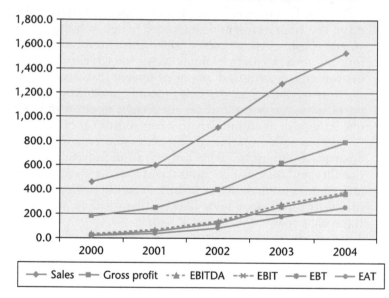

Figure 13.1 Puma's comparative income statements (2000–2004)
Source: Puma Annual Reports 2000–2004

In Table 13.2(A) we show each income statement item as a percentage of sales. This is the common-size analysis of income statement. In Table 13.2(B), we took the data of 2000 as the base of our trend analysis and recast each income statement item in percentage terms using that base.

Sales

Sales represent a high-growth driver increasing by EUR 1,067.9 million or 231 per cent from EUR 462.4 million in 2000 to EUR 1,530.3 million in 2004.

Table 13.2 Puma's common-size and trend analysis of income statements (2000–2004)
(A) Common-size statements (% of sales)

	2004	2003	2002	2001	2000
Sales	**100.0%**	**100.0%**	**100.0%**	**100.0%**	**100.0%**
Cost of sales	48.1%	51.3%	56.4%	58.1%	61.9%
Gross profit margin	**51.9%**	**48.7%**	**43.6%**	**41.9%**	**38.1%**
Royalty and commission income	2.9%	3.2%	4.9%	6.2%	6.3%
SG&A	29.6%	29.6%	33.4%	36.9%	38.0%
EBITDA	**25.1%**	**22.2%**	**15.1%**	**11.3%**	**6.4%**
Depreciation and amortisation	1.3%	1.6%	1.4%	1.4%	1.5%
EBIT	**23.8%**	**20.6%**	**13.7%**	**9.9%**	**4.9%**
Financial result	0.4%	0.1%	0.0%	−0.3%	−0.3%
EBT	**24.2%**	**20.7%**	**13.7%**	**9.6%**	**4.6%**
Taxes	7.3%	6.6%	4.4%	2.9%	1.4%
Earnings before minority interests	16.9%	14.1%	9.3%	6.7%	3.1%
Minority interests	0.1%	0.0%	0.0%	−0.1%	0.0%
EAT	**16.81%**	**14.1%**	**9.3%**	**6.6%**	**3.8%**

(B) Trend statements (2000 = 100%)

	2004	2003	2002	2001	2000
Sales	**331%**	**276%**	**197%**	**129%**	**100%**
Cost of sales	257%	229%	179%	122%	100%
Gross profit	**450%**	**351%**	**225%**	**142%**	**100%**
Royalty and commission income	151%	140%	155%	129%	100%
SG&A	258%	215%	173%	125%	100%
EBITDA	**1,298%**	**957%**	**465%**	**227%**	**100%**
Depreciation and amortisation	284%	295%	184%	122%	100%
EBIT	**1,600%**	**1,154%**	**548%**	**259%**	**100%**
Financial result	−356%	−56%	36%	100%	100%
EBT	**1,748%**	**1,246%**	**587%**	**271%**	**100%**
Taxes	−1,667%	1,257%	594%	258%	100%
Earnings before minority interests	1,786%	1,241%	584%	277%	100%
EAT	**1,470%**	**1,025%**	**485%**	**227%**	**100%**

Source: Puma Annual Reports 2000–2004

Today analysts often look at the growth of sales and related income statement items in terms of *compound annual growth rate* (CAGR). The CAGR is a mathematical formula that provides a 'smoothed' rate of growth. It is determined by taking the nth root of the total percentage growth rate where 'n' is the number of years in the period being considered:

$$CAGR = n\sqrt{\frac{Ending\ value}{Beginning\ value}} - 1$$

Year	2000	2001	2002	2003	2004		
Sales (millions of euro)	462.4	598.1	909.8	1274.0	1530.3		
Growth compared with the previous year		29%	52%	40%	20%	**CAGR** 35%	**Average** 35%

Check

	2000	2001	2002	2003	2004
Sales (millions of euro)	462.4	623.7	841.2	1134.6	1530.3
CAGR		35%	35%	35%	35%

For Puma the CAGR and average growth rate are the same, as the sales increased each year for the period 2000–2004. However, if the sales were volatile, the average growth rate and CAGR would be different.

The following graph (Figure 13.2) compares the actual sales to the CAGR and illustrates two things:

- First, the graph shows how the CAGR proxy relates to the actual values.

- Second, the difference between the actual values and the CAGR values illustrates the volatility of sales.

As you can see from Figure 13.2, as Puma's sales are not volatile, CAGR is a good proxy of the actual ones.

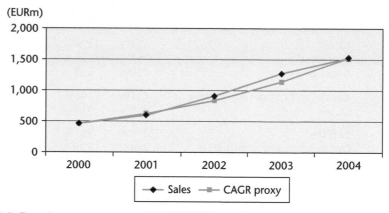

Figure 13.2 Puma's actual sales and CAGR (2000–2004)
Source: Puma Annual Reports 2000–2004

Gross profit and gross profit margin

The gross profit margin is a particularly important indicator of the company's positive performance. As a percentage of sales, the margin in the 2004 reporting year rose to 51.9 per cent, up from the previous year's level of 48.7 per cent. It was the highest gross profit margin in company history, which positions the company at the upper end of the margin spread within the sporting goods industry. In absolute figures, gross profit was up by a total of 28.1 per cent, rising from EUR 620.0 million to EUR 794 million.

The next graph (Figure 13.3) shows the trend both in gross profit (amounts in millions of euro) and in gross profit margin (%).

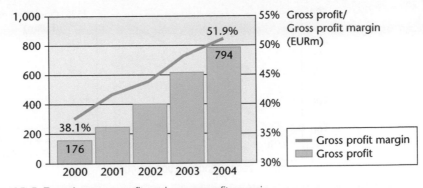

Figure 13.3 Puma's gross profit and gross profit margin
Source: Puma Annual Report 2004

Operating expenses

Operating expenses, consisting of selling, general and administrative expenses, have increased at a lower rate than sales, as shown in Figure 13.4. Over 2004, they rose by 20.2 per cent to EUR 453.4 million.

Operating expenses as a percentage of sales were maintained at the previous year's level of 29.6 per cent. The fact that expenses remained relatively low compared to sales suggests a more efficient cost management over time.

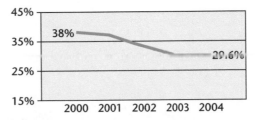

Figure 13.4 Puma's operating expenses as percentage of sales
Source: Puma Annual Report 2004

Depreciation and amortisation

Total depreciation and amortisation decreased slightly by EUR 0.8 million or 4 per cent between 2003 and 2004, from EUR 20.1 million to EUR 19.3 million.

Profitability

Increase in sales, higher gross profit margin and unchanged operating expenses to sales, in comparison with the previous year, led to a sustained improvement in profitability.

In 2004 operating profit or EBIT grew by 38.7 per cent from EUR 263.2 million in 2003 to EUR 365 million. Thus, EBIT as a percentage of sales grew from 20.6 per cent in 2003 to 24 per cent in 2004. Figure 13.5 shows the trend in EBIT over the period 2000–2004.

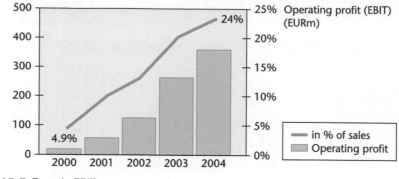

Figure 13.5 Puma's EBIT

Source: Puma Annual Report 2004

Tax expenses rose from EUR 84.2 million to EUR 111.7 million. There was a further drop in the average tax rate from 31.9 per cent to 30.1 per cent.

Net profit (EAT) grew more strongly than sales over the period 2000–2004. With an increase of 43.5 per cent, net profit reached a new record high of EUR 257.3 million, compared to EUR 179.3 million in 2003. The return on sales of 14.1 per cent was successfully stepped up to 16.8 per cent (see Figure 13.6).

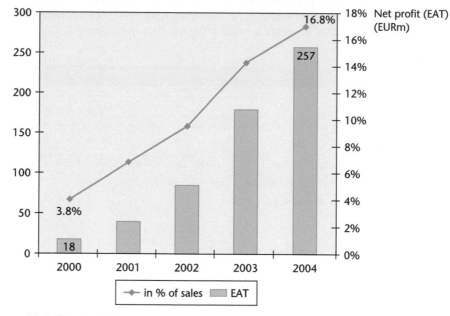

Figure 13.6 Puma's EAT

Source: Puma Annual Report 2003

13.4.2 Analysis of balance sheet

Balance sheets for Puma are presented in Table 13.3. As you can see from Table 13.4(A), a common-size balance sheet expresses each item on the balance sheet as a percentage of total assets. For the trend analysis we use 2000 data as the base numbers for other years.

Table 13.3 Puma's comparative balance sheets (2000–2004)

Amounts in millions of euro	31 Dec 2004	31 Dec 2003	31 Dec 2002	31 Dec 2001	31 Dec 2000
Cash and cash equivalents	369	191	114	35	43
Inventories	201	196	168	144	95
Trade and other receivables	190	176	136	120	109
Other short-term financial assets	0	2	8	7	1
Total current assets	**760**	**564**	**425**	**306**	**248**
PPE, net	85	67	57	50	30
Goodwill, net	20	22	14	15	3
Other intangible assets, net	7	6	5	5	1
Long-term financial assets	6	5	1	2	1
Deferred tax asssets, net	42	33	24	17	29
Total non-current assets	**160**	**100**	**77**	**72**	**35**
Total assets	**920**	**697**	**526**	**395**	**312**
Short-term borrowings	13	17	19	43	38
Trade payables	137	133	118	89	70
Other liabilities	123	69	47	28	17
Tax provisions	34	27	26	2	1
Other provisions (warranties and purchase risks)	18	18	23	17	14
Total current liabilities	**324**	**263**	**233**	**179**	**140**
Pension provisions	21	19	18	17	14
Other provisions (structural adjustments and other)	36	31	22	20	25
Long-term interest bearing liabilities and minorities	2	1	1	2	2
Total non-current liabilities	**60**	**51**	**41**	**39**	**41**
Shareholders' equity	**536**	**383**	**252**	**177**	**131**
Total liabilities and equity	**920**	**697**	**526**	**395**	**312**

Source: Puma Annual Reports 2000–2004

Total assets

Total assets increased by EUR 223 million or 32 per cent to EUR 920 million compared to EUR 697 million in the previous year. The increase was due to the increase in working capital, the new acquisition and in particular the strong increase in cash and cash equivalents.

Equity ratio

Despite a 23 per cent increase in current liabilities, the equity ratio was up from 54.9 per cent to 58.2 per cent (see Figure 13.7). Thus Puma has a very solid net worth and financial position. The non-current liabilities in 2004 increased by 18 per cent only over 2003.

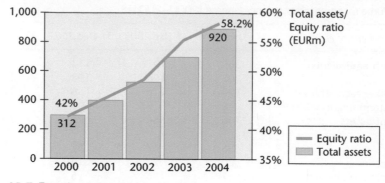

Figure 13.7 Puma's equity ratio and total assets
Source: Puma Annual Report 2004

Table 13.4 Puma's common-size and trend analysis of assets, liabilities and equity (2000–2004)
(A) Common-size statements (% of total assets)

	31 Dec 2004	31 Dec 2003	31 Dec 2002	31 Dec 2001	31 Dec 2000
Cash and cash equivalents	40.1%	27.3%	21.6%	8.9%	13.8%
Inventories	21.9%	28.2%	31.9%	36.5%	30.4%
Trade and other receivables	20.6%	25.2%	25.9%	30.4%	34.9%
Other short-term financial assets	0.0%	0.3%	1.5%	1.8%	0.3%
Total current assets	**82.6%**	**81.0%**	**80.9%**	**77.5%**	**79.5%**
PPE, net	9.2%	9.5%	10.8%	12.7%	9.6%
Goodwill, net	2.2%	3.2%	2.6%	3.8%	1.0%
Other intangible assets, net	0.8%	0.8%	0.9%	1.3%	0.3%
Long-term financial assets	0.6%	0.7%	0.2%	0.5%	0.3%
Deferred income taxes, net	4.6%	4.7%	4.5%	4.3%	9.3%
Total non-current assets	**17.4%**	**14.3%**	**14.6%**	**18.2%**	**11.2%**
Total assets	**100.0%**	**100.0%**	**100.0%**	**100.0%**	**100.0%**
Short-term borrowings	1.4%	2.4%	3.7%	10.9%	12.2%
Trade payables	14.9%	19.0%	22.4%	22.5%	22.4%
Other liabilities	13.4%	9.9%	9.0%	7.1%	5.4%
Tax provisions	3.7%	3.9%	4.9%	0.6%	0.3%
Other provisions (warranties and purchase risks)	1.9%	2.5%	4.4%	4.3%	4.5%
Total current liabilities	**35.3%**	**37.8%**	**44.3%**	**45.4%**	**44.9%**
Pension provisions	2.3%	2.7%	3.4%	4.3%	4.5%
Other provisions (structural adjustments and other)	3.9%	4.5%	4.2%	5.1%	8.0%
Long-term interest bearing liabilities and minorities	0.3%	0.1%	0.2%	0.5%	0.6%
Total non-current liabilities	**6.5%**	**7.3%**	**7.8%**	**9.9%**	**13.1%**
Shareholders' equity (Equity ratio)	**58.2%**	**54.9%**	**47.9%**	**44.8%**	**42.0%**
Total liabilities and equity	**100.0%**	**100.0%**	**100.0%**	**100.0%**	**100.0%**

Table 13.4 (Cont'd)
(B) Trend statements (2000 = 100%)

	31 Dec 2004	31 Dec 2003	31 Dec 2002	31 Dec 2001	31 Dec 2000
Cash and cash equivalents	858.8%	443.3%	264.1%	81.4%	100.0%
Inventories	211.7%	206.6%	176.7%	151.6%	100.0%
Trade and other receivables	173.9%	161.1%	124.8%	110.1%	100.0%
Other short-term financial assets	30.0%	190.9%	793.7%	700.0%	100.0%
Total current assets	**306.6%**	**227.5%**	**171.5%**	**123.4%**	**100.0%**
PPE, net	282.3%	221.7%	189.5%	166.7%	100.0%
Goodwill, net	666.7%	743.3%	460.7%	500.0%	100.0%
Other intangible assets, net	720.0%	588.8%	493.1%	500.0%	100.0%
Long-term financial assets	590.0%	500.0%	103.2%	200.0%	100.0%
Deferred tax asssets, net	144.8%	113.8%	82.1%	58.6%	100.0%
Total non-current assets	**456.6%**	**284.8%**	**218.9%**	**205.7%**	**100.0%**
Total assets	**294.9%**	**223.4%**	**168.5%**	**126.6%**	**100.0%**
Short-term borrowings	33.9%	44.2%	50.7%	113.2%	100.0%
Trade payables	195.6%	189.5%	168.4%	127.1%	100.0%
Other liabilities	725.3%	406.0%	277.9%	164.7%	100.0%
Tax provisions	3,370.0%	2,706.8%	2,575.6%	249.0%	100.0%
Other provisions (warranties and purchase risks)	125.7%	126.4%	164.3%	121.4%	100.0%
Total current liabilities	**231.7%**	**188.0%**	**166.5%**	**128.2%**	**100.0%**
Pension provisions	151.4%	132.4%	128.0%	121.4%	100.0%
Other provisions (structural adjustments and other)	144.8%	125.2%	88.0%	80.0%	100.0%
Long-term interest bearing liabilities and minorities	120.0%	50.0%	50.0%	100.0%	100.0%
Total non-current liabilities	**145.9%**	**124.0%**	**99.8%**	**95.1%**	**100.0%**
Shareholders' equity	**409.0%**	**292.4%**	**192.4%**	**135.1%**	**100.0%**
Total liabilities and equity	**294.9%**	**223.4%**	**168.6%**	**126.8%**	**100.0%**

Source: Puma Annual Reports 2000–2004

Significant improvement in liquidity

The strongest asset growth was in the area of cash and cash equivalents. Overall, at EUR 369 million, liquid assets as of the year-end nearly doubled compared with the previous year's amount of EUR 191 million. At the same time short-term borrowings were reduced from EUR 17 million to EUR 13 million. Accordingly, the net cash position rose from EUR 174 million to EUR 356 million thus reflecting a very positive cash flow.

'Accounting' working capital

Inventories were up by EUR 5 million or 2.6 per cent increasing from EUR 196 million to EUR 201 million. The inventory turnover was kept at the high level of the previous year. Receivables were up by EUR 14 million or 8 per cent, rising from EUR 176 million to EUR 190 million and growing in proportion with sales. These developments confirm Puma's systematic and effective working capital management.

Working capital at the end of 2004 totalled EUR 436 million compared to EUR 301 million in 2003 and EUR 108 million in 2000 and represented 28.5 per cent of sales compared to 23.6 per cent in 2003 and 23.4 per cent in 2000. The calculation of working capital is slightly different from that given in Puma's annual reports, as we have reclassified certain provisions.

	31 Dec 2004	31 Dec 2003	31 Dec 2002	31 Dec 2001	31 Dec 2000
Total current assets	760	564	425	306	248
Total current liabilities	324	263	233	179	140
Working capital (*)	*436*	*301*	*192*	*127*	*108*

(*) Note that we shall deal with 'trade on operating working capital' in Chapter 14.

Non-current assets

Non-current assets (property, plant and equipment, intangible assets and financial assets) increased by EUR 60 million or 60 per cent from EUR 100 million to EUR 160 million. This increase reflects the strategic expansion of Puma.

Activity 13.1 Trend analysis of cash flow statement

What follows is Puma's comparative cash flow statements (2000–2004) (amounts in millions of euro):

	2004	2003	2002	2001	2000
Net cash from operating activities	286	165	119	44	16
Net cash used in investing activities	(29)	(58)	(19)	(41)	(7)
Free cash flow	*257*	*107*	*100*	*3*	*9*
Net cash used in financing activities:					
• Reduction of financial liabilities – net	(3)	(3)	(24)	(10)	(1)
• Dividend payments	(11)	(9)	(5)	(2)	(2)
• Capital increase (conversion of share options issued to management)	23	10	10	1	
• Purchase of own shares	(79)	(21)			
	(71)	*(23)*	*(18)*	*(11)*	*(2)*
Effect of exchange rates on cash	(7)	(7)	(4)	0	0
Net increase (decrease) in cash	*179*	*77*	*78*	*(8)*	*7*

Questions:

1. Prepare a trend analysis of cash flow items.
2. Comment on the trends of those items.
3. Find on Puma's website the trend of its share price over the period 2000–4. How do you relate this trend with those of cash flow statement items?

Solutions to activities can be found at www.pearsoned.co.uk/kothari

Summary

- Investors need to understand what financial data reveal about an enterprise's economic activities and financial condition. They should also know how to adjust the reported numbers, when necessary, to overcome distortions caused by the accounting standards adopted or by management's accounting and disclosure choices.

- Financial analysts use common-size and trend statements to help spot changes in an enterprise's cost structure and profit performance.

- Common-size income statements recast each statement item as a percentage of sales. Common-size balance sheets recast each item as a percentage of total assets.

- Trend statements also recast each income statement and balance sheet item in percentage terms, but they do so using a base year number rather than sales or total assets.

- CAGR or compound annual growth rate provides a smoothed rate of growth of financial statement items or investment yields.

References and research

The following are examples of books that take the issues of this chapter further:

- Stephen N. Penman, *Financial Statement Analysis and Security Valuation*, McGraw-Hill, 2004
- Lawrence Revsine, Daniel W. Collins and W. Bruce Johnson, *Financial Reporting & Analysis*, 2nd Edition, Prentice Hall, 2002
- Gerald I. White, Ashwinpaul C. Sondhi and Dov Fried, *The Analysis and Use of Financial Statements*, 3rd Edition, Wiley, 2003, Chapters 3 and 4

Questions

13.1 The first step to informed financial statement analysis is a careful evaluation of the quality of the reported accounting numbers. No tool of financial statement analysis is completely immune to distortions caused by accounting standards or by management's reporting choices. Discuss.

13.2 (a) Give three sources of information for investors besides accounting information.
(b) Explain what CAGR is.

13.3 Following is the income statement for Deutsche Post for the years ended 31 December 2004 and 2003 (amounts in millions of euro):

in EURm	Deutsche Post World Net 2003	Deutsche Post World Net 2004
Revenue and income from banking transactions	40,017	43,168
Other operating income	1,203	1,365
Total operating income	**41,220**	**44,533**
Materials expense and expenses from banking transactions	−18,466	−20,546
Staff costs	−13,329	−13,744
Depreciation and amortization expense excluding goodwill amortization	−1,392	−1,451
Other operating expenses	−5,058	−5,445
Total operating expenses excluding goodwill amortization	**−38,245**	**−41,186**
Profit from operating activities before goodwill amortization (EBITA)	**2,975**	**3,347**
Goodwill amortization	−319	−370
Profit from operating activities (EBIT)	**2,656**	**2,977**
Net income/loss from associates	−28	4
Net other finance costs	−713	−825
Net finance costs	**−741**	**−821**
Profit from ordinary activities	**1,915**	**2,156**
Income tax expense	−573	−431
Net profit for the period before minority interest	**1,342**	**1,725**
Minority interest	−33	−137
Consolidated net profit for the period	**1,309**	**1,588**
in EUR		
Basic earnings per share	1.18	1.43
Diluted earnings per share	1.18	1.43

Source: Deutsche Post Annual Report 2004

Prepare a common-size income statement for Deutsche Post.

13.4 Following is the income statement for Coloplast for the year ended 30 September 2004 (amounts in millions of euro):

	2003/04	2002/03
Revenue	816	755
Cost of sales	−314	−289
Gross profit	**502**	**466**
Distribution costs	−246	−223
Administrative expenses	−97	−98
Research and development costs	−27	−22
Other operating income	5	5
Other operating expenses	−3	−6
Operating profit	**134**	**122**
Separate items	0	0
Income from investments in group enterprises before tax		
Income from investments in associates after tax	0	0
Financial income	6	12
Financial expenses	−18	−14
Profit before tax	**122**	**120**
Tax on profit for the year	−43	−41
Net profit for the year	**79**	**79**
Minority interests	−1	−3
Coloplast's share of profit for the year	78	76

Source: Coloplast Annual Report 2003/4

Prepare a common-size income statement for Coloplast.

13.5 Download the annual reports of Bayer for the last five years.

Prepare a trend analysis for Bayer's balance sheet items.

13.6 Download the annual reports of Gucci Group N.V. for the last three financial years.

(a) Prepare a trend analysis for Gucci's balance sheet, income and cash flow statements.

(b) Comment on trend analysis.

Case study   adidas-Salomon (A)

PART I

Download the annual reports of adidas-Salomon for the last five years. Concentrate on its balance sheets.

Questions:
After having reported the comparative data on an Excel worksheet:

1. Prepare common-size balance sheets at the end of each year.
2. What do the common-size statements reveal about the company's financial structure?
3. Prepare a trend analysis of adidas-Salomon's balance sheets.
4. What does the trend analysis reveal about the company's financial structure?
5. Which approach – common-size or trend analysis – was most revealing? Why?

PART II

Now print out adidas-Salomon's income statement for the last five years.

Questions:
After having reported the comparative data on an Excel worksheet:

1. Prepare common-size income statements for each year.
2. What do the common-size statements reveal about the company's operating results?
3. Prepare a trend analysis of adidas-Salomon's income statements.
4. What does the trend analysis reveal about the company's operating results?
5. Which approach – common-size or trend analysis or CAGR – was most revealing? Why?

PART III

Report on an Excel worksheet the comparative cash flow statements for adidas-Salomon covering the last five years.

Questions:

1. What is the purpose of preparing common-size statements of cash flows? What can a financial analyst learn about an enterprise by preparing a set of common-size cash flow statements?
2. Prepare common-size cash flow statements expressed as a percentage of sales.
3. Interpret your common-size cash flow statements referred to in the last question. What interesting features of the enterprise's operating, financing and investing activities do they reveal?

14 Corporate liquidity and solvency

Objectives

When you have completed this chapter you should be able to:

- understand how short-term liquidity risk differs from long-term solvency risk
- use ratio analysis to assess these two dimensions of credit risk
- use liquidity ratios, including working capital ratios, to assess an enterprise's ability to meet its current obligations
- use debt ratio to analyse an enterprise's financial structure.

14.1 Introduction

Credit risk refers to the ability and willingness of a borrower (an individual or an enterprise) to pay its debt. Ability and willingness of the borrower influence the likelihood that the lender (typically a bank or insurance enterprise) will receive the contracted principal and interest payments when due. In the corporate arena, two factors must be kept in mind:

- An enterprise's *ability to repay* debt is determined by its capacity to generate cash from operations, disposal of assets, or external financial markets.
- An enterprise's *willingness to pay* depends on which of the competing cash needs is viewed by management as most pressing at the moment. Those needs include working capital and plant capacity requirements to sustain current operating activities, capital expenditures for new products and service development or market expansion, and shareholder dividends or debt service requirements.

There are numerous and interrelated risks that influence an enterprise's ability to generate cash. Multinational enterprises, for example, must cope with possible changes in host government regulations, potential political unrest, and fluctuating currency exchange rates. Domestic enterprises are exposed to the kind of risk associated with political or demographic changes, recession, inflation, and interest fluctuations. Enterprises within a particular industry confront risk related to the technological change, shifting competition, regulation, and availability of raw materials and labour. Management competency, litigation and the enterprise's strategic direction are additional sources of risk. Each of these risks ultimately affects an enterprise's operating performance, net profit, and cash flows. In fact, the cash flow statement, which reports the net amount of cash generated or used by operating, investing and financing activities, as we saw in Chapter 12, is an important source of information for analysing an enterprise's credit risk.

Although cash flow statements contain information enabling a user to assess an enterprise's credit risk, financial ratios are also useful for this purpose. Credit risk analysis using financial ratios typically involves an assessment of liquidity and solvency. Liquidity refers to the enterprise's short-term liquidity to generate cash for working capital needs and immediate debt repayment needs. Solvency refers to the long-term ability to generate cash internally or from external sources in order to satisfy plant capacity needs, fuel growth and repay debts when due.

In this chapter, our discussion of financial ratios as an analytical tool for assessing credit risk is based on the distinction between concerns for short-term liquidity and long-term solvency.

14.2   Short-term liquidity

Short-term liquidity problems arise because operating cash inflows do not match outflows. To illustrate the mismatching problem, let us consider the operating cycle of a retailer, Discount World. It acquires personal computers, TVs, air conditioners and other items for resale from suppliers on credit, undertaking to pay within 30 or 60 days. All these items are first shipped to Discount World warehouses. Later they are sent on to Discount World stores where they are displayed for sale and promoted through in-store and external advertising. Discount World pays for transportation, labour and advertising costs immediately and delays payment for other costs. Eventually, Discount World sells goods to customers, who pay by cash or credit card; receivables (if any) are collected some time later; and the enterprise then pays the amounts owed to suppliers and others. Liquidity problems arise when cash inflows from customers lag behind the cash outflows to employees, suppliers and others.

The operating cycle must not only generate sufficient cash to supply working capital needs, it must also provide cash to service debt as payments become due. For some enterprises, interest expense is a very significant cost. Such enterprises may discover that operating cash flows are sufficient to cover periodic interest payments but that the need to repay the loan principal causes a liquidity problem. Enterprises that are not sufficiently liquid and are therefore not able to pay obligations as they become due may be forced into bankruptcy.

14.2.1 Current ratio, quick ratio and cash ratio

We saw in Chapter 3 that one of the ratios used to assess an enterprise's short-term liquidity is the current ratio:

$$\text{Current ratio} = \text{Current assets} \div \text{Current liabilities}$$

Current assets include cash and 'near cash' items. For example, trade and other receivables become cash as they are collected, so they are converted into cash in only one step. Inventories are converted into cash in two steps:

1. They are sold, usually on credit.
2. The resulting receivables are collected later.

By including receivables and inventory in current assets, the current ratio reflects existing cash as well as amounts soon to be converted into cash in the normal operating cycle.

A more short-term reflection of liquidity is the quick ratio:

$$\text{Quick ratio} = (\text{Current assets} - \text{Inventory}) \div \text{Current liabilities}[1]$$

As only few enterprises such as supermarkets can instantaneously convert their inventories into cash, the quick ratio does not include inventory in the numerator and thus provides a measure of immediate liquidity.

Lastly the cash ratio, defined as

$$\text{Cash ratio} = \text{Cash and cash equivalents} \div \text{Current liabilities}$$

is the most conservative of these measures of cash resources as only cash and securities easily convertible to cash are used to measure cash resources.

Activity 14.1 Liquidity ratios for Puma

Question:

Refer to Table 13.3 (on page 275) – Puma's comparative balance sheets (2000–2004) and calculate its liquidity ratios. Show your computations. Comment on the trends they present.

Solutions to activities can be found at www.pearsoned.co.uk/kothari

---

14.2.2 Analysis of working capital

Working capital to sales ratio

Both the current and quick ratios are the most widely used measures of short-term liquidity but a problem with them is that they are static. They reflect values at a point in time only, i.e. at the balance sheet date. It is possible to 'window dress' a company's accounts so that they look good on this one day.

The 'working capital to sales' ratio meets this objection to a certain extent.

This ratio gives a glimpse of the liquidity position from another point of view. This measure shows up features that cannot be ascertained easily from the previous two measures.

Walsh (2002) notes that, whereas the current and quick ratios use balance sheet figures only, here we take into account the ongoing operations by including a value from the income statement. The 'sales revenue' figure reflects, to some extent, the operating cash flow cycle. This ratio, therefore, relates the short-term surplus liquidity to the annual operating cash flow.

This ratio highlights a trend the other ratios miss. It is possible to have a stable 'current' or 'quick' ratio while working capital to sales ratio is deteriorating or increasing faster than the sales. This would happen if sales were increasing rapidly but the levels of working capital were static. This is a condition known as overtrading.

The term 'overtrading' is used to describe a situation where there are not sufficient resources to carry on the level of existing business. It arises in an enterprise that has grown too fast or has been underfunded in the first place. The symptoms show up as a constant shortage of cash to meet day-to-day needs. There is a danger of bankruptcy. Probably the only solution is an injection of long-term cash funds (Walsh 2002).

In order to look at the role of working capital in a company's operations, we define it as follows:

$$\text{Inventory} + \text{Trade receivables} - \text{Trade payables}$$

The reason why we are ignoring cash and short-term investments, and are concentrating only on those three items is that they are:

1. the dominant accounts, and
2. their behaviour is spontaneous (i.e. they react very quickly to changes in levels of company turnover).

For operating management purposes, this narrow definition, commonly known as *trade or operating working capital*, is more useful from the business point of view than the other we have used, 'accounting' working capital (i.e. current assets less current liabilities).

A negative figure for working capital as defined here denotes the fact that the enterprise had, at the year-end, more trade payables than inventory and trade

---

Liquidity Ratios I–III ///	The liquidity ratio measures the extent to which a company can quickly liquidate assets to cover short-term liabilities. They are calculated as follows:
	Liquidity I: The sum of cash and short-term financial assets divided by current liabilities multiplied by 100.
	Liquidity II: The sum of cash and short-term financial assets as well as accounts receivable divided by current liabilities multiplied by 100.
	Liquidity III: The sum of cash and short-term financial assets as well as accounts receivable and inventories divided by current liabilities multiplied by 100.

Figure 14.1 Definition of liquidity ratios

Source: adidas-Salomon Annual Report 2004

receivables. This is acceptable, providing creditors have confidence in the continuing ability of a company to pay its bills when they fall due. Normally such confidence is directly linked to the enterprise's business sector and its proven record of cash flow generation.

Generally, the lower the trading working capital to sales percentage, the better it is for the business, i.e. from the viewpoint of managing trade working capital. It follows that the enterprise is 'locking' up lower cash and cash equivalents in the trade working capital and therefore incurring lower interest expense than would otherwise be the case.

Activity 14.2 Working capital to sales ratio for Puma

Refer to Table 13.1 (on page 270) – Puma's comparative income statements (2000–2004) and Table 13.3 (on page 275) – Puma's comparative balance sheets (2000–2004).

Question:

Determine Puma's working capital to sales ratio for the period 2000–2004. Comment on its trend.

Solutions to activities can be found at www.pearsoned.co.uk/kothari

---

Working capital days

To understand in more detail the way in which cash flows around the business we can determine certain working capital ratios.

To see how long an enterprise's cash is tied up in inventories and thus how effectively inventories are managed, we can use the **inventory turnover**:

$$\text{Inventory turnover} = \text{Cost of sales} \div \text{(Year-end) Inventory}$$

An alternative 'rough and ready' way to determine inventory turnover is given by: Net sales ÷ (Year-end) Inventory. The inventory turnover can be used to determine the average **days inventory held** as follows:

$$\text{Days inventory outstanding (DIO)} = 365 \text{ days} \div \text{Inventory turnover}$$

The longer inventories are held, the longer financial resources are tied up in a non-profit-generating item. The lower the number of days in inventory, the faster the turnover of the inventory. Each time inventory is turned the enterprise makes a profit and generates cash.

However, an enterprise in practice should ensure that its inventory levels are sufficient to meet the needs of its customers. Otherwise, there is a risk that customers will go elsewhere. Poor performance in DIO suggests possible weakness in the forecast-to-fulfilment processes covering the inbound supply chain, manufacturing and outbound supply chain. However, strategic decisions can also cause inventory to vary.

For example, a company with a single distribution centre may optimise inventory but take, say, three days to deliver its product to customers, while a company with several distribution centres may be able to deliver products faster but must keep more inventory on hand.

In section 6.8, we found that in 2004, Puma had an inventory turnover of 3.66 and held its inventory on average for 100 days (365/3.66), i.e. more than three months.

To see the level of credit being offered to customers (trade receivables), we use the **trade receivables turnover**. This ratio can help us to understand whether receivables are being collected in line with industry practice or more slowly.

$$\text{Trade receivables turnover} = \text{Net (credit) sales} \div$$
$$\text{(Year-end) Trade receivables (net of VAT and provision for doubtful debts)}$$

Most enterprises just report a single 'Sales' number that is the sum of cash plus credit sales. Using total 'Sales' rather than the amount of sales made on credit in the trade receivables turnover calculation can sometimes produce misleading results. However, cash sales are rare in most enterprises today.

Trade receivables turnover can also be used to spot changing customer payment patterns. For example, if we divide 365 days by the trade receivables turnover, the result tells us the number of days that on average trade receivables are 'on the books' before being collected:

$$\text{Days sales outstanding (DSO)} = 365 \text{ days} \div \text{Trade receivables turnover}$$

A decrease in DSO represents an improvement, while an increase in DSO means deterioration in collection. An increasing in DSO would indicate a weakness in cash collection management. Enterprises with a high proportion of cross-border sales need to monitor carefully DSO because of long payment terms in some countries. In Italy, for example, terms can often be in excess of 100 days compared with an average of 58 days in France and 40 in Germany.

Trade payables turnover and **days payables outstanding** help management and analysts understand the enterprise's pattern of payments to suppliers:

$$\text{Trade payables turnover} =$$
$$\text{Inventory purchases} \div \text{(Year-end) Trade payables (net of VAT)}$$

$$\text{Days trade payables outstanding (DPO)} = 365 \text{ days} \div \text{Trade payables turnover}$$

A positive change in DPO is an improvement, a negative change indicates deterioration. Increasing DPO improves working capital and increases cash and cash equivalents, but must be weighted against the possibility of deterioration in relations with suppliers. An unusually high DPO is often a sign of weakness in cash management.

In the following example we piece these ratios together to get a picture that will help us analyse the financial condition of an enterprise. Cash flows out of the bank into inventory; from inventory into customers as trade receivables; and then back into the bank on collection of receivables. The suppliers of the inventory are paid in cash (or cash equivalents) and the cash cycle is now complete.

Example

DIO, DSO and DPO

AF&J Ltd's financial statements show the following items (in millions of euro):

Net sales:		1,500
Cost of sales:		900
Beginning inventory	170	
Add Purchases	876	
Deduct Ending inventory	(146)	
Trade receivables, net		200
Year-end trade receivables, net of VAT	250	
Deduct Bad debt provision	(50)	
Year-end trade payables, net of VAT		120

Let us determine DIO, DSO and DPO:

$$\text{Inventory turnover} = \frac{900}{146} = 6.08 \qquad \text{DIO} = \frac{365 \text{ days}}{6.08} = 59 \text{ days}$$

$$\text{Trade receivables turnover} = \frac{1,500}{200} = 7.5 \qquad \text{DSO} = \frac{365 \text{ days}}{7.5} = 49 \text{ days}$$

$$\text{Trade payables turnover} = \frac{876}{120} = 7.3 \qquad \text{DPO} = \frac{365 \text{ days}}{7.3} = 50 \text{ days}$$

Now we know that:

- Inventory is held on average for about 59 days;
- Inventory is sold and another 49 days on average elapse before cash is collected from customers;
- AF&J Ltd pays its suppliers on average 50 days after inventory is purchased.

Cash outflows and inflows are mismatched by 58 days (59 – 50 + 49) as shown in Figure 14.2.

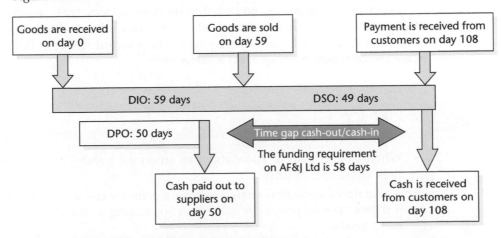

Figure 14.2 DIO, DSO and DPO combined together

14.3   Long-term solvency

Solvency refers to the ability of an enterprise to generate a stream of cash inflows sufficient to maintain its productive capacity and still meet the interest and principal payments on its long-term debt. An enterprise that cannot make timely payments of the amount required becomes insolvent and may be compelled to reorganise or liquidate. The two ratios that give insights on this ability of an enterprise are debt ratio and interest cover ratio and were illustrated in Chapter 8.

Debt ratio provides information about the amount of long-term debt in an enterprise's financial structure. The more an enterprise relies on long-term borrowing to finance its business activities, the higher its debt ratio and the greater the long-term solvency risk. Enterprises use different definitions of this ratio. The most used is the following:

Long-term debt to assets = Non-current liabilities ÷ Total assets

Although debt ratio is useful for understanding the financial structure of an enterprise, it does not provide information about its ability to generate a stream of cash inflows sufficient to make principal interest payments. The financial ratio commonly used for this purpose is the interest cover ratio:

Interest cover ratio = EBIT ÷ Interest expenses

This ratio, often referred to as times interest earned, indicates how many times interest expense is covered by operating profits before taxes and interest. It reflects the cushion between operating profit inflows and required interest payments. If the enterprise is also required to make periodic principal payments, then the analyst would include those amounts in the calculation.

A criticism of the traditional interest coverage ratio is that it uses earnings rather than operating cash flows in the numerator. Therefore we can compute a cash flow coverage ratio in which the numerator represents operating cash flows before interest and taxes:

Cash flow coverage ratio =
Operating cash flows before interest and tax payments ÷ Interest expenses

When operating profits and cash flow move in tandem, both versions of the ratio will yield similar results. However, when the two measures do diverge as during a period of high growth, income may be a poor substitute for cash flow, and in that case the cash flow coverage ratio is preferable.

Summary

- When lenders want to know about an enterprise's ability to pay debts on time, they assess its credit risk.
- A cash flow statement is often the starting point for credit risk assessment because it shows the enterprise's operating cash flows along with its financing and investment needs.
- Liquidity and solvency ratios are additional tools the lender can use to assess and monitor credit risk.

- Liquidity refers to an enterprise's short-term liquidity to generate cash for working capital needs and immediate debt repayment needs. Ratios used to assess short-term liquidity are current ratio, quick ratio and cash ratio. However, as they are static measures, working capital to sales ratio is used to meet this objection.

- Certain working capital ratios such as inventory turnover, trade receivables turnover and trade payables turnover are used to understand in more detail the way in which cash is flowing around the business.

- Solvency refers to the long-term ability to generate cash internally or from external sources in order to satisfy plant capacity needs, fuel growth and repay debts when due. To assess solvency, interest cover ratio and various debt ratios are used.

References and research

The following are examples of books and research papers which take the issues of this chapter further:

- Stephen N. Penman, *Financial Statement Analysis and Security Valuation*, McGraw-Hill, 2004, Part II
- Gerald I. White, Ashwinpaul C. Sondhi and Dov Fried, *The Analysis and Use of Financial Statements*, 3rd Edition, Wiley, 2003, Chapter 4
- Lawrence Revsine, Daniel W. Collins and W. Bruce Johnson, *Financial Reporting & Analysis*, 2nd Edition, Prentice Hall, 2002, Chapter 5
- REL Consultancy Group, *Seventh Annual Working Capital Scorecard*, September 2004. (www.relconsult.com)

Questions

14.1 Precious Toys Ltd wrote off EUR 100,000 of obsolete inventory at 31 December 2004. What effect did this write-off have on the company's 2004 current and quick ratios?

14.2 Melissa SpA has current assets of EUR 90,000 and current liabilities of EUR 180,000.

Compute the effect of each of the following transactions on Melissa's current ratio:

(a) Refinancing a EUR 30,000 long-term loan with a short-term loan.
(b) Purchasing EUR 50,000 of goods.
(c) Paying EUR 20,000 of trade payables.
(d) Collecting EUR 10,000 of trade receivables.

14.3 Lollo's inventory and other related accounts for the year ended 31 March 2005 follow:

Sales	EUR 6,000,000
Cost of sales	EUR 4,400,000
Inventory as at 31 March 2005	EUR 1,200,000

How many times did the inventory turn over during the financial year ended 31 March 2005?

14.4 An extract from the financial statements of a wholesaler for the years ended 31 December 2004 and 2003 follows (amounts in thousands of euro):

Balance sheet data	As at 31 December	
	2004	2003
Trade and other receivables	500,000	470,000
Deduct: Allowance for doubtful debts	(25,000)	(20,000)
Net trade and other receivables	475,000	450,000
Inventories	600,000	550,000

Income statement data	Year ended 31 December	
	2004	2003
Net credit sales	2,500,000	2,200,000
Net cash sales	500,000	400,000
Net sales	3,000,000	2,600,000
Cost of sales	2,000,000	1,800,000
Selling, general and administrative expenses	300,000	270,000
Other operating expenses	50,000	30,000
Net operating expenses	2,350,000	2,100,000

(a) What is the trade receivables turnover for 2004 and 2003?
(b) What is the inventory turnover for 2004 and 2003?
(c) Comment on the trend.

14.5 On 1 January 2004 Amit & Frances Co's inventory was EUR 400,000. During 2004 the company purchased EUR 1,900,000 of additional inventory, and on 31 December 2004 the total inventory was EUR 500,000.
    What is the inventory turnover for 2004?

14.6 Refer to Table 3.8 Consolidated balance sheet of Puma as at 31 December 2004, Table 4.4 Puma management income statement for 2004 and Table 12.1 Puma consolidated cash flow statement for the years ended 31 December 2004 and 2003. Determine the ratios you consider appropriate to assess the long-term solvency of Puma.

Case study   adidas-Salomon (B)

Refer to the financial statements of adidas-Salomon for 2000–2004 for the case study in Chapter 13.

Questions:

1. Analyse adidas-Salomon's short-term liquidity for the years 2002–2004.
2. Analyse its working capital over the same period.
3. Analyse its long-term solvency.
4. Comment on your findings.

Note

[1] From the numerator prepaid expenses should also be deducted.

15

Operating performance

Objectives

When you have completed this chapter you should be able to:

- understand what return on investment is and how it can be calculated and interpreted
- distinguish between shareholders' return and return on the total resources available to an enterprise
- subdivide ROTA and ROE into their components
- understand how the deductibility of interest expense may make the use of debt less costly than the issue of new shares.

15.1   Introduction

This chapter is concerned with an analysis of profitability. In Chapters 5 and 13 we have looked at the profit margin ratios when dealing with a vertical analysis of the income statement. Here we will use ratios to measure an enterprise's profitability or its 'return on investment'. This is a generic terminology which relates to one of the most important concepts in business finance.

Walsh (2002) states:

Each [euro] of assets has to be matched by a [euro] of funds drawn from the financial markets. These funds need to be paid for at the market rate. Payment can come only from the operating surplus derived from the efficient use of the assets. It is by relating this surplus to the value of the underlying assets/funds that we find a measure of return on investment.

If this return on investment is equal to or greater than the cost of funds, then the business is currently viable. However, if the long-term rate is less than the cost of funds, the business has no long-term future.

The concept of return on investment is universal, but the methods of measurement vary widely.

This lack of consistency may cause confusion. In general we evaluate the overall success of an investment by comparing our investment return with the amount of investment we initially made:

$$\text{Rate of return on investment} = \frac{\text{Profit}}{\text{Invested capital}}$$

Which profit and what assets shall we use?

Profit

A rate of return may be produced using the gross profit, EBITDA (earnings before interest, taxation, depreciation and amortisation), EBIT (earnings before interest and taxes), EBT (earnings before tax) or EAT (earnings after tax).

EBIT, also known as operating profit makes comparisons across companies more transparent. In fact, by removing interest and taxes from earnings, it does not take into account the impact that differences in capital structure and taxation may have on earnings. However, EBIT is not a cash flow measure and it may overstate or understate the degree to which operating cash is available to service debt.

EBITDA is currently enjoying favour among analysts as a financial benchmark for measuring an enterprise's cash flow and thus its ability to service debt. EBITDA removes from the profit calculation two non-cash items, depreciation and amortisation, that are major expense items for many enterprises today, especially technology and telecommunications companies. Enterprise value, i.e. total assets of an enterprise, today is commonly determined in terms of a multiple of EBITDA.

Invested capital

It is represented by the capital invested in the enterprise by shareholders and other financiers.

In this chapter we will explore two ratios of return on investments: return on total assets or ROTA and return on equity or ROE[1].

These two separate measures are necessary because they throw light on different aspects of the business, both of which are important:

- ROTA looks at the operating efficiency of the *total* enterprise.
- ROE considers how that operating efficiency is translated into benefit for the owners.

15.2   Return on total assets (ROTA)

Because the measurement of operating performance should not be influenced by how assets are financed, it is best measured by pretax operating rate of return on total assets, also called return on total assets (ROTA):

$$ROTA = \frac{EBIT}{Total\ assets} \times 100$$

ROTA calculation for Puma for 2004 is shown as follows:

$$ROTA = \frac{EUR\ 365.0m}{EUR\ 929.6m} \times 100 = 39.26\%$$

We have already defined EBIT as the amount remaining after the deduction of total operating expenses from total revenues, but before the charges for interest and tax. Total operating expenses include cost of sales, selling, distribution and administration overheads.

EBIT is compared with the total assets figure in the balance sheet. The percentage relationship between the two values gives the rate of return being earned by the total assets. Therefore, this ratio measures how well management uses all the assets in the business to generate an operating surplus independently of how those assets are financed.

15.2.1 The components of ROTA

Although the ROTA is a powerful tool in directing management's day-to-day activities it simply provides a target or benchmark.

To be useful in the decision-making process we should look at its component parts:

- margin on sales
- asset turnover.

We have seen that ROTA is calculated by the fraction EBIT/Total assets. If we introduce the figure for 'sales' and link it to each variable we will get two fractions instead of one, as shown in Figure 15.1.

An enterprise's overall profitability is the product of an activity ratio and a profitability ratio. A low ROTA can result from low turnover, indicating poor asset management, low profit margin or a combination of both factors.

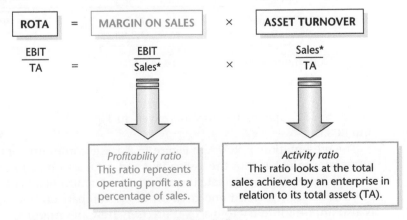

* Note that 'sales' cancel out above and below the line

Figure 15.1 The components of ROTA

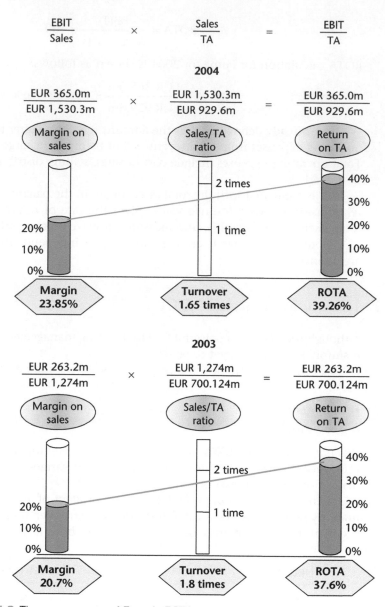

$$\frac{EBIT}{Sales} \quad \times \quad \frac{Sales}{TA} \quad = \quad \frac{EBIT}{TA}$$

2004

$$\frac{EUR\ 365.0m}{EUR\ 1,530.3m} \quad \times \quad \frac{EUR\ 1,530.3m}{EUR\ 929.6m} \quad = \quad \frac{EUR\ 365.0m}{EUR\ 929.6m}$$

Margin on sales   Sales/TA ratio   Return on TA

2 times   40%
30%
20%   20%
10%   10%
0%   1 time   0%

Margin 23.85%   Turnover 1.65 times   ROTA 39.26%

2003

$$\frac{EUR\ 263.2m}{EUR\ 1,274m} \quad \times \quad \frac{EUR\ 1,274m}{EUR\ 700.124m} \quad = \quad \frac{EUR\ 263.2m}{EUR\ 700.124m}$$

Margin on sales   Sales/TA ratio   Return on TA

2 times   40%
30%
20%   20%
10%   10%
0%   1 time   0%

Margin 20.7%   Turnover 1.8 times   ROTA 37.6%

Figure 15.2 The components of Puma's ROTA

Figure 15.2 applies the formula given in Figure 15.1 to Puma's ROTA in 2004 and 2003.

The presentation of ROTA in Figure 15.3 as the combining of the two component ratios is a useful basis for the assessment and comparison of an enterprise's performance. It is essential to calculate the overall rate of return of an enterprise for a number of years to see the trend and to allow direct comparison with other companies. It is also important to try to discover precisely how an enterprise is achieving its level of profitability. What is the relationship between the margin on sales and asset turnover? Is it consistent, and if not, why is it changing?

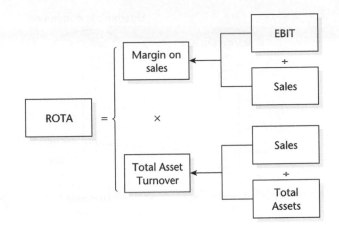

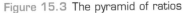

Figure 15.3 The pyramid of ratios

Figure 15.4 shows typical values of ROTA and its components for enterprises from different industrial sectors.

As Walsh (2002) explains, the first enterprise has a relatively low margin, combined with a high turnover ratio. This may indicate a distribution-type company.

The opposite applies to the second enterprise. Very high margins and low asset turnover are typical of companies that require large investment in non-current assets. The telecommunication sector generates sales margins in the region of 25 per cent. However, enormous investment in fixed assets with correspondingly low asset turnover means that this margin is only just adequate to make a reasonable return on total assets.

The third and last enterprise shows average values under both headings. Quite a number of medium-sized manufacturing companies have this kind of pattern. The difference between success and mediocrity in this type of business is often less than 2 per cent on margin and a small improvement in asset turnover.

15.3   Relationship between ROE, ROTA and leverage

In Chapter 9 we analysed the ROE and stated that this ratio is arguably the most important in business finance. It measures the absolute return delivered to shareholders:

$$\text{ROE} = \frac{\text{EAT}}{\text{Owners' funds}} \times 100$$

An above-average figure represents success for an enterprise – it results in a high share price and makes it easy to attract new funds. These will enable the company to grow, given suitable market conditions, and this in turn will lead to greater profits and continued growth in the wealth of its owners (Walsh 2002). It should, however, be remembered that the assertion just made is true only when earnings after tax represent core or recurring earnings and are not affected by non-recurring or abnormal gains.

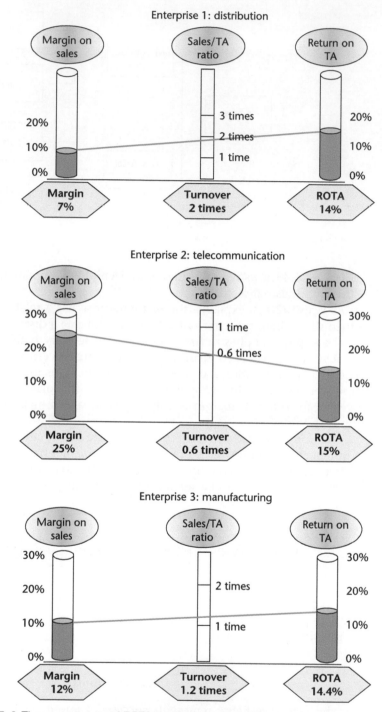

Figure 15.4 The components of ROTA in different enterprises

Source: adapted from Walsh (2002)

ROE is a critical feature of individual companies and overall market economy:

- At the level of the individual enterprise, an above-average ROE will keep in place the financial framework for a thriving, growing enterprise.

- At the level of the total economy, ROE drives industrial investments, growth in gross national product, employment, government tax receipts, and so on.

Now we will look in more depth at ROE, highlighting the relationships between it and ROTA and leverage.

The greater the debt, the greater the risk in terms of solvency of an enterprise.

All debt in the balance sheet gives third parties legal claims on the company. These claims are for interest payments at regular intervals, plus repayment of the principal on a given date. The principal is repaid either by periodic instalments or a single lump sum at the end of the loan period.

Therefore when a company raises debt, it takes on a commitment to substantial fixed cash outflows for some time into the future. The company does not have a guaranteed cash inflow over the same period. Indeed the cash inflow may be uncertain and volatile.

A fixed cash outflow combined with an uncertain cash inflow gives rise to financial risk. It follows that the greater the loan, the greater the risk.

The following example, based on Walsh (2002), illustrates the impact of different debt-to-equity ratios on ROE.

Let us look at an enterprise for which the mix of funds has not yet been decided. It has:

- assets of EUR 100,000

- sales of EUR 120,000

- operating profit or EBIT of EUR 15,000.

The effect of different levels of gearing or leverage on ROE is illustrated. In Figure 15.5 (on page 300), just one level of leverage is analysed to show you how the figures work.

Option 1 illustrates a situation with EUR 100,000 equity and no debt. Accordingly there is no interest charge. The total profit of EUR 15,000 is applied to shareholders' investment of EUR 100,000. The ROE is 15 per cent.

In **option 2**, the funding mix has changed to EUR 80,000 equity and EUR 20,000 debt. The interest charge at 10 per cent is EUR 2,000. This is deducted from the profit of EUR 15,000 to leave EUR 13,000 for the shareholders. Because the equity investment is now EUR 80,000 the ROE is 16.25 per cent (EUR 13,000 ÷ EUR 80,000 × 100).

As a result of introducing 20 per cent debt into the company, the ROE has increased from 15 per cent to 16.25 per cent. This is financial leverage in action.

In Table 15.1 (on page 300), the leverage has been extended in steps all the way up to 90 per cent. With each additional slice of debt, the ROE increases until it reaches 60 per cent at the 90 per cent level of debt.

Extraordinarily high levels of return can thus be achieved by highly leveraged companies. The price that is paid for these high returns is the additional exposure to risk. The relationship between ROE, ROTA, interest paid to lenders, and debt-to-equity ratio (D/E) is shown in the following equation:

$$\text{ROE (pre-tax)} = \text{ROTA} + [(\text{ROTA} - \text{Interest}) \times \text{D/E}]$$

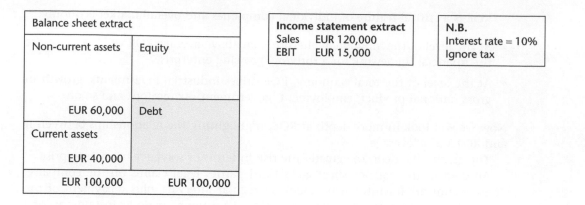

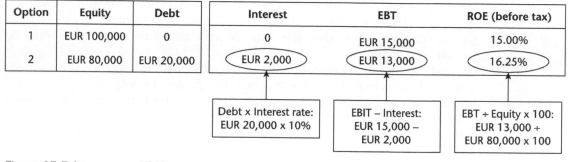

Figure 15.5 Leverage and ROE
Source: Walsh (2002)

When ROTA is higher than the interest rate paid on borrowing, higher gearing has a positive impact on ROE. Therefore, the debt/equity or leverage decision is of great importance to management.

There is a risk return trade-off. The impulse to achieve high returns for the shareholders must be restrained by the company's risk profile.

Even a very well-managed company can suffer an unexpected deterioration in its financial position either from a default on the part of a major customer or a general worsening of business conditions. Such deterioration can be very difficult to recover from. It is prudent to keep some liquidity in reserve to guard against such an eventuality.

Table 15.1 Degrees of leverage and impact on ROE

Option	Equity	Debt	Interest	EBT	ROE (before tax)
1	EUR 100,000	0	0	EUR 15,000	15.00%
2	EUR 80,000	EUR 20,000	EUR 2,000	EUR 13,000	16.25%
3	EUR 60,000	EUR 40,000	EUR 4,000	EUR 11,000	18.33%
4	EUR 50,000	EUR 50,000	EUR 5,000	EUR 10,000	20.00%
5	EUR 40,000	EUR 60,000	EUR 6,000	EUR 9,000	22.50%
6	EUR 20,000	EUR 80,000	EUR 8,000	EUR 7,000	35.00%
7	EUR 10,000	EUR 90,000	EUR 9,000	EUR 6,000	**60.00%**

Source: Walsh (2002)

15.3.1 Dangers of high gearing

The more a company relies on debt the less control it has over its finances and the more it is at risk, because banks are less likely to accept changes in the terms of a loan agreement than shareholders are to accept a lower or even no dividend if the company is short of cash or needs money to invest in assets.

High gearing can bring high volatility in the level of profit available to the equity shareholders. For a highly geared company, a small movement in profit can have a dramatic influence on equity earnings. A small drop would eat up in debt service all the profit that would otherwise be available to distribute as dividends.

When business is booming, a company may regard an increase in gearing as not only attractive but also essential. It can be seen as a sign of poor management called covenants not to borrow more to achieve returns in excess of the cost of borrowing. During inflationary times, when the real cost of debt decreases, the pressures can be irresistible. However, if the boom slows and/or ends and there is a recession, the highly geared company faces difficulties as profits decline, and the loan falls due for repayment.

A further danger inherent in high gearing is that as the providers of debt see gearing rise they may, to reduce their own exposure, insist that certain restrictions, called covenants, are built into loan agreements – for example, an upper limit for gearing or tougher levels for interest cover or liquidity. The company may lose some degree of control and flexibility of approach in its financial management. If it is unable to respect the loan restrictions, it may be held in default and forced to make immediate repayment.

15.4   A note on income tax effect

Because interest payments are deductible as an expense for income tax purposes but dividends are not, all other things being equal, the use of debt is less costly to the company than is equity. Moreover, it can be used to increase the returns to owners provided the returns generated from borrowed funds exceed the cost of paying interest, as we saw in section 15.3.

The following example illustrates this point.

Example

Income tax effects of high leverage

Consider raising additional capital of EUR 10 million either through long-term debt or through the issue of new shares. In the following table we show the effect on net profit and on the cost of capital raised in both hypotheses.

Amounts in millions of euro	EUR 10 million long-term debt	EUR 10 million new shares
EBIT (assumed)	5,000	5,000
Interest expense (10% of long-term debt)	1,000	–
EBT	4,000	5,000
Income tax expense at 40%	1,600	2,000
EAT	*2,400*	*3,000*
Dividends (on 'new' capital)	–	1,000
EAT less dividends	2,400	2,000
Pretax cost of capital raised	10%	10%
After tax cost of capital raised:		
EUR 600,000(*) ÷ EUR 10,000,000	6%	
EUR 1,000,000 ÷ EUR 10,000,000		10%

* Interest expense	1,000,000
Income tax 'savings' because of interest deduction:	
EUR 10,000,000 × 40%	400,000
Interest expense net of tax	600,000

As you can see from the example, interest is tax deductible so its after-tax cost is considerably less than that of dividends (6 per cent versus 10 per cent). In other words, net earnings attributable to shareholders can be significantly higher if debt is used wisely.

You should also consider that interest is an expense whereas dividends are not. Thus, net profit is higher in the instance additional capital is raised through the issue of new shares instead of long-term debt (EUR 3 million versus EUR 2.4 million).

Summary

- The concept of return on investment is universal, but the methods of measurement vary widely.

- A rate of return is determined comparing a profit (i.e. gross profit, EBITDA, EBIT, EBT, EAT) with the capital invested (i.e. total assets, owners' equity, etc.).

- ROTA is the return on total assets invested in an enterprise and is equal to EBIT divided by total assets. The ratios that drive ROTA are margin on sales and asset turnover.

- ROTA is the most important driver of ROE, which is the return on equity and is calculated by comparing EAT with owners' equity.

- When ROTA is higher than the interest rate paid on debt, extraordinarily high levels of ROE can be achieved by highly leveraged companies. However, high gearing can expose a company to higher risk.

- Because interest payments are deductible as an expense for income tax purposes but dividends are not, all other things being equal, the use of debt is less costly to the corporation than is equity.

References and research

The following are examples of books that take the issues of this chapter further:

- Stephen N. Penman, *Financial Statement Analysis and Security Valuation*, McGraw-Hill, 2004
- Lawrence Revsine, Daniel W. Collins and W. Bruce Johnson, *Financial Reporting & Analysis*, 3rd Edition, Prentice Hall, 2002
- Ciaran Walsh, *Key Management Ratios: Master the Management Metrics that Drive and Control Your Business*, 3rd Edition, Financial Times Prentice Hall, 2002.
- Gerald I. White, Ashwinpaul C. Sondhi and Dov Fried, *The Analysis and Use of Financial Statements*, 2nd Edition, Wiley, 2003

Questions

15.1 Which measures of operating performance are combined to give ROTA?

15.2 'The tax law discriminates against share capital but favours debt.' Do you agree? Explain why.

15.3 As the manager of Lene division of Elenia SpA, you are interested in determining the division's return on investment. As division manager you have no control over financing assets, but you control acquisition and disposition of assets. The division controller has given you the following data for the division to aid you in calculating return on investment:

Accounting period 1 January–31 December 2004 (amounts in thousands of euro)

Total assets (1 January)	800
Total assets (31 December)	1,050
Non-current liabilities (1 January)	150
Non-current liabilities (31 December)	192
Equity (1 January)	556
Equity (31 December)	606
EAT	108
Interest expense on non-current liabilities	8.4
Tax rate = 30%	

Which method would be most appropriate for calculating the division's return on investment? Why? Using this method, what is the return on investment for 2004?

15.4 Casa Comfort is a leading retailer in the home improvement industry. Certain data from its financial statements for the years ended 31 March 2004 and 31 March 2005 follow (euro in millions):

	2005	2004
Sales	38,434	30,219
EBIT	3,795	2,661
EAT	2,320	1,614
PPE, net	10,227	8,160
TA	17,081	13,465
Equity	12,341	8,740

(a) Compute ROTA for the years ended 31 March 2004 and 31 March 2005.

(b) Compute the margin on sales and total asset turnover. Show how these two ratios determine the ROTA.

15.5 Oltre il Giardino SpA, a medium-sized listed company, is considering two schemes to finance its next expansion.

1. The first is to raise EUR 8 million by means of a long-term loan from its bankers. Interest would be charged at 2 per cent above base rate which you should assume currently stands at 5 per cent. The loan would be repayable in equal annual instalments over five years starting on 1 April 2007 and finishing on 1 April 2011. The bank requires an agreement to the following covenants. Firstly, an interest cover of at least two times must be maintained and, secondly, the debt-to-equity ratio is not to exceed 1.

2. The other scheme is to raise EUR 8 million by issuing 2 million ordinary shares at EUR 4 each.

The following extracts have been taken from the company's records:

Years ended 30 September	2005	2004	2003
No. of EUR 1 ordinary shares (millions)	10	10	10
Amounts in millions of euro			
Shareholders' equity	36	34	32
Loans	26	20	18
	62	54	50
EBIT	9.3	5.2	8
Interest expense	3	2.8	2.4

EBIT for the year ending 30 September 2006 is forecast at EUR 10 million and the dividends are forecast at EUR 0.20 per share. Use a corporate tax rate of 35 per cent in your calculations.

(a) Calculate the following ratios for 2006 for each of the debt-and-equity alternative:
   (i) interest cover
   (ii) debt-to-equity ratio.

(b) Using the information just mentioned, and any other ratios you consider relevant, state with reasons which scheme you would recommend.

15.6 One of your main suppliers of raw materials is a family-owned company. It is the only available supplier and your company purchases 60 per cent of its output from it. Currently, it requires extra finance to re-equip its factory with modern machinery, which is expected to cost EUR 8 million. The machinery's life is expected to be 10 years, and savings, before depreciation, arising from its installation, will be EUR 3 million per annum. It has approached you to see if you are able to help and has mentioned that if it can acquire the new equipment your company will be able to share in the benefits through reduced prices for its purchases. An extract of some recent financial statements of the supplier company appears as follows:

Income statement data (amounts in millions of euro)
for the years ended 30 September

	2005	2004	2003
Sales	9.5	8.0	11.5
EBIT	1.9	(2.0)	(0.2)
Interest charge	1.5	2.4	1.2
EBT	0.4	(4.4)	(1.4)

There was no charge for tax in these years nor any dividend paid out.

Balance sheets at 30 September (amounts in millions of euro)

	2005	2004	2003
Non-current assets			
PPE	24.0	23.0	22.1
Deduct Accumulated depreciation	(14.0)	(12.0)	(10.0)
PPE, net	10.0	11.0	12.1
Current assets			
Inventory	3.8	3.5	4.3
Trade receivables	4.1	2.6	2.8
	7.9	6.1	7.1
Deduct **Current liabilities**			
Trade payables	(1.9)	(1.7)	(1.4)
Bank overdraft	(4.2)	(4.1)	(2.7)
	(6.1)	(5.8)	(4.1)
Net current assets	1.8	0.3	3.0
Total assets less current liabilities	11.8	12.2	14.9
Deduct Long-term loan	(7.4)	(8.2)	(6.5)
Net assets	4.4	4.0	8.4
Financed by:			
Owners' equity			
Capital	1.0	1.0	1.0
Retained earnings	3.4	3.0	7.4
	4.4	4.0	8.4

(a) Calculate for each year and comment upon each of the following ratios for the supplier:
  i.   ROTA
  ii. interest cover
  iii. debt ratio.

(b) Using the ratios you have determined and any other you consider relevant, prepare a short report stating the financial assistance, if any, your company would be prepared to provide to the supplier. Your recommendations should also state the form that the assistance should take, its amount, and what terms and conditions your company would seek to impose.

Case study   Kerry Group

Kerry Group is a leader in the global food industry based in Ireland. In 2004 it achieved a strong business and financial performance and sales grew by 11.8 per cent.

Prepare an analysis of Kerry's profitability for 2003 and 2004. Assume a 40 per cent tax rate. You can follow the steps below:

Step 1: Determine Kerry's return on total assets (ROTA) for 2003 and 2004.

Step 2: What is the effective interest rate (i.e. net of income tax effect) that Kerry has been paying for its debt? Analyse the portion of total assets that Kerry has been financing with debt and comment on any apparent strategy.

Step 3: Determine Kerry's return on equity for each year. Has leverage benefited Kerry's shareholders? How can you tell?

Table 15.2 Kerry Group's income statement for the year ended 31 December 2004

	2004 €000	2003 €000
Turnover	4,128,736	3,693,410
Operating costs	3,779,830	3,384,891
Operating profit before intangible amortisation and exceptional items	**348,906**	**308,519**
Goodwill and other intangible amortisation	69,252	48,103
Exceptional restructuring costs	41,108	–
Operating profit	238,546	260,416
Profit on sale of fixed assets	15,592	942
Interest payable and similar charges	48,982	37,356
Profit before taxation	205,156	224,002
Taxation	59,371	63,025
Profit after taxation and attributable to ordinary shareholders	**145,785**	**160,977**
Dividends – paid	8,483	7,625
– proposed	17,751	15,985
	26,234	23,610
Retained profit for the year	**119,551**	**137,367**

Source: Kerry Group Plc Annual Report 2004

Table 15.3 Kerry Group's consolidated balance sheet at 31 December 2004

	2004 €000	2003 €000
Fixed assets		
Tangible assets	968,480	844,701
Intangible assets	1,283,237	837,301
	2,251,717	1,682,002
Current assets		
Stocks (Inventory)	457,662	383,899
Debtors	566,938	482,955
Cash at bank and in hand	65,328	56,862
	1,089,928	923,716
Creditors: Amounts falling due within one year	(858,305)	(709,872)
Net current assets	231,623	213,844
Total assets less current liabilities	2,483,340	1,895,846
Creditors: Amounts falling due after more than one year	(1,350,908)	(899,024)
Provisions for liabilities and charges	(60,681)	(48,333)
	1,071,751	948,489
Capital and reserves		
Called-up equity share capital	23,356	23,234
Capital conversion reserve fund	340	340
Share premium account	375,032	365,229
Profit and loss account	654,177	531,149
	1,043,905	919,952
Deferred income	27,846	28,537
	1,071,751	948,489

Source: Kerry Group Plc Annual Report 2004

Note

[1] An alternative ratio of return on investments is return on capital employed or ROCE. This is determined by dividing EBIT by capital employed (i.e. non-current assets plus working capital).

16 Investment ratios

Objectives

When you have completed this chapter you should be able to:

- understand why earnings per share figure is important and how it is used by shareholders
- calculate basic and diluted EPS under different circumstances
- use the PE ratio to decide whether the shares are currently over- or undervalued
- determine the main stock-market-related ratios.

16.1 Introduction

The value of listed companies is determined by the stock market. For the majority of shareholders, it is the price quoted on the stock exchange that determines the value of their investment. Many factors influence a company's share price. Some are obvious and quantifiable; others are more esoteric and ephemeral. A company issuing a profit warning can expect a drop in share price. Rumours of a takeover, a technological breakthrough, changes on the board, a new or a loss of a big order can all influence the share price of an enterprise. Share price will partly reflect the general mood of the market, which in turn is linked to the domestic and global economic, political and social environment. Today the increase or decrease in the US stock exchanges has in all probability an effect on the Asian stock exchanges the next morning, and during the day the EU stock exchanges will be affected by both the movements on the US and Asian (especially the Japanese) stock exchanges.

The prime trigger for a movement in share price is a change in investors' confidence about the ability of a company to produce profits in the future. Shares may have been purchased on the basis of the past performance of a company, but they are held in expectation of future returns: dividends and capital gains.

The industry in which a company operates can also influence share price. If it is one that is seen as being static or mature, this will hold back the share price, whereas the reverse is true for a dynamic or glamorous industry.

The value of those companies not publicly listed is greatly influenced by the same market. It is therefore important to understand the most commonly used stock-market-related ratios. In this chapter we will look at them and show what drives corporate value.

16.2   Earnings per share (EPS)

A popular measure of company performance is earnings per share (EPS). This ratio is produced by dividing EAT for the year, deducting minority interests and any non-voting share dividends, by the average number of equity shares in issue (see section 9.4).

$$EPS = \frac{EAT - \begin{array}{c} \text{profit attributable} \\ \text{to minority shareholders} \end{array} - \begin{array}{c} \text{preference} \\ \text{dividends} \end{array}}{\text{Number of shares in issue}}$$

It is a mistake to assume you can compare profitability based on EPS. A difference in earnings per share can be brought about simply by differences in the share capital structure. Two companies could have an identical EAT, for example EUR 50,000, and share capital of EUR 100,000. But if one company (A) had issued shares of EUR 0.25 (i.e. 400,000 shares) and the other (B), shares of EUR 0.1 (i.e. 1,000,000 shares) the EPS would be very different. EUR 0.125 and EUR 0.05.

	A	B
EAT (EUR)	50,000	50,000
Number of shares	400,000	1,000,000
EPS (EUR)	**0.125**	**0.05**

Diluted EPS

As we have already seen in section 9.4, this arises where a company has issued securities which carry the right to be converted into equity shares at some future date. The diluted earnings per share is calculated assuming that this conversion has taken place, showing the position where all the possible options are taken up and shares are issued. Often a significant factor for determining the fully diluted earnings per share will be the share options of directors and other employees.

Creative EPS

Because shareholders as well as financial analysts place considerable weight on earning per share, directors are naturally keen that the figure they report is a good one, often providing an example of 'what you measure is what you get'. Temptation to succumb to such action, sometimes euphemistically referred to as 'aggressive earnings management', is greatest during economic uncertainty and recession. When looking at EPS it is important to see how extraordinary or exceptional items have been treated. It is possible for a dramatic improvement in EPS to be brought about by the sale of an asset, thus producing a large profit that has nothing to do with the real trading activity of a company.

16.2.1 How to determine basic EPS

EPS is frequently used by shareholders and directors to demonstrate the growth in a company's performance over time. Care is required to ensure that the number of shares is stated consistently to avoid distortions arising from changes in the capital structure that have changed the number of shares outstanding, without a corresponding change in resources during the whole or part of a year. Such changes occur, for example, with bonus issues, share splits, new issues etc. during the year. In such cases (i.e. bonus issues, share splits, exercise of conversion rights, etc.) the number of shares used in the basic EPS calculation should be adjusted.

Bonus issues

A bonus issue, or capitalisation issue, arises when a company capitalises its reserves (i.e. transfers part of its reserves to share capital). A bonus issue involves the issue of new shares to existing shareholders in proportion to their existing shareholdings. However, shareholders do not have to pay for the new shares issued. This means that neither the shareholders nor the company gives or receives any immediate financial benefits. A reason why a company might want to make a bonus issue is to lower the value of each share, without reducing the shareholders' collective or individual wealth.

Activity 16.1 Adjusting the number of shares used in the basic EPS calculation in a bonus issue

Refer to the data provided in the first example in section 9.4, where we assumed that XYZ plc had a net profit for 2004 of EUR 1,250,000 and an issued share capital of EUR 1,500,000 comprising 1,000,000 ordinary shares of EUR 0.50 each and 1,000,000 of EUR 1 10 per cent preference shares.

Now assume that XYZ increased its shares in 2004 by the issue of 1,000,0000 new ordinary shares and achieved identical earnings in 2004 as in 2003.

Questions:

1. Determine the basic EPS for 2004 for XYZ plc.
2. How would you restate the basic EPS of 2003 in order to compare the performance between the two years on a like-for-like basis?

Solutions to activities can be found at www.pearsoned.co.uk/kothari

Share splits

When the market value of a share becomes too high some companies may decide to increase the number of shares held by each shareholder by changing the nominal value of each share. The effect is to reduce the market price per share but in terms of value nothing changes for the shareholders. A share split would be treated in the same way as a bonus issue, as illustrated in the following example:

Example

Adjusting the number of shares used in the basic EPS calculation in the event of a share split

Refer to the data provided in Activity 16.1. Assume that XYZ plc split the 1,000,000 shares of EUR 0.50 each into 2,000,000 shares of EUR 0.25 each. As 2004 basic EPS would be calculated using 2,000,000 shares, it would seem that the basic EPS had halved in 2004.

This is misleading and 2003 basic EPS is therefore restated using 2,000,000 shares. The total market capitalisation of XYZ is therefore restated using 2,000,000 shares. The total market capitalisation of XYZ would remain unchanged. For example, if prior to the split, each share had a market value of EUR 4 and the company had a total market capitalisation of EUR 4,000,000, after the split each share would have a market price of EUR 2, and the company's market capitalisation would remain unchanged at EUR 4,000,000.

New issue of shares

Elliott and Elliott (2005) explain that:

> Issuing more shares to raise additional capital should generate additional earnings. In this situation we have a real change in the company's capital and there is no need to adjust any comparative figures. However, a problem arises in the year in which the issue took place. Unless the issue occurred on the first day of the financial year, the new funds would have been available to generate profits for only a part of the year. It would therefore be misleading to calculate the EPS figure by dividing the earnings generated during the year by the number of shares in issue at the end of the year. The method adopted to counter this is to use a time-weighted average for the number of shares.

Activity 16.2 Time-weighted number of shares for the basic EPS calculation

Assume that the following information is available for ABC plc:

Number of shares (nominal value EUR 0.50 each) in issue at 1 July 2004:	1,000,000
Number of shares issued for cash at market price on 31 December 2004:	500,000

Question:

Determine the time-weighted number of shares for EPS calculation at 30 June 2005.

Solutions to activities can be found at www.pearsoned.co.uk/kothari

Exercise of conversion rights during financial year

Shares actually issued will be in accordance with the terms of conversion and will be included in the basic EPS calculation on a time-apportioned basis from the date of conversion to the end of the financial year. The example below, based on an example in Elliott and Elliott 2005, illustrates such a calculation.

Example

Calculation of basic EPS assuming that convertible loan has been converted and options exercised during the financial year

Let us assume that the following information is available for Lollo & Luca SpA for 2005:

- An issued capital of 1,000,000 ordinary shares of EUR 0.50 each as at 1 January 2005.
- Convertible 10 per cent loan of EUR 1,000,000 converted on 1 April 2005 into 250,000 ordinary shares of EUR 0.50 each;
- Share options for 500,000 ordinary shares of EUR 0.50 each exercised on 1 August 2005.

The weighted average number of shares for 2005 for the basic EPS calculation is determined as follows:

1 January 2005	Ordinary shares in issue	$1,000,000 \times 3/12$	250,000
1 April 2005	Issued on conversion of the 10% loan	$\dfrac{250,000}{1,250,000} \times 4/12$	416,667
1 August 2005	Issued on exercise of options	$\dfrac{500,000}{1,750,000} \times 5/12$	729,167
31 December 2005	**Weighted average number of shares**		**1,395,834**

16.2.2 How to determine diluted EPS

In section 9.4, we saw that when a company has potential ordinary shares we need to add them to the basic weighted average number if they are dilutive. Where there are convertible bonds or convertible preference shares, we should adjust the net profit for:

- any dividends on dilutive potential ordinary shares that have been deducted in arriving at the net profit attributable to ordinary shareholders
- interest recognised in the period for the dilutive potential ordinary shares
- any other changes in income or expense that would result from the conversion of the dilutive potential ordinary shares, e.g. the reduction of interest expense related to convertible bonds results in a higher net profit.

The example below based on an example in Elliott and Elliott 2005, illustrates the calculation of diluted EPS for convertible bonds.

Example

Diluted EPS calculation for convertible bonds

Let us assume that for 2004 B&B plc had:

- An issued capital of 1,000,000 ordinary shares of EUR 0.50.
- Net profit of EUR 1,150,000.
- A 10 per cent loan of EUR 1,000,000 convertible into 250,000 ordinary shares of EUR 0.50 each.
- An average market price per share of EUR 4.
- The tax rate is 40 per cent.

The basic and diluted EPS are determined as shown below:

	Per share EUR	Earnings EUR	Number of shares
Net profit		1,150,000	
Weighted average share during 2004			1,000,000
Basic EPS = EUR 1,150,000 ÷ 1,000,000 =	*1.15*		
Number of shares resulting from conversion			250,000
Interest expense on convertible loan		100,000	
Deferred tax liabilities relating to interest expense		(40,000)	
Adjusted earnings and number of shares		1,210,000	1,250,000

Diluted EPS = EUR 1,210,000 ÷ 1,250,000 =   0.97

16.3   Price earnings ratio (P/E)

One of the most widely publicised ratios for a public company is the price/earnings or P/E ratio. The P/E ratio is significant because, by combining it with a forecast of company earnings, analysts can decide whether the shares are currently over- or undervalued.

The P/E ratio is calculated by dividing the market price of a share by the earnings that the company generated for that share:

$$Price/Earnings = Share\ price \div EPS$$

Alternatively, the P/E figure may be seen as a multiple of the earnings per share, where the multiple represents the number of years' earnings required to recoup the price paid for the share.

Example

P/E ratio

Assume the following data for three companies:

	A	B	C
Share price (EUR)	3.00	1.00	1.50
Earnings per share (EUR)	0.30	0.50	0.117
P/E	**10**	**2**	**12.9**

For company A a P/E of 10 means that when a share is purchased for EUR 3.00 this represents the equivalent of 10 years' earnings of EUR 0.3 a year, other things being equal: in other words, a payback period of 10 years. While it would take a shareholder in company B 2 years to recoup his/her outlay, and it would take a shareholder in company C about 13 years.

The P/E ratio for a company will reflect investors' confidence about the international scene, national economy and industry sector, as well as about the current year's performance of the company. It is difficult to interpret a P/E ratio in isolation without a certain amount of information about the company, its competitors and the industry within which it operates.

For example, a *high P/E ratio* might reflect investor confidence in the existing management team: people are willing to pay a high multiple for expected earnings because of the underlying strength of the company. Conversely, it might also reflect lack of investor confidence in the existing management, but an anticipation of a takeover bid which will result in transfer of the company assets to another company with better prospects for achieving growth in earnings than has the existing team.

A *low P/E ratio* might indicate a lack of confidence in the current management or a feeling that even a new management might not easily surmount the problems inherited. For example, there might be extremely high gearing, with little prospect of organic growth in earnings or new capital inputs from rights issues to reduce it.

These reasons for difference in the P/E ratios of companies, even though they are in the same industry, are market-based and not simply a function of earnings. However, the current EPS figure and the individual investor's expectation of future growth relative to that of other companies also have an impact on the share price.

16.4 Other stock-market-related ratios

Dividend per share, dividend cover and payout ratios

Dividend per share (DPS) can be calculated in the same way as earnings per share. The total dividend for the year is divided by the number of shares in issue:

$$\text{DPS} = \text{Dividends} \div \text{Number of equity shares in issue}$$

If EAT attributable to ordinary shareholders is divided by the dividend, the result is the number of times the dividend is covered. As with interest cover, the higher the dividend cover ratio the better or safer is the position of a company. However, levels of what is considered acceptable vary across business sectors. If a company is operating in a sector that is reasonably unaffected by economic downturns, such as food manufacturing and retailing, a lower dividend cover ratio is more acceptable because the risk is lower:

$$\text{Dividend cover} = \text{EAT} \div \text{Dividend} = \text{EPS} \div \text{Dividend per share}$$

Another way of looking at the safety level of dividend payments is to show what proportion of profit is being distributed to shareholders:

$$\text{Payout ratio} = 100 \div \text{Dividend cover}$$

The higher the payout ratio the lower is the dividend cover; the level of profit cover for dividend is just being expressed in a different way. In the example below, B has a dividend cover of 1.25 times. To put it differently, it has distributed in dividends 80 per cent of its profit of EUR 25. A company with a high payout ratio may not be retaining enough profit to reinvest in the business. You should always try to understand why. Is management not confident about the future prospects of the business, or are they taking a short-term view of keeping shareholders happy with a dividend payment rather than providing for future long-term growth?

	A	B	C
Dividend (EUR)	25	20	87
Number of shares	250	500	1,500
DPS (EUR)	0.10	0.40	0.58
EAT (EUR)	75	25	160
Dividend cover	3	1.25	2
Payout (%)	33	80	50

Earnings and dividend yields

To obtain an indication of the return flowing from an investment, the current share price and earnings per share can be combined to give the earnings yield:

$$\text{Earnings yield} = 100 \times (\text{EPS} \div \text{Share price})$$

Dividend yield links the current share price to the dividend received:

$$\text{Dividend yield} = 100 \times (\text{Dividend per share} \div \text{Share price})$$

	A	B	C
EPS (EUR)	0.30	0.5	0.117
Dividend per share (EUR)	0.10	0.40	0.58
Share price (EUR)	3.00	1.00	1.50
Earnings yield (%)	10	5	7.8
Dividend yield (%)	3.3	4.0	3.9

Changes in share price bring about a change in the dividend yield. As share price changes there is an automatic adjustment in dividend yield, illustrated as follows for company A, whose share price moves between EUR 1.50 and EUR 6.00:

	A	B	C
Dividend (EUR)	10	10	10
Share price (EUR)	3.00	1.50	6.00
Dividend yield	**3.3**	**6.7**	**1.7**

As the share price increases the dividend yield, i.e. the return for potential investors, decreases.

Market to book ratio

The market to book ratio gives the final and the most thorough assessment by the stock market of an enterprise's overall status, i.e. its management, profits, liquidity, and future prospects. This ratio expresses the relationship between a company's value on the stock exchange and the underlying net assets book value as shown in the balance sheet:

Market to book ratio = Market capitalisation ÷ Book value of owners' equity

The ratio relates the total market capitalisation to the shareholders' funds. In other words, it compares the value in the stock exchange with the shareholders' investment in the company.

It is the investors' perception of the performance of the company in terms of profits, liquidity, growth, and so on that determines the value of this ratio.

A value lower than one means that the shareholders' investment has diminished in value. The investing community has given a 'thumbs down' signal to the company, as it does not anticipate that future profits will be sufficient to justify the current owners' investment in the company.

On the other hand, when this ratio is higher than one, it means that the investment has been multiplied by the market to book factor. A high ratio does not simply mean that the value of the company has increased over time by means of its retained earnings. The multiplier acts in addition to this. Each euro of original investment plus each euro of retained earnings is multiplied by a factor equal to the market to book ratio.

In order to identify the factors that drive the market to book ratio, we should look at ROE and earnings yield. ROE is the rate of return that the company is delivering to its shareholders, while the earnings yield is the rate of return investors require to hold the share. Market to book ratio can thus be expressed as follows:

$$\text{Market to book ratio} = \frac{\text{ROE}}{\text{Earnings yield}} = \frac{\dfrac{\text{EAT}}{\text{Equity}}}{\dfrac{\text{EPS}}{\text{Share price}}}$$

This relationship is of crucial importance, as it illustrates that investors decide on the rate necessary for a particular business. Then they mark that business at a premium or a discount, depending on whether the return delivered by the enterprise is higher or lower than the required rate.

Summary

- Basic EPS is the net profit or loss for the period attributable to ordinary shareholders divided by time-weighted average number of ordinary shares outstanding during the period.
- In order to calculate diluted EPS the net profit attributable to ordinary shareholders and the weighted average number of shares outstanding should be adjusted for the effect of all dilutive potential ordinary shares (i.e. bonus issues, share splits, exercise of conversion rights, etc.)
- A company's EPS can be used to calculate another ratio which represents a payback measure: the price/earnings ratio. It is calculated by dividing the market price of a share by the earnings that the company generates for that share.
- Dividend per share, dividend cover, payout ratio, earnings yield and dividend yield are the most commonly used stock-market-related ratios.
- Market to book ratio expresses the relationship between a company's market capitalisation and the book value of its net assets. It is driven by ROE and earnings yield.

References and research

The IASB document relevant for this chapter is IAS 33 – *Earnings per Share*.

The following are examples of books that take the issues of this chapter further:

- Barry Elliott and Jamie Elliott, *Financial Accounting and Reporting*, 9th Edition, Financial Times-Prentice Hall, 2005, Chapters 26 and 28
- Tim Koller, Marc Goldhart and David Wessels, *Valuation: Measuring and Managing the Value of Companies*, Fourth Edition, John Wiley and Sons, 2005
- Hennie Van Greuning, *International Financial Reporting Standards: A Practical Guide*, The World Bank, 2005, Chapter 36
- Ciaran Walsh, *Key Management Ratios*, 3rd Edition, Financial Times-Prentice Hall, 2002, Part IV

Questions

16.1 Explain:
    (a) basic earnings per share
    (b) diluted earnings per share
    (c) potential ordinary shares
    (d) limitation of EPS as a performance measure.

16.2 In connection with IAS 33 – *Earnings per Share*:

    (a) Define the earnings figure used to determine basic and diluted EPS.
    (b) Explain the relationship between EPS and the PE ratio. Why is the PE ratio important as a stock market indicator?

16.3 The issued and fully paid share capital of Angli Inc remained unchanged at the following amounts since the date of incorporation until the financial year ended 31 March 2004:

- 1,200,000 ordinary shares with no par value
- 300,000 6 per cent participating preference shares of EUR 1 each.

The company has been operating at a profit for a number of years. As a result of a very conservative dividend policy followed by the directors during previous years, there is a large accumulated profit balance on the balance sheet. On 1 July 2004, the directors decided to issue to all ordinary shareholders, two shares for every one previously held.

The following abstract was taken from the (non-compliant) consolidated income statement for the years ended 31 March 2005 and 2004 (amounts in euro):

	2005	2004
Profit after tax	400,000	290,000
Minority interest (not IFRS compliant)	(30,000)	(20,000)
Net profit from ordinary activities	370,000	270,000
Extraordinary item (not IFRS compliant)	–	(10,000)
Profit for the year	370,000	260,000

The following dividends were paid or declared at the end of the reported periods (amounts in euro):

	2005	2004
Ordinary	165,000	120,000
Preference	34,500	30,000

The participating preference shareholders are entitled to share profits in the same ratio in which they share dividends, after payment of the fixed preference dividend. The shareholders will enjoy the same benefits during liquidation of the company.

(a) Calculate EPS for 2004 and 2005.
(b) Determine dividend per share for 2004 and 2005. Show your calculations.

16.4 L.J. Pathmark reported net profit of EUR 250,000 for 2005. The company had 125,000 ordinary shares of EUR 1 and 30,000 convertible preference shares of EUR 40 outstanding during the year. The dividend rate on the preference shares is EUR 2 per share. Each convertible preference share can be converted into two shares of L.J. Pathmark ordinary shares. During the year no convertible preference shares were converted.

(a) Calculate L.J. Pathmark's basic earnings per share.
(b) Calculate L.J. Pathmark's diluted earnings per share.

16.5 Find on the Internet the share price of Puma at the end of 2004. Then referring to Table 13.1 and Table 13.3 determine five stock-market-related ratios.

16.6 Find on the Internet the share price of adidas-Salomon at the end of 2004. Then referring to the data reported in the case study in Chapter 13, determine five stock-market-related ratios. Compare them with those calculated for Puma. Comment on the differences found.

Halma is a cash generative and highly profitable group which develops, makes and markets products worldwide that are used to enhance public safety and minimise hazards at work.

Its six specialist business groupings are:

- Fire and gas detection
- Water leak detection and UV treatment
- Elevator and door safety
- Bursting discs and sequential locking for process safety
- High power electrical resistors
- Optics and specialist technology

Its over-riding objective is to create *shareholder value* by:

- Building global businesses that sustain a leading position in specialised markets in areas of long-term sales growth.
- Concentrating on high margin activities where products and services are differentiated on the basis of performance, not price, and where barriers to entry are high.
- Tightly managing its asset base in order to maintain its outstanding operating ratios and powerful cash generation.
- Investing in marketing, new product development and innovation to maintain high organic growth.
- Acquiring businesses and intellectual assets that extend its existing activities, add value, contribute to growth and produce its exceptional operating ratios.
- Maintaining a high return on capital employed to self-fund organic growth, acquisition activity and rising dividends.
- Recruiting and retaining top quality management by preserving an entrepreneurial culture within a framework of rigorous financial planning, reporting and control.

Asked to describe his company's style, Stephen O'Shea says, 'We try to hide as much as we can.' Mr O'Shea [was] chief executive [until his retirement in March 2005 and now replaced by Andrew Williams], of Halma, an engineering company based in Amersham, a town tucked away in Buckinghamshire. It specialises in what he calls 'unrecognisable niches' of the fast-growing health and safety industry.

Its corporate style explains why, even though it is the world's second largest producer of fire detectors, it remains a little-studied success story.

In the past year, Mr O'Shea – who took up the CEO's job in 1995 – has emerged from the shadow of David Barber, the iron-willed chairman of Halma who dominated from 1972 until his retirement last year. Mr Barber was famously reluctant to spell out Halma's management approach to outsiders, which is one reason why the company remains so poorly known.

By contrast, Mr O'Shea is far happier to talk about the way his company does business. He does not share his former chairman's worry that other companies might copy Halma's approach and become competitors. 'I'd like to see more companies, particularly in the UK, try to emulate what we've done,' he says.

As Mr O'Shea spells it out, Halma's strategy boils down to producing a continual series of new technical ideas which can be turned into novel products. These include safety interlocks for industrial equipment, sensors to stop lift doors closing on people, high-power resistors used in electrical plants and, of course, fire detectors.

At the same time, it aims to maintain close contacts with a disparate group of customers – 10,000 of them around the world.

Halma relies on suppliers to do most of the work in making components, with its manu-facturing role predominantly concerned with final assembly. As a result, its resources are mainly focused on intellectual, rather than physical, assets.

That is how Halma's pre-tax return on net tangible assets – the capital employed – has, since the mid-1990s, been more than 40 per cent. This is a high figure for the engineering industry, which generally has a poor record for converting money invested in machinery into profits.

Last year, Halma turned in pre-tax profits of £36.7m on sales of £293m, of which 74 per cent came from outside the UK. Even though the pre-tax earnings (which take into account a £13.3m charge from exceptional items and amortisation of goodwill) were down on the previous year's, Halma's 12 per cent pre-tax earnings ratio for 2003/04 is well above the equivalent for most European engineering companies. Excluding exceptionals, pre-tax profits have risen more than 60 per cent since 1995.

Halma's shares hit a rocky patch in the late 1990s, as its earnings growth stumbled somewhat, but they have recovered in recent years, outperforming the London stock exchange as a whole by 150 per cent since 2000.

Mr O'Shea says that Halma is a beneficiary of the trend towards tighter legislation over health and safety. 'As globalisation continues, multinationals are exporting their safety pro-cedures everywhere in the world. Safety legislation isn't fast or dramatic. But it's a creeping tide going only one way.'

In particular, he says, there is a growing interest from countries in guaranteeing clean water by using detection and purification techniques. To meet this demand, Halma has been devising gadgets that use ultraviolet light to rid water of unwanted bacteria. 'Clean water is not part of a 10- or 20-year market,' he notes. 'It's much more fundamental – it's about the survival of the species.' Halma has nine broad product divisions, each covering a specific area such as gas detection or process safety, divided into nearly 50 smaller businesses.

A typical Halma business sells complex products, costing from £15 to £1,000, to an industrial customer in a niche market that is worth a few tens of millions of pounds annu-ally. In products representing 30 per cent of Halma's sales, Mr O'Shea says the company is the biggest in the world. In most of the other areas, it is one of just a few competitors.

To preserve its competitive edge, Halma endeavours to achieve a long-lasting quality in its products. 'In some of our products, such as the sensors that go inside fire detectors, we ensure that each one lasts 1,000 years before it fails,' claims Mr O'Shea. Such an exacting performance costs money, which is why Halma focuses on product development and final assembly, rather than component manufacture.

Illustrating Halma's way of doing business, Mr O'Shea points to the example of Palmer Environmental, a subsidiary that detects leaks in underground water pipes. 'We build this from four basic components that are mainly made for us by outsiders: a special microphone, pattern recognition [signal processing] software, a high-security radio and a water-proof casing. The people in our plants are mainly assembling items and using computers, rather than turning out products on lathes.'

Halma relies heavily on its suppliers, but Mr O'Shea says he keeps them in the dark about what the parts they supply actually do – a policy that fits in with the company's generally secretive style.

'Our suppliers generally do not know how their parts are put together. It's not in our interest to share this information. And we don't apply for many patents.

'If you do this, you have to disclose your ideas, and we'd rather not tell customers or competitors about how they might be able to use our ideas to make things for themselves.'

Even if Halma does not want to give too much detail about product engineering to its customers, it treasures its bond with them.

'Most companies do not want to kill or injure people they employ, or who use their products. That's a good reason for them to keep buying from us. We could cut 30 per cent of our worldwide employees of 3,000 [1,800 of which are in the UK] if we got rid of all the people who deal with customers. But that would do our business a lot of harm in the long run.'

As to where Halma goes from here, Mr O'Shea recognises the stock market perception that the company will have to do well to replicate its 30-year pattern of growth. But he thinks a decent level of expansion should be within Halma's capabilities. Two-thirds of Halma's potential sales and profits growth in the next few years could come from existing broad product areas, and the rest from fields that Halma has yet to discover. 'I don't know what these will be. But I am fairly confident they will be part of markets with long-term growth potential, be linked to increasingly rigorous legislation and involve a large amount of intellectual property where there is a high technological barrier to entry,' says Mr O'Shea.

He cites two promising areas. One is based on a tiny spectrometer for measuring small amounts of chemicals. This could be used in water purification or process control. The other is built around specialist pumps for transferring fluids, with applications in high-tech equipment for analysing blood samples, for instance.

It is difficult to predict precisely where these developments are going – but that, says Mr O'Shea, is a key to the company's growth.

'I get irritated when people describe a market as a neat pie chart with lines drawn on it to denote who is supplying what part of it, or what the applications are. Markets aren't like that. They are messy, multi-layered and incoherent. And they will probably change tomorrow. If you recognise this, then you have a chance to do well.'

Strategy to track financial progress

Under Halma's strategy, each operating division keeps track of eight items of financial information – communicated regularly to the head office in Amersham, outside London – that provide a way to monitor the financial progress of the group.

The eight items cover elements of the profit and loss account such as the cost of goods, and selling and administrative expenses, plus various ratios measuring return on different aspects of physical and financial capital. Stephen O'Shea, Halma's chief executive, says looking at this data is enough for senior managers to work out whether Halma is turning ideas into profits in an efficient manner. He says this approach is shared through the group. 'We have gone to some effort to ensure people a long way down the business have a deep-seated and logic-based understanding of how the company works. If I fell down dead tomorrow there would be a number of others in the company who could easily take over and run the company in the same way as me,' he says.

'A very secretive success story', Peter Marsh, Financial Times, 17 August 2004

After reading the article on Halma, answer these questions (you might need to obtain additional information from the website www.halma.com).

Questions:

1. Long-lasting quality of its products, contacts with its customers, focus on intellectual rather than physical assets, and tighter international legislation over health and safety are key issues in determining Halma's success. How have these elements driven value generation for Halma's shareholders?

2. Referring to those elements, are there any performance indicators which tell us whether value is being created?

3. 'Under Halma's strategy, each operating division keeps track of eight items of financial information . . .' Of these eight items, three relate to the income statement and one to the balance sheet and the remaining three are ratios. Which eight items might they be, in your view?

4. Whilst the importance of non-financial drivers is well understood, they are often hard to measure. How should we measure the 'softer' dimensions of Halma's performance?

5. How can you relate non-financial indicators and measures to financial ones to explain the success of Halma?

6. Do you think that the market recognises and rewards the softer dimension of Halma? How?

Part Five Current developments in corporate governance

17 Corporate reporting and corporate governance

Part of the text of Chapter 17 is an extract from *'Rebuilding Public Confidence in Financial Reporting: An International Perspective'* of the Task Force on Rebuilding Public Confidence in Financial Reporting, published by the International Federation of Accountants (IFAC) in July 2003 and is used with permission.

Objectives

When you have completed this chapter you should be able to:

- understand what corporate governance is and how it is linked to corporate reporting
- identify and analyse the causes of the loss of credibility in corporate reporting
- understand the role played in this process by all the participants in the financial reporting supply chain.

17.1 Introduction

Companies have changed the way people eat, work and play. As Joseph Schumpeter, the Austrian economist, observed 'it was not enough to produce satisfactory soap. It was also necessary to induce people to wash'. It is a company – McDonald's – that is credited with teaching the Chinese how to queue (James Watson, ed., *Golden Arches East: McDonald's in East Asia*, Stanford University Press, 1998). Moreover, companies were erecting the first towering offices in Manhattan and despoiling the Belgian Congo. They were battling with labour unions and challenging politicians.

Over the years, companies have proved enormously powerful, because they are able to create enormous wealth. As a result of their legal status, they are 'artificial persons' with the same ability to do business as real persons; they can issue tradable shares to any number of investors practically in any part of the world, and those investors can have limited liability and can lose only the money they have invested in the firm.

Because companies can be so powerful, they need to be well directed and controlled for the smooth functioning of the market economy:

Corporate governance is one key element in improving economic efficiency and growth as well as enhancing investor confidence. Corporate governance involves a set of relationships between a company's management, its board, its shareholders and other stakeholders. Corporate governance also provides the structure through which the objectives of the company are set, and the means of attaining those objectives and monitoring performance are determined. Good corporate governance should provide proper incentives for the board and management to pursue objectives that are in the interests of the company and its shareholders and should facilitate effective monitoring. The presence of an effective corporate governance system, within an individual company and across an economy as a whole, helps to provide a degree of confidence that is necessary for the proper functioning of a market economy. As a result, the cost of capital is lower, and firms are encouraged to use resources more efficiently, thereby underpinning growth.

Corporate governance is only part of the larger economic context in which firms operate that includes, for example, macroeconomic policies and the degree of competition in product and factor markets. The corporate governance framework also depends on the legal, regulatory, and institutional environment. (OECD Principles of Corporate Governance, 2004)

It is this framework that should ensure that timely and accurate disclosure is made on all material matters regarding the company, including the financial situation, performance, ownership and governance of the company. In addition, factors such as business ethics and corporate awareness of the environmental and societal interests of the communities in which a company operates can also have an impact on its reputation and its long-term success.

Awareness of corporate governance and its role in the global economy has grown steadily in recent years. In developed economies, where active markets for corporate control and dispersed ownership structures make it more difficult for shareholders to monitor management, governance concerns are increasingly articulated by shareholder activists, and companies' governance practices are regularly scrutinised in the public domain. The recent corporate failures of prominent companies in the US and Europe have resulted in greater attention being paid to corporate governance as a standalone risk factor in developed markets. In the emerging markets, the financial crises in Russia and east Asia in the late 1990s also revealed great gaps in corporate governance practices.

Stock exchanges and regulators around the world are increasingly looking to set standards or codes of best practice for corporate governance. Moreover, investors have started to review more systematically a company's corporate governance practices as part of the investment decision-making process. Increasingly, the debate on corporate governance extends beyond a company's own shareholders to include other stakeholders such as creditors, employees, customers, environmentalists and the local community.

As we will see in this chapter, poor corporate governance practices and business failure are closely linked to poor financial reporting and corporate disclosure. This, in turn, affects investors' confidence in financial information, resulting in a higher cost of capital. To understand more fully the reasons for the loss of credibility and to identify possible remedies, we will look at the role played by various participants involved in the financial reporting process. We will reach the conclusion that the foundation of any structure of corporate governance is disclosure of reliable financial information. Transparency is the basis of public confidence in the corporate system and funds will flow to centres of economic activity that inspire trust.

17.2 The loss of credibility in financial reporting

Failures of businesses in which deficiencies in financial reporting and corporate disclosure have figured prominently are not new. However, high-profile cases of the recent past, such as Enron, WorldCom, Global Crossing, Adelphia Communications, Tyco, Xerox, HealthSouth (all US), Vivendi (French), Royal Ahold (Dutch), Parmalat (Italian), Adecco (Swiss) and Shell (UK-Dutch), together with a host of smaller-scale examples worldwide, have drawn attention to this area throughout the developed market economies. At the same time, there is evidence of an increased frequency in restatement of financial statements (see Figure 17.1). All of this has had a negative and cumulative impact on the way informed opinion views financial reporting.

Also, there is a great concern regarding the proper functioning of the market economy, where shareholders, employees in general and pensioners have lost large sums of money, while those running companies, and seen as responsible for those losses, enriched themselves as their businesses collapsed. The scale of this issue is illustrated in the US by a calculation that executives of 25 companies whose stock price fell by 75 per cent or more between January 1999 and May 2002, many of which had both business and reporting problems, 'walked away' with $23 billion (*Fortune*, 2 September 2002, page 64). Though involving smaller amounts, similar concerns about the level and terms of corporate compensation have arisen in other countries. These concerns have reduced the credibility of all those involved in the process of providing reliable financial and other information, and increased the difficulty of restoring credibility.

This loss of credibility has been widespread across capital markets. Moreover, the increasingly global nature of the markets and businesses has resulted in concerns crossing national boundaries.

A key factor in the scale of the problem was the unprecedented high level of share prices in many markets, as shown in Figure 17.2. Maintaining these price levels was the main objective of top management. Reliable management turned to fraud, or at

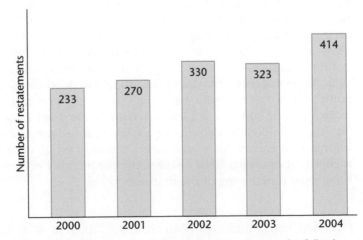

Figure 17.1 Number of restatements of American corporate results following accounting errors

Source: *2004 Annual Review of Financial Reporting Matters*, Huron Consulting Group

Figure 17.2 Share prices from January 1996 through July 2005

Source: Thomson Datastream

least deception, to achieve very large personal gains mainly through most favourable compensation schemes and stock options. To present a perception of high and
stable growth, earnings disclosed in financial statements became unconnected to
net operating cash flows, and were 'managed' by smoothing peaks and troughs by
means of reserve accounts from year to year. And when it became clear that the
supposed level and trend in profitability justifying the levels of share prices did not
exist, the share prices collapsed. This was said to be the result of bad strategy, reck-
lessly and even fraudulently implemented by management. However, that could
not have happened without dysfunctional corporate governance.

In some instances, fraud and deception extended to the auditors, legal counsel,
and the board of directors. Financial statements have historically been one of the
main ways in which information has been provided by a company to its shareholders and investors considering an investment. Reduced confidence in financial
information and corporate disclosures produces an investor retreat, and results in a
higher cost of capital. This weakens the productivity of an economy and threatens
the proper functioning of the market economy.

17.2.1 Relationship between business failure and reporting failure

Almost all the high-profile failures are the result of the combined effect of deficiencies
in management, in governance and in reporting. The financial information that
should be communicated to users of the financial statements is not properly

disclosed and/or is unreliable, governance structures fail to detect or to prevent this, and a reporting failure results. As an entity moves closer to business failure, the incentive to distort reporting increases and, therefore, the chance of reporting failure increases.

The close relationship between business and reporting failure stems from the quality of corporate governance, as highlighted by Jon Symonds in this extract:

> *Recent corporate failures should be blamed on poor corporate governance rather than accounting standards. Strong accounting standards are not a substitute for good corporate governance, but weak standards and differences in generally accepted accounting principles (GAAP) have not helped.*
>
> *But some change is coming. The International Accounting Standards Board is aiming for a single set of what it calls 'high quality, understandable and enforceable global accounting standards'. Its standards are intended to be based on principle – rather than rule – to allow practical application in a range of jurisdictions and business circumstances without supplementary guidance. They are now, or will be, the accepted guidance in more than 90 countries and from next January are scheduled to become the standards by which most of the European Union's 7,000 listed companies must prepare their group accounts.*
>
> *With uniform standards, capital market confidence in financial information will increase, global investment will be facilitated and the cost of capital will fall. There is another important potential benefit. Although the US is not going to adopt international standards, its standard setter, the Financial Accounting Standards Board, is committed to international convergence and has done much work already with the IASB.* From 'Accounts harmony is too big a prize to let go', Jon Symonds, *Financial Times*, 12 February 2004

17.2.2 The pattern of the loss of credibility

There has been a long history of corporate failure linked to governance and reporting failure. The recent high-profile corporate failures may have involved enormous numbers, but many of the issues highlighted are similar to those raised by cases in the past. The cumulative impact of high-profile cases has led to a steady loss in the credibility of financial statements and of the participants charged with producing and reporting on them.

The 1980s and 1990s are littered with examples of reporting failure, generally associated with governance and business failure. In the UK, these include Maxwell, BCCI, Polly Peck and Barings; France has Credit Lyonnais; Germany has Metalgesellschaft and Schneider; Italy provides Banco Ambrosiano and Ferruzzi/ Montedison; Australia provides AWA, Bond, Spedley Securities and Tricontinental; Canada has Canadian Commercial Bank, Castor Holdings and Roman Corporation; Japan has Yamaichi; and the US has many examples from the savings and loan industry as well as cases such as Cendant, Sunbeam, Waste Management, Wedtech and ZZZZ Best.

The east Asian financial crisis in the second half of 1997 raised questions about the reliability of financial statements and about the role of the large international accounting firms reporting on them. A report issued by the United Nations Conference on Trade and Development (UNCTAD) in March 1999 considered the corporate reporting implications of the crisis: 'The failure or near failure of many financial institutions and corporations in the East Asian region resulted from a highly leveraged corporate sector, growing private sector reliance on foreign currency borrowings and lack of transparency and accountability . . . A crucial role was played by disclosure deficiencies . . . And the lack of the appropriate disclosure requirements indirectly contributed to the deficient internal controls and imprudent risk management practices of the corporations and banks.'

However, the concerns raised were seen, and in retrospect, rather narrowly, as matters for certain Asian countries and not for the US, Western Europe, Japan or elsewhere.

As we can see from Figure 17.2, in the period 1999–2000, the stock market prices in many of the developed countries rose rapidly to historically high levels. In certain sectors, such as telecommunications and e-business, the surge was particularly dramatic. The pressures to deliver performance in line with the expectations of the market were correspondingly high and, in many cases, increasingly focused on maintaining share prices in the short term.

The collapse of Enron and the related accounting and audit issues are seen by many as the events that initiated the changed perception of the reliability of financial reporting. However, it might be better to consider Enron as the event that confirmed a trend and, by its sheer size, awoke many to issues that had been prevalent for some time. Enron gave the issues greater visibility. The larger reporting failure at WorldCom and issues raised by Global Crossing, Tyco, Adelphia and Xerox added further examples, reinforcing the perception that financial reporting was not as reliable as it should be.

Recent UK cases include Independent Insurance and Equitable Life. In respect of Ireland's Elan, a pharmaceutical company, questions were raised in relation to accounting, auditor independence and governance issues. The large French multinational Vivendi added false accounting and inadequate disclosure to the use of complex deals between entities in an international group. ABB, the Swiss–Swedish engineering group, raised significant governance and accounting issues in addition to its severe business problems.

Other recent mainland European examples include Comroad, where 97 per cent of revenue came from a non-existent company; Babcock-Borsig, Kirch, Philipp Holzmann and EM.TV in Germany; and Lernout & Hauspie in Belgium.

In February 2003, the Dutch retailer, Royal Ahold, was tagged Europe's Enron given the large amounts involved and the reports of aggressive earnings management, accounting irregularities, ineffective governance, and questions on auditor performance.

At Skandia, Sweden's biggest insurer, executives told shareholders that they got SKr 356 million (EUR 38.73 million) in bonus payments between 2000 and 2002, but in fact pocketed a further SKr 550 million (EUR 59.84 million). Moreover, some executives took corporate flats for themselves and their relatives. The flats were renovated at company expense.

The collapse into bankruptcy of Parmalat, an Italian dairy-products group in December 2003 became Europe's latest Enron. Over EUR 14 billion were missing. All the facts are not yet known: criminal investigations were still in progress in July 2005. This European scandal shares many elements with the US examples, from corrupt management and a complacent board of directors to complicated financial dealings in offshore tax havens via international banks, which seem to have been only too willing to underwrite the deals that kept a massive fraud alive for years. As at Enron, at the heart of the fraud lay an accounting and auditing fiasco.

Just over a year before the dairy group's debacle, Cirio, another Italian food group, had also defaulted. At the beginning of 2004, investors in Finmatica, a software firm, learnt that the chairman, three other members of the board and three statutory auditors had been placed under investigation for, among other things, making misleading statements about its health. Its share price fell sharply and the company went bankrupt in December 2004.

Adecco, in Switzerland, the world's largest temporary-employment agency, at the beginning of 2004 announced a delay in its 2003 results because of 'possible accounting, control and compliance issues . . . in certain countries'.

Royal Dutch/Shell, one of the most admired companies in the world, at the beginning of 2004 for three times in four months restated its 'proved' oil and gas reserves, a key measure of how much oil and gas a company can get to market quickly.

Each of these examples provides evidence of reporting failure. Many of the reports suggest the existence of fraud, and all point to the failure of corporate governance mechanisms. Now, many question the effectiveness of the audit process.

Governments and other bodies around the world have seen a need to take action, conduct reviews and commission reports. Some regulatory bodies have claimed that 'it could not happen here', but history has shown otherwise.

17.3   Financial reporting supply chain and its participants' roles

To understand more fully the reasons for the loss of credibility and to identify possible remedies, it is useful to review the many participants involved in the financial reporting process and the roles that they play.

Although the reporting of financial and other corporate information is an interactive process, involving constant discussion and contact between the participants at many points, we can simplify the process and consider it as a process flow (see Figure 17.3). It starts with corporate management, which, under the general direction of the board of directors, prepares the financial information for the eventual approval by the board and, in most countries, the general meeting of shareholders. The auditors interact with management and the board and provide independent opinions on the 'true and fair view' of the financial statements and the related disclosures. The media and others distribute information, and analysts and credit-rating agencies evaluate it. The process ends with the investors and other stakeholders,

Figure 17.3 Financial reporting supply chain

Source: *Building Public Trust* by Samuel DiPiazza and Robert Eccles, PricewaterhouseCoopers. © 2002 PricewaterhouseCoopers. All rights reserved. For further information see http://www.valuereporting.com/. 'PricewaterhouseCoopers' refers to the network of member firms of PricewaterhouseCoopers International Limited, each of which is a separate and independent legal entity.
In addition, the text in this Section 17.3 includes information which is summarised from the above PricewaterhouseCoopers publication.

who are the users of financial information. Sitting beside this flow are the standard setters, who set the rules; the regulators, who enforce them; and those, such as investment bankers and lawyers, who provide advice to the other participants. The access and use of financial information by investors is facilitated by developments in information technology.

Corporate management

The management of the company, led by the CEO and CFO, has direct responsibility for the preparation of financial statements and for the establishment of the processes and systems of control to ensure that the information necessary for supporting the statements is reliable and available on a timely basis. Management is responsible for ensuring that the statements reflect economic reality and comply with the relevant accounting and reporting standards.

Board of directors

The board has oversight over the actions of management on behalf of the shareholders, appoints the CEO and often appoints or approves the appointment of other senior members of management. In most countries the board also approves the financial statements. This governance role may be performed by the supervisory board in a two-tier structure or, in part, through committees, such as an audit committee, where there is a unitary board. The board is responsible for ensuring that management has performed its role effectively and that the financial statements reflect the performance of the company and are in conformity with accounting and reporting standards.

Independent auditors

The auditor's role is to give an independent opinion on the company's financial statements, assessing whether there is a material misstatement in them or failure to conform to relevant accounting standards. In carrying out this responsibility, the auditor needs to follow appropriate auditing standards with competence, diligence and integrity and to give an independent opinion that is appropriate. Because it is independent and objective, the auditor's opinion should add credibility to the reported information, thereby facilitating its use by shareholders and others.

Information distributors

They are basically data vendors that consolidate reported information and provide it for others to use. This group also includes news media, Web sites, and so on, which provide an important communication channel for financial information, as well as providing analysis and comment on that financial information. Balanced comment can provide shareholders with useful additional material to assist in their decision-making.

Third-party analysts

They use the information reported by companies, usually in combination with other information and research, to evaluate a company's prospects and performance:

- *Credit-rating agencies* – Credit-rating agencies evaluate the business and financial statements of companies so as to provide information to the market and assist banks and bond market lenders in providing financing to companies. Good-quality and timely evaluations that take account of the underlying business circumstances and risks facing a company provide an additional perspective that assists in the making of business decisions.

- *Financial analysts* – Based on their analysis of the financial statements, analysts provide investors and potential investors with evaluations of individual companies. These evaluations normally include comments on the financial performance, strengths and weaknesses of the business, benchmarking with other similar companies, and future prospects or performance. If these evaluations are unbiased, they provide additional information to facilitate decision-making by the investing community.

- *Investment banks* – Investment banks employ many of the financial analysts and are also providers of finance and facilitators of transactions. In performing these roles, the banks provide advice to companies, and information supporting companies in major transactions. Where these functions are performed with probity and with appropriate segregation of activities to avoid conflicts of interest, the banks can be useful facilitators in the market.

- *Internal and external lawyers* – Internal and external lawyers provide extensive advice on the appropriateness and structuring of individual business transactions, including, in some cases, the applicability of accounting standards. Legal advice which takes account of best practice and gives priority to fair financial reporting and disclosure, and does not focus only on what is not illegal, can protect the interests of the company and assist other participants in performing their roles.

Investors and other stakeholders

They are the ultimate consumers of corporate reporting information. Investors include company shareholders but may also refer to those who are contemplating stock purchases. Other stakeholders are the myriad other users of reported information including company employees, business partners, customers and suppliers. They also include tax authorities, community members, social and environmental groups, and other non-governmental organisations (NGOs) that may have a stake in a company's performance.

Standard setters

The standard setters for accounting and reporting and for auditing and professional ethics, establish the standards that companies use for reporting their results and that auditors use for delivering their opinion on those results. In a large number of countries, standard setting is the responsibility of the professional accounting body. In other countries standard setting is handled by government agencies or other independent bodies. In the European Union, the task of standard setting is delegated to the International Accounting Standards Board (IASB). Effective standards make the language of reporting comprehensible and responsive to users' needs, make comparisons possible and restrict the actions of those who wish to mislead or disguise.

Market regulators

Regulators impact the financial reporting process in two main ways: through regulation of the capital markets and the financial statements used in those markets, and through regulation of auditors. Regulation may be directly by government and indirectly through delegation to stock exchanges and professional or other bodies. In some cases, the regulatory role is combined with that of standard setter. The regulator's role is to assess compliance with standards and handle any breaches of them. An effective regulatory regime makes it more difficult to ignore the standards and easier to bring culprits to justice, resulting in increased trust among investors.

Enabling technologies

These refer to Internet technologies and Extensible Business Reporting Language (XBRL), in particular, that enable the widespread distribution and use of reported information both inside and outside of companies. They also refer to hardware and software developed by technology companies for collecting and analysing information.

17.4   Financial reporting supply chain and its weaknesses

All the participants inevitably operate in an environment that places continuous pressure on them. Those pressures, which may be personal, financial or political, will be heightened if they combine or if the checks and balances that the system is supposed to provide fail to operate. A brief analysis of the more significant pressures may help in appreciating how they produce the weaknesses in the system.

17.4.1 Environmental pressures

Preparers of information have profit and performance expectations to meet. They have their jobs to protect. And in many cases, particularly where options have been granted, they have profit to be earned. These pressures primarily impact on management, including executive directors.

Standard setters face 'political' pressures. For example, the pressures from industry explain the inadequacy, until recently[1], of US accounting standards on share options and the ineffectiveness of standards on special purpose entities. The US standard setter had been strongly criticised for the inadequacy of standards in these areas, but the irony is that the criticism had come from some of the same politicians whose lobbying on behalf of preparers prevented the production of effective standards in the first place. Standard setters around the world may also be pressured through inadequate funding. Regulators face similar problems.

Auditors face many pressures. They are required to give their paymaster an opinion that is by definition independent. They also face pressures with respect to the timing of completion of work, fees and retention of the audit assignment. These pressures affect the audit firm as a whole as well as the career of the individual auditor. Individual auditors may also be under pressure to sell or retain both audit and non-audit services if they wish to further their own careers.

Credit-rating agencies, analysts and others who provide information and assessments to the marketplace face conflicts of interest either because those on whom they report pay them or because their organisations are dependent on the sale of other products or services to the firms they report on. Similar pressures affect key advisers such as lawyers and investment bankers.

There is one significant factor that has affected many of the participants: their inability to respond effectively to market expectations. Each of the participants is assigned a role and each has expectations of a level of performance assigned to it by the other participants in the market. This performance level may or may not be achievable in a realistic time frame or at an economic cost. In some cases, it may be possible to move closer to expectations. In others, the expectations may be impossible. As a result, an 'expectation gap' exists. This expectation gap, the gap between what investors and other stakeholders believe the participant does and what is professionally required, is particularly relevant in relation to the role of the independent auditor. The auditor's role in the deterring and detection of fraud is a good example. The marketplace almost certainly has unrealistically high expectations, but for many years auditors have also been able to use this as a justification for performing at a level below that which it should have been possible to achieve without huge additional cost. The audit expectation gap has been recognised for many years, but the profession's attempts to eliminate it by informing stakeholders as to what is realistic to expect, and by raising auditor performance through improved practices and stricter ethical standards, do not appear to have been sufficient to reduce this expectation gap significantly.

The general level of expectation regarding financial statements is also particularly relevant. This issue can be simply put by considering the frequently asked question: are the statements accurate? This question assumes a degree of precision that is unrealistic and fails to reflect the combination of estimating and judgement that underlie all sets of financial statements. However many improvements there are in accounting standards, however much managements improve their accounting systems, however effectively boards of directors oversee management, and however strong auditing standards and practices are, the financial statements will still require exercising judgement on many issues, where honest and competent individuals doing their jobs conscientiously will reach different conclusions. It will never be possible to eliminate such differences, but it should be possible to narrow the range and to provide information which will allow users to understand the more significant estimates and judgements which have been made.

17.4.2 Key weaknesses

Given the number of participants, the relationships between the participants, and the range of pressures they face, it is not surprising that the market has significant structural weaknesses that need to be guarded against. Some have argued, at least pre-Enron, that these weaknesses, most of which have been recognised for many years, were being handled appropriately with the safeguards in place. In assessing the extent to which this view has validity, and how much further change, if any, is needed, we first need to look more closely at those weaknesses.

The incentives provided to management

The incentives provided to management through direct remuneration and stock options, and their relationship to a company's share price, can and have produced unacceptable behaviour. Managers are seen as having to protect their jobs by meeting the market's profitability expectations. Where their incomes are linked to the short-term or a point-in-time share price through bonus arrangements or the ability to exercise stock options, pressures to manage the share price are intensified.

Company internal controls

Focus on growth and share prices has, in some cases, resulted in a neglect of basic internal discipline, including effective internal controls. Internal audit, which should be an important element both in assessing the effectiveness of controls and in improving them, may have been overlooked or neglected. The focus of senior management, especially the CFO, may be more on strategic issues than on the operations and controls relating to the preparation of the financial statements. Many CFOs are now actively involved in strategic planning, information technology and managing investor relations. As a result, some have failed to give basic accounting and reporting requirements and internal controls the attention they deserve. Where the CFO is not central to the reporting process, the roles of the board and the audit committee in relation to financial reporting are made more difficult.

Oversight of management by boards of directors

Some boards have failed to build a healthy governance structure or to see that management sets an appropriate 'tone at the top', and gives adequate attention to reporting matters. A healthy governance culture requires a clear understanding of each party's role and must provide the opportunity to challenge management in a constructive and mature way that leaves both management and directors feeling comfortable. To fulfil their responsibilities, directors need independence, skills, resources, information and adequate time. Audit committees, which in many companies assume the key oversight role in relation to financial reporting, have often devoted inadequate time, and have not always had the skills, resources or independence to handle their responsibilities.

Auditor independence

Auditors' independence is a crucial factor in maintaining public confidence in financial reporting. Given that auditors are paid by the entity on which they report, they cannot be considered independent in the full sense of the term. More frequent criticisms relate to the impact the provision of additional services has on independence, or the closeness of the auditor to management, and to the individual auditor's reliance on the audit relationship with management. Auditors have traditionally had their primary relationship with management, and, in practice, are often appointed by them and have their fees determined by them. Both the firm and the individual auditor are dependent on that relationship for income, for the continuation of that income and, in the case of the individual auditor, for his or her future career. As we have seen, individual auditors can also come under pressure to sell additional services. Pressures to keep fees down may impact on the level of work or individual decisions on the audit. As a result, safeguards are needed.

To enhance auditors' independence, compulsory rotation of either audit firms or audit partner within the same firm has been proposed. In the extract from Thomas Healey's article we have the pros and cons of auditors' rotation:

> *There is heated debate over the merits and shortcomings of mandatory auditor rotation . . . The potential benefits fall into three main areas. First, mandatory rotation creates an effective 'peer review' system that discourages aggressive accounting practices. Second, it prevents the conflicts of interest that can easily arise from long-standing client relationships. Last, it promotes a more competitive market for audit firms, leading to better audits.*
>
> *Rotation's opponents, however, are not impressed. They cite the significant start-up costs – both financial and non-financial – that rotation entails for auditors, clients and the public. They also claim that disrupting the ongoing relationship between client and auditor results in inferior audits. This, they say, is because only a steady, long-term relationship can give an auditor comprehensive knowledge of clients' operations.*   From 'The best safeguard against financial scandal', Thomas Healey, *Financial Times*, 12 March 2004

We are against mandatory auditor rotation. In Italy where we reside and work, there is mandatory auditor rotation. And yet Italy has produced examples of notable corporate and audit failures such as Parmalat, Cirio, Giacomelli and Finmatica. There is no proven evidence that mandatory auditor rotation provides quality audits. Because of the mandatory rotation, auditors are encouraged to 'relax' during the last term of their engagement. Businesses are increasingly becoming more complex so auditors need to be knowledgeable of complex business issues to deliver a quality service to the shareholders and other stakeholders in whose interests they are required to act. The accountancy profession needs to re-emphasise professional rather than commercial standards: professional pride, professional competence, professional duty, professional authority and professional career paths. All this implies that auditors should be adequately remunerated for their professional services and thus their services should not be considered a commodity.

Audit quality

Ineffective consultation processes, weak independent partner reviews and superficial quality review programmes are the most frequently mentioned issues. Relying on other auditors' work may be also an issue. Failure to set an appropriate environment in which quality is the overriding objective is also a concern. A firm's quality control system may be ineffective in picking up errors of judgement by individual auditors or in identifying systemic weakness in controls or procedures. The input of a firm's technical arm may be inadequate, or may be overridden for business reasons. Fraud is difficult to detect, particularly where it involves collusion among senior management or between senior management and third parties. Thus, auditors have long argued that they cannot be expected to detect it in all instances, even instances of material fraud. This is reflected in current auditing standards, but is not in line with market expectations.

> *The big four accounting firms – Deloitte, Ernst & Young, KPMG and PwC – all struggle to manage public expectations that their audit work should be able to root out fraud. And not every business failure is an audit failure. But the big four know they must demonstrate a new commitment to audit quality after getting distracted from their core competence during the 1980s and 1990s by lucrative consulting and tax work.*   From 'We have to prove our own quality', Andrew Parker, *Financial Times*, 21 July 2005

Accounting standards

Besides questions of adequacy of standards in individual countries, there are significant variations among countries, leading to confusion and difficulty in comparing financial statements between them. With investments across national boundaries now commonplace, this increases the difficulty of making informed investment decisions, as well as creating problems for preparers who have to handle more than one set of standards. The difficulties at the national level may arise because individual standards are weak, poorly grounded in principles, fail to consider assets such as intangibles, or have inadequate emphasis on forward-looking information or on risks. Further factors contributing to these weaknesses may include standard setters being subject to political pressures, having inadequate resources, having sources of finance which raise questions about their independence, and being insufficiently timely in responding to market needs. Not many companies in developed capital markets today use IASs/IFRs in presenting their financial statements. National standards show a wide range of variations from international standards. This will be reduced, as all listed companies in the EU are required to use IASs/IFRs from January 2005. However, there are still a number of significant barriers to convergence, including the complex nature of certain significant international standards, the tax-driven nature of current national standards, disagreement on certain standards, such as that on financial instruments, language problems, and so on. All this suggests that actual convergence will be less rapid than is desirable. As a result, the existence of a wide variation in reporting practices among countries is likely to remain a weakness and there will be a resultant impact on the credibility of financial reporting for some time.

Regulation

The effectiveness of regulation varies among countries. Many countries allocate inadequate resources to the task. The regulation of the profession also varies in effectiveness, with perceptions of weakness being high where the degree of independent monitoring of the regulation undertaken by professional bodies is low. Regulators, whether professional bodies performing self-regulatory functions or government agencies, may lack skills or resources; their role may be narrowly defined; the rules they work with may be ineffective; and they may be subject to political pressures to do too little or too much. If self-regulation lacks effective monitoring, it may lack credibility, however worthy the activities undertaken.

Behaviour of investment banks, lawyers and other advisers

Investment banks have sold products which, upon inspection, have often produced misleading financial statements. Loans have been structured to appear as sales, off-balance sheet finance has been structured to conceal the reality of the transaction, and special purpose entities have been set up to avoid disclosure of losses and borrowings. Without considering the need for a true and fair presentation, lawyers and others have given opinions relying on technicalities that have supported accounting approaches that are now seen as unacceptable.

Many of the examples of reporting failure show a serious lack of ethical standards practised by some participants. This list is lengthy: misleading of auditors, auditors looking the other way, disguising transactions, withholding information, providing unbalanced advice, abuse of trust, and misusing insider information. Participants have been seen as following self-interest without concern for the interests of the company, its shareholders and other stakeholders. Where the participants are members of a professional body, they have been seen as ignoring the body's ethical guidance.

Summary

- There has been a long history of corporate failures linked to governance and reporting failure. The cumulative impact of high-profile cases has led to a steady loss in the credibility of financial statements and of the participants involved in producing and reporting on them.

- To understand the reasons for the loss of credibility, it is crucial to look at the role played by the many participants involved in the financial reporting process (i.e. board of directors, management, auditors, standard setters, regulators, and so on).

- Public reporting is by definition a public-interest activity for which a company is required, by law, to publish financial statements that show a 'true and fair view'. Companies have an obligation to provide to shareholders and other stakeholders the information needed to make informed decisions.

References and research

The following are examples of research papers and books that take the issues of this chapter further:

- Richard C. Breeden, *Restoring Trust*, August 2003
- Adrian Cadbury, *Corporate Governance and Chairmanship: A Personal View*, Oxford University Press, 2002
- Samuel A. DiPiazza Jr. and Robert G. Eccles, *Building Public Trust: The Future of Corporate Reporting*, John Wiley & Sons, New York 2002
- International Federation of Accountants (IFAC), *Rebuilding Public Confidence in Financial Reporting: An International Perspective*, July 2003
- John Micklethwait and Adrian Wooldridge, *The Company: A Short History of a Revolutionary Idea*, Weidenfeld & Nicolson, 2003
- John Plender, *Going Off the Rails: Global Capital and the Crisis of Legitimacy*, John Wiley & Sons, 2003
- Hervé Stolowy, 'Nothing like this could happen in France(!)', *European Accounting Review*, Vol. 14 No. 2, 2005
- Alison Thomas, Kurt Ramin and Mike Willis, 'New languages of transformation, *EBF European Business Forum*, Issue 18, Summer 2004, pp. 84–86 (http://www.ebfonline.com/)
- United States General Accounting Office (GAO), *Public Accounting Firms: Required Study on the Potential Effects of Mandatory Audit Firm Rotation*, November 2003

Questions

17.1 'To get reliable access to international financial markets and to regain investors' confidence, big companies in Italy and other European countries shaken by corporate scandals need to adopt better standards of governance. Given the international nature of the problem, it is not surprising that the European Commission is interested in the issue' (*The Economist*, 15 January 2004). Discuss.

17.2 Expectations about corporate governance reform need to be managed. Good corporate governance is not an insurance policy against fraud. Even very vigilant company directors, credit-rating agencies and investors can be misled by forged documents. Regulators can only hope to make it more difficult for fraud to occur. Discuss.

17.3 Corporate reporting should be determined by the needs of investors, but fortunately there is a large overlap between investors' needs and other stakeholders'. Moreover, modern technology will allow multiple stakeholders to access precisely the information they want. Discuss.

17.4 Corporate reporting plays an important role in investors' decisions but there needs to be recognition of the importance of other sources of information such as direct experience of the business or contact with management. Many reformers give reporting a more important and comprehensive role and attribute stock market volatility, bubbles and slumps to the alleged defects in today's reporting. Discuss.

17.5 There is no other effective way of ensuring that reporting is comparable and meets users' needs than regulation. Without regulation there is no comparability, and bad reporting drives out good. Discuss.

17.6 Efforts to strengthen and improve corporate governance around the world are ineffective without the cooperation of those involved in the production of financial information. Discuss.

Case study   Parmalat

When the Parmalat scandal first began to unfold in December (2003), it was easy to jump to the conclusion that the collapse of this huge publicly-quoted group, still 51 per cent-owned by the Parma-based family of its founder Calisto Tanzi, exemplified little more than the dark side of Italian business. But as more and more details of the company's disappearing billions have come to light, it is clear that this is no uniquely Italian affair.

At the heart of the scandal lies a letter, purportedly from the Bank of America – founded a century ago this year (with no little irony) as the Bank of Italy – in which the bank confirmed that Bonlat, a Parmalat subsidiary based in the Cayman Islands, had deposits of close to EUR 4 billion ($5.5 billion) with the bank. Fausto Tonna, Parmalat's former chief financial officer and one of ten people (including his wife) who are currently under arrest over the affair, has told prosecutors that he benefited personally from funds held by subsidiaries in Luxembourg, and he has alleged that the company took kickbacks from the Swedish packaging group Tetra-Pak – an allegation that the Swedish company has denied. The splat from Parmalat is spreading far and wide.

As in the comparable scandal at Enron, the attention of investigators has been sharply focused on the auditors. Until 1999, Grant Thornton, an international network of accounting firms, was Parmalat's main auditor. But Italy's rules on the mandatory rotation of auditing firms at regular intervals forced the group to switch that year to Deloitte & Touche, one of the big four global accounting firms.

Rotation of auditors – one of the more controversial measures introduced in July 2002 by the Sarbanes-Oxley act, America's response to Enron, WorldCom and other corporate scandals – seems to have been of little use here. Grant Thornton continued as the auditor of Bonlat and relied on the Bank of America letter for evidence of the Parmalat subsidiary's assets until, in mid-December 2003, Bank of America said that the document had been forged: the cash simply did not exist. Without the money, Parmalat's empire came crashing down. It is now operating under a new bankruptcy law – protected from immediate liquidation by its creditors – which was rushed through Italy's parliament at the end of last year.

Last week, Grant Thornton expelled its Italian member from the network. 'We do not tolerate behaviour that deviates from our ethical standards,' it said, mindful no doubt of the fate of Arthur Andersen, the auditing firm which was forced to disband after the disclosure of its role in the scandals at its erstwhile client, Enron. But how could Grant Thornton's Italian arm have failed to detect the forgery? Standard practice is for auditors to write independently to banks for confirmation of cash balances. Grant Thornton, it seems, relied on Parmalat's internal mail to deliver its letters seeking confirmation, an astonishing lapse that allowed the fraud to continue. Several of the firm's employees are now under investigation, and on January 8th magistrates called in the first Deloitte partners to explain their firm's role in the affair.

The parallels with America's corporate scandals do not end with the fallibility of auditors. The lack of independence of non-executive directors on the board is another issue in common. Parmalat's was stuffed with family members and local cronies. Despite a 1999 reform that imposed independent directors on listed Italian companies, big ones such as Parmalat were allowed to opt out.

Moreover, Mr Tanzi was both chairman and chief executive of the group, now acknowledged in America and Britain as a potentially dangerous combination. There also seems to have been close complicity between him and the chief financial officer, with Mr Tanzi and Mr Tonna echoing the roles of Jeff Skilling and Andrew Fastow at Enron, of Bernie Ebbers and Scott Sullivan at WorldCom, and of Dennis Kozlowski and Mark Swartz at Tyco. And everywhere there were employees who either knew or suspected what was going on but who, for one reason or another, were dissuaded from blowing the whistle.

The Parmalat case may seem to differ in the simplicity of its fraud. The audited statements from Bonlat were used to show cash balances that were reported by the parent company as offsetting high levels of debt on its balance sheet. Each quarter a set of forged documents would show purported cash holdings at Bonlat that matched the head office's requirements. Deloitte seems to have accepted Grant Thornton's audits unquestioningly, while bankers and investors took the audited group figures as reassurance that, although complex, the group's finances were essentially sound. They failed to ask why a company with so much cash needed to borrow so much.

The deceit continued for several years and might have originated as an effort to cover up losses at the group's Brazilian operation (said to be considerable), or to conceal the Tanzi family's siphoning off of cash, or to retrieve complicated financial derivatives deals that went badly wrong. Whatever the case, and it may have been a combination of several things, matters clearly got wildly out of control.

But the fraud may have been more sophisticated than it might at first appear. 'What is the one line in an audited balance sheet that no one questions?' asks a former auditor with Deloitte & Touche. 'Answer: the cash and other short-term assets line. And that is precisely where this fraud was directed.' Moreover, it was not sufficient for Bonlat and other group entities merely to claim fictitious cash balances. They also had to generate a paper trail of false sales to show where the money was supposedly coming from.

'The lessons of the Parmalat scandal', *The Economist*, 15 January 2004

Questions:

1. What lessons do you draw from the scandal at Europe's largest dairy-products group?

2. What transatlantic similarities in corporate scandals exist other than the fallibility of auditors?

3. Parmalat's CEO was the dominant shareholder. What checks and balances should exist in quoted companies to ensure proper corporate governance?

Note

[1] FAS 123 R – *Share-based payment* issued by FASB in 2004 requires most public companies to recognise in their financial statements, from the fiscal year beginning after 15 June 2005, the compensation cost relating to stock options, stock appreciation rights, employee stock purchase plans and other share-based payments.

18 Public trust in corporate reporting

Objectives

When you have completed this chapter you should be able to:

- describe the key elements that create public trust in capital markets
- comment on how regulators and stakeholders have responded to the crisis in corporate reporting
- illustrate the weakness of the current reporting practices
- consider how transparency in corporate reporting may enhance the value of an enterprise in the long run.

18.1 Introduction

The interaction between national and international developments in corporate governance and corporate reporting is critical. In fact, globalisation may increase the risks of a failure to understand foreign markets and to exert proper control over foreign subsidiaries.

In this chapter, after focusing on the key elements of public trust in capital markets, we consider whether the changes in regulation and standards that are being made are consistent with the overall objective of raising the credibility of financial reporting on a worldwide basis.

Then we illustrate the current reporting model and its weakness in communicating the value of an enterprise.

Finally, we describe a new model of corporate transparency, which allows financial performance to be evaluated more accurately and the company's future sustainability to be assessed more easily.

18.2   The three key elements of public trust

Business failures are not the most important issue in the loss of public trust in the capital markets. Instead, it is how the aftermath of these failures can serve as a lens to sharpen our collective focus on the key elements that create public trust in markets and, therefore, allow those markets to allocate capital efficiently:

- transparency
- accountability
- integrity.

Transparency

Corporations have an obligation to provide willingly to shareholders and other stakeholders the information needed to make decisions. This responsibility ultimately rests with the board of directors, which determines the level of transparency which it considers appropriate.

For a variety of reasons, management and boards do not consistently make available information that they know investors would want. Sometimes the lack of transparency is simply a result of management's failure to understand the information needs of its stakeholders. However, too often, this failure is based on the belief that playing the earnings game – managing and bearing the market's expectations about next period's earnings – will increase shareholder value. Or in other situations we find that business leaders want to hide such issues as compensation policies and conflicts of interest, which they know would not meet public approval if they became visible. Today, shareholders and other stakeholders are demanding a much higher level of transparency, recognising that transparency is necessary to create and protect value.

Accountability

Providing information is not enough. It should be accompanied by a firm commitment to accountability by participants in the corporate reporting supply chain.

Commitment means taking responsibility, and this can only occur when an ethos exists that values and understands accountability. This accountability is collective: every member of the corporate reporting supply chain must commit to collaborating with all the others. However, this chain is only as strong as its weakest link. Management must hold itself accountable for using shareholders' money to make decisions that will create value for those shareholders. Independent boards exist to see that this accountability is recognised and maintained both by managements and the board itself.

Accounting firms are responsible for providing assurance on the information that management produces and reports. In addition, accounting firms should never forget that their work serves the interests of shareholders and other stakeholders, not just the companies that write their cheques.

Analysts are responsible for using the reported information to produce high-quality research that investors need to make informed decisions. Further, analysts are responsible for providing research that is free from any bias due to economic conflict of interest.

Standard setters are responsible for establishing principles and rules for making this information useful and reliable. Regulators are responsible for ensuring that all these groups fulfil their roles, and through careful oversight regulators are responsible for proactively identifying problems. Information distributors are responsible for making sure that information they cite or analyse from corporate reporting sources is delivered without distortion to the public. Hardware and software suppliers need to be constantly monitoring and introducing useful new technologies.

Finally, investors must bear the ultimate responsibility for obtaining, understanding and analysing the information they use as they make personal judgements about risk and return and invest accordingly. Today, investors and other stakeholders are demanding greater accountability from those on whom they depend for information. Yet they must hold themselves ultimately accountable for their decisions and avoid investments where full information is unavailable or their understanding of available information has gaps.

Integrity

Even transparency and accountability are not enough to establish public trust. In the end, both depend on people of integrity. Rules, regulations, laws, concepts, structures, processes, best practices and the most progressive use of technology cannot ensure transparency and accountability. This can only come about when individuals of integrity are trying to 'do the right thing', not what is expedient or even necessarily what is permissible. What matters in the end are the actions of people, not simply their words. Without personal integrity as the foundation for reported information, there can be no public trust.

Source: *Building Public Trust* by Samuel DiPiazza and Robert Eccles, PricewaterhouseCoopers. © 2002 PricewaterhouseCoopers. All rights reserved. For further information see http://www.valuereporting.com/. 'PricewaterhouseCoopers' refers to the network of member firms of PricewaterhouseCoopers International Limited, each of which is a separate and independent legal entity.

18.3   Credibility as an international issue

Globalisation of markets continues to be a major factor both for goods and services and for the provision of finance. Securities offerings are no longer limited to an entity's home country, but are frequently offered in multiple jurisdictions. Securities of many companies are now traded on exchanges in a number of countries.

However, regulation is, and is likely to remain, a national matter and therefore the standards which determine how financial statements are presented are national standards. A company with securities listed in more than one country will continue to be subject both to the rules in its home country and those in the other countries in which it is listed. The presence in the market of sets of information that are different, but each of which purports to be a fair presentation, undermines the credibility of each set. This increases the inefficiency of the market as well as adding unnecessary costs.

The solution to this is not to have every country adopt one country's standards. While prior to Enron, some argued that the solution was for all countries to adopt US accounting principles and associated practices, adopting one country's standards was never likely to be acceptable politically even if it were possible to agree on which country's standards to adopt. The alternative is to agree on a 'neutral' set of standards which can be accepted by every country and either adopted as the country's standards or incorporated into them.

A further matter that makes credibility an international question is the position of the large firms of auditors. These firms are multinational, but organised differently from their large clients, the multinational enterprises. They are networks of independent firms with common processes and basic policies and standards, but without the enterprises' common central ownership. Each independent firm is subject to national laws and professional regulations in the country in which it operates. They share certain central costs. When performing audit work for a multinational enterprise, the reporting office will assign a team and issue instructions so that work can be performed in line with the requirements of the client's home country. As a result, a large firm's name is associated with financial reports presented using a wide variety of national standards; if these reports comply with the relevant national standards, they will receive unqualified reports or 'clean' opinions. This will continue to be the case until one set of accounting standards is widely accepted.

18.4   The seeds of change

To date, the efforts of regulatory bodies to drive reform have focused on two key areas:

- a desire to harmonise global accounting standards
- a need to define more clearly the roles and responsibilities of corporate executives and directors.

Some of the more visible of these initiatives are highlighted on the map in Figure 18.1. While all these initiatives are, to a greater or lesser degree, shaping tomorrow's reporting agenda, some stand out as exemplars of the process of change.

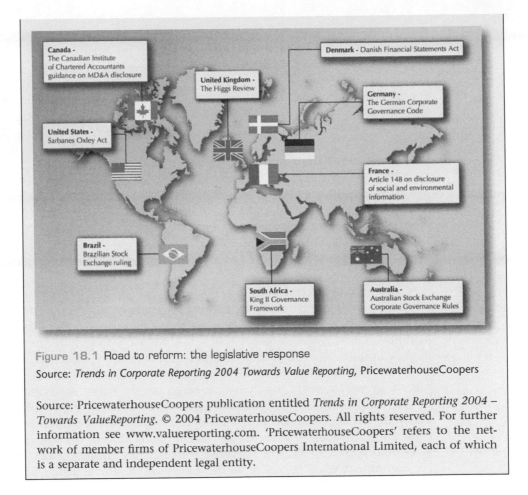

Figure 18.1 Road to reform: the legislative response

Source: *Trends in Corporate Reporting 2004 Towards Value Reporting*, PricewaterhouseCoopers

18.4.1 Global accounting standards and capital markets

Almost every country with a public capital market currently uses its own set of generally accepted accounting principles (GAAP) or one based on other national or international standards. The quality of these standards varies from country to country, with many permitting a range of accounting principles that lead to relatively little consistency and comparability.

As recently as a few years ago, the prospect of converging accounting standards in most of the world's major countries would have been viewed as desirable, but not likely, at least within the short term. With a dramatically changed corporate reporting environment, characterised at least in part by high-profile corporate scandals and a much greater focus on corporate transparency and accountability, the potential and opportunity to deliver on the vision is within our grasp.

Spring 2001 saw the creation of the International Accounting Standards Board (IASB). After great efforts on both sides of the Atlantic, and from the rest of the world, businesses and the accounting professions agreed to fund a full-time board to improve and extend the existing IASs. In addition, the IFRSs are now mandatory across the EU, in Australia, Russia and elsewhere, from Singapore to South Africa. Soon we will see ourselves in the previously unexpected position, where only two bodies – the IASB and the Financial Accounting Standards Board (FASB) in the US – will set the accounting standards for the vast majority of the global capital markets.

Despite this enormous step forward, the standard setters are not resting on their laurels. November 2002 saw the arrival of the Norwalk agreement through which the International and US standards bodies agreed to reduce the differences between the two sets of standards. Global GAAP – where all entities use standards that should be identical in their outcome – is a prospect, transforming our ability to compare and contrast the financial performance of companies around the world.

The process of convergence is no trivial matter. The two standards bodies are rightly filled with opinionated thinkers from very different environments. The magnitude of the challenge to arrive at consistent accounting solutions should not be underestimated: realising that goal will require the willingness and commitment of all parties, including regulators and politicians. To date, the level of interaction between the two standards bodies has been extensive, and both are working hard to achieve convergence over major areas of accounting.

The difficulties of implementing global financial reporting standards do not stop there. Even if the text and meaning of standards can be harmonised, the considerable challenge of ensuring consistent application of the agreed principles regardless of territory still remains. Meeting this challenge will require the commitment of such bodies as the IASB's International Financial Reporting Interpretations Committee (IFRIC) and the FASB's Emerging Issues Task Force (EITF), as well as enforcement agencies, such as the US Securities and Exchange Commission (SEC) and the Committee of European Securities Regulators (CESR).

Source: PricewaterhouseCoopers publication entitled *Trends in Corporate Reporting 2004 – Towards ValueReporting*. © 2004 PricewaterhouseCoopers. All rights reserved. For further information see www.valuereporting.com. 'PricewaterhouseCoopers' refers to the network of member firms of PricewaterhouseCoopers International Limited, each of which is a separate and independent legal entity.

18.4.2 Regulators and governance

As mentioned earlier, in addition to corporate reporting, a second key area of focus for regulators has been improving corporate governance. In contrast to the reforms underway in financial reporting, changes to the governance structures are occurring territory by territory, as shown on the map in Figure 18.1. To offer an insight into the differences among various approaches, we will examine three in greater depth.

First approach

A common approach has been for regulators to define far more precisely the composition and responsibilities of the board of directors. Exemplified by the Higgs Review in the UK, the German Corporate Governance Code and the Australian Stock Exchange's Corporate Governance Rules, regulators in these markets have focused on the transparency of the governance process, the roles of company executives and independent directors, and their relationship with shareholders. Although whether or not to apply such recommendations within a particular company is typically left to the discretion of management, a decision to ignore any element must be explained to the market.

Second approach

US regulators have adopted a less forgiving – and far more wide-ranging – approach to the governance question. Enacted on 30 July 2002, the Sarbanes-Oxley Act:

- places increased accountability on companies' executives as well as others involved in the corporate reporting process
- defines a higher level of responsibility, accountability, and financial reporting transparency to restore the credibility of corporate accounting and reporting.

Moreover, the Act underscores the government's commitment to compliance with the full weight of the law.

Source: PricewaterhouseCoopers publication entitled *Trends in Corporate Reporting 2004 – Towards ValueReporting.* © 2004 PricewaterhouseCoopers. All rights reserved. For further information see www.valuereporting.com. 'PricewaterhouseCoopers' refers to the network of member firms of PricewaterhouseCoopers International Limited, each of which is a separate and independent legal entity.

Designed to repair damaged investor confidence following an outbreak of corporate boardroom scandals, Sarbanes-Oxley set important new baselines for financial reporting and disclosure by companies. It also imposed tight new regulations on auditors and virtually single-handedly changed the face of corporate governance. Critics (. . .) charge that it swung the pendulum too far, imposing enormous compliance costs on companies (and indirectly on their shareholders) that outweigh the potential benefits of reduced fraud. So what has Sarbanes-Oxley really accomplished? (. . .) A study of 2,500 international companies by GovernanceMetrics International found that the reforms have led to a 10 per cent improvement in the corporate governance performance of large US companies compared with their foreign counterparts. The reaction of the equity markets underscores the progress we have made in improving corporate governance. The US stock market has rebounded 40 per cent since the act was signed by President George W. Bush on July 30, 2002, compared with the nearly 20 per cent it tumbled during the first seven months of that year in the wake of the Enron and WorldCom scandals. Today, the markets are once again performing efficiently and there are more initial public offerings. (. . .) Additionally, the finance and audit committees of corporate boards are taking their roles much more seriously and imposing greater accountability on their members. Gone are the days when Enron's directors could approve a stock split, place shares in a compensation plan, purchase a corporate jet, launch an investment in a Middle East power plant and grant Andrew Fastow, chief financial officer, exemption from the energy trader's code of conduct – all in a single, one-hour teleconference. (. . .) The legislation might not have been perfect but it accomplished its paramount goal: to boost investor confidence and bring the markets back to life.   From 'Sarbanes-Oxley has let fresh air into boardrooms', Thomas Healey and Robert Steel, *Financial Times*, 29 July 2005

Third approach

Probably the most visionary governance framework, however, is King II in South Africa. Emerging from a period of isolation, the new South African regime recognised the need to rebuild public trust in its corporate sector both within the country and globally. The far-reaching document that resulted from these efforts discusses the relationship between the company and all its key stakeholders. As one might expect, transparency, accountability and responsibility are three of the seven primary pillars of good corporate governance identified. Investors, it is argued, deserve a forward-looking approach to reporting, and while acknowledging that financial reporting provides a valuable record of where a company has been, non-financial information provides an indication of where a company is going and how it will get there. All corporate communication should therefore offer a comprehensive and objective assessment of the activities of the company that gives shareholders and relevant stakeholders a full, fair and honest account of performance. This can only be achieved if disclosures embody six key characteristics: relevance, reliability, clarity, comparability, timeliness and verifiability.

Regardless of where change is happening, no evidence is available yet to determine clearly which approach, if any, is the most appropriate to restore investor confidence and to improve corporate transparency and accountability. What is clear however, is that there is a greater and greater scrutiny of corporate management.

Source: PricewaterhouseCoopers publication entitled *Trends in Corporate Reporting 2004 – Towards ValueReporting*. © 2004 PricewaterhouseCoopers. All rights reserved. For further information see www.valuereporting.com. 'PricewaterhouseCoopers' refers to the network of member firms of PricewaterhouseCoopers International Limited, each of which is a separate and independent legal entity.

18.4.3 Stakeholders' initiatives

Regulators are not alone in responding to the perceived crisis in corporate reporting. A number of key stakeholders and companies themselves have recognised that they too have a responsibility to work towards meaningful, positive change.

Non-governmental organisations (NGOs)

For a number of decades, non-governmental organisations (NGOs) have been vocal in challenging the role of business in society. Among the earliest was the Brundtland Commission. In 1987, it developed a report titled 'Our Common Future', which introduced the now ubiquitous phrase 'sustainable development'. This report emphasised that issues of balance and equity are essential to long-term development. This fundamental tenet was developed by SustainAbility, a British consulting firm, into what is now known as the 'triple bottom line'.

Triple bottom line refers to the expansion of the traditional financial bottom line to three areas:

- economic prosperity
- environmental quality
- social justice.

These concepts should permeate all levels of corporate governance and strategy in order to achieve long-term success.

This framework has made a significant impact on the reporting world. Nonetheless, the triple bottom line model is insufficiently prescriptive to allow stakeholders to compare performance over time and among industry peers. Overcoming this limitation was one of the original motivations for forming the Global Reporting Initiative (GRI). Originally convened by the Coalition for Environmentally Responsible Initiative (CERES) and the United Nations Environment Programme (UNEP), the GRI is an ambitious effort to develop a set of non-financial reporting standards. A long-term, multi-stakeholder initiative, it aims to develop and disseminate globally applicable 'sustainability reporting guidelines'. Companies would then use the guidelines to communicate voluntarily their management of the triple bottom line (an example of such companies is given by Shell).

Investors

Given the recent uncertainty about and lack of confidence in corporations and the markets as a whole, investors have increasingly accepted their responsibility to take an active interest in the ongoing debate, to question the sustainability of performance, to insist on good corporate governance. Evidence of this new mindset is clearly emerging. At the market level we have seen the introduction of new indices and rankings that rate companies according to a broader set of indicators. High-profile examples include the Dow Jones Sustainability Index, FTSE4Good[1], and the Standard & Poor's Transparency and Disclosure Study, to name but a few.

This shift in mindset is even more pervasive than these headline indices might first suggest. There are prominent examples of fund management organisations that are redefining the terms of engagement for the assets that they own. Notable among them is the International Corporate Governance Network (ICGN) – a global network that includes CalPERS in the US, the world's largest pension fund, Hermes in the UK, and ABP, Europe's largest pension fund. The draft code this network has produced aims to 'energise' investors, 'turn up the heat' on company executives, and strengthen the faith of investors in the ability of pension fund trustees to manage their savings effectively. In a series of proposals, the ICGN urges pension funds to be more activist and interventionist, urging board members to ensure that fund managers 'act fully independently from corporate management or other conflicting relationships'.

▶

Similarly, in 2002 Hermes published 10 'Hermes Principles' (see http://www.hermes.co.uk/pdf/corporate_governance/Hermes_Principles.pdf) that underscore its commitment to corporate governance and shareholder activism:

> *As a pension fund manager, Hermes needs to have the confidence that the companies in which we invest our clients' money create value for the long-term. To instil that confidence, companies need to be more open in discussing their strategic positioning, the ways they maximise long-term financial returns, and how they manage the risks that they face. It was this thinking which led us to publish the Hermes Principles, which outline the information we believe all long-term investors need to understand the companies they own. Where companies do not meet the expectations we have set out in the principles, we will work with the board and senior management to encourage change.*   (Tony Watson, Hermes CEO)

How pervasive is this desire for greater transparency and better communication of corporate – not just financial – information? In the last part of this section we highlight a few examples of the many companies around the world that have proactively moved beyond the regulatory model of reporting. Whether through intellectual capital statements, a breakdown of risk-based return, or an analysis of the impact of environmental protocols on value creation, their effort towards broader reporting demonstrates a growing recognition in recent years of the competitive advantage that can accrue from a commitment to greater corporate transparency.

Companies

Although today there is no single company providing a truly comprehensive picture of its corporate performance, a number of encouraging trends are worthy of note:

- First, companies are showing an increased understanding of the need to report in an integrated fashion – to think not in informational silos but in a 'joined up' fashion: to offer the reader a vision of the 'front of the jigsaw box' rather than merely a jumbled collection of jigsaw pieces. In the EU, Novo Nordisk communications offers an example of this trend (see, for example, its economic stakeholder model we reproduced in Chapter 1, Figure 1.2).

- The second notable trend has been the announcement by a number of global major corporations of their decision to break the vicious circle of the earnings game. The focus on short-term earnings that quarterly reporting imposes on management – so evident in the US – levies a significant economic cost. It is this cost that companies such as Coca-Cola, PepsiCo, Gillette, AT&T, McDonalds, Porsche and *The Washington Post* hope to mitigate through a commitment to communicating their long-term strategy rather than short-term financial objectives.

    Coca-Cola, for example, announced in late 2002 that it will no longer publish quarterly earnings guidance. Instead the company said it would continue to provide investors with 'perspectives on its value drivers, its strategic initiative, and those factors critical to understanding its business and operating environment'. Douglas N. Daft, CEO of Coca-Cola, explained, 'Establishing short-term guidance prevents a more meaningful focus on the strategic initiatives that a company is taking to build its business and succeed over the long run. Our share owners are best served by this because we should not run our business based on short-term expectations. We are managing this business for the long-term.'

Source: PricewaterhouseCoopers publication entitled *Trends in Corporate Reporting 2004 – Towards ValueReporting*. © 2004 PricewaterhouseCoopers. All rights reserved. For further information see www.valuereporting.com. 'PricewaterhouseCoopers' refers to the network of member firms of PricewaterhouseCoopers International Limited, each of which is a separate and independent legal entity.

This section has touched on only a handful of the myriad initiatives underway to improve corporate reporting. All have stimulated a healthy debate about the roles and responsibilities of the different links in the Corporate Reporting Supply Chain. When pieced together, however, do they establish a new reporting framework that meets the primary objective of allowing the user to evaluate corporate performance in a coherent and cost effective fashion? This is not something that any single company, institution or government can do in isolation. All must work as one: the social and economic penalties of disunity or inaction are too great for any of us to ignore.

Source: PricewaterhouseCoopers publication entitled *Trends 2005 – Good Practices in Corporate Reporting*. © 2005 PricewaterhouseCoopers. All rights reserved. For further information see www.valuereporting.com. 'PricewaterhouseCoopers' refers to the network of member firms of PricewaterhouseCoopers International Limited, each of which is a separate and independent legal entity.

18.5   The traditional reporting model

Would you buy a ticket for a train if you did not know where it was going? Would you board it if you did not know whether the engines and the crew could get you to your destination safely? Of course not. Yet some of the most important decisions affecting our lives and livelihoods are made with just such a lack of critical information.

Employees, for example, join companies based on 'trust' (and little else) that the company will make good on its promise to treat its people as the 'number one asset'. Customers buy a product in the hope and belief that the company has not exploited workers in its manufacture. Fund managers make decisions about which company to invest in without gaining essential information about the business from management. And because so many make such critical decisions based on so little information, the inefficient – and even the dishonest – can prosper, while the long-term engines of economic growth go unrewarded.

Why does this situation persist? The answer can be traced to the way in which companies are required to communicate their performance.

In this section we will illustrate the current reporting model and its failure to communicate, among other things, the value of intangible assets. In section 18.6 we will describe the three-tier model of corporate transparency, which in our opinion offers a new vision of corporate reporting.

The current financial reporting model, by its very nature, focuses largely on a backward assessment of short-term financial performance. Consequently, it does not provide all information necessary to evaluate the quality or sustainability of corporate performance, to differentiate good management from bad, or to know whether success results from luck or from skill.

The current model's dependence on a generic set of financial indicators encourages companies to play the 'earnings game,' leaves stakeholders suspicious of managerial intent, and some would say, forces investors to 'fly blind'. The potential outcome from continuing this model is a wholesale misallocation of scarce resources. Within an individual business, for example, managers may forsake investments that might negatively affect their short-term earnings numbers. Within industries and the market as a whole, investors are unable to analyse accurately the risks and returns associated with any given investment decision.

Observations like these are far from new. For many years, academic literature, government findings, and respectable news and business media have conscientiously and ceaselessly catalogued shortcomings of the current financial reporting model and the economic consequences that could ensue. What has changed now, however, is the growing recognition among companies that they are responsible to a wider group of stakeholders, and not just shareholders.

After the recent scandals, corporate failures and dramatic market declines, the world has become painfully aware of the profound impact that inadequate attention to corporate governance – notably to transparency, accountability and integrity – can have on public trust. For too long the issues have been debated out of the direct public eye. Now they are front-page headlines, and all stakeholders have become uncompromisingly insistent on change.

Source: PricewaterhouseCoopers publication entitled *Trends in Corporate Reporting 2004 – Towards ValueReporting*. © 2004 PricewaterhouseCoopers. All rights reserved. For further information see www.valuereporting.com. 'PricewaterhouseCoopers' refers to the network of member firms of PricewaterhouseCoopers International Limited, each of which is a separate and independent legal entity.

18.5.1 Development of the corporate reporting model

So what has gone wrong with the corporate reporting model? A brief detour into the history of its development offers some insight.

The origins of the reporting model used today may be traced to the era when mass manufacturers dominated the industrial base. The need to attract funding into these capital-intensive industries prompted a search for a practical tool that would allow factory managers to assure investors that their money was being wisely deployed.

The success of the regulated reporting model in fulfilling this role is widely accepted and, to this day, its structure remains particularly pertinent for evaluating the quality and sustainability of the performance of such businesses. It is equally well understood that this model is less relevant when applied to enterprises for which success is a function of intangibles such as brand, employees and the organisational capabilities of the firm to innovate. Such firms dominate the industrial landscape today, further lessening the traditional reporting model's relevance.

So why have regulators been slow to respond to these new challenges? It is probably less a lack of willingness, but more a reflection of the complexity of the task at hand and the need for collective action among all the various individuals and organisations that directly affect the corporate reporting supply chain, discussed in Chapter 17.

Source: PricewaterhouseCoopers publication entitled *Trends in Corporate Reporting 2004 – Towards ValueReporting*. © 2004 PricewaterhouseCoopers. All rights reserved. For further information see www.valuereporting.com. 'PricewaterhouseCoopers' refers to the network of member firms of PricewaterhouseCoopers International Limited, each of which is a separate and independent legal entity.

18.5.2 Intangibles and corporate reporting

When a traditional commodity manufacturer wants to signal its long-term strength, it needs to demonstrate that it generates an adequate return on its investment in fixed assets and that it is a low-cost manufacturer. When a technology company wants to signal its future prospects, however, it faces the challenge of communicating the strength and value of its intellectual capital. In contrast to physical assets, intellectual capital derives much of its value from the fact that it can be deployed simultaneously in multiple tasks and that it can have increasing returns to scale, as knowledge is cumulative.

Even though they have very different attributes from traditional fixed assets, intangibles could still be evaluated if there were an organised exchange where they were traded. This is not typically the case. Even if a pricing mechanism existed, the issue of intellectual property rights would remain. Except in the case where intellectual property is protected by a watertight patent, the ownership of such assets is often in question, making them inherently more risky than fixed assets.

Figure 18.2 illustrates the scale of this issue. It highlights the mismatch between assets that are readily measurable and those that underpin competitive advantage.

To date, accounting standards have focused on evaluating the tangible goods to the left of the flow chart. The FASB in the US and the IASB in Europe have begun to move into the second column, intangible goods. The sources of competitive advantage in today's economy, however, lie firmly to the right in the diagram. The very nature of these assets means that their value is highly unlikely to be communicated through the current financial reporting framework.

Tangible assets where ownership is clear and enforceable	Rights that can be bought, sold, stocked and readily traded in disembodied form and (generally) protected	Non-price factors of competitive advantage	Potentially unique competition factors that are within the firm's capability to bring about
'Hard' Commodities (disembodied) ←——————————————————————————————→			'Soft' – difficult to isolate and value (embodied)
TANGIBLE ASSETS	INTANGIBLE GOODS	INTANGIBLE COMPETENCES	LATENT CAPABILITIES
PHYSICAL ASSETS	MATERIAL SUPPLY CONTRACTS	COMPETENCY MAP	CAPABILITIES
PPE		Distinctive competences	Leadership
Inventory	Licences, quotas & franchises	Core competences	Workforce calibre
Other	REGISTRABLE IPR (intellectual property rights)	Routine competences	Organizational (including networks)
FINANCIAL ASSETS			
Cash & cash equivalents	Copyright or patent protected originals – film, music, artistic, scientific, etc. including market software		Market/reputational
Securities			Innovation/R&D in-process
Investments			Corporate renewal
	Trademarks		
	Designs		
	OTHER IPR		
	Brands, know-how & trade secrets		

Figure 18.2 The resources of 21st century enterprises

Source: PRISM Report 2003, Report series 2, October 2003.
www.euintangibles.net/research_results/finalreport.pdf. © PRISM, 2003

Yet these are the resources and competencies that need to be understood for resources to be allocated efficiently.

Having recognised the need to improve our ability to 'measure the measurable', we must focus attention and effort on alternative methods for communicating the performance of companies across the full spectrum of assets that underpin value and growth today, with a view to drawing some strong conclusions about the structure and content of the information required to piece together a complete picture of a company's performance – to measure both the hard goods to the left in the diagram and to evaluate the sources of competitive advantage to the right.

18.6   ## The three-tier model of corporate transparency

Among several proposals for new reporting models, which have been summarised in the report 'Information for Better Markets: New Reporting Models for Business' (Institute of Chartered Accountants in England and Wales, November 2003 www.icaw.co.uk/bettermarkets), we will illustrate the three-tier model of corporate reporting (see Figure 18.3). This model builds on the current model but takes into account the needs for broader and more dynamic reporting.

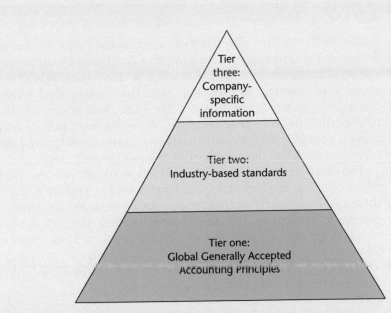

Figure 18.3 The three-tier model of corporate transparency

Source: *Building Public Trust* by Samuel DiPiazza and Robert Eccles, PricewaterhouseCoopers. © 2002 PricewaterhouseCoopers. All rights reserved. For further information see http://www.valuereporting.com/. 'PricewaterhouseCoopers' refers to the network of member firms of PricewaterhouseCoopers International Limited, each of which is a separate and independent legal entity.

The three-tier model of corporate transparency offers a new vision of corporate reporting:

- Tier one: a set of global generally accepted accounting principles (global GAAP)
- Tier two: industry-specific standards for measuring and reporting performance, consistently applied and developed by the industries themselves
- Tier three: company-specific information including strategy, plans, risk management practices, compensation policies, corporate governance and performance measures unique to the company.

These three tiers should not be viewed as separate, discrete reporting levels. Rather, they should serve as an integral model for improving corporate transparency overall.

Tier one: global generally accepted accounting principles

Today, every country with a public capital market uses its own set of generally accepted accounting principles (GAAP) or one based on other national or international standards (IFRSs). The quality of these standards varies widely from country to country, as does how well they are applied by companies and checked by independent auditors. Even the 'best country GAAP' have come under criticism, since they are all based for the most part on an historical cost model. Today's complex business environment challenges the relevance of historical cost information and is putting strain on this model.

The creation of a set of global standards would allow companies to access the world's capital markets more easily and with less cost. If global GAAP existed, investors could more easily and accurately compare the performance of any company, in any country, thus broadening their range of investment choices. In adopting new global standards, market regulators worldwide could agree to allow any company using global GAAP to list on the exchanges within their jurisdictions. Global GAAP would also require addressing interpretation of, and compliance with, standards on a global basis.

Tier two: industry-specific standards

Investors need the ability to compare companies in any given industry in ways that go beyond required financial reporting. In order to meet these information needs, companies should supplement GAAP with other financial and non-financial information regarding past performance and future prospects. Examples of supplemental financial information include pro forma earnings and free cash flow, neither of which is covered by any form of GAAP. Examples of non-financial information include performance measures relating to intangibles such as brands, customers and innovation (see Table 18.1).

Companies also need to compare their own performance with that of industry peers. Therefore, it is in their own best interest voluntarily and collaboratively to develop industry-wide tier two standards based on the critical value drivers unique to their industries. These standards would define what industry-specific information should be reported as a supplement to GAAP.

Table 18.1 shows the 'measures that matter' across four very different industries. It offers an insight not only into the differences among key measures across the industries, but also the emphasis that is placed on contextual or non-financial measures. It is important to note that we are referring here only to the industry-specific measures and not the financial measures such as EBITDA, EBIT, WACC, EPS, etc., that would apply universally across most industries.

Table 18.1 Industry-specific performance measures

Advertising	Banking	Petroleum	Retail
Market growth	Market growth	Supply, demand, and prices for petrolium products by region	Market growth
Market share	Customer retention	CAPEX	Market share
Key accounts	Customer penetration	Exploration success rate	CAPEX
New business (billings)	Asset quality	Refinery utilisation	Store portfolio changes
Customer demographics	Capital adequacy	Refinery capacity	Expected return on new stores
Performance by business segment	Assets under management	Volume of proven and probable reserves	Customer satisfaction
	Loan loss	Reserve replacement costs	Some store/like store for like sales

Tier three: company-specific information

Even if investors had all the information provided in the first two tiers, they would still need additional information specific to individual companies. This information would include management's views of the business and the competitive environment, company strategies, unique company value drivers and the company's commitments to other stakeholders. Such company-specific information forms the basis of tier three. While well-defined external standards cannot be developed for tier three content, general guidelines for content, as well as external standards for the format of reporting such information, certainly could be developed.

18.7   A framework for reporting the full array of information

In order to gain comfort with the sustainability of current corporate performance, investors and managers alike demand a body of information that covers both the external environment in which the company operates, and the resources and competencies that the management can harness to execute its strategy. The ultimate success of these endeavours will be measured in terms of financial performance.

The ValueReporting™ Framework (see Figure 18.4), developed by PricewaterhouseCoopers, embodies these needs.

This reporting model builds on a number of underlying principles, the key being transparency. Enterprises that embrace it can create their own comprehensive, cohesive information set that satisfies the needs of all stakeholders – not just investors. The underlying philosophy of this reporting model is that while investors have primacy, the needs (including information) of all stakeholders must be addressed if value is to be optimised in the long run. The approach also assumes that information should be communicated consistently across all media, with particular attention to reporting forward-looking information. This does not mean issuing profit forecasts. Rather, it encourages greater transparency regarding, but not limited to, lead indicators of future performance such as expected trends in the marketplace, other external forces that could affect the enterprise, high-level targets, performance milestones and relevant non-financial operating data. Nor does it mean giving away competitively sensitive information.

Source: PricewaterhouseCoopers publication entitled *ValueReporting Review 2003 – Transparency in Corporate Reporting.* © 2003 PricewaterhouseCoopers. All rights reserved. For further information see www.valuereporting.com. 'PricewaterhouseCoopers' refers to the network of member firms of PricewaterhouseCoopers International Limited, each of which is a separate and independent legal entity.

It is also important to note that although they are presented separately, the four categories should not be considered in isolation. Each one represents a logical building block in forming a complete and coherent picture of corporate performance. The challenge for management is to construct this view across all

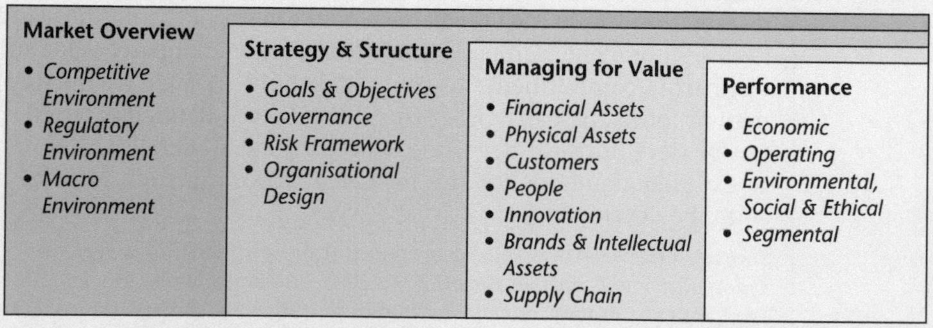

Figure 18.4 ValueReporting™ Framework

four categories of information to show that its thinking is not only aligned and linked, but also reflected in the systems and metrics used to run the business on a day-to-day basis.

For example, the first category of information that stakeholders need is an analysis of the economic and competitive landscape of the enterprise (*market overview*), followed by an articulation of the *strategy and structure* required to compete in this landscape. Next come the risks, resources and relationships that will enable the enterprise to put in place its strategy (*managing for value*). Last but not least are the financial and non-financial outcomes of corporate activities (*performance*).

By reporting across these four categories, enterprises enable users of their publicly reported information to evaluate and compare the performance of different enterprises (to the extent that other enterprises report similarly). Through this type of structured reporting, stakeholders can assess financial results within the context of total corporate performance, which in turn allows them to evaluate more accurately the 'quality' of the enterprise today and its future sustainability.

In the next four sections we will examine each of the four categories more closely and give examples of best practices.

Source: PricewaterhouseCoopers publication entitled *Trends 2005 – Good Practices in Corporate Reporting.* © 2005 PricewaterhouseCoopers. All rights reserved. For further information see www.valuereporting.com. 'PricewaterhouseCoopers' refers to the network of member firms of PricewaterhouseCoopers International Limited, each of which is a separate and independent legal entity.

18.7.1 Market overview

This category represents the starting point of any analysis and presentation of performance, as factors in the external marketplace typically constitute a dominant force in determining a company's current performance and future prospects. Corporate managers should therefore communicate their views on areas such as the market in which the company is competing, how the market has been defined, who the competitors are, the company's position within the competitive landscape, the macroeconomic environment and the regulatory challenges facing the company. This is critical information, though this is an area that is often less well communicated and consequently more poorly understood than one might expect.

The lack of communication by management in this area is all the more surprising given its fundamental importance for understanding the rationale and logic for the chosen strategic direction and thus evaluating a company's current performance and future prospects. Managers often justify their silence in this area by claiming that analysts can glean market information from other sources. Advocates for better disclosure, on the other hand, contend that market overview information is too critical for the evaluation of an enterprise's performance to rely on analysts, competitors or other market commentators to provide it. For this reason, enterprises with a more enlightened, active view prefer to provide

▶

their own descriptions, analyses and opinions of the environment in which they operate.

Source: PricewaterhouseCoopers publication entitled *ValueReporting Review 2003 – Transparency in Corporate Reporting.* © 2003 PricewaterhouseCoopers. All rights reserved. For further information see www.valuereporting.com. 'PricewaterhouseCoopers' refers to the network of member firms of PricewaterhouseCoopers International Limited, each of which is a separate and independent legal entity.

The market overview category includes three main elements:

- *Competitive environment:* market factors and dynamics that can affect the current or future business environment in which a company operates, such as competitors and industry outlook.
- *Regulatory environment:* current or future legal, agency or other regulatory factors that impose requirements on the conduct of business activity, such as deregulation and privatisation.
- *Macro environment:* current or future macro-economic factors that could have a material impact on corporate performance, such as interest rates, demographics, and economic outlook.

Figure 18.5 shows the description of the macro environment of Puma.

Sources: PricewaterhouseCoopers publications entitled *Trends 2005 – Good Practices in Corporate Reporting* and *ValueReporting Review 2003 – Transparency in Corporate Reporting.* © 2005 and 2003 PricewaterhouseCoopers. All rights reserved. For further information see www.valuereporting.com. 'PricewaterhouseCoopers' refers to the network of member firms of PricewaterhouseCoopers International Limited, each of which is a separate and independent legal entity.

Development of the World Economy

According to a value assessment of the 'Kiel Institute for World Economics,' the world economy maintained its upswing in 2004 but lost some momentum from the spring onward. This weakening is attributable in part to a tightening of previously expansive economic policy. Although the impetus of US fiscal policy had lost most of its momentum, monetary conditions nevertheless remained clearly positive. China took administrative measures to slow down the excessive economic boom. Economic activities were additionally dampened by the steep rise in oil prices. However, the negative effects of oil price increases were buffered by economic expansion in various regions of the world.

The economic recovery also continued in the Euro zone over the course of the year. Real gross domestic product grew faster than in the second half of 2003. In general, however, development in the Euro zone differed significantly from country to country.

The major sports events in the year 2004 also had a positive impact on the sporting goods industry. Despite limited consumer spending, additional growth was reported in nearly all markets. Overall, Puma has achieved strong global positioning as a Sportlifestyle brand, resulting in a competitive advantage and enabling adaptation to constantly changing market conditions. The selective distribution strategy will anchor and further expand the desirability of the brand.

Figure 18.5 Market overview: an example
Source: Puma Annual Report 2004

Strategy of the Puma Group

The course was set for lasting future success as early as 1993; in subsequent years, the strategic development of the brand was implemented by means of systematic corporate planning. The focus of Phase I (1993–1997) was on restructuring with the aim of establishing a sound financial base for the future. The main emphasis of Phase II was on brand investment and the transformation from a traditional sporting goods manufacturer to a Sportlifestyle Group.

Following the successful completion of Phases I and II, the year 2002 saw the rollout of Phase III of corporate planning a year earlier than originally planned. The goal of Phase III is to achieve full utilization of the brand potential by further increasing the desirability of the brand.

The main cornerstones of strategic corporate planning during phase III (2002–2006) are:

Brand
With its successful positioning as a unique Sportlifestyle brand, Puma wants to get a clear edge over competition.

Marketing
Unconventional and creative concepts ensure the seamless interplay of elements from sports, lifestyle and fashion that give the brand its unique image.

Product and Market Segmentation
With clear product and market segmentation, Puma is able to appeal equally to athletes as well as lifestyle consumers. Puma incorporates influences from the entire spectrum of Sportlifestyle to develop creative and innovative products. From a marketing perspective, Puma responds to the different requirements of consumers in four product stations.

Distribution
A selective distribution policy ensures that the various products reach their respective consumer group.

Retail
The targeted expansion of Puma's own retail outlets is a component of the company's strategic planning and offers an ideal platform for presentation of the brand and its products. Moreover, Puma benefits from direct contact with end consumers.

Profitability and Value-Based Management
Profitability and sustained increase in corporate value provides the standards for strategic and operative decisions.

Figure 18.6 Strategy and structure: an example
Source: Puma Annual Report 2004

18.7.2 Strategy and structure

Within the context of an enterprise's market overview, management should clearly communicate how its strategy and corporate structures enable the enterprise to compete and thrive (see Figure 18.6). In addition, management should support its strategy with quantified medium-term targets and relevant milestones, including a description and rationale for its chosen mix of risk (e.g. the cost of capital) and return (e.g. cash flow) for the enterprise as a whole and for each business segment. Furthermore, management should distinguish clearly the portion of its growth strategy which will be achieved organically compared to the portion that requires acquisitions.

Any strategy should derive from an understanding of the key areas in which an enterprise has competitive advantage. Accordingly, the enterprise's success in creating value will depend on management's ability to identify these key areas, invest resources in them, and manage them to deliver the financial performance investors expect. Inextricably linked to all of this is how well the enterprise's underlying organisational and governance structures, systems and processes and risk management frameworks are aligned with strategy.

The elements within the strategy and structure category are:

- *Goals and objectives:* a clear statement of strategic goals and objectives, preferably covering plans for both the long and short–medium terms. These targets should be quantifiable and measurable, and should demonstrate the link between strategy and shareholder value creation, for both the company as a whole and the individual business segments.
- *Governance:* communication of management's commitment to transparency and how governance issues are managed. This may include supervision, oversight, and accountability of the board of directors and management through guidelines, policies, procedures and actions. Such open dialogue can greatly enhance the public credibility of management.
- *Risk framework:* a company's risk management strategy and its risk profile for the different types of risks that it faces in the day-to-day operation of the business.
- *Organisational design:* alignment of current and corporate structure, and segmentation of business with value-creating activities. Management should clearly communicate how the organisational design of the company supports the overall strategy.

Source: PricewaterhouseCoopers publication entitled *Trends 2005 – Good Practices in Corporate Reporting.* © 2005 PricewaterhouseCoopers. All rights reserved. For further information see www.valuereporting.com. 'PricewaterhouseCoopers' refers to the network of member firms of PricewaterhouseCoopers International Limited, each of which is a separate and independent legal entity.

18.7.3 Managing for value

Having communicated its strategy and structure, management must clearly communicate at a more detailed level the complex web of assets, relationships, capabilities and processes it has in place for executing strategy. Although the components of this web may vary in relative importance relating to industry dynamics and corporate strategy, they include:

- an enterprise's *financial and physical assets*
- its *'people'* assets such as employees' abilities and skills
- the interaction and relationships with its *customers*

- how the enterprise protects and enhances the value of its *brands and intellectual assets*
- the structure of and the nature of the relationships within the enterprise's *supply chain*.

Without this information, investors must often make decisions based on a much less than optimal understanding of how the enterprise actually creates value or seeks this information from external sources outside the enterprise's control. On the other hand, those enterprises that have learned how to link their disparate value-creating elements to strategy and then manage them effectively are positioned to report to the investment community the kind of information it needs to assess both current performance and future prospects. An example of how enterprises have begun to incorporate such information into their public communication is given in Figure 18.7.

Source: PricewaterhouseCoopers publications entitled *Trends 2005 – Good Practices in Corporate Reporting*. © 2005 PricewaterhouseCoopers. All rights reserved. For further information see www.valuereporting.com. 'PricewaterhouseCoopers' refers to the network of member firms of PricewaterhouseCoopers International Limited, each of which is a separate and independent legal entity.

Sustainable supply chain management benefits bottom line

Working with suppliers on social and environmental issues can benefit a company's financial bottom line, according to a model commissioned by Novo Nordisk. The model indicates that the return on investment for sustainable supply chain management is created through financial and reputational benefits for both parties.

The model concludes that there are both direct and indirect implications which can be identified if not yet quantified. According to the model, effective sustainable supply chain management can affect the bottom line in two ways: through costs and through turnover. Total costs, in turn, are affected by production costs and cost of capital.

Benefits include higher product quality and reduced risk as well as a positive impact on the company brand. In a broader perspective there are benefits to society, such as reduced pollution and fewer work-related injuries and accidents. Suppliers can measure the effects of improving labour standards and environmental

Like ripples in the water: Novo Nordisk is encouraging its suppliers to look at their own supply chains.

management in terms of fewer costs related to compensation, reduced pollution charges, etc. As important, perhaps, is closer collaboration and sharing of better practices between Novo Nordisk and its suppliers, and better self-regulation and documentation towards regulatory authorities.

Novo Nordisk has had a comprehensive supply chain management programme since 2001, when it began requiring its suppliers to complete a self-evaluation questionnaire regarding their environmental and social performance. The latter deals with treating employees fairly in terms of wage and benefits, working hours, child labour, collective bargaining and other issues described in The United Nations Universal Declaration of Human Rights and the International Labour Organisation's Core Conventions.

The programme, which now includes audits, is expected to cover all major areas of purchase by 2005.

Now reaching out to second-tier suppliers, Novo Nordisk has developed a new toolbox for its suppliers and other companies who intend to engage in a programme with their suppliers which is available at suppliertoolbox.novonordisk.com

Read more, and see the research behind the model of the financial impacts, at novonordisk.com/annual-report-2004

Figure 18.7 Managing for value: an example
Source: Novo Nordisk Annual Report 2004

18.7.4 Performance

This category is a key focus both internally and externally. It is the test of whether or not an enterprise has delivered results in line with expectations, and implicitly, of how well management has understood its market, executed its strategy and managed its value-creating resources and relationships.

Whether or not investors and stakeholders understand the impact of the results achieved depends, of course, on how well management can communicate all the information to them. In other words, it is in this category where the elements of risk, return and growth come together in the form of performance outputs.

Traditional financial reporting provides most of the information needed on financial performance. The other three elements within the performance category have been largely ignored or given little attention. While financial performance remains at the heart of corporate reporting, it needs to be expanded. Performance should be approached in a more holistic way, adding *economic* measures to financial accounting measures and including results of *operating* performance, such as customer satisfaction, average revenue per customer, and revenue from new products.

Performance also includes reporting on how well the enterprise is meeting its commitments to *environmental, social and ethical responsibility*, as well as reporting on important aspects of performance by major individual business segments. While great importance is placed on financial performance, it is not the exclusive focus of the reporting model described in this section. Figure 18.8 gives an example of reporting on performance.

Source: PricewaterhouseCoopers publications entitled *Trends 2005 – Good Practices in Corporate Reporting*. © 2005 PricewaterhouseCoopers. All rights reserved. For further information see www.valuereporting.com. 'PricewaterhouseCoopers' refers to the network of member firms of PricewaterhouseCoopers International Limited, each of which is a separate and independent legal entity.

18.8 Conclusions

The economic and reputational rewards of providing such a comprehensive picture of performance are substantial and well documented. Increased management credibility, lower stock price volatility, and competitive advantage in the labour market are benefits typically highlighted by empirical analysis and case studies.

However, despite the benefits of greater transparency, the corporate sector has been slow to respond. The tendency seems to remain for management to rely largely on financial measures for evaluating performance and making strategic decisions. At the same time, others, including some sell-side analysts and large institutional investors, prefer the uneven playing field that a lack of transparency may create. That uneven playing field could mean a competitive advantage for some in terms of access to more accurate, more complete or more timely information.

In contrast, non-governmental organisations and an increasing number of politicians recognise the critical role that the corporate sector can play in

Performance highlights

Financial performance

In 2004, Novo Nordisk's sales were 29,031 million Danish kroner (DKK), up 11% from DKK 26,158 million in 2003. Measured in local currencies this is an increase of 15%. Operating profit in 2004 increased by 9% from 2003 to DKK 6,980 million. A lower level of non-recurring income reduced operating margin in 2004 to 24.0% from 24.6% in 2003. Return on invested capital increased by 21% in 2004 from 20% in 2003.

The cash to earnings ratio for 2004 ended at 85% up from 80% in 2003. Earnings per share (diluted) increased by 5% in 2004 to DKK 14.83 from DKK 14.15.

Environmental performance

Novo Nordisk continued to produce 'more with less' in 2004. The eco-productivity indices, which express the ability to utilise resources effectively, showed an improvement of 7% for water and 8% for energy, and thereby reaching the targets for 2004. The implementation of certified environmental management in Japan is progressing according to plan. Detailed accounts for performance can be found at novonordisk.com/annual-report-2004

Social performance

In 2004 Novo Nordisk created 1,484 new full-time positions, mainly outside Denmark. The year-end number of employees in 2004 was 20,725. The employee turnover rate for 2004 was 7.3%. The frequency of occupational injuries was 5.6 per million working hours, compared to 5.4 in 2003. Detailed accounts for performance can be found at novonordisk.com/annual-report-2004

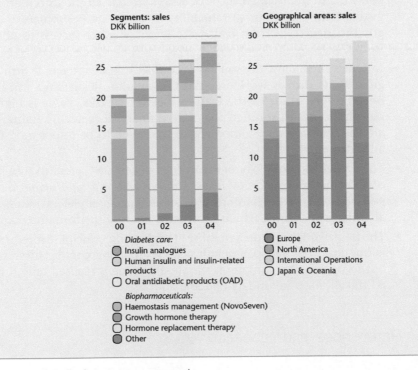

Figure 18.8 Performance: an example

Source: Novo Nordisk Annual Report 2004

creating a civil economy. For these groups, transparency and better information on key areas of corporate performance are seen as critical to the process of changing corporate behaviour. Ultimately, it is difficult to see a world where better information is not demanded. The challenge for all those involved is to ensure it is really better information, and not just more information involving more process and more bureaucracy.

Source: PricewaterhouseCoopers publication entitled *Trends in Corporate Reporting 2004 – Towards ValueReporting*. © 2004 PricewaterhouseCoopers. All rights reserved. For further information see www.valuereporting.com. 'PricewaterhouseCoopers' refers to the network of member firms of PricewaterhouseCoopers International Limited, each of which is a separate and independent legal entity.

Summary

- The key elements that create public trust in capital markets and, therefore, allow those markets to allocate capital efficiently are: (1) transparency (2) accountability (3) integrity.

- To date, the efforts of regulatory bodies to drive reform have focused on two key areas: (1) a desire to harmonise global accounting standards (2) a need to define more clearly the roles and responsibilities of corporate executives and directors.

- The current financial reporting model focuses largely on short-term financial performance. Consequently, it does not provide all the information necessary to evaluate the quality or sustainability of corporate performance, to differentiate good management from bad, or to know whether success results from luck or from skills.

- In today's economy, the sources of competitive advantage lie firmly in the intangible assets such as workforce skills, reputation, leadership, innovation, and so on. The very nature of these assets means that their value is highly unlikely to be communicated through the current financial reporting framework. Yet these are the resources and competencies that need to be understood for them to be allocated efficiently.

- The ValueReporting™ Framework developed by PwC presents four basic categories of information: *market overview*, *strategy and structure*, *managing for value* and *performance*. Together they create a coherent and complete medium-term picture of an enterprise, against which short-term financial performance can be explained.

- The framework builds on a number of underlying principles, foremost among them is the notion of transparency. It assumes that shareholder interests are primary, but recognises that long-term sustainable value is realised only if the interests of all stakeholders are understood and addressed.

References and research

The following are examples of research papers and books that take the issues of this chapter further:

- Vivien Beattie, Bill McInnes and Stella Fearnley, *Through the Eyes of Management: A Study of Narrative Disclosures*, ICAEW, London, 2002

- Business Reporting Research Project, *Improving Business Reporting: Insights Into Enhancing Voluntary Disclosures*, Financial Accounting Standards Board, Norwalk, 2001
- The European Commission, *Modernizing Company Law and Enhancing Corporate Governance in the European Union – A Plan to Move Forward*, May 2003
- Florian Gimbel and Simon Targett, 'The big picture: new index highlights corporate standards, FT Fund Management', *Financial Times*, 1 March 2004
- International Federation of Accountants (IFAC), *Enterprise Governance: Getting the Balance Right*, February 2004

Questions

18.1 The existing conceptual framework of the accounting standards needs to be revisited to reflect the needs of all stakeholders for non-financial and forward-looking information. Discuss.

18.2 Corporate reporting cannot achieve transparency. In fact, transparency in corporate reporting is significantly constrained by considerations of cost, competition, confidentiality and litigation. Discuss.

18.3 Information is the lifeblood of the capital markets. Investors risk their hard-earned capital in the markets, and they rely on information they receive from enterprises in making their investment decisions. They need reliable information on a timely basis. They want it in a language they can understand, and they should receive it in formats they can easily use for analysis. Investors have the right to expect that the benefits or losses they experience will result from the decisions they make, not from flawed information. Discuss.

18.4 'Economies are increasingly based on knowledge . . . what is new is that a growing chunk of production in the modern economy is in the form of intangibles, based on the exploitation of ideas, rather than material things . . .' (*The Economist*, 23 September 2000). What are, in your opinion, the implications for corporate reporting of the growing importance of intangibles as the key drivers of corporate performance?

18.5 For the efficient functioning of market economy, reliable, timely and transparent financial information is indispensable not only for the shareholders but for all other stakeholders. Discuss.

18.6 Assets like leadership, talent and speed cannot be valued. Discuss.

Case study   Good ethics means more than ticking boxes   FT

Corporate governance codes have proliferated and business ethics is a fast-growing industry. But has corporate behaviour changed? The scandals just keep coming: Citigroup, AIG, Volkswagen and SK Corp have all had to defend themselves against allegations of ethical misconduct in recent months. Meanwhile, boardroom pay and golden goodbyes continue to escalate far beyond any corresponding improvement in corporate performance. The actors may have learnt their cues better, but they appear to have lost the plot. Why is this? And what can and should be done about the serious ethical shortcomings in finance and business?

In an environment where much boardroom pay is in the form of equity or stock options, most scandals today involve cooking the books to keep the share price up. Add in the fact that chief executives are under greater pressure than ever before from fund managers and analysts to 'hit the numbers' and you have the nub of the problem. Incentive structures in the boardroom and below, and the business strategies of the consultants, all push in a direction that is at odds with ethical behaviour and, it should be said, long-run corporate performance. Ordinary financial market participants and business people feel penalised, not supported, for raising ethical questions.

This misalignment between individual incentives and ethical behaviour is not adequately addressed by the Sarbanes-Oxley Act in the US. Its requirement for companies to have a code of ethics for the CEO and the chief financial officer assumes that you can legislate companies into good behaviour. Conversely, the extraordinary expansion of legislation and governance codes since Enron has exacerbated the problem by encouraging a compliance culture.

Ethics and governance are today reduced to a box ticking exercise, while many codes are cynical public relations exercises. Too many boards have delegated the task to ethics officers, who in turn have outsourced the task of defining the company's values to consultants. These 'values' are then ignored by directors and employees as meaningless puff. Cynicism is not universal. But even where ethics are taken seriously, the rate of corporate change, with takeovers, divestments and redundancies, makes it harder for employees to hold on to core values.

The law alone is not enough to ensure that corporate behaviour does not act against the wider interests of society. It invariably codifies the lowest common denominator, while lagging behind changes in the way the economy and markets evolve. And corporate activity has side-effects – externalities – that are not adequately regulated by the market or by laws and regulations. So there is a need for ethical behaviour that goes beyond complying with the law, especially in the grey areas where managers face conflicting priorities. A further case for business ethics is that trust is fundamental to business relations and to the efficient working of markets. Economies contract when trust breaks down. The more transactions have to be governed by contract the more cumbersome and costly business becomes as everything has to be negotiated, agreed, litigated and enforced. Put crudely, ethical standards are a low-cost substitute for internal control within the company and for outside external regulation. While many financial participants grapple with new rules on operational, market and credit risks they should remember that ethics plays a role in risk-management at both the macro and micro level. The collapse of Andersen, Enron and WorldCom demonstrates what can happen when ethics go out of the window.

Restoring trust and establishing a more ethical corporate culture are therefore worthwhile objectives. That means addressing personal behaviour. But we should not forget the corporate incentives that lie behind that behaviour.

A MORI poll in the UK last year showed that, when prompted, only 42 per cent of institutional investors said they took into account honesty and integrity of corporate leaders in making investment decisions. When not prompted, this figure fell to 6 per cent. The short-term bias of institutional investors may actually conspire to support unethical behaviour. Perhaps greater research and analysis is required to help investors measure unethical behaviour and weigh up its real long-term consequences. This is not a pipe dream. It is one of the objectives of the recently announced Enhanced Analytics Initiative of leading fund managers.

Meanwhile, it is important to remain focused on changing individual behaviour. After all, it is individuals who make unethical decisions, not faceless, corporate bodies. It is vital that managers engage employees throughout the company when they draw up ethical standards. A code handed down from on high, without consultation, will be treated with deserved scepticism. Managers must also convey the message that beating targets and winning business at any cost fly in the face of what the company is about. They should avoid the crass error perpetrated at Enron where people who violated the company's stated values were treated as heroes if the violation helped the bottom line. Managers also have to show by example that they do not expect employees to shed their moral values when they walk through the company door.

The attributes of ethical leadership, according to the London-based Institute of Business Ethics, are openness, fair-mindedness, courage, honesty and the ability to listen. It would be nice if all managers had these attributes - now that is a pipe dream - but more effective than an attractive personality is a sound framework to make ethical choices. We believe this is easier to do than it sounds. A simple starting point is for decision makers to query any business decision routinely, asking whether it will cause harm to anyone; whether the decision has been influenced by disguised conflicts; and whether a situation has been contrived that disadvantages others.

Those accused of perpetrating market timing abuses during the last stock market boom may have forgotten the first question. Those who puffed new issues to their clients deuring that boom failed to consider the second question. Citibank's European government bond traders probably failed to ask themselves the third question when they tried to corner the market in September 2004.

For some, a heavy judicial penalty is the only route to ensuring good behaviour. But for many in business, asking good questions is the starting point to making an ethical culture work.

Ethical Framework

The intricate ethical guidelines laid down in the Sarbanes-Oxley Act and elsewhere can relegate business ethics to a box-ticking exercise. We propose a simpler approach: the following five simple questions provide a minimum framework. Whatever the answers, if managers and employees are not even asking these simple questions you should expect a problem.

- Who are all the people affected by this business decision: from employees, shareholders, counter-parties and clients to the wider community and environment?
- Does this decision cause harm to any of those affected and are there reasonable things you can do to mitigate this harm?
- Is your behaviour deceptive? Would you regard it that way if you were in the counter-party's position?
- Are there any disguised conflicts between yourself, shareholders and those affected by the business decision? Transparency can help reinforce ethical behaviour.
- What would happen if everyone were to behave in the same way in relation to each player in the transaction? This is like every driver at an intersection deciding to jump the traffic lights. If harm would be caused by everyone treating clients, counter-parties, whistle-blowers and shareholders as you do, you should refrain from doing it.

From 'Good ethics means more than ticking boxes',
Avinash Persaud and John Plender, *Financial Times*, 23 August 2005

As the article indicates, the scandals just keep coming and the law alone is not enough to ensure that corporate behaviour does not act against the wider interests of society. What are the solutions to corporate misbehaviour in your view? Relate your arguments to your own country's ethical environment.

Note

[1] The FTSE4 Good selection criteria cover three areas: working towards environmental sustainability, developing positive relationships with stakeholders and upholding and supporting universal human rights.

Glossary

This glossary primarily represents the terminology and language used by the International Accounting Standards Board. However, there are numerous cross-references to terminology commonly used in the United States.

Terms used in an entry that are defined elsewhere in the glossary are shown in small capitals.

AAA *See* AMERICAN ACCOUNTING ASSOCIATION.

Accelerated depreciation DEPRECIATION at a faster rate than an even allocation of cost over an asset's expected life. This is prevalent in many European countries, usually as tax concessions intended to encourage investment in certain class of fixed assets or regions.

Account *See* ACCOUNTS.

Accounting Process of identifying, measuring and communicating information to permit informed judgements and decisions by users of the information. It also relates to the preparation, presentation and interpretation of financial statements.

Accounting convention Another way of referring to the fundamental conceptual rules of accounting. *See* ACCOUNTING PRINCIPLES.

Accounting equation Mathematical representation of a transaction under the DOUBLE-ENTRY system. The total of assets and expenses (all debits) equal the total of liabilities, capital and revenues (all credits).

Accounting period *See* FINANCIAL YEAR.

Accounting policies The specific principles, bases, conventions, rules and practices adopted by an enterprise in preparing and presenting its financial statements.

Accounting principles Fundamental rules or conventions as to how assets and liabilities should be measured or valued and accounting statements prepared.

Accounting Principles Board (APB) APB was set up in 1959 in the USA and was replaced in 1973 by the FINANCIAL ACCOUNTING STANDARDS BOARD. It issued 31 opinions and 4 statements which mostly have not been replaced and therefore they are still an integral part of the GENERALLY ACCEPTED ACCOUNTING PRINCIPLES.

Accounting profit The profit or loss for a period before deducting income tax expense.

Accounting standards Technical accounting rules of valuation, measurement, recognition and disclosure. Each country today has its own denomination (i.e. UK FRS, US GAAP, IAS/IFRS etc.).

Accounts Records of the Bookkeeping entries dealing with a particular item. In the Double-entry system there is a Debit side (left) and a Credit side (right). Accounts also mean financial statements in the UK terminology.

Accounts payable *See* Trade and other payables

Accounts receivable *See* Trade and other receivables

Accruals *See* Accrued expenses and Accrued revenues.

Accrual basis of accounting The effects of transactions and events are recognised when they occur (and not as cash and cash equivalents are received or paid) and they are recorded in the accounting records and reported in the financial statements of the periods to which they relate. For example, accountancy fees or the cost of electricity consumed in an accounting period should be accounted for as a charge in the income statement and as liabilities in the balance sheet even though these costs have not been paid and invoices have not yet been received.

Accrued expenses Expenses related to an accounting period and outstanding or unpaid at the end of it. Accrued expenses are paid or settled subsequent to the accounting period.

Accrued revenues Revenues related to an accounting period which will be cashed or settled subsequent to the accounting period.

Accumulated depreciation Total amount by which the cost of Fixed assets has been reduced to take account of the wear and tear and/or obsolescence at a given date (see Depreciation).

Acid test *See* Quick ratio.

Acquisition A business combination in which one of the enterprises, the acquirer, obtains control over the net assets and operations of another enterprise, the acquiree, in exchange for the transfer of assets, incurrence of liability or issue of equity.

AGM *See* Annual general meeting.

AICPA *See* American Institute of Certified Public Accountants.

Allowances Provision in the US terminology. An allowance represents an amount charged against Profit or Income to recognise reductions in value of an asset (i.e. allowance for depreciation, allowance for doubtful debts, etc.).

American Accounting Association (AAA) An organisation of accounting academics in the US. It organises conferences annually and publishes *The Accounting Review* and *Accounting Horizons*.

American Institute of Certified Public Accountants (AICPA) Founded in 1887, it is responsible for professional and ethical guidance for its members and the educational standards. It is also responsible for setting Auditing standards which are known as Generally accepted auditing atandards.

Amortisation The systematic allocation of the depreciable amount of an intangible asset (such as goodwill, patents, licences, etc.) over its economic or contractual life.

Annual general meeting (AGM) Annual meeting of the shareholders of a COMPANY which normally takes place after the end of the company's financial year to approve the annual financial statements and other matters, such as the appointment of directors and auditors.

Annual report A document containing the financial statements, notes, the directors' report and the report by the auditors issued to shareholders and stakeholders after a COMPANY's year end.

Articles of association Regulations for the management of a COMPANY registered in the UK which sets out the rights and duties of the shareholders and directors, and the relationship between different types of shareholders. Together with the MEMORANDUM OF ASSOCIATION they form the COMPANY's constitution. Called BYLAWS in the US or statutes in the mainland Europe.

Asset A resource owned by an enterprise as a result of past events and from which future economic benefits are expected to flow to the enterprise. The NET ASSETS are determined by deducting the LIABILITIES from the total assets.

In a balance sheet the following categories of assets are listed: current assets – cash, bank deposits, inventories, trade receivables and trade investments; non current (tangible) assets – land, buildings, plant and machinery, vehicles and furniture; non-current (intangible) assets – goodwill, patents, and so on. Financial assets can be either current or non-current assets.

Associated company An enterprise in which an investor has significant influence and which is neither a subsidiary nor a joint venture of the investor. The significant influence is presumed when an investor holds 20 per cent or more of the voting power of the investee.

Audit committee A COMPANY committee, usually made of non-executive directors of the company, on all matters of internal control, accounting issues and disclosures in the financial statements. Such audit committee is also responsible for approving the auditors' fees.

Audit report The auditor's report contains a clear written expression of opinion on the financial statements. An unqualified opinion is expressed when the auditor concludes that the financial statements give a true and fair view or are presented fairly, in all material respects, in accordance with the applicable financial reporting framework.

Auditing An examination conducted by auditors which involves checking the physical existence and valuation of ASSETS and examining the internal control's system to ensure the correct recording of transactions. The objective of an audit of financial statements is to enable the auditor to express an opinion whether the financial statements are prepared, in all material respects, in accordance with an applicable financial reporting framework.

Auditing practices board The Consultative Committee of the Accountancy Bodies committee responsible for preparing AUDITING STANDARDS and guidelines in the UK.

Auditing standards Regulations or standards to be observed by external auditors in preparing their work and issuing their AUDIT REPORT.

Authorised share capital The maximum amount of capital that a registered company is authorized to issue under its MEMORANDUM OF ASSOCIATION or bylaws or statutes.

AVCO   *See* AVERAGE COST.

Average cost (AVCO)   In the context of INVENTORY valuation, a method of determining the historical cost of an item of inventory. The cost is obtained by dividing all purchases for a period (i.e. month or year) by the total quantity bought in that period (weighted average cost). *See* FIFO and LIFO.

Bad debts   Amounts owed by customers which are or are expected to be uncollectible, probably because the customer has become insolvent. Bad debts are recorded as an EXPENSE against INCOME and the related amount in the Trade and other receivables is written down to nil.

Balance   Amount required to be inserted in one of two columns of a T-account to make the totals of debits and credits equal (double-entry bookkeeping). A debt bank balance represents cash receivable by an enterprise while a credit bank balance represents an overdraft i.e. a liability of the enterprise.

Balance sheet   A statement of the ASSETS, LIABILITIES and capital of an enterprise as at a given date, usually at the end of an accounting period, as distinct from income statement, which presents transactions for a period. The balance sheet has two sections: assets on the left-hand side or at the top, and liabilities on the right-hand side or at the bottom. The assets of the company – receivables, property, cash – are equal to the claims or liabilities of the persons or organisations owing them: creditors, lenders and shareholders. This is the basis of double-entry bookkeeping.

Basic earnings per share   The amount of net profit for the period that is attributable to ordinary shareholders divided by the weighted average number of ordinary shares outstanding during the period.

Bear   Investor on the STOCK EXCHANGE who expects a fall in prices and so sells securities. A bear market is one in which investors are pessimistic as opposed to a BULL market in which investors expect share prices to rise.

Big Four   A title which describes the four largest international accounting firms: Deloitte Touche Tohmatsu, Ernst & Young, KPMG and PriceWaterhouseCoopers. Before the demise of Arthur Andersen, there were the 'Big Five' and at one time there were the 'Big Eight'.

Bill of exchange   Acknowledgement of a debt in the form of an order in writing addressed by one party to another requiring the latter to pay on demand or at a fixed time a specified amount. Can be transferred to others, i.e. they are negotiable. Bills of exchange are divided into the categories of bank bills, trade bills, fine trade bills and finance bills. Called notes in the US.

Bonds   Represent long-term debentures issued under a contract by a COMPANY for a fixed term, normally a fixed INTEREST rate and a fixed redemption value.

Bonus shares   Shares issued for free to shareholders in proportion to their shareholding generally with the aim of lowering or diluting the share price. There is no transfer or movement of cash. An enterprise's retained earnings or reserves are 'converted' into share capital by an accounting entry.

Bookkeeping   Describes the mechanical aspects of accounting which involves the recording of transactions of an enteprirse (see DOUBLE-ENTRY for further details).

Book value (gross)   Value of the Assets and Liabilities of a business as stated in its Financial statements.

Book value (net)   Amount at which an Asset is stated in the Balance sheet depending on the system of accounting being used. It does not necessarily represent the amount for which the asset can be sold.

  The net book value of a long-lived asset is given by its historical cost less accumulated depreciation/amortisation and impairment loss.

Borrowing costs   Interest and other costs incurred by an enterprise in connection with the borrowing of funds.

Budget   A financial plan to guide a business to prepare, monitor and control its activities during the year.

Bull   Investor on a Stock exchange who expects a rise in price and so buys securities with the aim to sell them again later at a profit. Also describes an optimistic state of the market as opposed to a Bear market.

Business combination   The bringing together of separate enterprises into one economic entity as a result of one enterprise obtaining control over the net assets and operations of another enterprise (see Consolidated financial statements).

Business segment   A distinguishable component of an enterprise that is engaged in providing an individual product or service or a group of related products or services and that is subject to risks and returns that are different from those of other business segments.

Bylaws   The rules concerning the operations of an enterprise in the US. *See* Memorandum of association.

Cadbury committee   A UK government appointed committee, which in December 1992 put forward proposals for good corporate governance.

Called-up share capital   Amount of the capital due from the shareholders where the shares are being paid in instalments or in calls.

Capital employed   There is no universally agreed definition of the term. It is often referred to as the sum of owners' equity and non-current liabilities.

Capital gains tax   A tax applied to the gain realised on disposal of an asset.

Capital lease   US term for Finance lease.

Capital reserves   Accounts, such as the Share premium account, which can be distributed by a Company only if certain conditions are met under the law. Restricted surplus in US terminology.

Capitalisation   What an enterprise is worth considering the total market price of all the Shares (market capitalisation of an enterprise).

  Recognising an expenditure as an Asset rather than an Expense (capitalisation of development expenditure under IFRS).

Carrying value (or amount)   Amount at which an item is shown on a Balance sheet. In the case of asset, it represents the amount at which an asset is recognised in the balance sheet after deducting accumulated depreciation (amortisation) and accumulated impairment losses thereon.

Cash   Cash on hand and demand deposits.

Cash equivalents   Short-term, highly liquid investments that are readily convertible to known amounts of cash and which are subject to an insignificant risk of changes in value.

Cash flow   Represents the flow of money entering (cash inflow) or leaving (cash outflow) the enterprise during a period of time.

Cash flow statement   A financial statement focusing on the cash flow of various activities of an enterprise such as operating, investing and financing activities for a period or year.

Chart of accounts   Detailed and standardised system of account codes for ASSETS, LIABILITIES, Capital, REVENUES and EXPENSES.

Class of assets   Grouping of assets of a similar nature and use in an enterprise's operations.

Closing rate method   In UK terminology, method of CURRENCY TRANSLATION under which the financial statements of foreign subsidiaries are translated into the parent company's currency at current exchange rates.

Commercial code   Code, a part of the legal system, containing specific accounting rules applicable to companies.

Commissione nazionale per le società e la borsa (CONSOB)   Italian equivalent of the SECURITIES AND EXCHANGE COMMISSION in the US.

Common stock   US terminology for ORDINARY SHARES, that represent equity capital of a company.

Companies' Acts   *See* COMPANY LAW.

Company   A legal entity which is the vehicle for a business and is separate from its owners, the shareholders.

Company law   The law that deals with companies and their operations.

Conceptual framework   A theoretical framework accompanying the technical accounting rules such as the one published by the International Accounting Standards Committee in 1989.

Conservatism   *See* PRUDENCE.

Consistency   Concept whereby an enterprise should use each year identical rules for measurement, valuation and recognition in its FINANCIAL STATEMENTS in order to allow for proper comparison of figures from year to year. The purpose of consistency is to ensure proper comparison of a year's profits and values with those of the previous years.

CONSOB   *See* COMMISSIONE NAZIONALE PER LE SOCIETÀ E LA BORSA.

Consolidated financial statements   Presentation of the financial position and results of a PARENT and its SUBSIDIARIES (bringing together their balance sheets and profit and loss accounts) as if they were a single entity. Generally, the FINANCIAL STATEMENTS of all the enterprises in a GROUP are aggregated and consolidation adjustments are made to eliminate all intercompany transactions and their effects.

Contingent liability

(a) A possible obligation that arises from past events and whose existence will be confirmed only by the occurrence or non-occurrence of one or more uncertain future events not wholly within the control of the enterprise; or

(b) a present obligation that arises from past events but is not recognised because:

  (i) it is not probable that an outflow of resources embodying economic benefits will be required to settle the obligation; or

  (ii) the amount of the obligation cannot be measured with sufficient reliability.

Contract   An agreement between two or more parties that has clear economic consequences that the parties have little, if any, discretion to avoid, usually because the agreement is enforceable at law. Contracts may take a variety of forms and need not be in writing.

Control (of an asset)   The power to obtain the future economic benefits that flow from an asset.

Control (of an enterprise)   The power to govern the strategic, financial and operating policies of an enterprise so as to obtain benefits from its activities.

Corporate governance

Corporate governance is concerned with holding the balance between individual and communal goals. The governance framework is there to encourage the efficient use of resources and equally to require accountability for the stewardship of those resources. The aim is to align as nearly as possible the interests of individuals, corporations and society.

The incentive to corporations and to those who own and manage them to adopt internationally accepted governance standards is that these standards will help them to achieve their corporate aims and to attract investment. The incentive for their adoption by states is that these standards will strengthen the economy and discourage fraud and management.

The foundation of any structure of corporate governance is disclosure. Openness is the basis of public confidence in the corporate system, and funds will flow to centres of economic activity that inspire trust.   (Sir Adrian Cadbury in a foreword to the World Bank publication, *Corporate Governance: A Framework for Implementation*)

Corporation tax   A tax levied on the taxable profits of companies.

Cost   The amount of cash or cash equivalent paid or the fair value of other consideration given to acquire an asset at the time of its acquisition or construction.

Cost of an acquisition   The amount of cash or cash equivalents paid or the fair value, at the date of exchange, of other purchase consideration given by the acquirer in exchange for control over the net assets of the other enterprise, plus any costs directly attributable to the acquisition.

Cost of capital   Cost of capital is a means by which an investor who provides capital can expect a return that is commensurate with the risk to which that capital is exposed. The term can also be used to describe the cost of raising money.

Cost of disposal   Incremental costs directly attributable to the disposal of an asset, excluding finance costs and income tax expense.

Cost of goods sold   *See* COST OF SALES.

Cost of inventories   All costs of purchase, costs of conversion and other costs incurred in bringing the inventories to their present location and condition.

Cost of sales   It is equal to beginning inventory plus the cost of goods purchased during a specified period, less the ending inventory.

Cost method   A method of accounting for investments whereby the investment is recorded at cost. The income statement reflects income from the investment only to the extent that the investor receives distributions from accumulated net profits of the investee arising subsequent to the date of acquisition.

Credit   An entry made on the right-hand side of an account in double-entry bookkeeping.

Creditors   *See* TRADE AND OTHER PAYABLES.

Currency translation   *See* FOREIGN CURRENCY TRANSLATION.

Current assets   ASSETS that are expected to turn into cash within one year. Such assets normally include INVENTORY, TRADE AND OTHER RECEIVABLES, and CASH.

Current cost accounting   Method of adjusting accounting to reflect the changing prices of the enterprise's ASSETS. It is often included under the generic heading INFLATION ACCOUNTING, although its normal form does not involve adjustments for inflation but for specific price changes relating to the enterprise's assets.

Current liabilities   Liabilities that will be paid within a year. Thus they will include TRADE AND OTHER PAYABLES, certain tax liabilities, and declared DIVIDENDS. Bank overdrafts are included on the grounds that they fluctuate in size and are technically repayable at short notice.

Current purchasing power accounting (CPP)   UK term for a method of adjusting HISTORICAL COST ACCOUNTING financial statements to take into consideration inflation. The US equivalent is GENERAL PRICE LEVEL ADJUSTED or constant dollar.

Current ratio   CURRENT ASSETS divided by CURRENT LIABILITIES of an enterprise at a particular date.

Date of acquisition   The date on which control of the net assets and operations of the acquirer is effectively transferred to the acquirer.

Debentures   Loans, often long-term and usually secured on company ASSETS.

Debit   Records what is owed and is on the left-hand side of an account in double-entry bookkeeping. Total debits should always equal total CREDITS.

Debt–equity ratio   *See* GEARING.

Debtors   Amount of money owed to the business by customers who have been invoiced for goods or services but who have not yet paid what they owe. Recorded as CURRENT ASSET. See TRADE AND OTHER RECEIVABLES.

Deferred revenue   See UNEARNED REVENUE.

Deferred tax assets   The amounts of income taxes recoverable in future periods in respect of:

(a) deductible temporary differences;
(b) carryforward of unused tax losses; and
(c) carryforward of unused tax credits.

Deferred tax liabilities   The amounts of income taxes payable in future periods in respect of temporary differences.

Depreciable amount   The cost of an asset, or other amount substituted for cost in the financial statements, less its residual value.

Depreciation   The systematic allocation of the DEPRECIABLE AMOUNT of an asset over its useful life. Annual depreciation can be determined using the straight-line method or the diminishing-balance method or the sum-of-the-units method.

Deprival value   The amount by which a business would be worse off if it were deprived of a particular asset. This is sometimes referred to as its 'value to the business' or 'value to the owner'.

Derivative   Financial instrument, such as financial options, futures and forwards, interest rate swaps and currency swaps, which create rights and obligations that have the effect of transferring between the parties to the instrument one or more of the financial risks inherent in an underlying primary financial instrument. Derivative instruments do not result in a transfer of the underlying primary financial instrument on inception of the contract and such a transfer does not necessarily take place on maturity of the contract.

Development   The application of research findings or other knowledge to a plan or design for the production of new or substantially improved materials, devices, products, processes, systems or services prior to the commencement of commercial production or use.

Diluted earnings per share   The amount of net profit for the period that is attributable to ordinary shareholders divided by the weighted average number of ordinary shares outstanding during the period, both adjusted for the effects of all DILUTIVE POTENTIAL ORDINARY SHARES.

Dilutive potential ordinary shares   Potential ordinary shares whose conversion to ordinary shares would decrease net profit per share from continuing ordinary operations or increase loss per share from continuing ordinary operations.

Direct method of reporting cash flows from operating activities   A method which analyses major classes of gross cash receipts and gross cash payments.

Discontinued/discontinuing operation   A component of an enterprise:

(a) that the enterprise, pursuant to a single plan, is:
   (i)   disposing of substantially or in its entirety, such as by selling the component in a single transaction, by demerger or spin-off of ownership of the component to the enterprise's shareholders;
   (ii) disposing of piecemeal, such as by selling off the component's assets and settling its liabilities individually; or
   (iii) terminating through abandonment;
(b) that represents a separate major line of business or geographical area of operations; and
(c) that can be distinguished operationally and for financial reporting purposes.

Distributable profits and reserves   Usually covers the year's profit as well as any undistributed profit from previous years which is available for distribution to shareholders as DIVIDENDS.

Dividend cover   Number of times the most recent annual dividend could have been paid out of the most recent PROFIT which indicates how secure future dividend payments are.

Dividend yield   Indication of the potential cash return on buying shares calculated by dividing the most recent total annual dividend per share by the market price.

Dividends   PROFIT after tax paid out to the shareholders (usually in the form of a half yearly or annual payment).

The company directors decide how much profit will be paid out as dividends, if any, and how much will be retained in the business to help finance future operations.

Double-entry   Describes the routine recording of two aspects, DEBIT and CREDIT, of monetary transactions of a business in ACCOUNTS kept in LEDGERS. Each transaction will result in both a credit and a debit entry. The credit entry effectively represents the source of financing, while the debit entry represents how that finance has been used. This method will ensure that the business's assets always equal its liabilities. This is essential if the business wishes to have its balance sheet balance.

The system was devised in Italy in the Middle Ages.

Earnings   Amount of PROFIT available to the ordinary shareholders, i.e. the profit after all operating expenses, interest charges, taxes and dividends on PREFERRED/PREFERENCE STOCK.

Earnings per share (EPS)   EARNINGS of the most recent year divided by the WEIGHTED AVERAGE NUMBER OF ORDINARY SHARES OUTSTANDING DURING THE PERIOD.

Earnings yield   EARNINGS PER SHARE divided by the market price of the shares.

EBIT   EARNINGS before interest and tax.

EBITDA   EARNINGS before interest, tax, DEPRECIATION and AMORTISATION.

Economic life   The period over which an asset is expected to be economically usable by one or more users or the number of production or similar units expected to be obtained from the asset by one or more users.

Employee benefits   All forms of consideration given by an enterprise in exchange for service rendered by employees.

EPS   *See* EARNINGS PER SHARE.

Equity   Generally refers to a proprietor's share in a business. Short for STOCKHOLDERS' EQUITY in the US.

See SHAREHOLDERS' FUNDS.

Equity method   A method used as part of the preparation of CONSOLIDATED FINANCIAL STATEMENTS, for the accounting of ASSOCIATED COMPANIES.

Events after the balance sheet date   Events, both favourable and unfavourable, that occur between the balance sheet date and the date when the financial statements are authorised for issue. Two types of events can be identified:

(a) those that provide evidence of conditions that existed at the balance sheet date (adjusting events after the balance sheet date); and

(b) those that are indicative of conditions that arose after the balance sheet date but before the issue of the financial statements (non-adjusting events after the balance sheet date).

Exchange difference   The difference resulting from reporting the same number of units of a foreign currency in the reporting currency at different exchange rates.

Exchange rate   The ratio for exchange of two currencies.

Expenses   Decreases in economic benefits during the accounting period in the form of outflows or depletions of assets or incurrences of liabilities that result in decreases in equity, other that those relating to distributions to equity participants.

Exposure drafts   Documents preceding the issue of ACCOUNTING STANDARDS to which companies, auditors, academics, financial analysts and so forth respond.

Extraordinary general meeting   A general meeting of a company held for an unusual event, such as dealing with a takeover. Normally the shareholders meet at the ANNUAL GENERAL MEETING.

Fair value   The amount for which an asset could be exchanged, or a liability settled, between knowledgeable, willing parties in an arm's length transaction.

FASB   *See* FINANCIAL ACCOUNTING STANDARDS BOARD.

Fédération des Experts Comptables Européens (FEE)   A Brussels-based body of European professional accountancy institutes.

FEE   *See* FÉDÉRATION DES EXPERTS COMPTABLES EUROPÉENS.

FIFO   *See* FIRST-IN, FIRST-OUT.

Finance lease   A capital lease, i.e. a LEASE treated as if the lessee had borrowed money and bought the leased ASSETS.

A lease that transfers substantially all risks and rewards incident to ownership of an asset. Title may or may not eventually be transferred.

Financial Accounting Standards Board (FASB)   The US non-governmental body set up in 1973 to lay down ACCOUNTING STANDARDS for the measurement, valuation and disclosure practices to be complied with when preparing financial statements. FASB replaced Accounting Principles Board (APB).

Financial asset   Any asset that is:

(a) cash;
(b) a contractual right to receive cash or another financial asset from another enterprise;
(c) a contractual right to exchange financial instruments with another enterprise under conditions that are potentially favourable; or
(d) an equity instrument of another enterprise.

Financial instruments   Any contract that gives rise to both a financial asset of one enterprise and a financial liability or equity instrument of another enterprise.

Financial liability   Any liability that is a contractual obligation:

(a) to deliver cash or another financial asset to another enterprise; or
(b) to exchange financial instruments with another enterprise under conditions that are potentially unfavourable.

Financial position   The relationship of the assets, liabilities, and equities of an enterprise, as reported in the balance sheet.

Financial reporting standards (FRS)   The UK accounting standards issued by the Accounting Standard Board since 1990.

Financial statements   A financial statement is a quantitative description of the business's current financial position. A complete set of financial statements includes the following components:

(a) balance sheet;
(b) income statement;
(c) a statement showing either:
    (i)   all changes in equity; or
    (ii) changes in equity other than those arising from capital transactions with owners and distributions to owners;
(d) cash flow statement; and
(e) accounting policies and explanatory notes.

Financial year   Period for which FINANCIAL STATEMENTS or ACCOUNTS are prepared in UK terminology. Also known in the US as FISCAL YEAR.

Financing activities   Activities that result in changes in the size and composition of the equity capital and borrowings of the enterprise.

First-in, first-out (FIFO)   The assumption that the items of inventory which were purchased first are sold first, and consequently the items remaining in inventory at the end of the period are those most recently purchased or produced.

Fiscal year   US term for the period for which a company prepares FINANCIAL STATEMENTS. The date commonly selected is 31 December as it coincides with the year end for tax purposes. See FINANCIAL YEAR.

Fixed assets   Tangible assets intended for a continuous use in the enterprise, such as plant and machinery, buildings, furniture and fixture, subject to depreciation. Under US terminology, these are called 'property, plant and equipment'.

Fixed costs   Fixed costs incorporate all business costs, which do not change, regardless of the volume of production or sale. Typically, fixed costs can be related to overheads, such as the rent of the premises, lease payments on equipment, or other predictable costs which remain static.

Foreign currency   A currency other than the reporting currency of an enterprise.

Foreign currency transaction   A transaction which is denominated in or requires settlement in a foreign currency.

Foreign currency translation (*See* CURRENCY TRANSLATION)   Accounting operation whereby the financial statements of a foreign SUBSIDIARY are 'translated' into the currency of the parent company (reporting currency) to facilitate the preparation of CONSOLIDATED FINANCIAL STATEMENTS.

Foreign entity   A foreign operation, the activities of which are not an integral part of those of the reporting enterprise.

Foreign operation   A subsidiary, associate, joint venture or branch of the reporting enterprise, the activities of which are based or conducted in a country other than the country of the reporting enterprise.

FRS   *See* FINANCIAL REPORTING STANDARDS.

Fundamental errors   Errors discovered in the current period that are of such significance that the financial statements of one or more prior periods can no longer be considered to have been reliable at the date of their issue.

Future economic benefit   The potential to contribute, directly or indirectly, to the flow of cash and cash equivalents to the enterprise. The potential may be a productive one that is part of the operating activities of the enterprise. It may also take the form of convertibility into cash or cash equivalents or a capability to reduce cash outflows, such as when an alternative manufacturing process lowers the costs of production.

GAAP   *See* GENERALLY ACCEPTED ACCOUNTING PRINCIPLES.

Gearing   A measurement of the degree to which a business is funded by loans rather than SHAREHOLDERS' EQUITY. The US expression is LEVERAGE.

General price level adjusted accounting (GPLA)   A US term for a system of adjusting historical cost accounting by price indices to account for inflation. See GENERAL PURCHASING POWER APPROACH.

General purchasing power approach   The restatement of some or all of the items in the financial statements for changes in the general price level.

Generally accepted accounting principles (GAAP)   Mainly US technical term encompassing the Accounting standards of the Financial Accounting Standards Board and rules of the predecessor bodies. The SEC requires companies registered with it to comply with GAAP when preparing their financial statements.

Generally accepted auditing standards   Rules to be followed by auditors when carrying out an audit of financial statements.

Geographical segments   A distinguishable component of an enterprise that is engaged in providing products or services within a particular economic environment and that is subject to risks and returns that are different from those of components operating in other economic environments.

Going concern   The enterprise is normally viewed as a going concern, that is, as continuing in operation for the foreseeable future. It is assumed that the enterprise has neither the intention nor the necessity of liquidation or of curtailing materially the scale of its operations.

Goodwill   The amount paid for a business above the Fair value of its Net assets upon Acquisition. This means that there is a premium in terms of its value compared with the business's existing and identifiable assets and liabilities. It can represent various things such as customer loyalty, knowledgeable and skilled management or its ability to earn more profit than similar newly-formed businesses.

Government grants   Assistance by government in the form of transfer of resources to an enterprise in return for past or future compliance with certain conditions relating to the operating activities of the enterprise. They exclude those forms of government assistance which cannot reasonably have a value placed upon them and transactions with government which cannot be distinguished from the normal trading transactions of the enterprise.

GPLA   *See* General price level adjusted accounting.

Gross profit   The difference between the value of sales and the related Cost of sales.

Group   A Parent and all its Subsidiaries.

Group accounts   The financial statements of a group of companies, i.e. of a parent company and its subsidiaries. UK expression for Consolidated financial statements.

Hedging   Designing one or more Hedging instruments so that their change in fair value is an offset, in whole or in part to the change in fair value or cash flows of a hedged item.

Hedging instrument   A designed derivative or (in limited circumstances) another financial asset or liability whose fair value or cash flows are expected to offset changes in the fair value or cash flows of a designed hedged item. A non-derivative financial asset or liability may be designated as a hedging instrument for hedge accounting purposes only if it hedges the risk of changes in foreign currency exchange rates.

Historical cost   Assets are recorded at the amount of cash or cash equivalents paid or the fair value of the consideration given to acquire them at the time of their acquisition. Liabilities are recorded at the amount of proceeds received in exchange for the obligation, or in some circumstances (for example, income taxes), at the amounts of cash or cash equivalents expected to be paid to satisfy the liabilities in the normal course of business.

Historical cost accounting Conventional accounting system widely established throughout the world except in some countries where inflation is endemic and high. Even in the latter countries, the GENERAL PURCHASING POWER APPROACH is a set of simple adjustments carried out annually from historical cost records.

Holding company Company that owns or controls other companies, that does not itself actively trade but operates via its subsidiaries. CONSOLIDATED FINANCIAL STATEMENTS are required for the group. Holding company is also known as PARENT Company.

Hyperinflation Loss of purchasing power of money at such a rate that comparison of amounts from transactions and other events that have occurred at different times, even within the same accounting period, is misleading.

IASB *See* INTERNATIONAL ACCOUNTING STANDARDS BOARD.

IASC *See* INTERNATIONAL ACCOUNTING STANDARDS COMMITTEE.

Impairment The loss of value of an ASSET below its book value (i.e. generally its depreciated cost). This is measured by comparing the book value with the RECOVERABLE AMOUNT.

Impairment loss The amount by which the carrying amount of an asset exceeds its recoverable amount.

Income Increases in economic benefits during the accounting period in the form of inflows or enhancements of assets or decreases of liabilities that result in increases in equity, other than those relating to contributions from equity participants.

Income statement The statement of revenues and expenses of a particular period, leading to the calculation of net income or net profit. The equivalent UK statement is the PROFIT AND LOSS ACCOUNT.

Indirect method of reporting cash flows from operating activities Under this method, net profit or loss is adjusted for the effects of transactions of a non-cash nature, any deferrals or accruals of past or future operating cash receipts or payments, and items of income or expense associated with investing or financing cash flows.

Inflation accounting Inflation accounting aims to provide financial comparisons over a period of time in which the value of money has changed, because of inflation.

Intangible assets ASSETS, such as goodwill, patents, brand names, trademarks, copyrights and franchises, that are not physical or tangible.

Interest rate risk A price risk – the risk that the value of a financial instrument will fluctuate due to changes in market interest rates.

Interim financial report A financial report containing either a complete set of financial statements or a set of condensed financial statements for an interim period.

Interim period A financial reporting period shorter than a full financial year.

International Accounting Standards Board (IASB) An independent, privately-funded accounting standard-setter based in London, UK. The IASB is committed to developing, in the public interest, a single set of high quality, understandable and enforceable global accounting standards that require transparent and comparable information in general purpose financial statements. In addition, the IASB co-operates with national accounting standard-setters to achieve convergence in accounting standards around the world.

International Accounting Standards Committee (IASC)   IASC was founded in June 1973 as a result of an agreement by accountancy bodies in Australia, Canada, France, Germany, Japan, Mexico, the Netherlands, the United Kingdom and Ireland and the United States, and these countries constituted the Board of IASC at that time. It operated from 1973 until 2001, when it was substituted by the IASB.

International Organisation of Securities Commissions (IOSCO)   An international body of governmental regulators of stock exchanges.

Inventories   ASSETS:

(a) held for sale in the ordinary course of business;
(b) in the process of production for such sale; or
(c) in the form of materials or supplies to be consumed in the production process or in the rendering of services.

Inventories encompass goods purchased and held for resale including, for example, merchandise purchased by a retailer and held for resale, or land and other property held for resale. Inventories also encompass finished goods produced, or work in progress being produced by the enterprise and include materials and supplies awaiting use in the production process.

In the UK, the word 'stock' is generally used instead of inventory.

Investing activities   The acquisition and disposal of long-term assets and other investments not included in cash equivalents.

Investment property   Property (land or building – or part of a building – or both) held (by the owner or by the lessee under a finance lease) to earn rentals or for capital appreciation or both, rather than for:

(a) use in the production or supply of goods or services or for administrative purposes; or
(b) sale in the ordinary course of business.

Properties held by a business for investment or rental income rather than for owner-occupation.

Investment securities   Securities acquired and held for yield or capital growth purposes, usually held to maturity.

IOSCO   *See* INTERNATIONAL ORGANISATION OF SECURITIES COMMISSIONS.

Issued share capital   The amount of share capital of a company, at NOMINAL VALUE that has been issued to the shareholders.

Joint control   The contractually agreed sharing of control over an economic activity.

Joint venture   A contractual arrangement whereby two or more parties undertake an economic activity which is subject to joint control.

Jointly controlled entity   A joint venture which involves the establishment of a corporation, partnership or other entity in which each venturer has an interest. The entity operates in the same way as other enterprises, except that a contractual arrangement between the venturers establishes joint control over the economic activity of the entity.

Key Performance Indicators (KPI)   Metrics that a company's managers have identified as the most important variables reflecting mission success or organisational performance.

KPI   *See* KEY PERFORMANCE INDICATORS

Last-in, first-out (LIFO)   The assumption that the items of inventory which were purchased or produced last are sold first, and consequently the items remaining in inventory at the end of the period are those first purchased or produced. This method is not allowed by IASs/IFRSs.

Lease   An agreement whereby one party (the lessor) conveys to another party (the lessee) in return for a payment or series of payments the right to use an asset for an agreed period of time.

Ledger   A ledger is a group of accounts. In a manual system, it may be a bound book with the title 'general ledger' printed on the cover. Inside are one (or more) pages for each account. All the accounts of a small enterprise could be maintained in such a book. It may also consist of a set of loose-leaf pages, or, with, computers, as a set of impulses on a magnetic disc or tape.

Legal merger   Usually a merger between two companies in which either:

(a) the assets and liabilities of one company are transferred to the other company and the first company is dissolved; or

(b) the assets and liabilities of both companies are transferred to a new company and both the original companies are dissolved.

Legal obligation   An obligation that derives from:

(a) a contract (through its explicit or implicit terms);

(b) legislation; or

(c) other operation of law.

Legal reserve   Requirement in some countries (France, Germany, Italy, but not the US or the UK) to set up Undistributable reserves out of profit in order to protect Creditors.

Leverage   US term for Gearing.

Liability   A present obligation of the enterprise arising from past events, the settlement of which is expected to result in an outflow from the enterprise of resources embodying economic benefits (usually cash). They include long-term loans, bank overdrafts and amounts owed to suppliers. There are current and non-current liabilities.

LIFO   *See* Last-in, first-out.

Liquidity   The availability of sufficient funds to meet deposit withdrawals and other financial commitments as they fall due.

Liquidity risk   The risk that an enterprise will encounter difficulty in raising funds to meet commitments associated with financial instruments. Liquidity risk may result from an inability to sell a financial asset quickly at close to its fair value.

Listed company   A Company whose shares are listed or quoted on an official Stock exchange.

Losses   Decreases in economic benefits and as such they are no different in nature from other expenses.

Lower of cost and net realisable value (NRV)   Rule for the valuation of Current assets, particularly Inventories. In conventional accounting cost means the historical purchase price of the inventory, plus the costs of work done on it. NRV is what inventory could be sold for in the normal course of business when ready for sale (market value less any expected costs involved in finishing and selling it).

Market risk The risk that the value of a financial instrument will fluctuate as a result of changes in market prices whether those changes are caused by factors specific to the individual security or its issuer or factors affecting all securities traded in the market.

Market value The amount obtainable from the sale, or payable on the acquisition, of a financial instrument in an active market.

Marking to market Accounting for investments or commodities by constantly updating their values to the current market value in the BALANCE SHEET and taking any resulting gains or LOSSES to INCOME immediately.

Matching of costs with revenues Expenses are recognised in the INCOME STATEMENT on the basis of a direct association between the costs incurred and the earning of specific items of income. This process involves the simultaneous or combined recognition of revenues and expenses that result directly and jointly from the same transactions or other events.

Materiality Information is material if its non-disclosure could influence the economic decisions of users taken on the basis of the financial statements.

Measurement The process of determining the monetary amounts at which the elements of the financial statements are to be recognised and carried in the balance sheet and income statement.

Memorandum of association A legal document drawn up as part of the registration of a company. It includes a record of the company's name, its registered office, its purpose and its AUTHORISED SHARE CAPITAL.

Merger accounting A method of accounting for a business combination. In US terminology it is known as pooling of interests. The IFRS equivalent term is UNITING OF INTERESTS.

Minority interest That part of the net results of operations and of net assets of a subsidiary attributable to interests which are not owned, directly or indirectly through subsidiaries, by the parent.

Monetary items (monetary assets; monetary financial assets and financial liabilities; monetary financial instruments) Money held and assets (financial assets) and liabilities (financial liabilities) to be received or paid in fixed or determinable amounts of money.

Money measurement convention Financial statements include only those items that can be measured in monetary terms with reasonable OBJECTIVITY. Thus the value (to the enterprise) of skilled management or of loyal staff or customers, is not normally shown in financial statements. This is because it is virtually impossible to measure reliably its worth in money terms. This convention is linked to the use of HISTORICAL COST ACCOUNTING, where ASSETS are measured at their purchase price or production cost.

NBV *See* NET BOOK VALUE.

Negative goodwill Any (remaining) excess, as at the date of the acquisition of an enterprise, of the acquirer's interest in the fair values of the identifiable assets and liabilities acquired over the cost of the acquisition.

Net assets The worth of an enterprise in accounting terms as measured or represented by its BALANCE SHEET. It is the total of all the recorded ASSETS less the LIABILITIES that are owed to outsiders. The net assets equal the owners' equity.

Net book value (NBV)   The net amount at which an asset is stated in the BALANCE SHEET of an enterprise.

Net current assets   The net current assets or (accounting) working capital of an enterprise is the excess of the current assets (such as cash, inventories and accounts receivable) over the current liabilities (such as accounts payable and overdrafts).

Net income   *See* NET PROFIT OR LOSS.

Net investment in a foreign entity   The reporting enterprise's share in the net assets of that entity.

Net present value (NPV)   A current estimate of the present discounted value of the future net cash flows in the normal course of business.

Net realisable value (NRV)   Usually represents the current selling price of the assets, net of the estimated costs of completion and selling costs.

Net selling price   The amount obtainable from the sale of an asset in an arm's length transaction between knowledgeable willing parties.

Net worth   *See* NET ASSETS.

Neutrality   Freedom from bias of the information contained in financial statements.

Nominal value   Most shares (and bonds) have a nominal or par value. When a company issues new shares the share capital is recorded at nominal value, any excess being recorded as SHARE PREMIUM.

Non-adjusting events after the balance sheet date   *See* EVENTS AFTER THE BALANCE SHEET DATE.

Non-profit   The description applied to an organisation whose main aims are not commercial; for example, a university or a charity. Depending on the legal structure of such bodies, they may not be subject to normal accounting rules.

NPV   *See* NET PRESENT VALUE.

NRV   *See* NET REALISABLE VALUE and LOWER OF COST AND NET REALISABLE VALUE.

Objectivity   An accounting measurement is said to be objective if it is reasonably independent of the judgement of management. There is a trade-off between objectivity and relevance. For example, today the price of a building acquired ten years ago is objective but may be irrelevant from the point of view of the current value of that building today or for a decision about what to do with it.

Obligation   A duty or responsibility to act or perform in a certain way. Obligations may be legally enforceable as a consequence of a binding contract or statutory requirement. Obligations also arise, however, from normal business practice, custom and a desire to maintain good business relations or act in an equitable manner.

Offsetting   *See* SET-OFF, LEGAL RIGHT OF.

Onerous contract   A contract in which the unavoidable costs of meeting the obligations under the contract exceed the economic benefits expected to be received under it.

Operating activities   The principal revenue-producing activities of an enterprise and other activities that are not investing or financing activities.

Operating and financial review   A statement included in the Company's ANNUAL REPORT which examines and explains important features of the company's financial results. The US equivalent is 'management discussion and analysis'.

Operating cycle   The time between the acquisition of materials entering into a process and its realisation in cash or an instrument that is readily convertible into cash.

Operating lease   A lease other than a finance lease.

Operating profit   *See* EBIT.

Option   A financial instrument that gives the holder the right to purchase ordinary shares.

Ordinary activities   Any activities which are undertaken by an enterprise as part of its business.

Ordinary share   An equity instrument that is subordinate to all other classes of equity instruments. The normal type of shares is called COMMON STOCK in the US. They can be distinguished from PREFERENCE SHARES.

Own shares   *See* TREASURY STOCK and TREASURY SHARES.

Pacioli, Luca   A Franciscan monk widely attributed as the inventor of double-entry bookkeeping. In 1494, Pacioli documented the double-entry system practised at the time by merchants in Venice in his famous book *Summa de arithmetica, geometria, proportioni et proportionalita* (The Collected Knowledge of Arithmetic, Geometry, Proportion and Proportionality). The section of the book which made him famous was *Particularis de Computis et Scripturis*, a treatise on accounting. *De Scripturis* has been described as 'a catalyst that launched the past into the future'.

Paid-in surplus   US expression for SHARE PREMIUM.

Parent   An enterprise or HOLDING COMPANY that has one or more SUBSIDIARIES.

Partnership   A business arrangement whereby two or more persons (individuals) pool their capital and skills, and share the risks and profits. Normally, most or all of the partners are directly involved in the management of the business. Partners are jointly and severally liable (they do not normally have limited liability) for the debts of the enterprise. In the US and UK (except Scotland), partnerships are not legal entities. In continental Europe there are several different forms of partnerships and many do have a legal personality.

Pay-back period   A widely used technique for appraising the likely success of investment projects. It involves an analysis of the expected future net cash inflows, followed by a calculation of how many years it will take for the original capital investment to be recovered. It is simple to use and, perhaps more importantly, simple to explain to non-financial managers.

P/E ratio   *See* PRICE/EARNINGS RATIO.

Pension fund   ASSETS set aside for the eventual payment of the pension obligation.

Percentage of completion method   A method by which contract revenue is matched with the contract costs incurred at each stage of completion, resulting in the reporting of revenue, expenses and profit which can be attributed to the proportion of work completed. The objective of the method is to account for profits or losses as they are earned or incurred. This is opposite to the completed contract method under which the profit or loss is only accounted for at the time of completion of the contract.

Performance   The relationship of the income and expenses of an enterprise, as reported in the income statement.

Post balance sheet events   *See* EVENTS AFTER THE BALANCE SHEET DATE.

Post-employment benefit plans   Formal or informal arrangements under which an enterprise provides post-employment benefits for one or more employees.

Pre-acquisition profits Profits of a Subsidiary earned before the subsidiary was purchased by its present Parent company. Thus undistributed pre-acquisition profits are not accounted for as reserves of that group in Consolidated financial statements, but as an element of the cost of the investment in the subsidiary.

Preference shares Preference shares pay a fixed dividend, and compared with ordinary shares they offer greater security to the investor, as they are repayable in full before any distribution to ordinary shareholders. Unlike ordinary shares, however, preference shares do not normally have voting rights. Preferred stock is the US term for preference shares.

Preliminary expenses Expenses relating to the setting up of a company (i.e. those relating to the issue of shares or preparation of legal documents, etc.). Preliminary expense is a UK term; the US term is start-up costs.

Prepayments Amounts recorded in a Balance sheet (generally in the Current assets section) which represent payments made in advance with respect to expenses relating to a subsequent period (for example, rent or insurance premiums). The parallel accounting treatment for expenses paid in arrears gives rise to Accrued expenses in the balance sheet.

Price/earnings ratio (P/E ratio) This ratio compares the market price of an Ordinary share with the earnings per share of that company, based on the most recently available year's Profit after interest, tax, Minority interest and preference dividend.

Price risk There are three types of price risk: currency risk, interest rate risk and market risk. The term 'price risk' embodies not only the potential for loss but also the potential for gain in terms of price.

Prior-year adjustment This arises when a business discovers an error of material size in its financial statements of previous years, or if there is a change in accounting policies.

Private company Company which is not allowed to sell its shares or loan stock on an open market. *See* Private limited company.

Private limited company A company that is not allowed to create a market in its securities. It should be distinguished from Public limited company. In most countries where this distinction exists, private companies are much more numerous than public companies. Rules for disclosures, audit, profit distribution, etc., are normally less onerous for private companies.

Profit The residual amount that remains after all expenses (including capital maintenance adjustments, where appropriate) have been deducted from income.

Profit and loss account *See* Income statement.

Property, plant and equipment Tangible assets that:

(a) are held by an enterprise for use in the production or supply of goods or services, for rental to others, or for administrative purposes; and
(b) are expected to be used during more than one period.

Proportional consolidation *See* Proportionate consolidation.

Proportionate consolidation A method of accounting and reporting whereby a venturer's share of each of the assets, liabilities, income and expenses of a jointly controlled entity is combined on a line-by-line basis with similar items in the venturer's financial statements or reported as separate line items in the venturer's financial statements.

Provision   A liability which represents uncertain timing or amount. The term is also used in the United States to mean an ALLOWANCE against the value of an asset. *See* RESERVE.

Prudence   The inclusion of a degree of caution in the exercise of the judgements needed in making the estimates required under conditions of uncertainty, such that assets or income are not overstated and liabilities or expenses are not understated.

In the US, CONSERVATISM is the word generally used for this concept.

Public company   *See* PUBLIC LIMITED COMPANY.

Public limited company   A company whose SECURITIES may legally be publicly traded. In the US it is a corporation that is registered with the SECURITIES AND EXCHANGE COMMISSION. Often, the expression PUBLIC COMPANY is used loosely to mean companies whose shares are traded on a stock exchange.

Purchase accounting   US term for the normal method of BUSINESS COMBINATION.

Qualified audit report   Report which states that the financial statements give a True and Fair View except for certain qualifying remarks. The qualifications may concern the under- or overstatement of profit (loss) and assets or liabilities, infringement of company law or accounting standards. *See* AUDIT REPORT.

Quarterly report   Unaudited document, reporting the financial results for the quarter and noting any significant changes or events in the quarter. Quarterly reports contain financial statements, a discussion from the management, and a list of 'material events' that have occurred with the company (such as a stock split or acquisition).

Quick ratio   Measure of a company's liquidity. It compares CURRENT ASSETS (net of INVENTORY) to CURRENT LIABILITIES. An alternative measure comparing all Current Assets to all Current Liabilities is called the CURRENT RATIO.

Quoted company   An alternative expression for a LISTED COMPANY.

R&D   *See* RESEARCH AND DEVELOPMENT.

Rate of return   Measure of the profitability of a business or an investment. It normally compares Profit of the business or on investment with the amount of Capital invested in it.

Ratios   A ratio expresses a relation between two items appearing in the financial statements. A ratio value in isolation tells us little. To get an objective view of a situation we should use numerous ratios and must apply appropriate benchmarks. These benchmarks can be derived from various sources, such as historical data, competitors' accounts and published data of all kinds. It is the trend over time rather than the absolute number that gives the most valuable information.

Realisable value   The amount of cash or cash equivalents that could currently be obtained by selling an asset in an orderly disposal.

Receivables   The IFRS and US expression for amounts of money due to an enterprise. It is often known as Trade and other receivables or as ACCOUNTS RECEIVABLE. The UK term is DEBTORS.

Recognition   The process of incorporating (recording) in the BALANCE SHEET or INCOME STATEMENT an item that meets the definition of an element and satisfies the following criteria for recognition:

(a) it is probable that any future economic benefit associated with the item will flow to or from the enterprise; and

(b) the item has a cost or value that can be measured reliably.

Recoverable amount The higher of an asset's net realisable value and its value in use.

Related parties Parties are considered to be related if one party has the ability to control the other party or exercise significant influence over the other party in making financial and operating decisions.

Related party transaction A transfer of resources or obligations between RELATED PARTIES, regardless of whether a price is charged.

Relevance Information has the quality of relevance when it influences the economic decisions of users by helping them evaluate past, present or future events or confirming, or correcting, their past evaluations.

Reliability Information has the quality of reliability when it is free from material error and bias and can be depended upon by users to represent faithfully that which it either purports to represent or could reasonably be expected to represent.

Replacement cost accounting A system of preparing financial statements in which all ASSETS (and expenses relating to them, such as DEPRECIATION) are valued at current Replacement Costs (the amount a business would have to pay in order to replace an asset).

Replacement cost of an asset Represents the current acquisition cost of a similar asset, new or used, or of an equivalent productive capacity or service potential.

Reportable segment A BUSINESS SEGMENT or a GEOGRAPHICAL SEGMENT for which segment information is required to be disclosed under IFRS or equivalent accounting standards.

Reporting currency The currency used in presenting the financial statements.

Reporting enterprise An enterprise for which there are users who rely on the financial statements as their major source of financial information about the enterprise.

Research Original and planned investigation undertaken with the prospect of gaining new scientific or technical knowledge and understanding.

Research and development (R&D) Examples of research activities are:

(a) activities aimed at obtaining new knowledge;
(b) the search for, evaluation and final selection of, applications of research findings or other knowledge;
(c) the search for alternatives for materials, devices, products, processes, systems or services; and
(d) the formulation, design, evaluation and final selection of possible alternatives for new or improved materials, devices, products, processes, systems or services.

According to IAS 38, expenditure on research should be recognised as an expense when it is incurred. No CAPITALISATION is permitted.

Examples of development activities are:

(a) the design, construction and testing of pre-production or pre-use prototypes and models;
(b) the design of tools involving new technologies
(c) the design, construction and testing of a chosen alternative for new or improved materials, devices, products, processes, systems or services.

According to IAS 38, expenditure relating to development activities can be capitalised as intangible assets under certain conditions.

Reserve   An amount voluntarily or compulsorily set aside out of profit. In the case of voluntary allocation profits are retained in the enterprise for growth; whereas in the case of compulsory allocation profits are retained to protect generally the interests of the creditors.

Residual value   The net amount which an enterprise expects to obtain for an asset at the end of its useful life after deducting the expected costs of disposal.

Restricted surplus   US expression for amounts of retained earnings or profit that are unavailable for distribution to shareholders. *See* UNDISTRIBUTABLE RESERVES.

Retained earnings   US expression for RETAINED PROFIT. *See* RESERVE.

Retained profit   Amount of profit, earned in the current and prior years, that have not yet been paid out as DIVIDENDS, but retained in the enteprise. RETAINED EARNINGS is a typical US expression for such amounts.

Retirement benefit plans   Arrangements whereby an enterprise provides benefits for its employees on or after termination of service (either in the form of an annual income or as a lump sum) when such benefits, or the employer's contributions towards them, can be determined or estimated in advance of retirement from the provision of a document or from the enterprise's practices. *See also* POST-EMPLOYMENT BENEFIT PLANS.

Return on capital employed (ROCE)   EBIT divided by CAPITAL EMPLOYED.

Return on equity (ROE)   NET PROFIT divided by EQUITY.

Revalued amount of an asset   The fair value of an asset at the date of a revaluation less any subsequent accumulated depreciation.

Revenue   The gross inflow of economic benefits during a period arising in the course of the ordinary activities of an enterprise when those inflows result in an increase in equity, other than increases relating to contributions from equity participants.

Revenue reserve   UK expression for RETAINED PROFIT.

Rights issue   The sale of additional Shares by a company to its existing shareholders usually at a discount on market prices. The rights to buy the shares are given to the existing shareholders in proportion to their shareholdings. Rights issues should be distinguished from BONUS SHARES where no money is paid to the company, but where existing shareholders receive shares for 'free' in proportion to their share-holdings and the profits so 'distributed' are relabelled as share capital.

ROCE   *See* RETURN ON CAPITAL EMPLOYED.

ROE   *See* RETURN ON EQUITY.

Sale-and-leaseback transactions   The sale of an asset by a vendor and the leasing of the same asset back to the vendor. The rentals and the sale price are usually interdependent.

SEC   *See* SECURITIES AND EXCHANGE COMMISSION.

Securities and Exchange Commission (SEC)   The US government agency set up in 1934 after the Wall Street Crash of 1929. Its function is to control the issue and exchange of publicly traded shares, with the aim to protect US investors against malpractice in the securities market. Listed companies are required to register with the SEC, and then comply with a mass of detailed regulations.

Security   An instrument representing ownership (shares), a debt agreement (BONDS), or the rights to ownership (DERIVATIVES).

Segmental reporting   The disclosure of Sales, PROFIT or ASSETS by line of business or by geographical area. *See also* GEOGRAPHICAL SEGMENT and REPORTABLE SEGMENT.

Set-off, legal right of   A DEBTOR's legal right, by contract or otherwise, to settle or eliminate all or a portion of an amount due to a CREDITOR by applying against that amount a RECEIVABLE from the same creditor.

Share premium   Amounts received by a company in excess of the Nominal Value of the shares from the shareholders on purchase of shares from the company.

Shareholders' equity

1. The total of the shareholders' interest in a company. This will at a given date include the share capital, amounts contributed in excess of the Par Value of shares (i.e. SHARE PREMIUM or PAID-IN SURPLUS), and retained profits.
2. The difference between Total Assets and Total Liabilities.

Shareholders' funds   *See* SHAREHOLDERS' EQUITY.

SIC   *See* STANDING INTERPRETATIONS COMMITTEE.

Significant influence   The power to participate in the financial and operating policy decisions of an economic activity but not control or joint control over those policies. According to IFRSs, this is presumed to exist when an investor has a 20 per cent or more interest in the enterprise. See ASSOCIATED COMPANY.

Solvency   The availability of cash and cash equivalents on a continuous basis to meet financial commitments as they fall due.

Standing Interpretations Committee (SIC)   Set up in 1997 by the INTERNATIONAL ACCOUNTING STANDARDS COMMITTEE (now IASB) to publish interpretations of international accounting standards.

Statement of total recognised gains and losses   A financial statement required from the UK companies since 1993. It includes gains and losses that are not recorded in the PROFIT AND LOSS ACCOUNT, such as those on FOREIGN CURRENCY TRANSLATION and on the revaluation of fixed assets.

Stock exchange   An organised market for the issue of new securities and the exchange of existing securities. Companies whose shares may be sold on such exchanges are called LISTED or QUOTED COMPANIES. In addition to accounting regulations, listed companies are required to comply with the listing requirements of their particular stock exchange.

Stockholders' equity   *See* SHAREHOLDERS' EQUITY.

Straight-line depreciation   A method of calculating the annual DEPRECIATION charge for a FIXED ASSET. Under this method, annual depreciation charge equals the cost of the asset less any estimated residual value divided by the number of years of useful life.

Subsidiary   An enterprise that is controlled by another enterprise (known as the PARENT). Control is presumed when an enterprise has a more than 50 per cent interest in another enterprise.

Substance over form   The principle that transactions and other events are accounted for and presented in accordance with their substance and economic reality and not merely their legal form.

T-account   *See* ACCOUNTS.

Tangible assets   Assets having a physical existence, such as PROPERTY, PLANT AND EQUIPMENT.

Tax base of an asset or liability   The amount attributed to that asset or liability for tax purposes.

Tax expense (tax income)   The aggregate amount included in the determination of net profit or loss for the period in respect of current tax and deferred tax. Tax expense (tax income) comprises current tax expense (current tax income) and deferred tax expense (deferred tax income).

Taxable profit (tax loss)   The profit (loss) for a period, determined in accordance with the rules established by tax authorities, upon which income taxes are payable (recoverable).

Temporary difference   A difference between the carrying value of an asset or liability in the balance sheet and its tax base.

Termination benefits   Employee benefits payable as a result of either:

(a) an enterprise's decision to terminate an employee's employment before the normal retirement date; or
(b) an employee's decision to accept voluntary redundancy in exchange for those benefits.

Trade and other payables   Suppliers of goods or services to the business who are not paid immediately at the time of purchase. At a BALANCE SHEET date, outstanding amounts owed to them are shown as Trade and other paybles as part of CURRENT LIABILITIES. 'Trade creditors' is a UK term. The equivalent US expression is ACCOUNTS PAYABLE.

Trade and other receivables   Buyers of an enterprise's goods or services who do not pay immediately at the time of purchase. At a BALANCE SHEET date, outstanding amounts owed by them will be shown as Trade and other receivables as part of CURRENT ASSETS. 'Trade debtors' is a UK term. The equivalent US expression is ACCOUNTS RECEIVABLE.

Trademark   A name or design that an enterprise has a right to use in connection with its products. Management will put a value on this for BALANCE SHEET purposes only if the trade mark was bought. Thus the value of a trade mark will be recorded as its COST. Trade marks are an example of INTANGIBLE ASSETS.

Transfer price   The notional or arm's length prices charged by one Group COMPANY to another Group Company when goods or services are sold.

Treasury shares   Equity instruments re-acquired and held by the issuing enterprise itself or by its subsidiaries.

Treasury stock   US expression for a company's shares that have been bought back by the company and not cancelled. They receive no dividends and carry no votes at company meetings. The UK equivalent is 'own shares' and the IFRS term is TREASURY SHARES.

Trial balance   A trial balance is a list of accounts and their balances at a given point in time. It proves that the ledger is in balance (that is, that total debits equal total credits in the ledger accounts). If errors are made in journalising and posting, they would be detected in the process of preparing a trial balance. It is a starting point for organising the information to be reported in the financial statements.

Turnover   UK expression for sales revenue.

Understandability   Information provided in financial statements has the quality of understandability when it is comprehensible to users who have a reasonable knowledge of business and economic activities and accounting and who are willing to study the information diligently.

Underwriting expenses   Costs incurred for instructing an institution to underwrite an issue of new shares.

Undistributable reserves   Amounts not available for distribution to the shareholders as DIVIDENDS. SHARE PREMIUM and RESERVES arising from the revaluation of fixed assets are examples of such reserves. Called RESTRICTED SURPLUS in the US.

Unearned revenue   Also called DEFERRED REVENUE, it represents the amount received during the year for which no services have yet been provided. Such unearned revenue will be accounted for normally in the following accounting period when the services/products are provided/delivered.

Uniting of interests   A business combination in which the shareholders of the combining enterprises combine control over the whole, or effectively the whole, of their net assets and operations to achieve a continuing mutual sharing in the risks and benefits attaching to the combined entity such that neither party can be identified as the acquirer.

Useful life   Either:

(a) the period over which a depreciable asset is expected to be used by the enterprise; or

(b) the number of production or similar units expected to be obtained from the asset by an enterprise.

Value in use   The present value of estimated future cash flows expected to arise from the continuing use of an asset and from its disposal at the end of its useful life.

Variable costs   Costs, such as raw material costs or direct labour, which varies in proportion to the volume of production or sales.

Venturer   A party to a joint venture that has joint control over that joint venture.

Weighted average number of ordinary shares outstanding during the period   Number of ordinary shares outstanding at the beginning of the period, adjusted by the number of ordinary shares cancelled, bought back or issued during the period multiplied by a time-weighting factor.

Window dressing   The manipulation of figures in financial statements in order to make them appear better than they otherwise would be. A company might wish to do this in order to influence the judgement of existing or potential shareholders or lenders, the government, or other readers of financial statements.

Working capital   Either:

(a) the difference between CURRENT ASSETS and CURRENT LIABILITIES (accounting working capital); or

(b) Inventory plus TRADE RECEIVABLES less TRADE PAYABLES (trade or operating working capital).

Index

Terms in **bold** are defined in the glossary.